Propagandists of the Book

Propagandists of the Book

Protestant Missions, Christian Literacy, and the Making of Brazilian Evangelicalism

PEDRO FEITOZA

OXFORD
UNIVERSITY PRESS

Oxford University Press is a department of the University of Oxford.
It furthers the University's objective of excellence in research, scholarship,
and education by publishing worldwide. Oxford is a registered trade mark of
Oxford University Press in the UK and in certain other countries.

Published in the United States of America by Oxford University Press
198 Madison Avenue, New York, NY 10016, United States of America.

© Oxford University Press 2024

All rights reserved. No part of this publication may be reproduced, stored in
a retrieval system, or transmitted, in any form or by any means, without the
prior permission in writing of Oxford University Press, or as expressly permitted
by law, by license or under terms agreed with the appropriate reprographics
rights organization. Inquiries concerning reproduction outside the scope of the
above should be sent to the Rights Department, Oxford University Press, at the
address above.

You must not circulate this work in any other form
and you must impose this same condition on any acquirer

CIP data is on file at the Library of Congress

ISBN 9780197761779

DOI: 10.1093/9780197761809.001.0001

Printed by Integrated Books International, United States of America

For Priscila

Contents

Acknowledgments ix
List of Abbreviations xiii

Introduction 1

1. Protestant Origins: Migrants, Missionaries, Local Leaders, and Religious Institutions 20
2. Bibles and Tracts in Motion 58
3. Doctrines in Motion 96
4. The Dynamics of Religious Change 131
5. The Idea of Christian Cooperation 165
6. The Rise of an Evangelical Intelligentsia 205

Conclusion 247

Bibliography and Sources 259
Index 279

Acknowledgments

I began to do research for this book nearly seven years ago and carried this project with me from Brasília to Cambridge, São Paulo, and Edinburgh. I accumulated debts to a great number of people over the years, and I want to express my gratitude here. This book started as a doctoral dissertation at the University of Cambridge and my greatest intellectual debt is to David Maxwell. He offered vital encouragement when I started my studies with tentative research questions and broken English, and he helped to bring this project into being. David's comments on chapter drafts pushed me to be comparative, to query the sources reflexively, and to have confidence in my ideas. He continues to be an inspiration and to provide friendship and support and I feel that I owe him too much. Paul Freston and David Lehmann examined the thesis, made insightful comments at different times, and helped in the journey toward publication.

Through a postdoctoral fellowship at the Brazilian Center of Analysis and Planning (CEBRAP) in São Paulo, I entered this exciting academic community amidst the uncertainties and isolation of the coronavirus pandemic. I am thankful to Angela Alonso, Maria Hermínia Tavares, and Vera Schattan Coelho for their support. My colleagues at the International Postdoctoral Program offered detailed and valuable comments on chapter drafts during our weekly meetings and shared their experiences and trials as junior academics in such turbulent times in informal conversations. I am especially grateful to Leonardo Fontes, Gustavo Mesquita, Leonardo Nóbrega, and Jaciane Pimentel. Thank you also to Angela Alonso, Ronaldo Almeida, and Paula Montero for welcoming me into their research groups and to the participants for their insightful suggestions.

Beyond that, a small army of academics took their time to read drafts and make comments that opened new vistas and prevented me from making mistakes. I thank Maria Lúcia and Peter Burke, Joel Cabrita, Manoela Carpenedo, Joseph Florez, Richard Graham, and Brian Stanley for their generosity. Gabriela Ramos made valuable comments in the first-year assessment of the PhD. Bernice Martin and the late David Martin read almost the entirety of the thesis that forms the basis of this book. The last stages of writing and revision were done in Edinburgh. I thank Alex Chow, Kirsty Murray, and Emma Wild-Wood for welcoming me into the School of Divinity, and Helen Bond, Morgane Jarles, and Julie Robertson for their support. At Oxford University Press, I am grateful to Theo Calderara, Alexandra Rouch, and Rachel Ruisard for their editorial work.

Funding for this research came from various sources. The Brazilian Federal Agency for Support and Evaluation of Graduate Education (CAPES) and the Cambridge Commonwealth, European, and International Trust funded my doctoral studies. A generous grant from the São Paulo Research Foundation (#2019/14369-2) enabled me to carry out additional research for this book amidst the ordeals of the pandemic. Emmanuel College and the University of Cambridge Fieldwork Fund financed research trips to Brazil and the United States.

Librarians and archivists helped me find crucial resources for this book. I thank the personnel of the *Biblioteca Nacional* in Rio de Janeiro, the Presbyterian Historical Society in Philadelphia, the *Biblioteca Central* of the University of Brasília, the New College Library in Edinburgh, the Theology Faculty at Mackenzie University in São Paulo, the SOAS Library in London, and the University Library in Cambridge. Onesimus Ngundu introduced me to the vast collections of the British and Foreign Bible Society in Cambridge. Jim Berwick welcomed me at the archives of the International Baptist Mission Board in Richmond, Virginia, and helped me locate valuable material. The late Enos Moura provided a warm welcome at the *Arquivo Histórico Presbiteriano* in São Paulo. Sonia Mabel and Claudia Santiago granted access to the rich collections of the *Centro de Documentação e História Rev. Vicente Themudo Lessa* at the Independent Presbyterian Church of São Paulo. And Esther Marques Monteiro helped me find important missionary correspondence at the *Biblioteca Fernandes Braga* of the Fluminense Evangelical Church in Rio de Janeiro.

My parents, Carlinhos and Cláudia, supported this project in every possible way: from listening to inchoate ideas and offering comments, to looking after my children and offering shelter. They encouraged me to go ahead even when no one had an idea of where this career would take us. I cannot even begin to repay them for their love and support, but I try my best. I am also grateful to my siblings and their spouses, Anna and André, Cézar and Lud, and their readiness to cheer us up and make us laugh. Thank you also to Ronaldo and Mírian, Camila and Rogério, Pedro and Heidi for their enormous generosity and hospitality.

Maria, Clara, and Francisco were all born as this project unfolded. Their fast growth offered a telling contrast to the sluggish development of this book, and it is a pleasure to see them becoming wonderful people. By taking me to playgrounds and parks, they dragged me away from obscure libraries, rescued me from the dullness of my desk, and made me see what lies ahead with great hope. Priscila embraced this project from the beginning. She listened to immature ideas attentively and encouraged me to go on when I thought I had reached dead ends. We celebrated together every little achievement and comforted each other after our failures. She bore the burden of our mobile lives with three children and little money across the Atlantic with astounding strength and I dedicate this book to her, knowing that she deserves much more.

New College, Edinburgh
June 2023

List of Abbreviations

ABS	American Bible Society
AHP	Arquivo Histórico Presbiteriano, São Paulo, Brazil
BFB-IEF	Biblioteca Fernandes Braga, Igreja Evangélica Fluminense, Rio de Janeiro, Brazil
BFBS	British and Foreign Bible Society
BFM-PCUSA	Board of Foreign Missions of the Presbyterian Church of the United States of America
BN	Biblioteca Nacional, Rio de Janeiro, Brazil
BSA	Bible Society Archives, Cambridge, UK
BSET	Brazilian Society of Evangelical Tracts
CCLA	Committee on Cooperation in Latin America
CDH-VTL	Centro de Documentação e História Vicente Themudo Lessa, Catedral Presbiteriana de São Paulo, Brazil
CSWC	Center for the Study of World Christianity, New College, University of Edinburgh, UK
IBMB	International Baptist Mission Board, Richmond, USA
PHS	Presbyterian Historical Society, Philadelphia, USA
RTS	Religious Tract Society
SBC	Southern Baptist Convention
SOAS	School of Oriental and African Studies, London, UK
YMCA	Young Men's Christian Association

Introduction

In the months of July and August 1928, members of the Spiritualist Crusade of Rio de Janeiro organized a series of meetings exploring the history, practices, and doctrines of an array of religious confessions and philosophies. This "Conference on Comparative Religions," as the event was called, was aimed at fostering a spirit of confraternity amongst practitioners of Christianity, Islam, Buddhism, Theosophy, Positivism, and others. In each of the eight meetings, the speakers took to the pulpit of a large auditorium in the center of the Brazilian capital to give their talks. The Presbyterian minister and writer Erasmo Braga was chosen to represent the Protestant tradition. On July 27, he gave his address. The auditorium was simply adorned: large posters with biblical verses were affixed to the walls, the choir of the Congregationalist Fluminense Evangelical Church sang hymns in Portuguese, and two large Bibles were placed on a table decorated with flowers.[1] These arrangements offered a clear contrast to other meetings. The conferences on Judaism, Buddhism, Islamism, and Catholicism featured statues and images of Christian saints, Moses, and the Buddha, while the music was sung in Hebrew, Pali, Arabic, and Latin.[2] The event seemed to reassert centuries-old stereotypes associated with Protestants, especially their iconoclasm and vernacularism. Braga's long and remarkable address explored the historical and social significance of evangelical Christianity. For him, both the early modern Reformation and the contemporary evangelical movement were animated by an impulse of "reversal to primitive Christianity." Protestants sought to restore the spiritual vigor and democratic egalitarianism of the apostolic age by leaning on the supreme authority of the Bible, rescuing the Christian church from centuries of ecclesiastical and doctrinal "distortions." Hence, he argued, on account of this close attachment to the written word

---

[1] *Jornal do Commercio*, August 31, 1928, n. 208.
[2] Gustavo Macedo, "Advertencia," in *Religiões Comparadas*, ed. Gustavo Macedo (Rio de Janeiro: Roland Rohe & C., 1929), iii–iv, at v.

"we [Protestants] became one of the greatest promoters of culture amidst mankind, for we are propagandists of the book."[3]

At the time of Braga's address evangelicals had indeed become agents of literacy in Brazil. When British and American Protestant missionaries opened the first mission stations in the country in the mid-nineteenth century, they demonstrated an extraordinary confidence in the power of the printed word. Believing that Christian texts could penetrate regions beyond their reach, missionaries resorted to modern print technologies to fill the land with Bibles, Christian books, periodicals, and tracts. In the evangelical imagination of that time, these "silent messengers" moved freely across the Brazilian territory and introduced the foundations of Christianity to people who would otherwise be suspicious of face-to-face interactions with Protestant evangelists. Based on these assumptions, Protestants devoted a great deal of energy and resources into the production and circulation of evangelical print. In his address, Braga estimated that, from the establishment of the first missionary ventures in the mid-nineteenth century up to that date, Protestants had put around three million Bibles and portions of the Bible in motion in the country.

But beyond its evangelistic ends, evangelical literacy served other purposes in the missionary enterprise. At the foundation of the Brazilian Society of Evangelical Tracts in September 1883, an organization created to produce and disseminate Protestant booklets, the influential Presbyterian minister Eduardo Carlos Pereira affirmed that this venture would bring his denomination into maturity. In demanding modest but systematic contributions from believers, the Society would deliver Brazilian Presbyterian churches from their dependence on foreign capital.[4] American Baptists and British Congregationalists believed in the civilizing effects of Christian literature, in their power to develop the mental abilities of readers and lift moral standards. Bible societies and mission bodies created a vast infrastructure comprising evangelical bookstores, local congregations, and itinerant booksellers through which Bibles and Christian literature moved widely across the country. Catholics, too, associated Protestants with their books. In the nineteenth century, bishops issued pastoral letters warning their flocks against the "false Bibles" of the evangelicals, and Capuchin friars in the twentieth century burned tracts and books in large bonfires aimed at

---

[3] Erasmo Braga, "Protestantismo," in *Religiões Comparadas*, ed. Macedo, 75–96, at 79–80.
[4] *Imprensa Evangelica*, September 29, 1883, n. 18.

cleansing their communities from Protestant pollution.[5] Catholics depicted the principle of the free examination of the scriptures and the operations of Bible societies as disruptive to the natural hierarchies inscribed by God in the world, usurping the authority of priests. Tellingly, Catholic periodicals attached a pejorative label to evangelicals by calling them *os bíblias*. From their material realities to their intellectual contents, from their potential to generate religious change to their capacity to disrupt the religious landscape of the country, texts were at the very heart of the Protestant missionary enterprise in Brazil.

They are also the central object of this book. In the period ranging from the mid-nineteenth century up until Erasmo Braga's address, the Protestant population of the country evolved from small congregations of Anglophone merchants and German immigrants scattered along the coast and the far south into a sizeable community of over 700,000 churchgoers spread across all states of the Brazilian territory. This growing evangelical population encompassed a wide range of denominations and independent churches, as well as an array of social and professional groups, including small farmers, artisans, urban workers, the emerging middle classes, and foreign immigrants. The majority of the agents who pushed these new religious frontiers were, to a greater or lesser extent, agents of literacy, including local ministers, evangelists, Bible-readers, itinerant booksellers, and schoolteachers. Believers depicted their encounter with God as an encounter with the word of God, the Bible, and associated evangelical conversion to reading and writing. The conversion narratives and spiritual autobiographies they produced illuminate the social configurations implicated in processes of religious change and provide insight into dynamics of cultural change and power relations within civil society. Missionaries and local ministers also set up small, artisanal printing presses at the back of church buildings or in private houses to produce periodicals, tracts, pamphlets, and short books. They took sermons, hymns, religious polemics, seminary lectures, catechisms, and devotional texts into these presses and had them run off in a few days. Some of these small presses evolved into large, respectable publishing houses with a professionalized bureaucracy. Through the pages of these texts Protestants took part in the

---

[5] Erika Helgen, *Religious Conflict in Brazil: Protestants, Catholics, and the Rise of Religious Pluralism in the Early Twentieth Century* (New Haven, CT: Yale University Press, 2020).

"printing culture" of Brazil and in the religious, political, and social debates circulating in the country.[6]

A close examination of Protestant texts, their production, ideas, and the infrastructure built to set them in motion sheds light into the intricacies of the religious encounter in modern Brazil. This book concentrates on the first wave of evangelical diffusion in the country, which was led by the Presbyterians in the Brazilian center-south, more specifically in the regions of São Paulo, Minas Gerais, and Rio de Janeiro, although it also considers the experiences of Congregationalists, Baptists, and Pentecostals for comparative purposes. I also look at non-denominational bodies, such as Bible and tract societies and independent faith missionaries. Some of the chapters concentrate on the intellectual dimension of evangelical texts and explore the ways in which Brazilian believers deployed modern theological discourse. Ordinary believers resorted to the Protestant conceptual repertoire to give meaning to processes of religious change and to narrate conversion. Ministers and religious specialists, by their turn, manipulated a vast array of intellectual traditions in their interactions with secular and Catholic writers, inventively weaving theological discourse into public argument. On the other hand, this study considers the materiality of the texts that circulated in Brazil and the Lusophone Atlantic. The constitution of Protestantism as a book religion depended crucially on the far-reaching networks devised to bring Bibles and tracts into the hands of the people. In considering both the conceptual and material dimensions of the missionary publishing enterprise, this book connects studies of discourse and diffusion and reconciles intellectual with social history.[7]

A Note on Sources and Approaches

My interest in this topic was stirred when I visited the Center of Documentation and History Vicente Themudo Lessa at the Independent Presbyterian Church of São Paulo and encountered a large collection of evangelical tracts published between the 1850s and the 1930s. This

---

[6] I take the expression "printing culture" from Karin Barber, "Hidden Innovators in Africa," in *Africa's Hidden Histories: Everyday Literacy and Making the Self*, ed. Karin Barber (Bloomington: Indiana University Press, 2006), 1–24, at 15.

[7] Robert Darnton, "Discourse and Diffusion," *Contributions to the History of Concepts* 1 (2005): 21–28.

compilation of over six hundred short books and tracts pointed to a complex, yet neglected, history of public intellectual exchange and debate. Catechisms, doctrinal pamphlets, conversion narratives, and religious controversies attacked the foundations of the Catholic Church and the modern renewal of Catholic worship and politics, while simultaneously translating central tenets, practices, and beliefs of evangelical religion to their Brazilian audiences. Periodicals and tracts projected Brazilian Protestants into debates on political change, abolitionism, and educational reform. High-level texts, such as theological treatises and religious controversies, provided insight into the thinking of the Protestant intellectual elites that emerged in this period. At the same time, popular, low-level texts, such as evangelical pamphlets, periodicals, and short tracts, captured the voices of "ordinary believers" who left little traces in other historical records but played a vital role in the making of this religious universe.[8] Additional forays into libraries and archives in Rio de Janeiro, Brasília, and the countryside of São Paulo enabled me to collect more evidence and delve into the intellectual climate of the age.

But there remained the challenge of identifying *who* read these texts and *how*. Given that in the late-nineteenth and early-twentieth centuries over eighty percent of the Brazilian population was illiterate, the evangelistic strategy of reaching out to the Brazilian public through the printed word seemed utterly misplaced. For sociologist Antonio Gouvêa Mendonça, Protestant attachment to the written word in an illiterate society helped to explain the failure of missionaries and their local collaborators.[9] This explanation, however, obfuscates the creative ways in which rural and urban communities in modern Brazil related to the written word and the reading practices that emerged at grassroots level. Additional research into missionary archives in Brazil, the United States, and Britain furnished important information about the circulation of evangelical texts. Missionary correspondence described in detail how Bibles, periodicals, and tracts were disseminated through the Brazilian countryside and uncovered how different social categories made use of print matter. Converts read aloud to congregations letters, hymns, and sermons printed in Protestant periodicals,

---

[8] I take the distinction between high- and low-level texts from Emma Hunter, "Recovering Liberties in Twentieth-century Africa," CRASSH work in progress seminar, Cambridge UK, October 2018.
[9] Antonio G. Mendonça, *O celeste porvir: A inserção do protestantismo no Brasil*, 3rd ed. (São Paulo: Editora da Universidade de São Paulo, 2008 [1984]), 225–227.

while the educated children of evangelical families recited biblical passages, catechisms, and devotional tracts to kin and neighbors in domestic meetings. These practices merged print and oral cultures and enabled Christian texts to reach reading publics and listening audiences simultaneously. Missionary reports and correspondence revealed how evangelical print culture was embedded into the religious practices of local congregations and illuminated the reading practices emerging "from below" in modern Brazil.

Missionary sources, however, require careful reading. The religious bodies that corresponded with missionaries in the field selected, organized, and published their reports with American and European audiences in mind. They resorted to powerful contrasts between civilization and savagery, darkness and light to account for the "redemptive" work of missionaries and elicit material and spiritual support for mission organizations at home.[10] Literary scholars of a postcolonial persuasion have depicted Western missions and their evangelistic endeavors as organizations and initiatives that "inevitably assisted the subjugation of indigenous peoples and the consolidation of white institutions of colonial control."[11] The works of Anna Johnston and Gareth Griffiths conceive missionary texts and conversion narratives as particular representations of colonized people that circulated as general knowledge in colonies and the metropolis, or as texts grounded in narrative conventions that were not apparently rooted in any specific culture, but shared "a broader set of concerns."[12] Such an approach runs the risk of obliterating the contingencies and historical specificities that characterized worldwide religious encounters and the ways in which they were chronicled.

Instead of viewing missionary and evangelical literacy simply as "representation," this study takes into account anthropologist John Peel's remark that missionary sources and materials require a "hermeneutic of deep suspicion": an analytical procedure that pays attention to the selective interest of missionaries in the customs and cultural practices they fought against and the ontological assumptions that lay behind their reportage.[13] Instead of dismissing missionary sources as expressions of the self-image of Western

[10] David Maxwell, "The Missionary Movement in African and World History: Mission Sources and Religious Encounter," *The Historical Journal* 58 (2015), 901–930.
[11] Anna Johnston, *Missionary Writing and Empire, 1800–1860* (Cambridge: Cambridge University Press, 2003), 19.
[12] Johnston, *Missionary Writing*, 4; Gareth Griffiths, "'Trained to Tell the Truth': Missionaries, Converts, and Narration," in *Missions and Empire*, ed. Norman Etherington (Oxford: Oxford University Press, 2005), 153–72, at 158.
[13] J. D. Y. Peel, *Religious Encounter and the Making of the Yoruba* (Bloomington: Indiana University Press, 2000), 12.

elites and their projection onto non-Western cultures, this book follows historian Tony Ballantyne and looks at them as situated texts, as "products of the interaction between evangelical worldviews, the sensibility and experience of individual missionaries, and their particular engagements with specific places, individuals, collectives, and events."[14] This way of analyzing missionary sources against the grain discloses important dynamics of worldwide religious encounters by *reading out* indigenous and local voices from missionary reports, and showing how these actors "seized hold of the material, spiritual, and intellectual resources of Christianity" in specific historical settings.[15] This study deploys similar analytical strategies to reconstruct the intellectual exchanges between Brazilian Protestants and their secular and Catholic interlocutors, the ideologies that motivated them to devise such a vast infrastructure to circulate Christian literacy, and to examine the changing social and cultural configurations related to processes of religious change.

The Study of Latin American and Brazilian Evangelicalism

Evangelical Christianity is the fastest growing religious movement in Brazil and Latin America. Its charismatic variants have been spreading rapidly across the continent since at least the 1960s, particularly amongst impoverished and marginalized communities, with significant consequences. In countries such as Brazil and Guatemala, evangelicals emerged as political actors in recent decades, successfully mobilizing their constituencies in favor of church leaders and fellow believers.[16] The remarkable growth of such religious communities and their contentious political ventures have attracted both popular and scholarly attention, notably after the election of far-right president Jair Bolsonaro in Brazil in 2018 and the substantial support he drew from evangelical voters.[17]

---

[14] Tony Ballantyne, *Entanglements of Empire: Missionaries, Maori, and the Question of the Body* (Durham, NC: Duke University Press, 2014), 14.
[15] Maxwell, "The Missionary Movement," 909.
[16] Paul Freston, "The Protestant Eruption into Modern Brazilian Politics," *Journal of Contemporary Religion* 11 (1996): 147–168.
[17] Two popular assessments of evangelical growth and politics in Brazil are Juliano Spyer, *Povo de Deus: Quem são os evangélicos e por que eles importam* (São Paulo: Geração Editorial, 2020); "Of Bibles and Ballots: Evangelical Churches are Political Players in Brazil." *The Economist*, Special report: Brazil on the Brink, June 5, 2021, https://www.economist.com/special-report/2021/06/05/of-bible-and-ballots. For an insightful, although somewhat dated summary of the academic

Some of the most influential explanations for this phenomenon came from the social sciences. Drawing upon quantitative data, ethnographic observations, and discourse analysis, sociologists related religious change to broader social and economic transformations in Latin America. Scholars such as Emilio Willems, Ronald Frase, and Antonio Gouvêa Mendonça viewed large-scale evangelical diffusion and conversion as consequences of larger processes of migration and mobility that released specific social categories from established cultural norms and social constraints and facilitated religious rupture.[18] However, functionalist explanations for religious change risk sidelining what was central for believers: worship, scripture, belief, religious practice, and the religious community. While such explanations rightly drive attention to the socioeconomic contexts in which conversion takes place, they see religious change as symptoms of broader quantifiable social transformations and fail to account for the power of ritual, myth, and belief in such religious realignments.[19]

The sophisticated literature on Pentecostalism has in many ways addressed the limitations of functionalism, and shed light on the history that unfolds in this book. The works of David Smilde, Elizabeth Brusco, and David Martin demonstrate how converts seize the spirit-infested language of charismatic evangelicalism to navigate contexts of everyday violence, alcohol consumption, and domestic abuse. They draw attention to changing notions of domesticity and the new economic cultures that emerge in Pentecostal communities, which "domesticates" male violence and behavioral excesses and enable nuclear families to accumulate.[20] David Lehmann's comparative study of the attitudes of progressive Catholics and Pentecostals

literature on Pentecostalism, see Paul Freston, "Pentecostalism in Latin America: Characteristics and Controversies," *Social Compass* 45 (1998): 335–358.

[18] Emilio Willems, *Followers of the New Faith: Culture Change and the Rise of Protestantism in Brazil and Chile* (Nashville, TN: Vanderbilt University Press, 1967); Emilio Willems, "Protestantism as a Factor of Culture Change in Brazil," *Economic Development and Cultural Change* 3 (1955): 321–333; Ronald G. Frase, "A Sociological Analysis of the Development of Brazilian Protestantism: A Study of Social Change" (unpublished PhD dissertation, Princeton Theological Seminary, 1975); Mendonça, *O celeste porvir*.

[19] For a study that contemplates the limitations of functionalist explanations of religious change, see Joseph Florez, *Lived Religion, Pentecostalism, and Social Activism in Authoritarian Chile: Giving Life to the Faith* (Leiden: Brill, 2021).

[20] David Smilde, *Reason to Believe: Cultural Agency in Latin American Evangelicalism* (Berkeley: University of California Press, 2007); Elizabeth Brusco, "The Reformation of Machismo: Asceticism and Masculinity among Colombian Evangelicals," in *Rethinking Protestantism in Latin America*, ed. Virginia Garrard-Burnett and David Stoll (Philadelphia: Temple University Press, 1993), 143–158; David Martin, *Tongues of Fire: The Explosion of Protestantism in Latin America* (Cambridge, MA: Basil Blackwell, 1990).

toward traditional culture situates evangelical growth firmly in its religious settings. Lehmann calls attention to the complex relationship between Pentecostals and the other religious players in contemporary Brazil, showing how evangelicals derive practices such as the collection of prayer requests and exorcism from Catholic petitioning to the saints and Afro-Brazilian possession cults.[21] In sum, they take the religious vocabulary of evangelicals seriously into account and examine how religious transformations generate new individual attitudes and sociocultural practices.

Part of the academic literature historicizes the intersections between religion, politics, and social change. The influential and sophisticated work of historian Jean-Pierre Bastian uncovered the "endogenous" nature of Protestantism in Latin America, locating the new religion into the political transformations of the nineteenth century. In a context of strong though waning Catholic influence over politics, Protestants drew near radical liberal groups in the continent that advocated the secularization of the state, full religious liberty, and foreign immigration. For Bastian, Protestantism was part of a broader culture of religious and political dissent that flourished around secret societies, such as Masonic lodges and the "societies of thought."[22] In the case of Mexico, these relations fermented over several decades in the tense political space under Porfirio Díaz's dictatorship and impelled Protestants to support revolutionary mobilization in 1910-1911.[23] Another group of scholars, however, view Latin American evangelicalism as an iteration, almost reproduction of American civil religion. They blame the conservatism and fundamentalism of foreign American missionaries as a source of sociopolitical alienation underlining Latin American Protestants' legitimation of existing and unjust social structures.[24] In recent years, scholars

---

[21] David Lehmann, *Struggle for the Spirit: Religious Transformation and Popular Culture in Brazil and Latin America* (Cambridge: Polity Press, 1996), 168, 209.

[22] Jean-Pierre Bastian, "The Metamorphosis of Latin American Protestant Groups: A Sociohistorical Perspective," *Latin American Research Review* 28 (1993): 33–61; Jean-Pierre Bastian, "Protestantism in Latin America," in *The Church in Latin America, 1492-1992*, ed. Enrique Dussel (Tunbridge Wells: Burns & Oates, 1992); Jean-Pierre Bastian, *Protestantismos y modernidad latinoamericana: Historia de unas minorías religiosas activas en América Latina* (Mexico, DF: Fondo de Cultura Económica, 1994), 91–105; Jean-Pierre Bastian, ed., *Protestantes, liberales y francmasones: Sociedades de ideas y modernidad en América Latina, siglo XIX* (Mexico, DF: Fondo de Cultura Económica, 1990).

[23] Jean-Pierre Bastian, *Los disidentes: Sociedades protestantes y revolución en México, 1872-1911* (Mexico, DF: Fondo de Cultura Económica, 1989).

[24] Pablo A. Deiros, "Protestant Fundamentalism in Latin America," in *Fundamentalisms Observed*, ed. Martin E. Marty and Scott R. Appleby (Chicago: University of Chicago Press, 1991), 142–196; Antonio G. Mendonça and Prócoro Velasques Filho, *Introdução ao protestantismo no Brasil* (São Paulo: Edições Loyola, 1990); Rubem Alves, *Protestantism and Repression: A Brazilian Case Study*,

have begun to conflate religious and political identities, locating the ideologies of evangelical and Catholics on either the left or the right of the turmoils of the Cold War.[25]

This study pursues different goals. First, unlike J. P. Bastian's scholarship, this book is concerned with the *publicness* of evangelical religion, the outward expressions of evangelical faith, worship, and practice, not the privacy of secret societies. Its central objects are the religious presses, the Bible and tract societies, and the evangelical institutions such as congregations, schools, seminaries, and associations that contributed to the constitution of civil society and public opinion. Additionally, up until the mid-twentieth century, Brazilian Protestants lacked the revolutionary leverage that characterized the experiences of religious dissidents in modern Mexico and early modern England.[26] Martin's assertion that religious change in Latin America assisted "peaceful evolution," individual processes of spiritual renewal, instead of radical upheaval accurately describes the Brazilian case.[27] While it is true that Protestants in modern Brazil, Mexico, and Guatemala supported a series of causes that resonated with the reformist agendas of political minorities, Brazilian Protestants held the revolutionary ferment of such radical groups in suspicion. The following chapters take the irreducibility of Brazilian evangelical politics seriously into account. Protestants developed complex and ambiguous responses to the social and political transformations of their age, and to conflate religious and political identities misrepresents these interactions and obliterates their significance.

---

trans. by John Drury (London: SCM Press, 1985); Mendonça, *O celeste porvir*; Frase, "A Sociological Analysis."

[25] David C. Kirkpatrick, *A Gospel for the Poor: Global Social Christianity and the Latin American Evangelical Left* (Philadelphia: University of Pennsylvania Press, 2019); Benjamin A. Cowan, *Moral Majorities across the Americas: Brazil, the United States, and the Creation of the Religious Right* (Chapel Hill: University of North Carolina Press, 2021). Some studies resist the temptation to overpoliticize evangelical politics and identities, see Virginia Garrard-Burnett, *Protestantism in Guatemala: Living in the New Jerusalem* (Austin: University of Texas Press, 1998); Israel B. de Azevedo, *A celebração do indivíduo: A formação do pensamento batista brasileiro* (Piracicaba, SP: Editora Unimep, 1996); Silas L. de Souza, *Pensamento social e político no protestantismo brasileiro* (São Paulo: Editora Mackenzie, 2005); Carlos Mondragón, *Like Leaven in the Dough: Protestant Social Thought in Latin America, 1920–1950*, trans. Daniel Miller and Ben Post (Madison, NJ: Fairleigh Dickinson University Press, 2011); Daniel Salinas, *Latin American Evangelical Theology in the 1970s: The Golden Decade* (Leiden: Brill, 2009).

[26] Christopher Hill, *The World Turned Upside Down: Radical Ideas during the English Revolution* (Harmondsworth: Penguin, 1978); Jean-Pierre Bastian, *Los dissidentes: Sociedades protestantes y revolución en México, 1872–1911* (Mexico, DF: Fondo de Cultura Econômica, 1989).

[27] David Martin, *Forbbiden Revolutions: Pentecostalism in Latin America, Catholicism in Eastern Europe* (London: SPCK, 1996), 37.

Second, this study examines the grassroots dynamics of Brazilian evangelicalism. Instead of portraying religious change as a sequel of broader social transformations, it concentrates on the strategies, aspirations, experiences, and ordeals of the local agents of religious diffusion, reconstructing the ways in which they navigated between multiple social and cultural worlds and expanded new religious frontiers.[28] Finally, engaging with scholarship on global intellectual history, or "intellectual history on an international scale," this book evaluates the multiple conceptual universes through which Brazilian Protestants navigated.[29] It also interrogates the ways in which Protestant ministers and writers domesticated, circumvented, and rejected exogenous ideas, deploying them in argument.[30] This study views their theological and doctrinal production less like grand abstractions than as "languages of claim-making and counter claim-making whose effects were shaped ... by complex struggles in specific contexts, played out over time."[31] By situating the thinking and ideologies of Brazilian Protestant intellectuals in multiple contexts, the book uncovers the unpredictable dynamics and unexpected outcomes of these conceptual exchanges. It also contemplates the specific responses of missionaries and converts to the religious and social challenges of their time, instead of locating their writings into the static categories of the left and right, conservative and liberal.

The terms *Protestants* and *evangelicals* are used interchangeably in this book. Brazilian converts called themselves and defined their religious identities as such. The earliest Protestant schools, publications, and congregations of the country carried the adjective *evangélico* or *evangélica* in their names. For the first generations of converts and missionaries, this word expressed their attachment to *the gospels* (*os evangelhos*) and encapsulated their urge to recover the practices and spirituality of the early Christian church. Brazilian

---

[28] Lyndon A. Santos, *Os mascates da fé: História dos evangélicos no Brasil (1855 a 1900)* (Curitiba: CRV, 2017); Émile G. Léonard, "L'illuminisme dans un protestantisme de constitution récente," *Revue de l'Histoire de Religions*, 1 (1952): 26–83, later published as Émile G. Léonard, *Iluminismo num protestantismo de constituição recente* (São Bernardo do Campo, SP: UMESP, 1988).

[29] David Armitage, *Foundations of Modern International Thought* (Cambridge: Cambridge University Press, 2013), 7. For further reviews and perspectives on global intellectual history, see Samuel Moyn and Andrew Sartori, "Approaches to Global Intellectual History," in *Global Intellectual History*, ed. Samuel Moyn and Andrew Sartori (New York: Columbia University Press, 2013), 3–30. For some insightful remarks on the "turn to the global," see Christopher Bayly, Sven Beckert, Matthew Connelly, Isabel Hofmeyr, Wendy Kozol and Patricia Seed, "AHR Conversation: On Transnational History," *American Historical Review* 111 (2006): 1441–1464.

[30] Shruti Kapila, "Preface," *Modern Intellectual History* 4 (2007): 3–6; Christopher Bayly, "Afterword," *Modern Intellectual History* 4 (2007): 163–169.

[31] Frederick Cooper, *Colonialism in Question: Theory, Knowledge, History* (Berkeley: University of California Press, 2005), 24.

Protestants were thus motivated by a "primivist impulse" akin to the first generations of Pentecostals in the United States and southern Africa,[32] although they were deeply suspicious of the pneumatic "signs and wonders" of glossolalia, prophecy, and healing. Yet, there are other reasons beyond self-definition. Historical and sociological categories have been deployed to define evangelical practice and belief in global and Latin American history in different ways. Historian David Bebbington offered the standard model in his foursquare definition of British evangelicalism. For him, the movement's distinctive features were conversionism (the idea that an individual encounter with God promoted spiritual regeneration), activism (the dedication of ordinary believers to evangelism and the church), Biblicism (the evangelical devotion to the Bible as the ultimate source of authority), and crucicentrism (the centrality of the doctrine of Christian atonement).[33] Although his ready-made model has been contested and updated,[34] sociologist Paul Freston regards it as a useful definition to understand the historical experience of Latin American evangelicals. Variations of these main characteristics can be found across various denominations.[35] Moreover, such a broad characterization avoids the risk of blurring political and religious identities within evangelicalism.[36] Historically, evangelicalism has been associated with the rise of non-Catholic forms of Christian religion in Latin America, encompassing both mainline Protestants and Pentecostals.[37] In this study I explore the tension between diversity and uniformity in the making of Brazilian Protestantism. Denominational differences and sectarian conflicts played an important part in the consolidation of evangelical religion in the country, and it is worth disaggregating the experiences of Presbyterians, Baptists, and

[32] Grant Wacker, *Heaven Below: Early Pentecostals and American Culture* (Cambridge, MA: Harvard University Press, 2001), 11–12; David Maxwell, *African Gifts of the Spirit: Pentecostalism and the Rise of Zimbabwean Transnational Religious Movement* (Oxford: James Currey, 2006), 14–15.
[33] David W. Bebbington, *Evangelicalism in Modern Britain: A History from the 1730s to the 1980s* (London: Unwin Hyman, 1989), 1–19.
[34] See, for instance, Timothy Larsen, "Defining and Locating Evangelicalism," in *The Cambridge Companion to Evangelical Theology*, ed. Timothy Larsen and Daniel J. Treier (Cambridge: Cambridge University Press, 2007).
[35] Paul Freston, "The Many Faces of Evangelical Politics in Latin America," in *Evangelical Christianity and Democracy in Latin America*, ed. Paul Freston (Oxford: Oxford University Press, 2008), 3–36, at 5–6.
[36] Paul Freston, *Evangelicals and Politics in Asia, Africa and Latin America* (Cambridge: Cambridge University Press, 2001), introduction.
[37] Todd Hartch, *The Rebirth of Latin American Christianity* (New York: Oxford University Press, 2014).

Congregationalists for analytical purposes, while also paying attention to the elements that brought non-Catholic religious minorities together.

Christian Literacy and the Multiple Arenas of the Public Sphere

This book deals with the category of the "public sphere." However, following historians Emma Hunter and Pablo Piccato, I use the concept loosely, exploring its explanatory and methodological potential and viewing the public sphere less like a descriptive ideal type than as a space of debate, exchange, and circulation of discourse.[38] The majority of works on the topic almost invariably refer to Jürgen Habermas's *The Structural Transformation of the Public Sphere*, which has remained widely influential since its publication in 1962. Habermas traced a history whereby monarchical and ecclesiastical forms of representation yielded to new forms of publicness in the wake of the social and political changes wrought by the advent of capitalist economy. The traffic in commodities and news, characteristic of early modern mercantilism, generated new power relations in Europe as the new markets reformed political authority and shaped the modern states. At the same time, the rise of the press enabled political authorities to address their subjects, *the public*, as an entity distinct from the realm of the state. In the early modern age, a variety of bourgeois institutions of sociability such as salons, coffeehouses, theatres, and clubs emerged in Britain, France, and Germany, from which Habermas drew his rich case studies. Along with the consolidation of art and literary criticism, these institutions facilitated the exchange of critical-rational debates and gave rise to the modern public sphere, that Habermas defined as "the sphere of private people come together as a public."[39]

Habermas's work has been the object of numerous reviews. Historians criticized his conception of the public sphere for the absence of "a feminine component," the elitism of his institutions of sociability, his neglect of the role of religious presses, and his emphasis on the structural transformations of the modern capitalist economy.[40] However, both the book and its critics

---

[38] Emma Hunter, *Political Thought and the Public Sphere in Tanzania: Freedom, Democracy and Citizenship in the Era of Decolonization* (New York: Cambridge University Press, 2015), 23–24; Pablo Piccato, "Public Sphere in Latin America: A Review of the Historiography," *Social History* 35 (2010): 165–192.

[39] Jürgen Habermas, *The Structural Transformation of the Public Sphere: An Inquiry into a Category of Bourgeois Society*, trans. Thomas Burger (Cambridge: Polity Press, 1989 [1962]), 15–27.

[40] For an insightful summary, see Massimo Rospocher, "Beyond the Public Sphere: A Historiographical Transition," in *Beyond the Public Sphere: Opinions, Publics, Spaces in Early Modern*

highlight two elements of crucial importance for this study. First, in contrast to historians such as Reinhart Koselleck, who emphasized the role of secret societies in the rise of such a culture of debate and exchange, Habermas focused precisely on the "principle of publicity" governing the European public sphere that was "held up in opposition to the practice of secrets of state."[41] Second, the following chapters will expand the scope of Habermas's elite institutions of sociability to include its religious and popular forms.

Latin Americanist historians engaged with and expanded the Habermasian model. Two insightful reviews by Piccato and Victor Uribe-Uran have shown how printing presses, clubs, scientific societies, and literary associations proliferated quickly in the decades preceding the independence of Latin American states. Even though there was an influential lettered elite in the colonies composed of aristocrats, high bureaucrats, and clergymen reminiscent of the European public sphere, Piccato and Uribe-Uran argue that popular forms of sociability also emerged around marketplaces, religious associations, taverns, and city councils. The coexistence of elite and popular sociabilities, as well as the interpenetration of print, manuscript, and oral forms of communications, dynamized these arenas of intellectual exchange and political criticism in the continent.[42] Historians have also explored the transnational dimension of the Latin American public sphere in the modern age, showing how ideas, texts, and debates flowed in multiple directions across the Atlantic in the Age of Revolutions.[43] From enslaved and indigenous people to artisans and landowners, a diverse social compound deployed the political vocabulary of such turbulent years, appropriating notions of citizenship and rights in various ways as discussions on independence and nation building emerged.[44] Elite socialization in clubs and salons

---

Europe, ed. Massimo Rospocher (Bologna: Il Mulino, 2012). On religion and science, see David Zaret, "Religion, Science, and Printing in the Public Sphere in Seventeeth-century England," in *Habermas and the Public Sphere*, ed. Craig Calhoun (Cambridge, MA: MIT Press, 1992).

[41] Habermas, *The Structural Transformation*, 52. See also Dena Goodman, "Public Sphere and Private Life: Toward a Synthesis of Current Historiographical Approaches to the Old Regime," *History and Theory* 31 (1992): 1–20.

[42] Piccato, "Public Sphere in Latin America"; Victor Uribe-Uran, "The Birth of a Public Sphere in Latin America during the Age of Revolution," *Comparative Studies in Society and History* 42 (2000): 425–457.

[43] Lúcia Maria B. P. das Neves, *Corcundas e constitucionais: A cultura política da independência (1820–1822)* (Rio de Janeiro: Revan/FAPERJ, 2003); François-Xavier Guerra, *Modernidad y independencias: Ensayos sobre las revoluciones hispánicas* (Madrid: Encuentro, 2009).

[44] James Sanders, *The Vanguard of the Atlantic World: creating Modernity, Nation, and Democracy in Nineteenth-century Latin America* (Durham, NC: Duke University Press, 2014); João José Reis, "'Nos achamos em campo a tratar da liberdade': A resistência escrava no Brasil oitocentista," in

projected into the public realm the symbolic prestige of aristocratic families, while training in schools and political associations consolidated their power.[45] In the nineteenth and twentieth centuries, the diffusion of a political press and the emergence of political organizations gave rise to new forms of collective mobilization and protest in Brazil and Latin America. In consequence of this, a good number of studies on the public sphere in the continent conceived the rise of associations and criticism in the light of notions of political culture and participation.[46]

Evangelical institutions of sociability such as congregations, associations of young people, women's societies, missionary schools, and seminaries are best understood when viewed as constituent and constitutive of the rich associational culture of modern Brazil. These institutions generated and empowered their own human capital amidst sweeping processes of social fragmentation. The religious presses and publishing houses of the age projected their homegrown intelligentsia into public life. Protestant ministers, missionaries, writers, and converts deployed these technologies to take part in public debates, discussing religious, political, and social topics from the reform of the Catholic Church to the abolition of slavery. A close attention to the periodicals, magazines, tracts, and books they published and set in motion captures the voices and experiences of the ordinary believers and religious experts who brought this religious world into being.

Another interdisciplinary body of work modified the Habermasian model once again and expanded scholarly understanding of the constitution of publics. For literary scholar Michael Warner, the public is an entity that comes into being "by virtue of being addressed." Unlike a concrete audience

---

Viagem incompleta: A experiência brasileira, 1500–2000, ed. Carlos G. Mota (São Paulo: Editora SENAC, 2000).

[45] Jeffrey Needell, *A Tropical Belle Époque: Elite Culture and Society in Turn-of-the-Century Rio de Janeiro* (Cambridge: Cambridge University Press, 1987); Andrew Kirkendall, *Class Mates: Male Student Culture and the Making of a Political Class in Nineteenth-century Brazil* (Lincoln: University of Nebraska Press, 2002); José Murilo de Carvalho, *A construção da ordem: A elite política imperial/ Teatro de sombras: A política imperial*, 3rd ed. (Rio de Janeiro: Civilização Brasileira, 2010).

[46] Marcello Basile, "O laboratório da nação: A Era Regencial (1831–1840)," in *O Brasil Imperial, Vol. II: 1831–1870*, ed. Keila Grinberg and Ricardo Salles (Rio de Janeiro: Civilização Brasileira, 2009); Marco Morel, *As transformações dos espaços públicos: Imprensa, atores políticos e sociabilidades na cidade imperial (1820–1840)* (São Paulo: Hucitec, 2005); Sandra L. Graham, "The Vintem Riot and Political Culture: Rio de Janeiro, 1880," *The Hispanic American Historical Review* 60 (1980): 431–449; James Woodard, "Pages from a Yellow Press: Print Culture, Public Life and Political Genealogies in Modern Brazil," *Journal of Latin American Studies* 46 (2014): 353–379; Hilda Sabato, *The Many and the Few: Political Participation in Republican Buenos Aires* (Stanford, CA: Stanford University Press, 2001); Hilda Sabato, "Citizenship, Political Participation and the Formation of the Public Sphere in Buenos Aires 1850s–1880s," *Past & Present* 136 (1992): 139–163.

or a crowd, this notion of the public is centered on the text and the imagined subjects it addresses. In this sense, publics are "virtual entities" conjured into being by the circulation of texts and performances, and so they can exist beyond institutions boundaries.[47] In a similar manner, literary scholar Isabel Hofmeyr and anthropologist Karin Barber have drawn attention to the historical specificity of publics. Examining the circulation of periodicals and Christian literature in Africa, these authors emphasized the importance of looking at the interpenetration of oral and written genres, textual genre and style, and to the specific ways in which texts were broadcast and adapted in the arenas in which they circulated.[48] In recent decades, historians and social scientists have begun to explore the theoretical implications of looking at texts as material objects, as things or commodities. For historian Mark Gamsa, bringing together analyses of intellectual flows and commodity transfers has the benefit of offering "a potentially new way of thinking about the global spread of ideas and the circuits of cross-cultural exchange."[49] This focus on the materiality of texts also highlights the specific uses of print matter in religious communities and the imaginary surrounding their local appropriations.

Over the past couple of decades scholars interested in the study of Christian and missionary literacies took part in these discussions and offered valuable contributions to the study of the worldwide diffusion of Christianity. Developments in communications and print in the modern era played an important role in connecting religious actors and organizations across the globe. The massive circulation of sacred texts and religious literature standardized religious doctrines, stabilized clerical authorities, and furnished missionaries and evangelists with a powerful technology of conversion.[50] Africanist scholars have been leading the way in the study of Christian literacy, showing how an in-depth analysis of Christian print illuminates the

---

[47] Michael Warner, *Public and Counterpublics* (New York: Zone Books, 2005), 67, 88–89.

[48] Karin Barber, *The Anthropology of Texts, Persons and Publics: Oral and Written Culture in Africa and Beyond* (Cambridge: Cambridge University Press, 2007); Isabel Hofmeyr, *The Portable Bunyan: A Transnational History of The Pilgrim's Progress* (Princeton, NJ: Princeton University Press, 2004); Isabel Hofmeyr, "Bunyan in Africa: Text and Transition," *Interventions* 3 (2001): 322–335.

[49] Mark Gamsa, "Translation and the Transnational Circulation of Books," *Journal of World History* 22 (2011): 553–575, at 574.

[50] Christopher Bayly, *The Birth of the Modern World, 1780–1914: Global Connections and Comparisons* (Oxford: Blackwell, 2004), 333–336; Christopher Clark and Michael Ledger-Lomas, "The Protestant International," in *Religious Internationals in the Modern World: Globalization and Faith Communities since 1750*, ed. Abigail Green and Vincent Viaene (Basingstoke: Palgrave Macmillan, 2012), 23–52.

intricacies of religious encounters. Although Western missionaries envisaged individual reading and writing as instruments for the development of the indigenous mind, a way of controlling and transforming the inner self,[51] African Christians appropriated Christian texts in unexpected ways. Missionary print culture intersected with flourishing oral cultures and established customs, enabling local converts to mobilize "scriptural authority in support of local practices," including polygamy and the notion that dreams served as vehicles of divine communication.[52] Charismatic Christian leaders in southern Africa created complex mechanisms involving collective reading of church histories, sermons, and correspondence to assert both their authority and the evangelical credentials of converts.[53] Other studies considered the materiality of Christian texts, highlighting patterns of scriptural reception and rejection in African societies, and examined how Christian literacy and mission schools stabilized local vernaculars and ethnicities.[54]

These insights shed light on different aspects of the missionary publishing enterprise in Brazil. By taking the circulation and materiality of texts into account, this book recovers the infrastructure devised by mission organizations and Bible societies to set texts in motion and highlight their specific uses in evangelical communities. They could be deployed in many ways: catechisms were used as reading primers in parish and Sunday schools, tracts and pamphlets served evangelistic purposes, while periodicals could be used to guide regular religious services or, in a mundane way, as wrapping paper. Texts could be carefully kept in private collections or carelessly abandoned by the roadside or at home. In any case, evangelicals believed that in *reading* they unlocked the transformative power of Bibles, periodicals, and tracts, enabling believers to encounter consolation, truth, and spiritual inspiration. In looking at the circulation of evangelical literature I recover some of the

---

[51] Jean Comaroff and John Comaroff, *Of Revelation and Revolution: Christianity, Colonialism, and Consciousness in South Africa* (Chicago: University of Chicago Press, 1991), 63.

[52] Patrick Harries, "Missionaries, Marxists and Magic: Power and the Politics of Literacy in Southeast Africa," *Journal of Southern African Studies* 27 (2001): 405–427, at 418.

[53] Joel Cabrita, *Text and Authority in the South African Nazaretha Church* (New York: Cambridge University Press, 2014); David Maxwell, "'Sacred History, Social History': Traditions and Texts in the Making of a Southern African Transnational Religious Movement," *Comparative Studies in Society and History* 43 (2001): 502–524.

[54] Thomas Kirsch, *Spirits and Letters: Reading, Writing and Charisma in African Christianity* (New York: Berghahn Books, 2008); Matthew Engelke, *A Problem of Presence: Beyond Scripture in an African Church* (Berkeley: University of California Press, 2007); J. D. Y. Peel, *Religious Encounter and the Making of the Yoruba* (Bloomington: Indiana University Press, 2000); David Maxwell, "The Creation of Lubaland: Missionary Science and Christian Literacy in the Making of the Luba Katanga in Belgian Congo," *Journal of Eastern African Studies* 10 (2016): 367–392.

assumptions that informed the evangelical attachment to the printed word and the individual and collective reading practices that emerged in Brazil.

Outline of Chapters

Chapters in this book follow a combination of chronological and thematic approaches. They have an overarching narrative that starts with the arrival of Protestant mission organizations in mid-nineteenth-century Brazil and closes with an examination of the rise of an evangelical intelligentsia in the twentieth century.

The opening chapter traces the first wave of Protestant expansion in Brazil between 1860 and 1900. It begins by situating this experience of evangelical diffusion into the social and political transformations of the age, interrogating what social categories embraced and propagated the new religion. It also recovers the experiences of Brazilian ministers and laypeople and the roles they played in the making of Protestant congregations and schools. The chapter concludes with an analysis of the evangelical publishing enterprise in this context of religious expansion and institution building, showing how converts seized the missionary bureaucratic machinery.

Chapter 2 is a case study of the operations of two London-based evangelical publishers in Brazil between 1870 and 1900: the British and Foreign Bible Society (BFBS) and the Religious Tract Society (RTS). It concentrates on the experiences of colporteurs, the itinerant booksellers who circulated an impressive number of Bibles and evangelical tracts throughout the country. The chapter reconstructs the interactions of colporteurs with customers, their encounters with Catholic priests and believers, and the reading practices that emerged out of the circulation of Christian texts. It also examines the rise of a Lusophone evangelical public sphere by tracing the flow of texts, people, and ideas throughout the transatlantic conduits of the BFBS and the RTS in Brazil, Portugal, Madeira, and Britain.

The following two chapters turn to the cultural and conceptual transformations involved in the making of Brazilian evangelicalism. Chapter 3 is an analysis of evangelical doctrines and ideas in the context of church–state conflicts and religious diversification in the last decades of the nineteenth century. By looking at the periodical *Imprensa Evangelica* (1864–1892) and the texts published by the Brazilian Society of Evangelical Tracts (1883–1897) it recovers the responses of Brazilian Protestants to the First Vatican

Council (1869–1870), the conservative Catholic renewal, and the secular ideologies of the time. The chapter also considers the tracts produced by Plymouth Brethren independent missionaries in Brazil and Portugal and their critique of the Brazilian religious landscape. Chapter 4 is concerned with conversion. Through an examination of conversion narratives, biographies of early converts, and missionary publications, it concentrates on the exchanges, objects, practices, and ideas that brought about evangelical conversion. The chapter analyzes the rhythms and ruptures of religious change in Brazil over two generations, unpacking the responses of neophytes and their offspring to new religious ideas and practices.

The book's last two chapters focus on the intellectual history of the movement. Chapter 5 examines how foreign missionaries and Latin American ministers appropriated and modified the idea of Christian cooperation of the World Missionary Conference in Edinburgh, 1910, in a series of missionary conferences in the Americas. Through an analysis of missionary correspondence and publications this chapter reconstructs the multiple interactions and exchanges that modified the missionary legacy of Edinburgh in 1910. The last part of the chapter concentrates on two books written by Brazilian ministers Erasmo Braga and Eduardo Carlos Pereira about the significance of the ideal of Christian cooperation to the social, political, and diplomatic life of the Americas. Finally, the last chapter in this monograph turns to the life-worlds and thought of a broader seminary-educated Protestant elite that emerged in Brazil. Straddling religious and secular domains, the protagonists of this chapter served as church pastors, mission theorists, and scholars who took part in the literacy academies and emerging universities of the country. The chapter examines their engagement with Anglophone Protestant theology; their participation in the social, literary, and religious debates of the country; and their scholarly interest in the rural traditions and language of the mixed-race rural populations of central Brazil.

1
Protestant Origins
Migrants, Missionaries, Local Leaders, and Religious Institutions

When foreign Protestant missionaries arrived in Rio de Janeiro in the nineteenth century their attention was immediately drawn to the magnificence of the surrounding landscape. They believed they were reaching a natural paradise of stunning beauty while navigating through the Guanabara Bay and looking at the multitude of small islands and high rocks emerging from the sea and the mountainous coastline covered with dense tropical vegetation. Presbyterian chaplain James C. Fletcher and Methodist missionary Daniel P. Kidder expressed their amazement by claiming that "The first entrance of any one to the Bay of Rio de Janeiro forms an era in his existence: 'an hour whence he may date thenceforward and forever.'"[1] On setting foot in the Brazilian capital, however, they were soon caught between mixed feelings of excitement and apprehension. The pioneer Presbyterian missionary Ashbel Simonton registered in his diary, in August 1859, the "conflicting emotions" that emerged as he entered the Rio de Janeiro bay on board of a steamship. He felt "contentment for the end of the long trip and fear for the great responsibilities and difficulties" that awaited him.[2] Others, like the Methodist pastor and agent of the American Bible Society Hugh Tucker, merged judgments about the religious landscape of the country into their astonishment with the city. Arriving in 1886, Tucker bemoaned the influence of the Catholic Church and sought to establish a contrast between the natural splendor of the Brazilian capital and the official religion: "There is perhaps no spot on the earth where the grandeur, beauty and harmonies of surrounding nature stand out in such bold contrast to the littleness, loathsomeness, and

---

[1] James C. Fletcher and Daniel P. Kidder, *Brazil and the Brazilians: Portrayed in Historical and Descriptive Sketches* (Philadelphia: Childs & Peterson, 1857), 15.

[2] Ashbel Green Simonton, *Diário, 1852–1867* (São Paulo: Casa Editora Presbiteriana, 1982), 142.

incongruity of the religious character and ideas of the people as in the city of Rio de Janeiro."[3]

These vignettes shed light on the expectations and worries that swirled around the minds of the first Protestant missionaries who landed in Brazil. They were entering a territory that had only recently begun to accept open religious dissidence after three centuries of colonial control. The social, political, and cultural prominence of the Catholic Church was impossible to circumvent, and episodes of anti-Protestant religious persecution soon began to occur. Some of the concerns of missionaries quickly became a reality: they found it difficult to learn the Portuguese language, felt uneasy with some of the customs of the country, encountered an orthodox and zealous Catholic clergy seeking to revitalize the Church, and met with some legal impediments enshrined in Brazilian law. At the same time, the religion of missionaries resonated with a set of religious traditions and social transformations in nineteenth-century Brazil. The rapid expansion of coffee plantations in the center south and the boom of commercial firms dynamized a region that was poorly served by the Catholic clergy. The influx of foreign European and American immigrants created Protestant communities in different parts of Brazil, especially in the region of São Paulo and the far south. A liberal Catholic clergy, that since the eighteenth century aimed to reform the Church, laid the basis for the settlement of Protestant missions. Brazilian converts rapidly seized the message of individual salvation and a set of evangelical religious practices, such as private reading of the Bible and domestic worship, and then adapted them to their own historical circumstances. A network of missionary schools gave rise to a local leadership that shared in the evangelistic fervor of the modern evangelical movement and played a key role in the diffusion of Protestantism in Brazil.

This chapter surveys some of the dynamics and interactions that characterized the earliest wave of evangelical expansion in Brazil, from the 1860s up until the twilight of the nineteenth century. It situates these experiences into the political and social transformations that enabled evangelical Christianity to gain a foothold in the country through the settlement of migrant communities and the operations of mission organizations. Special attention is given to the religious practices and institutional dynamics involved in the diffusion of Protestantism in the Brazilian center south. The chapter shows how the

---

[3] Hugh Tucker, *The Bible in Brazil: Colporteur Experiences* (New York: Young People's Missionary Movement of the United States and Canada, 1902), 29.

earliest generations of local converts and ministers shared in the voluntarist impulse of modern evangelicalism and took an active part in the missionary enterprise. The final section turns to the evangelical publishing endeavor, considering the religious imagination that underpinned it and the place of Protestant print in the religious encounter.

Immigrants and Missionaries

It was only in the nineteenth century that Brazil was included into the dense and far-reaching networks of global Protestantism. The incursions of French Huguenots in sixteenth-century Rio de Janeiro (1555–1567) and Dutch Calvinists in seventeenth-century Pernambuco (1630–1654) in the colonial era did not live long enough to inaugurate a sustained Protestant tradition in Brazil. The Portuguese re-conquest of these areas sought to wipe out these experiments in religious tolerance and dissidence from the Brazilian territory, with limited and dubious results despite the orthodox zeal of Jesuit missionaries and colonial authorities.[4] Legal concessions for the exercise of religious liberty emerged in the context of the crisis of the colonial enterprise in Brazil in the early nineteenth century. When the Portuguese court fled the Napoleonic invasion of the Iberian Peninsula with military support from the British navy and landed in the Brazilian coast in early 1808, they made a series of commercial and diplomatic concessions to the British. Some were intended to accommodate religious differences. A clause of the Treaty of Commerce and Navigation signed in 1810 determined that subjects of the British crown would be allowed to conduct religious services in the Brazilian territory as they saw fit, as long as they did not proselytize in the Portuguese language and their chapels did not look like churches.[5] After independence from Portugal in 1822, the Constitution of the Brazilian Empire extended the limits of religious freedom in the country. The Constitution established Catholicism as the state's official religion and determined that all other religious expressions could be practiced in the country as long as their private houses of worship did not resemble religious buildings. The traditional

---

[4] On the experience of tolerance and religious heterogeneity in colonial Brazil, see Stuart Schwartz, *All Can Be Saved: Religious Tolerance and Salvation in the Iberian Atlantic World* (New Haven, CT: Yale University Press, 2008), 177–206.

[5] Duncan A. Reily, *História documental do protestantismo no Brasil*, 3rd ed. (São Paulo: ASTE, 2003), 47–48.

interpretation of this legal clause was that non-Catholic churches could not have steeples and bells.[6] The Constitution also determined that religious persecution would be penalized.[7]

Another set of laws imposed a series of limits on the exercise of religious liberty. According to the Constitution, non-Catholics could neither vote nor be elected to the Chamber of Deputies and the Senate. Complementary laws approved in the late 1820s subjected public municipal cemeteries and registrations of marriage and births to ecclesiastical control.[8] Up until the electoral reform of 1881, elections for the parliament and the provincial assemblies took place in parish churches, a practice that "linked the social order to a holy one reaching to God himself" and surrounded electoral processes with religious "symbols of unquestioned authority."[9] From the 1860s onward, when the immigration of non-Catholic populations to Brazil took off, Protestant ministers, journalists, and liberal politicians started to object to these regulations and practices. For them, this set of limitations on the full exercise of religious liberty disenfranchised a growing number of people, including naturalized foreigners, and threatened the flow of foreign immigrants to the country.[10] The vagueness of these legal clauses defining the boundaries of religious liberty, along with the difficulties to enforce them, opened some room for maneuvering in negotiations between Protestants and public authorities. Throughout much of the nineteenth century, Protestant evangelization was carried out in the breaches of a poorly defined legislation. The same was not true for practitioners of African religions, frequent subjects of police investigation. According to historian João José Reis, "if the letter of the law stated that religions would be tolerated, the spirit of the law was intent at protecting religious freedom among white Protestant foreigners who resided in Brazil, such as Anglican British merchants. Religious freedom or tolerance was conceived with them in mind."[11]

---

[6] Alexander L. Blackford, *Sketch of the Brazil Mission* (Philadelphia: Presbyterian Board of Education, 1886), 3.
[7] *Collecção das leis do Império do Brazil de 1824* (Rio de Janeiro: Imprensa Nacional, 1886).
[8] Mercedes G. Kothe, "O Brasil no século XIX: restrições aos grupos não católicos," in *História em movimento: temas e perguntas*, ed. Albene M. Menezes (Brasília: Thesaurus, 1999), 92–103.
[9] Richard Graham, *Patronage and Politics in Nineteenth-century Brazil* (Stanford, CA: Stanford University Press, 1990), 114–115.
[10] Cláudia Rodrigues, "Sepulturas e sepultamentos do protestantes como uma questão de cidadania na crise do Império (1869–1889)," *Revista de História Regional* 13 (2008): 23–38.
[11] João José Reis, *Divining Slavery and Freedom: The Story of Domingos Sodré, an African Priest in Nineteenth-century Brazil*, trans. H. Sabrina Gledhill (New York: Cambridge University Press, 2015), 126–127.

Upholding a tradition that long characterized church–state relations in Portugal, the Brazilian Constitution incorporated into its legal apparatus the state patronage, which severely limited the autonomy of the Catholic Church. The Imperial state, not the Church, controlled elements of vital importance for the ecclesiastical management, such as the appointment of bishops, the collection of tithes, the opening of seminaries, and the creation of new bishoprics and parishes.[12] Dependent on the goodwill of imperial ministers, the Catholic Church received scant resources from the state. These policies deteriorated the Church's ecclesiastical institutions in the long run. Up until the republican *coup d'état* in 1889, imperial regulations on religious liberty and ecclesiastical administration proved to be disruptive for both the Catholic hierarchy and non-Catholic religious minorities.

Under these circumstances, two forces shaped Brazilian Protestantism in the nineteenth century: immigration and the missionary work. The settlement of immigrant communities in the newly independent Latin American states responded to internal sociopolitical pressures. National governments were interested in populating thinly occupied areas in their respective countries and opening their markets to international trade.[13] In the decades following the Brazilian independence, a few Anglican churches were created in different parts of the country, mostly in coastal cities such as Rio de Janeiro, Recife, Salvador, and Santos. At least until the arrival of American Episcopalian missionaries in the late 1880s, Anglican chaplains and priests catered to the religious needs of communities of British merchants, sailors, engineers, and railroad workers.[14]

German immigration was an important driver of Protestant growth. In the first half of the nineteenth century, when the Brazilian Empire faced international pressures to suppress the transatlantic slave trade, imperial ministers sought to stimulate foreign immigration to Brazil and attract workforce. In the racially charged discourse of political and intellectual elites, European immigrants would whiten Brazil's mestizo population and

---

[12] George Boehrer, "The Church in the Second Reign, 1840–1889," in *Conflict and Continuity in Brazilian Society*, ed. Henry H. Keith and S. F. Edwards (Columbia: University of South Carolina Press, 1969), 113–135; Guilherme P. das Neves, "A religião do Império e a Igreja," in *O Brasil Imperial, vol. I: 1808–1831*, ed. Keila Grinberg and Ricardo Salles (Rio de Janeiro: Civilização Brasileira, 2009), 377–428, at 395.

[13] José M. Bonino, *Rostros del protestantismo latinoamericano* (Buenos Aires: Nueva Creación, 1995), ch. 4.

[14] Richard Graham, *Britain and the Onset of Modernization in Brazil, 1850–1914* (Cambridge: Cambridge University Press, 1968), 278–279; Carlos Calvani, "Anglicanismo no Brasil," *Revista USP* 67 (2005): 36–47.

"civilize" the nation.[15] German and Swiss Lutheran immigrants began to settle in the Brazilian territory as early as 1819, establishing colonies and opening congregations in the provinces of Rio de Janeiro, Espírito Santo, Minas Gerais, and São Paulo.[16] It was in the south of Brazil, however, that German immigration flourished. During the long reign of Emperor Pedro II (1840–1889), studies on the viability of foreign immigration to Brazil were seriously debated in the houses of the parliament, leading the Empire to demarcate areas for immigrant settlement.[17] In the early twentieth century, Protestants, mostly of Lutheran origins, comprised the majority of the population of the southernmost state of Rio Grande do Sul.[18]

Another migratory wave played an important role in shaping Brazilian Protestantism. In the context of the American Civil War (1860–1865), a few thousand Confederate families from the American south made their way to Brazil and settled in different parts of the country, such as the Amazon region and Bahia. The majority of them settled in the province of São Paulo, attracted by the positive economic prospects of the region, its cheap lands, milder climate, and continued slavery. In the interior of São Paulo, the Confederates created Presbyterian, Methodist, and Baptist congregations with established elders and pastors prior to the arrival of foreign missionaries.[19] These religious communities were not driven by the same missionary fervor characteristic of the evangelical missionary enterprise. Lutherans and Anglo-Catholics did not consider Roman Catholics as suitable objects of mission work, let alone rebaptism.[20] Also, many German colonies were geographically and linguistically insulated in Brazil: they were poorly served by local schools and located at considerable distances from urban centers, which made interactions between immigrants and Brazilians a difficult affair.[21]

---

[15] Emília V. da Costa, *The Brazilian Empire: Myths and Histories* (Chicago: Univesity of Chicago Press, 1985).
[16] Martin N. Dreher, "Immigrant Protestantism: The Lutheran Church in Latin America," in *The Cambridge History of Religions in Latin America*, ed. Virginia Garrard-Burnett, Paul Freston and Stephen Dove (New York: Cambridge University Press, 2016), 304–318.
[17] João Klug, "Imigração no sul do Brasil," in *O Brasil Imperial, vol. III: 1870–1889*, ed. Keila Grinberg and Ricardo Salles (Rio de Janeiro: Civilização Brasileira, 2009), 201–231.
[18] Erasmo Braga and Kenneth Grubb, *The Republic of Brazil: A Survey of the Religious Situation* (London: World Dominion Press, 1932), 52.
[19] James Dawsey and Cyrus Dawsey, "The *Confederados*' Contributions to Brazilian Agriculture, Religion and Education," in *The Confederados: Old South Immigrants in Brazil*, ed. James Dawsey and Cyrus Dawsey (Tuscaloosa, AL: University of Alabama Press, 1995), 94–96; Frank P. Goldman, *Os pioneiros americanos no Brasil: educadores, sacerdotes, covos e reis* (São Paulo: Pioneira, 1972), ch. 1.
[20] Dreher, "Immigrant Protestantism," p. 305.
[21] Klug, "Imigração no sul do Brasil."

When the first American and British missionaries arrived in Brazil, they initially addressed communities of Protestant immigrants before turning to the Portuguese-speaking population. In the 1830s, two pastors of the Methodist Episcopal Church of the United States, Daniel P. Kidder and Justin Spaulding, established the first missionary work in the Brazilian territory. Attracted to Rio de Janeiro in 1836 by the settlement of lay migrants in South America, Kidder and Spaulding initially reached out to English-speaking sailors and Anglican chaplains in the country before establishing closer connections with Brazilian politicians and liberal Catholic clerics. They also circulated Bibles in Portuguese.[22] The death of Kidder's wife and the mission's financial problems put an end to this early Methodist experiment in 1841. After that, an American Presbyterian pastor, James C. Fletcher, who worked intermittently in Brazil from 1852 through the 1870s as a chaplain and agent of the American Bible Society (ABS), deployed missionary methods similar to those of the Methodists. Fletcher's flamboyant personality enabled him to enter diplomatic, intellectual, and political circles. His enthusiasm for the "virtues of Protestantism" and the "progress" of Brazil won important friendships in the political and literary establishments of the country, including the Brazilian Emperor Pedro II. Fletcher also circulated Bibles and opened small educational ventures in Rio de Janeiro.[23] Foreign missionaries and Protestant educators who later embarked to Brazil benefited from Fletcher's networks and were able to obtain political protection to open mission stations and schools in the country.

It was from the 1850s onward, after the quelling of a series of upheavals and slave revolts in the context of the Regency Period (1831–1840) that Protestant mission organizations turned their attention to Brazil. Five main denominational missionary fronts led Protestant expansion. The Scottish Congregationalist medical missionary, Dr. Robert Kalley, established a pioneer center in Rio de Janeiro. Prior to his arrival in Brazil, Kalley led a Presbyterian missionary work in the Island of Madeira, Portugal (1838–1846). There he became fluent in Portuguese and was able to assemble a large Protestant community. As Kalley's missionary initiatives succeeded, Portuguese ecclesiastical and political authorities launched a coordinated

---

[22] Walter Wedemann, "A History of Protestant Missions to Brazil, 1850–1914" (PhD diss., Southern Baptist Theological Seminary, 1977), 87–92; David Hempton, *Methodism: Empire of the Spirit* (New Haven, CT: Yale University Press, 2005), 157–158. On Daniel P. Kidder's experiences in Brazil, see his *Sketches of Residence and Travel in Brazil*, 2 vols. (Philadelphia, PA: Sorin & Ball, 1845).

[23] The best analysis of James C. Fletcher's significance is in David G. Vieira, *O protestantismo, a maçonaria e a Questão Religiosa no Brasil* (Brasília: Editora UnB, 1980), ch. 3–4.

effort to control evangelical diffusion in the island, sparking bursts of religious persecution. In 1846, after a violent episode, Kalley and a good number of Portuguese converts fled the island. A group of around a thousand Portuguese converts settled the cities of Springfield and Jacksonville in the US state of Illinois.[24] After some years wandering through Malta, Beirut, Britain, and the United States, Kalley moved to Rio de Janeiro in 1855, where he soon began to offer medical care during an outbreak of cholera, and where he opened a Sunday school.[25] Shortly after his arrival in Brazil, Kalley was joined by Portuguese exiles from Madeira, who worked as evangelists and colporteurs circulating religious literature in Rio de Janeiro and beyond. Together they founded the *Igreja Evangélica Fluminense* (Fluminense Evangelical Church) in 1858.[26]

American Presbyterians opened their first mission station in Brazil at around the same time. In 1859, Ashbel Simonton, from the Board of Foreign Missions of the Presbyterian Church of the United States, arrived in Rio de Janeiro carrying letters of introduction written by James C. Fletcher. Simonton's sister and brother-in-law, Elizabeth and Alexander Blackford, joined him in 1860 and opened another mission station in São Paulo in 1861, attracted by the communities of German and American immigrants in the region.[27] Southern American Presbyterians entered the Brazilian field in 1869 with the missionaries George Morton and Edward Lane, who settled in the city of Campinas in the province of São Paulo. What attracted Morton and Lane to Campinas was the presence of Confederate families in the region, and together they founded in 1870 the International School, which soon became a prestigious educational institution. In the early 1870s, Presbyterians expanded their work to Bahia and Pernambuco. It was in São Paulo, however, that the endeavors of American Presbyterian missionaries advanced at a faster pace. In the 1870s and 1880s, missionaries, Brazilian ministers, and laypeople opened dozens of churches and preaching places in the region.[28]

American Methodists opened two different missionary fronts in Brazil. The southern American Methodist Episcopal Church began operations

---

[24] Dennis Suttles, "Schism on the Prairie: The Case of the Free Portuguese Church of Jacksonville, Illinois," *Journal of Presbyterian History* 75 (1997): 211–222; Robert R. Kalley to Leonards, October 22, 1846. BSA/D1/2, Foreign Correspondence Inwards, Robert Reid Kalley.

[25] Wedemann, "A History of Protestant Missions," 107–108; Vieira, *O protestantismo*, ch. 6.

[26] João G. da Rocha, *Lembranças do passado*, 4 vols. (Rio de Janeiro: Centro Brasileiro de Publicidade, 1941), vol. I, 33–38.

[27] Vieira, *O protestantismo*, 135–141.

[28] Wedemann, "A History of Protestant Missions," 134–136.

in the city of Santa Bárbara, São Paulo, in 1867 with a preacher, Junius Newman, who served the communities of American immigrants. Years later Newman persuaded his home church to expand operations in Brazil and, in 1876, the missionary John James Ransom arrived in the countryside of São Paulo. A couple years later southern American Methodists expanded their work to Rio de Janeiro. In the south of Brazil, it was the Brazilian physician Dr. João da Costa Corrêa who became the pioneer Methodist agent. Dr. Corrêa was linked to the northern American Methodist *La Plata Mission* based in Uruguay, and he introduced Methodism in the province of Rio Grande do Sul in 1875.[29]

Whereas these ventures targeted the economically dynamic Brazilian center-south, the two last missionary societies occupied the north and the south of the country. Missionaries from the Southern Baptist Convention of the United States arrived in Brazil in 1881 with the couple William and Anne Bagby. They initially opened a mission station in Santa Bárbara, serving the communities of American immigrants, and they studied Portuguese with the Presbyterians in Campinas. In the following year, another competent missionary couple, Zachary and Kate Taylor, joined the Bagbys. Upon concluding that Presbyterians and Methodists had already occupied the most promising areas in the province of São Paulo, they decided to move the Baptist mission station to Bahia (Figure 1.3).[30] From this base, Baptists expanded their work nationwide. In 1884, the Bagbys moved to Rio de Janeiro where they encountered sectarian resistance from other church leaders who considered the Baptists as a "sect of narrow-minded and bigoted" people.[31] Finally, the American Episcopal Church entered Brazil with the ministers James Morris and Lucien Kinsolving. They opened their denomination's missionary operations in the province of Rio Grande do Sul in 1890, supported by Presbyterian and Methodist converts.[32]

Although Protestants shared a similar identity as a non-Catholic religious minority in Brazil, denominational differences loomed large. Presbyterians and Baptists, the most successful groups of this era, illustrate this. Regional

---

[29] Reily, *História documental*, 104–114.
[30] Wedemann, "A History of Protestant Missions," 145–149.
[31] *Proceedings of the Southern Baptist Convention* (Atlanta: J. P. Harisson & Co., 1885), appendix A, ix. Hereinafter cited as SBC Proceedings [year].
[32] *Brazilian Missions*, vol. IV, n. 7, July 1891, 53. A summary of the history of these five Protestant missionary ventures can be found in Léonard, *O protestantismo brasileiro*, 53–94; and in Elizete da Silva, Lyndon Santos, and Vasni Almeida, eds., *Fiel é a palavra: Leituras históricas dos evangélicos protestantes no Brasil* (Feira de Santana: UEFS Editora, 2011).

presbyteries and a national synod linked Presbyterian churches together, whereas Baptists adopted the congregational government, ensuring the independence of local churches. Baptist missionaries also practiced a more aggressive style of evangelism and were able to reach out to larger audiences, while Presbyterians proved to be competent institution builders.[33] Baptists also antagonized the sacramental practices of the other Protestant denominations and strongly opposed the baptism of infants.

In 1889, when Brazilian Emperor Pedro II was overthrown and a provisional republican government seized power, Protestant churches and small congregations had been established in the majority of eastern and southern provinces of Brazil. In 1888, Presbyterian missionaries from the north and the south of the United States decided to join their forces and create a unified national synod. The statistics gathered at that time showed that the Presbyterian Church of Brazil was comprised of approximately three thousand communicant members scattered in sixty-one congregations located in twelve of the twenty provinces of Brazil.[34] Among Baptists, the church of Bahia became their strongest missionary center. In 1889, the Bahia mission station counted a membership of 198 communicant members in four different churches. From this base Zachary Taylor undertook evangelistic trips and coordinated preaching points in other northern provinces, such as Maceio and Pernambuco (Figure 1.3).[35] The central stage of evangelical expansion in nineteenth-century Brazil was the province of São Paulo. Thirty-four of the sixty-one Presbyterian churches in the Brazilian territory in the late 1880s were located there. In 1884, for instance, there were Presbyterian congregations in the expanding cities of Sorocaba, Rio Claro, Campinas, and São Paulo, where a new church building had the capacity to accommodate six hundred people (see Figures 1.1 and 1.2). From the Rio Claro Presbyterian Church, the Portuguese pastor João Dagama oversaw dozens of preaching places across the surrounding villages and *sítios* (small farms).[36]

---

[33] H. B. Cavalcanti, "O projeto missionário protestante no Brasil do século 19: Comparando a experiência presbiteriana e batista," *Revista de Estudos da Religião* 4 (2001): 61–93.
[34] *The Fifty-second Annual Report of the Board of Foreign Missions of the Presbyterian Church in the United States of America* (New York: Mission House, 1889), 39. Hereinafter cited as BFM-PCUSA Annual Report [year].
[35] SBC Proceedings [1889], appendix A, xiv–xvii.
[36] BFM-PCUSA Annual Report [1884], 31–35.

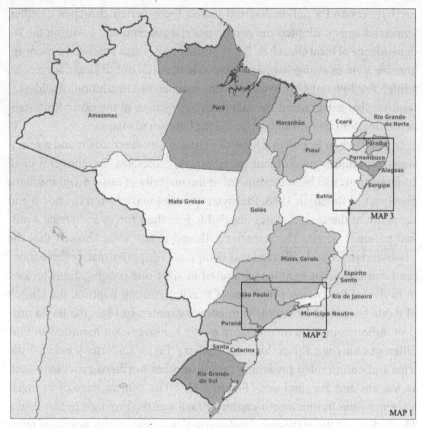

Figure 1.1 Map of Brazil at the start of the Republic, 1889.
Author: Milenioscuro, https://commons.wikimedia.org/wiki/File:Brazil_in_1889.svg.

Figure 1.2 Protestant nuclei and congregations in the states of São Paulo, Rio de Janeiro, and southern Minas Gerais.

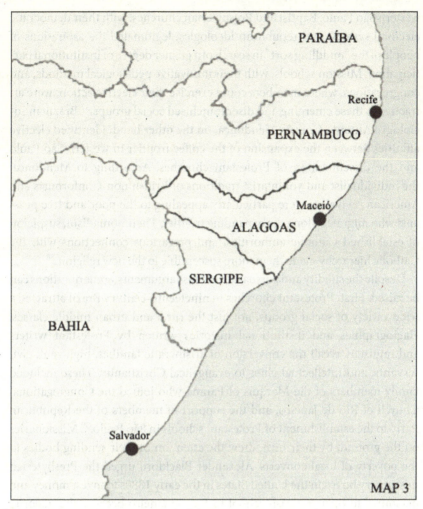

Figure 1.3 Protestant nuclei and congregations in the Brazilian northeast.

Religious Diffusion and the Rise of a Local Leadership

In the 1970s and 1980s, social scientists offered explanations for this earliest wave of evangelical expansion in Brazil's most dynamic economic centers. American sociologist and theologian Ronald Frase argued that Protestantism was particularly appealing to Brazil's emergent urban and rural middle classes, especially in the growing cities of São Paulo and Rio de Janeiro and the expanding agricultural frontiers of southern Bahia and western São Paulo. Baptist and Presbyterian churches, with their democratic electoral systems and republican ideologies, legitimated the aspirations of people of the "middling sort" in search of a greater degree of institutional participation. Mission schools, with their innovative pedagogical methods, and congregations, where members could exercise their elective action, were attractive to these emerging and disenfranchised social groups.[37] Brazilian sociologist Antonio Gouvêa Mendonça, on the other hand, identified elective affinities between the expansion of the coffee frontier in western São Paulo and the dissemination of Protestant churches. According to Mendonça, the individualist and voluntarist traditions of British non-Conformists and American revivalists were particularly appealing to the poor and free peasants who migrated along the expanding frontier. Their nomadism, suspicion of established Catholic authorities, and precarious connections with the Catholic hierarchy made them more susceptible to the new religion.[38]

Despite the solidity and persuasion of these arguments, some questions can be raised. First, Protestant churches in nineteenth-century Brazil attracted a wide variety of social groups, not just the rural and urban middle classes. Hagiographies and institutional histories written by Protestant writers and ministers recall the conversion of aristocratic families, high-rank civil servants, and intellectual elites to evangelical Christianity. These included family members of the Marquis of Paraná who joined the Congregational Church of Rio de Janeiro, and the support of members of the Republican Party to the establishment of Protestant schools in São Paulo.[39] Missionaries on the ground, by their turn, drew the attention of their sending bodies to the poverty of local converts. Alexander Blackford urged the Presbyterian missionary board in the United States in the early 1880s to invest money and personnel to open a parish school in Rio de Janeiro because the majority of church members were poor and unable to send their children to private schools.[40] A colleague of Blackford, the Portuguese missionary João Dagama,

---

[37] Ronald G. Frase, "A Sociological Analysis of the Development of Brazilian Protestantism: A Study of Social Change" (PhD dissertation, Princeton Theological Seminary, 1975), 248–249, 306–307, 330–331.

[38] Antonio G. Mendonça, *O celeste porvir: a inserção do protestantismo no Brasil*, 3rd ed. (São Paulo: Ed. USP, 2008), 220–224.

[39] João G. da Rocha, *Lembranças do passado, vol. I* (Rio de Janeiro: Centro Brasileiro de Publicidade, 1941), 82–83; Boanerges Ribeiro, *Protestantismo e cultura brasileira: aspectos culturais da implantação do protestantismo no Brasil* (São Paulo: Casa Editora Presbiteriana, 1981), 207, 224.

[40] A. L. Blackford to Rev. D. Irving. Bahia, August 15, 1882. PHS, BFM-PCUSA, Mission Correspondence, South American Letters.

wrote to his sending body in the early 1870s that the new converts of the Presbyterian Church of Rio de Janeiro came from various walks of life. His church, he claimed, was "attracting the attention of the small and larg [sic]; the poor and reach [sic]."[41] About a decade later, when Dagama was relocated to the flourishing Brotas mission station in São Paulo, he began to carry out an extensive itinerant work, preaching and administering sacraments in small towns, hamlets, and *sítios* across the province. In all these places he encountered impoverished and illiterate audiences.[42] The Presbyterian missionary George Chamberlain, who worked for several years in the city of São Paulo, wrote to the BFM that, in 1878, the five new members of his church touched "the extremes of society."[43] Protestant missionaries encountered mixed social categories interested in joining their congregations and schools.

Apart from that, the institutional machinery created by Presbyterian missionaries played a crucial role in the diffusion of Protestantism. Local congregations and parish schools furnished converts with a basic infrastructure that could be deployed to raise funds and provide elementary education to their children. Mission schools, seminaries, and publishing houses gave rise to a group of religious specialists, such as ministers and schoolteachers, and projected the religious energy of the first generations of Brazilian evangelicals into the public sphere. The expansion and consolidation of this religious bureaucracy involved two interrelated processes: the training of a Portuguese-speaking leadership and the involvement of the laity. Although the American missionaries controlled a large share of the financial resources and were in charge of corresponding with their sending bodies, the most active agents of religious expansion were either Portuguese immigrants or Brazilian converts. They served as ministers, itinerant evangelists, booksellers, and schoolteachers in the evangelistic enterprise.

The experiences of João Dagama, one of the busiest missionaries on the ground, illustrate this. He was recruited from among the community of Portuguese exiles who fled religious persecution in Madeira and settled in Illinois.[44] Upon his arrival in Brazil in 1870, Dagama worked in the cities of Rio de Janeiro and Brotas before establishing his residence in Rio Claro in

---

[41] J. F. Dagama to Rev. D. Irving. Rio de Janeiro, March 29, 1872. PHS, BFM-PCUSA, Mission Correspondence, South American Letters.
[42] J. F. Dagama to Rev. D. Irving. Brotas, May 9, 1873. PHS, BFM-PCUSA, Mission Correspondence, South American Letters.
[43] BFM-PCUSA Annual Reports [1879], 23.
[44] Suttles, "Schism on the Prairie," 211–222.

the countryside of São Paulo in 1873. From this base he coordinated a far-reaching itinerant ministry encompassing the surrounding cities of Brotas, Dois Córregos, Pirassununga, Belém, Bom Jardim, São Carlos do Pinhal, and some *sítios* around Serra and Cabeceira do Jacaré (see Figure 1.2).[45] By 1883, Dagama's missionary base in Rio Claro comprised twenty-seven preaching places scattered across the province of São Paulo. In all these places, it was local converts who conducted weekly religious services, gathered believers, taught at the parish schools, and carried out evangelistic work.[46]

Most of the Portuguese-speaking leaders of the Presbyterian Church of Brazil in the last decades of the Empire were either recruited or trained in churches and schools in São Paulo. The training of their personnel involved a long process of study for the pastoral ministry and preparatory work in schools, local churches, and the evangelical publishing enterprise. In the early 1870s, the Presbyterian Church had ordained two pastors in Brazil: the former Catholic priest José Manoel da Conceição, who did extensive itinerant work in São Paulo between his ordination in 1865 and death in 1873; and Modesto P. Carvalhosa, a Portuguese immigrant appointed to the Lorena church in 1871, whose work encompassed the surrounding cities.[47] Other potential ministers at that time trained as licensed preachers, schoolteachers, or journal editors under the supervision of foreign missionaries. In Rio de Janeiro, missionary Alexander Blackford employed a candidate for the pastorate, Cândido J. de Mesquita, as director of the primary and secondary Presbyterian school in the city of Petrópolis. Apart from his educational responsibilities, Mesquita also organized regular religious services in the city thrice a week.[48] Mesquita later abandoned the Presbyterian work in the early 1880s to join the Baptist mission in Rio.[49]

The Presbyterian Church had, in the mid-1870s, three other candidates for the pastoral work: the Brazilians Antônio de Cerqueira Leite and Miguel Torres, and the Portuguese Antônio Trajano. At that time, Cerqueira Leite was working in the church of Sorocaba as a licensed preacher under the

---

[45] Relação breve de meus trabalhos na pregação do Evangelho desde Agosto do anno pp. até o presente (J. F. Dagama, August 4, 1875). AHP, Coleção Carvalhosa—Relatórios Pastorais (1866–1875).
[46] BFM-PCUSA Annual Report [1884], 35.
[47] On Conceição, see Júlio A. Ferreira, *História da Igreja Presbiteriana do Brasil, vol. I*, 2nd ed. (São Paulo: Casa Editora Presbiteriana, 1992), 62–65. On the beginning of Carvalhosa's ministry, see his annual reports: AHP, Coleção Carvalhosa—Relatórios Pastorais (1866–1875).
[48] Relatório Annual de A. L. Blackford, apresentado ao Presbytério do Rio de Janeiro, em sessão no Rio de Janeiro, a 19 de Agosto de 1872. AHP, Coleção Carvalhosa—Relatórios Pastorais (1866–1875).
[49] SBC Proceedings [1885], appendix A, ix and x.

supervision of George Chamberlain, and he was ordained in 1876. Torres and Trajano trained in São Paulo and Rio de Janeiro respectively as evangelists and schoolteachers, and they were both ordained in 1875.[50] Throughout the 1880s, the Presbyterian Church of Brazil appointed other Brazilian and Portuguese men for ministry in local congregations, mainly in the province of São Paulo. Some of them eventually occupied prestigious positions in the hierarchy of the church. Trajano, for instance, after his ordination, worked in the churches of São Paulo and Brotas up until 1879, when he was appointed to the Presbyterian Church of Rio de Janeiro, the oldest and largest in the country where his preaching was highly appreciated.[51] Up until the overthrow of the Empire in 1889, the Presbyterian Church ordained four other Portuguese-speaking pastors: the Portuguese João de Carvalho Braga (1885) and the Brazilians José Zacarias de Miranda (1881), Benedito Ferraz Campos (1889), and Eduardo Carlos Pereira (1881). Some of them became prominent Protestant leaders.

Pereira's trajectory in the Presbyterian Church of Brazil illustrates the dynamics involved in the making of a local clergy (Figure 1.4). Born to a middle-class family in the city of Caldas, Minas Gerais, Pereira became a convert in 1875 and joined the São Paulo Presbyterian Church.[52] He spent four years preparing for the pastorate and in 1880 became a licensed preacher at the Presbyterian Church of Lorena, in the countryside of São Paulo.[53] In the following year, he was ordained and appointed to a church in the city of Campanha, Minas Gerais. In 1888, Pereira became the head pastor of the Presbyterian Church of São Paulo, one of the largest evangelical churches in the country. By the time of Pereira's nomination, this church had become self-supporting by relying on the contributions of its local members and acquiring some independence from the Presbyterian Board of Foreign Missions.[54] Throughout his career Pereira taught languages, especially Portuguese and Latin at the Presbyterian schools of São Paulo and Campanha. A talented writer, he contributed frequently with the *Imprensa Evangelica*, the first Protestant periodical of Latin America, and founded the

---

[50] Relatório dos trabalhos de G. W. Chamberlain durante o anno Presbyterial de 1874 a 1875. AHP, Coleção Carvalhosa—Relatórios Pastorais (1866–1875).
[51] BFM-PCUSA Annual Reports [1880], 20.
[52] Vicente T. Lessa, *Annaes da 1ª Egreja Presbyteriana de São Paulo (1863–1903): Subsidios para a historia do presbiterianismo brasileiro* (São Paulo: Edição da 1ª Igreja Presbiteriana Independente de São Paulo, 1938), 131–137.
[53] BFM-PCUSA Annual Reports [1881], 22.
[54] BFM-PCUSA Annual Reports [1889], 44.

Figure 1.4 Eduardo Carlos Pereira in 1899. CDH-VTL, Pasta de Fotos.

Brazilian Society of Evangelical Tracts in 1883, the periodical *O Estandarte* in 1893, and the Review of National Missions in 1888. The latter gained some prominence as the Presbyterian Church's flagship organ defending the emancipation of national churches from the American missionary boards.[55] As his trajectory illustrates, local ministers were able to enter missionary bureaucracies, rise in the institutional hierarchy, and ensure the independence of local churches from foreign missionary control.

[55] Lessa, *Annaes*, 229–230, 281–282.

Creating Evangelical Institutions

Evangelical organizations, especially the parish school and the local church, furnished local believers with an institutional framework within which they could organize themselves, apply their money, and supply their own needs apart from the structures of the state and the Catholic Church. In nineteenth-century Brazil, primary and secondary public schools were debilitated institutions, unable to provide instruction to a considerable part of the population. In the face of this, private education proliferated, either in the form of language and science courses or in fully equipped schools, such as those founded by the American missions.[56] At the same time, the terms of the Empire's state patronage subjected the hierarchy of the Catholic Church to imperial rulers and a somewhat anticlerical political elite. The Empire, not the Church, oversaw the collection of tithes and the appointment of bishops, whereas the Provincial Assemblies, not the ecclesiastical authorities, were constitutionally entitled to create new parishes.[57] Although Emperor Pedro II envisioned a general moral reform of the Brazilian clergy and invested in the careers of promising priests, the Church received scant resources during his long reign. Only a few dioceses were created, seminaries were depleted, and the state interfered even in religious orders, prohibiting them from accepting novices.[58] In the face of this institutional void, evangelical organizations evolved into respectable institutions and opened much room for lay involvement.

Under the leadership of George Chamberlain, the Presbyterian Church of São Paulo employed its own financial resources, collected from contributions and tithes, to purchase a lot in the city center in 1874. Missionaries and local leaders ran the church and a school at this lot for a decade.[59] In 1883, the mission station was able to inaugurate a new church building, a "beautiful and commodious house of worship" with capacity for six hundred people. It cost about $13,000, of which $5,000 had been collected in the United States and $8,000 locally amongst members of the São Paulo church.[60] In 1875, João

---

[56] José R. P. de Almeida, *História da instrução pública no Brasil (1500–1889)* (São Paulo: EDUC; Brasília: INEP, 1989); Maria L. Hilsdorf, *História da educação brasileira: leituras* (São Paulo: Pioneira, 2003).

[57] Neves, "A religião do Império," 395.

[58] Boehrer, "The Church in the Second Reign," 124–135.

[59] Relatório dos trabalhos de G. W. Chamberlain durante o anno Presbyterial de 1874 a 1875. AHP, Coleção Carvalhosa—Relatórios Pastorais (1866–1875).

[60] BFM-PCUSA Annual Report [1884], 34.

Dagama reported to his fellow missionaries that in the city of Palmeiras, São Paulo, members of the Presbyterian congregation donated a piece of land upon which they expected to build a church, a cemetery, and a house for a poor convert who would look after the church.[61] In the same year the Rev. Modesto P. Carvalhosa informed that believers in the churches of Borda da Mata and Caldas collected funds amidst congregations to build houses of worship and small cemeteries.[62] Brazilian converts seized the voluntarist impulse of evangelical Christianity to mobilize their constituencies and provide for their own religious, financial, and educational needs, a process that to a certain extent anticipated the strategies of Pentecostals in twentieth-century Latin America.[63]

Local fundraising had a broader significance. It implicated believers in a relationship with the global church. According to sociologist David Lehmann, the practice of tithing put believers into an abstract relationship with the organization. By giving to the local congregation, converts believed they were joining a larger, worldwide community.[64] Although Lehmann's study examines the experiences of contemporary Pentecostal believers, the first generations of Protestant converts experienced their religious commitment in similar ways. In 1910, when the pastor of the Presbyterian Church of Rio de Janeiro, Rev. Álvaro Reis, was invited to attend the World Missionary Conference in Edinburgh, members of his church volunteered to ensure the financial viability of the trip. They donated money and a luggage set to have their pastor represented in that prestigious event.[65] In a similar way, Baptist pastor Solomon Ginsburg challenged the members of his church in 1895 in the city of Campos, near Rio de Janeiro, to donate goods and money to the Foreign Mission Board of the Southern Baptist Convention, which was undergoing a financial crisis. Believers contributed golden rings, breast-pins, earrings, money, and even chicken eggs that amounted to twenty-five dollars, which was sent to the United States.[66] Even though it is unlikely

---

[61] Relação breve de meus trabalhos na pregação do Evangelho desde Agosto do anno pp. Até o presente (J. F. Dagama). AHP, Coleção Carvalhosa—Relatórios Pastorais (1866–1875).

[62] Relatório de M. P. B. Carvalhosa para o anno de 1875. AHP, Coleção Carvalhosa—Relatórios Pastorais (1866–1875).

[63] Paul Freston, "Pentecostalism in Latin America: Characteristics and Controversies," *Social Compass* 45 (1998): 335–358.

[64] David Lehmann, *Struggle for the Spirit: Religious Transformation and Popular Culture in Brazil and Latin America* (Cambridge: Polity Press, 1996), 207.

[65] *O Puritano*, March 3, 1910, n. 533.

[66] Henry Spittle to A. W. Armstrong, Campos, March 29, 1895. IBMB, Solomon Ginsburg papers.

that this modest aid relieved the financial pressure of the Baptist mission, their contributions nevertheless demonstrated the willingness of Brazilian evangelicals to participate actively in the worldwide missionary movement.

Local fundraising and lay involvement also enabled evangelical religion to create local roots. The activism of ordinary believers was a central aspect of modern evangelical culture, widely spread by missionaries worldwide.[67] But this was also a reality to Brazilian Catholics since the colonial era. Both the Portuguese and the Brazilian monarchies curtailed investment in the bureaucracy of the Church. By the time of the Brazilian independence there were little more than six hundred parishes in the entire country, meaning that each parish priest was in charge of flocks of around six thousand souls, on average, over vast stretches of remote territories.[68] Seminaries were also scarce, and the Catholic Church struggled to reach out to far-off communities, administer the sacraments to the faithful, and keep them within the fold. Consequently, lay initiative and leadership became crucial bearers of religious traditions and practices. Brotherhoods and associations played a central role in the consolidation of Catholic devotions, raising funds among ordinary believers to erect shrines and organize religious festivals for patron saints. Brazilian Catholicism was highly participatory by the time Protestant missionaries arrived, enabling missionaries and ministers to seize hold of these practices and channel them for different purposes.

Churches, local congregations, and parish schools opened multiple possibilities for the engagement of the laity in the missionary work. The Presbyterian Church of Brazil had, in 1886, thirty-three congregations with a membership of nearly 1,700 people.[69] There were also dozens of smaller preaching places spread throughout São Paulo, Rio de Janeiro, and Bahia. Ordained ministers, however, amounted to only sixteen. They could barely meet the needs of this expanding community of converts.[70] The individuals who took over the task of carrying out regular church work were ordinary believers who propagated the new religion at grassroots level. They took on various roles in the missionary work, depending on their training and skills, and most of these roles were somewhat related to schooling and literacy.

---

[67] On evangelical activism see David Bebbington, *Evangelicalism in Modern Britain: A History from the 1730s to the 1980s* (London: Unwin Hyman, 1989).

[68] Guilherme P. das Neves, "Igreja," in *Dicionário do Brasil colonial (1500–1808)*, ed. Ronaldo Vainfas (Rio de Janeiro: Objetiva, 2001), 292–296, at 294.

[69] Blackford, *Sketch*, 18.

[70] BFM-PCUSA Annual Report [1887], 44.

The majority of Presbyterian mission stations in the nineteenth century employed at least one colporteur to circulate evangelical literature, the periodical *Imprensa Evangelica*, and Bibles.

Presbyterian missionaries invested money and personnel in an array of ventures to prepare and ordain Brazilian ministers and other local leaders. This process involved the creation of a theological school in São Paulo and the establishment of a short-term theological class in the city of Brotas, aimed at preparing schoolteachers, Bible-readers, and evangelists. These initiatives were integrated into a broader plan devised in the 1870s intended to make Brazilian Presbyterian churches independent from the American mission boards and nationalize their personnel. As stated in a missionary report, "these Bible-readers, coming from among the people, and having been educated without losing their former habits of life, and therefore living just exactly as the people, will not only seem nearer to them and better able to sympathize with them, but will also require much less for their support."[71] Although the implementation of this plan was unsuccessful and the Presbyterians continued to prepare their staff in an improvised manner, Bible-readers acquired some prestige in the missionary work. They conducted religious services in the absence of ordained ministers, or they acted independently in smaller congregations. In 1880, Bible-readers coordinated parish schools and carried out weekly services in various cities and villages across São Paulo and Minas Gerais. In the city of Pirassununga, São Paulo, Innocencio Xavier conducted services and ran a small parish school relying solely on the contributions of church members.[72] The missionary Alexander Blackford also employed Bible-readers in Bahia in the early 1880s. The first of them was a widow, "a colored woman, sensible and devoted," whose mission was to reach out and instruct illiterate women at the same church.[73] In the same year, Blackford opened a second preaching place in Bahia, in which a Bible-reader read aloud manuscript sermons to the congregation.[74]

The material and human resources deployed in the preparation of a local religious leadership reflected wider debates about the nature, goals, and challenges of the worldwide missionary enterprise. These missiological

---

[71] BFM-PCUSA Annual Report [1878], 24.
[72] Annual Report of the Rio Claro Station from August 1, 1880 to January 31, 1881. PHS, BFM-PCUSA, Mission Correspondence, South American Letters.
[73] A. L. Blackford to D. Irving, Bahia, May 6, 1881. PHS, BFM-PCUSA, Mission Correspondence, South American Letters.
[74] BFM-PCUSA Annual Report [1882], 22.

principles emerged out of the ordeals of British and American missionaries in their fields and to intellectual exchanges between Anglophone mission organizations in the 1850s. The mission theorists Henry Venn, honorary secretary of the Church Missionary Society between 1841 to 1872, and Rufus Anderson, foreign secretary of the American Board of Commissioners for Foreign Missions from 1832 to 1866, played a key role in these debates.[75] Contemplating the financial hardship of mission societies and acknowledging that the evangelization of the world by Western missionaries alone was an impossible task, Venn and Anderson upheld the cause of the autonomy of indigenous churches.[76] They promoted the so-called three-self program, whose main formula asserted that local churches should become self-governing, self-supporting, and self-propagating. Venn and Anderson believed that this program would alleviate the financial burden of missionary organizations and avoid the alienation of indigenous leaders from their cultural surroundings.[77] Their defense of the autonomy of local churches should not be confounded with appreciation for indigenous cultures. According to historian Wilbert Shenk, Anderson and Venn accepted the superiority of Western culture as self-evident.[78] Nevertheless, the three-self program left room for multiple appropriations. When a series of disagreements between Brazilian Presbyterian ministers and the American missionaries about the administration of churches and seminaries began to escalate in the 1890s, ministers and elders of the São Paulo Church deployed the idea of the self-government of local churches to try and seize control of evangelical institutions.[79] Although these first attempts proved unsuccessful, the fact demonstrates that Anglophone missionary theory could be deployed in different ways, even weaponized at the hands of local religious leaders.

In the light of this, it may be useful to nuance Antonio Gouvêa Mendonça's argument that mainline Protestantism was not able to disseminate more

---

[75] Wilbert R. Shenk, "Rufus Anderson and Henry Venn: A Special Relationship?" *International Bulletin of Missionary Research* 5 (1981): 168–172.

[76] Andrew Porter, *Religion versus Empire? British Protestant Missionaries and Overseas Expansion, 1700–1914* (Manchester: Manchester University Press, 2004), 167–168. See also, Dana Robert, "Rufus Anderson," and C. P. Williams, "Henry Venn," in *The Blackwell Dictionary of Evangelical Biography: 1730–1860*, ed. Donald Lewis, 2 vols. (Oxford: Blackwell, 1995).

[77] Paul Harris, "Denominationalism and Democracy: Ecclesiastical Issues Underlying Rufus Anderson's Three Self Program," in *North American Foreign Missions, 1810–1914: Theology, Theory, and Policy*, ed. Wilbert R. Shenk (Grand Rapids, MI: William B. Eerdmans Publishing Co., 2004).

[78] Shenk, "Rufus Anderson and Henry Venn," 171.

[79] *Manifesto aos nossos irmãos, membros da Igreja Presbyteriana do Brazil* (São Paulo: Typ. da Sociedade Brazileira de Tratados Evangelicos, 1892).

widely in Brazil because of its excessive intellectualism and institutionalism.[80] It was precisely the creation and expansion of evangelical institutions and religious bureaucracies that accommodated the engagement of laypeople and created conditions for the rise of a Portuguese-speaking leadership. From the outset, these local agents domesticated the new religion by seizing the practices, beliefs, and institutions of evangelical Christianity. On Sundays, a few thousand converts gathered in various congregations spread across the Brazilian territory, opened the pages of Bibles and Christian texts, and discussed them. These congregations generated new forms of religious sociability separated from the state, the Catholic Church, and the aristocratic institutions of the secular public sphere in nineteenth-century Brazil. In a country with high rates of illiteracy and a debilitated educational system, Protestant churches and schools offered new paths to the acquisition of formal education.

Missionary Schools

Foreign missionaries, local ministers, and converts devoted a great deal of energy, material, and human resources to the creation of educational institutions. They opened a network of parish and secondary schools that introduced basic literacy and professional training to a growing public. Protestant education fulfilled the aspirations of both missionary organizations and the Brazilian state. Formal instruction embodied the late nineteenth-century ideal of Christian civilization upheld by mission societies and theorists in Europe and the United States. In Britain, America, and their worldwide mission fields, elementary and Sunday schools aimed to enable converts and their children to read the Bible and educate themselves in the fundamentals of Christian doctrine.[81] The expansion of basic schooling was also in the modernizing agenda of Brazil's political elites. Both monarchists and their republican rivals shared in the scientific enthusiasm of the modern era. The emperor and his ministers demonstrated some confidence in the modern pedagogic methods of secondary missionary

---

[80] Mendonça, *O celeste porvir*, 225–226.
[81] William R. Hutchison, *Errands to the World: American Protestant Thought and Foreign Missions* (Chicago: University of Chicago Press, 1987), ch. 4; Norman Etherington, "Education and Medicine," in *Missions and Empire*, ed. Norman Etherington (New York: Oxford University Press, 2005), 261–284.

schools.[82] Professional instruction offered in Protestant institutions was in tune with the interest of Positivist republicans in technical education and the creation of a technocratic elite.[83] Missionary education also realized the aspirations of upwardly mobile middle classes willing to harness the means of self-improvement and respectability.[84]

Parish schools were usually established alongside the new churches, providing elementary instruction to children and illiterate adults.[85] They sprang out of both the evangelical belief that converts should be able to read the Bible in their own language and, in the Presbyterian Church, of oaths undertaken by parents during baptismal celebrations stating that they would teach children to read and memorize the catechism, the Apostles' Creed, and the Lord's Prayer.[86] These parish schools occupied the same rooms and buildings of the congregations, and their teachers were usually pastors or other lettered members of churches.[87] Because mission societies were not always capable of providing financial support to all educational ventures carried out by its agents, mechanisms of fundraising played a central role in equipping and maintaining parish schools. In the countryside of the provinces of São Paulo and Minas Gerais, Presbyterian converts and churchgoers mobilized their funds and resources to keep the schools running. In the city of Pirassununga, the Bible-reader Innocencio Xavier was able to keep the parish school alive even though the mission had ordered its closure. Xavier relied on the contributions of the students' parents. Twenty-five boys and twelve girls attended classes and Xavier and his wife used the Bible and the Presbyterian catechism as reading primers.[88] Similarly, in Araraquara, the Rev. João Dagama opened a parish school in the *sítio* (small farm) that hosted the church. Again, it was the parents of students who mobilized and furnished a room for the school, purchased a blackboard, washed the clothes of students, and paid the teacher's salary.[89] Similar initiatives appeared in virtually every city or village where Presbyterian missionaries founded a church.

---

[82] Boanerges Ribeiro, *Protestantismo e cultura brasileira: Aspectos culturais da implantação do protestantismo no Brasil* (São Paulo: Casa Editora Presbiteriana, 1981), 183–221.

[83] Robert Nachman, "Positivism, Modernization, and the Middle Class in Brazil," *Hispanic American Historical Review* 57 (1977): 1–23, at 12–14.

[84] Frase, "A Sociological Analysis," 306–307.

[85] Mendonça, *O celeste porvir*, 144–153; Ribeiro, *Protestantismo e cultura brasileira*, 183–198.

[86] *Imprensa Evangelica*, n. 10, October 1881.

[87] Mendonça, *O celeste porvir*, 149, 169–170.

[88] Annual Report of the Rio Claro Station from August 1, 1880 to January 3, 1881. PHS, Philadelphia, Mission Correspondence, South American Letters.

[89] J. Dagama to the Rev. D. Irving. São João do Rio Claro, January 29, 1880. PHS, Philadelphia, Mission Correspondence, South American Letters.

In 1878, for instance, there were four evangelical elementary schools in the city of Brotas. Similar schools scattered throughout Rio Claro, Caldas, Borda da Mata, Sorocaba, Araras, Pirassununga, and Rio de Janeiro offered basic instruction to 206 pupils.[90] In Bahia, too, the missionary couple Alexander and Nannie Blackford organized weekly services, a catechetical class, and a Sunday school with an average attendance of thirty people. The Blackfords used the Bible, the Westminster Confession of Faith, and the Shorter Catechism as primers.[91]

These parish schools introduced an increasing number of people to literacy and print matter, generating new reading habits and disciplines amongst convert families and communities. Literacy rates were significantly higher in Brazilian Protestant congregations in comparison with the overall rate of Brazilian society in the nineteenth and twentieth centuries.[92] During a visit to the Presbyterian Church of Borda da Mata in 1873, where churchgoers kept at their own expenses a parish school for their children, the Rev. Modesto P. Carvalhosa observed that only one member of the church was illiterate.[93] In disseminating elementary education and literacy from below, Protestant parish schools, like Catholic educational institutions, opened new channels of upward social mobility and stimulated culture change.

Whereas missionary organizations in the United States and Britain were unable to provide financial support to all these smaller schools, they did finance a network of fully equipped educational institutions. American Methodists opened primary and secondary schools in the states of São Paulo, Minas Gerais, Rio de Janeiro, and Rio Grande do Sul beginning in the late nineteenth century.[94] Southern American Presbyterians founded the International School in the city of Campinas, São Paulo, in 1869. Although the Emperor Pedro II visited its facilities in 1875, the school attracted the children of republican families in the region.[95] An outbreak of yellow fever in Campinas in 1891 forced the closure of the school, and the

---

[90] BFM-PCUSA Annual Report [1878], 24.
[91] BFM-PCUSA Annual Report [1884], 32.
[92] Emilio Willems, "Protestantism as a Factor of Culture Change in Brazil," *Economic Development and Cultural Change* 3 (1955): 321–333, at 329–330.
[93] Relatorio annual que ao Presbyterio do Rio de Janeiro apresenta M. P. B. de Carvalhosa (1873). AHP, São Paulo, Coleção Carvalhosa, Relatórios Pastorais (1866–1875).
[94] For a list of schools and a brief history of each, see James L. Kennedy, *Cincoenta annos de methodismo no Brasil* (São Paulo: Impresa Methodista, 1928), 319–386.
[95] Ribeiro, *Protestantismo e cultura*, 199–221.

medical missionary Samuel Gammon decided to relocate it to the city of Lavras, Minas Gerais. In 1892, he reopened the Presbyterian school, which evolved into an agricultural and vocational college in the first decades of the twentieth century. Gammon's college also encompassed workshops and a model farm that offered employment to students.[96] In the city of São Paulo, the Presbyterians founded the American School in 1870. Over the next couple of decades, it received a good deal of material and human resources from the BFM of the Presbyterian Church in the United States and became a prominent educational institution in São Paulo. In 1890, there were eighteen teachers employed by the American School, with an attendance of 395 students.[97] An American lawyer and benefactor, John Theron Mackenzie, gave a grant of fifty thousand dollars to the American School in 1891, aimed at expanding the offer of higher education.[98] The school was named after Mackenzie and, in the early twentieth century, it encompassed a kindergarten, primary, intermediary, secondary, and higher education, including a normal school.[99] In the northeast of Brazil, it was the Baptists who made greater progress in the field of missionary education. A convert and captain of the Brazilian Army, Egydio Pereira de Almeida, alongside the missionary educator Laura Taylor, collected funds and opened a school in Bahia in 1898. A few years later, American Baptists opened a seminary (1902), an elementary school, and a secondary school (1906) in Pernambuco.[100]

As some scholars have shown, these Protestant educational institutions were not always successful in converting incoming students or keeping them within the evangelical fold. For example, although nine deputies of the Constitutional Assembly of 1934 had studied at the Mackenzie Institute in São Paulo, none were Protestant.[101] Sociologist David Martin's observations about contemporary Pentecostals help understand this phenomenon. Articulate Christians trained in evangelical communities may become well versed in literature, pedagogy, and music and be absorbed by a wider

---

[96] David C. Etheridge, "A Potent Agency: The Educational Ministry of Samuel Rhea Gammon," typescript, n/d. PHS, Philadelphia, RG 360, folder Samuel Rhea Gammon (1865–1928).
[97] BFM-PCUSA Annual Report [1890], 28–29.
[98] Lessa, *Annaes*, 453–454.
[99] *Eschola Americana—32°anno; Mackenzie College 12° anno* (São Paulo: n/p, 1902).
[100] Asa R. Crabtree, *História dos batistas do Brasil até o ano de 1906*, 2nd ed. (Rio de Janeiro: Casa Publicadora Batista, 1962), 155–156, 220, 228–229.
[101] Paul Freston, "Protestantes e política no Brasil: da Constituinte ao impeachment" (PhD dissertation, State University of Campinas, 1993), 53.

specialist culture.[102] Moreover, the aspirations of well-educated evangelicals were sometimes at odds with the ecclesiastical structures and ideologies of churches and missions.

Nevertheless, these schools played a central role in educating and training some of Brazil's most distinguished Protestant ministers and intellectuals. This was the case of Erasmo Braga. He was the son of a Portuguese shopkeeper João Ribeiro de C. Braga, who converted to Protestantism in Brazil, worked as a bookkeeper under the Presbyterian mission, and was ordained in 1885 to the Presbyterian pastorate.[103] Due to his father's involvement with the Presbyterian Church, Erasmo was able to undertake his secondary studies at the American School of São Paulo. At that time, the school's curriculum included all the basic subjects, such as mathematics, Portuguese grammar and literature, history, geography, and sciences, and also special language courses in English, French, and Latin.[104] A good number of Presbyterian ministers in the nineteenth and twentieth centuries trained as teachers in these evangelical schools and produced influential textbooks and educational material. The Rev. Eduardo Carlos Pereira taught Portuguese grammar at the American School. Later, in 1894, he occupied the first chair of Portuguese grammar at the prestigious Gymnasium of São Paulo, and he was acknowledged as one of Brazil's leading grammarians. Pereira's *Expository Grammar*, first published in 1907, reached as many as 147 editions throughout the first half of the twentieth century.[105] Similarly, after ordination Braga taught a variety of subjects at the Mackenzie College and in other educational institutions in São Paulo and Rio de Janeiro, including literature, Portuguese grammar, Greek, and Hebrew. Starting in 1909, Braga wrote a popular series of five reading primers known as *Série Braga* that were published for over forty years in Brazil and reached more than a hundred editions.[106]

---

[102] David Martin, *Forbidden Revolutions: Pentecostalism in Latin America and Catholicism in Eastern Europe* (London: SPCK, 1996), 31–32.

[103] Ferreira, *História da Igreja Presbiteriana*, 202–203. The best treatment of Braga's life and career is Alderi Souza Matos, *Erasmo Braga, o protestantismo e a sociedade brasileira: Perspectivas sobre a missão da igreja* (São Paulo: Cultura Cristã, 2008).

[104] Paul E. Pierson, *A Younger Church in Search of Maturity: Presbyterianism in Brazil from 1910 to 1959* (San Antonio: Trinity University Press, 1974), 153. On the American School's programme and curriculum, see *Programma e Regulamento do Instituto de S. Paulo, Escola Americana* (São Paulo: Typ. de Leroy King Bookwalter, 1885).

[105] Pierson, *A Younger Church*, 111.

[106] *Revista da Academia Paulista de Letras*, vol. 13 (1941), 131–132. Braga's series was also translated into Japanese, aimed at supporting the integration of newly arrived immigrants in Brazil. Pierson, *A Younger Church*, 111.

Networks of evangelical schools in Brazil created dynamic channels of social and intellectual mobility for individuals of different social ranks. In some cases, such as that of Braga, social change evolved across generational lines, beginning with his father. In other cases, missionary education and the missionary enterprise created opportunities for income improvement in the short run. Such was the case of Zacarias de Miranda, who had abandoned his secondary studies during his youth and resumed them as an adult with the Presbyterians in Campinas and São Paulo, working simultaneously as a tailor and music teacher. Upon ordination at the age of twenty-nine, in 1881, Miranda received from the Presbyterian BFM a regular salary of 150$000, a considerable sum for that time, which was complemented by his work as schoolteacher.[107] Instead of assuming that Baptist and Presbyterian schools aimed at reaching Brazilian elites and educating the upper classes,[108] they became dynamic vectors of social change. Formal education also created new reading habits and encouraged the use of print matter amongst religious communities in the country. The educational efforts of mission organizations were intimately connected to the missionary publishing enterprise and together they played an important role in transforming "communities of believers into communities of opinion."[109]

The Missionary Publishing Enterprise

Missionary writing and the publishing enterprise served evangelistic ends in Brazil. Presbyterian and Baptist missionaries, along with Bible and Tract Societies, put large amounts of Christian literature and Bibles in circulation, hoping that these books would introduce evangelical doctrines to broader audiences beyond the reach of missionaries. The publishing enterprise itself was a *locus* that facilitated the encounter between foreign missionaries and converts. For obvious reasons, Brazilian and Portuguese ministers and lay leaders had better control of the Portuguese language than the foreign

---

[107] Júlio A. Ferreira, *Galeria evangélica: Biografias de pastôres presbiterianos que trabalharam no Brasil* (São Paulo: Casa Editora Presbiteriana, 1952), 129.

[108] Mendonça, *O celeste porvir*, 153–167; Laura Premack, "'The Holy Rollers are Invading Our Territory': Southern Baptist Missionaries and the Early Years of Pentecostalism in Brazil," *Journal of Religious History* 35 (2011): 1–23, at 6, 9, 11–15.

[109] Abigail Green and Vincent Viaene, "Introduction: Rethinking Religion and Globalization," in *Religious Internationals in the Modern World: Globalization and Faith Communities since 1750*, ed. Abigail Green and Vincent Viaene (Basingstoke: Palgrave Macmillan, 2012), 1–19, at 1.

American and British missionaries. From the very beginning of the publication of *Imprensa Evangelica*, Presbyterian missionaries recruited Brazilian converts to contribute to it.[110] José Manoel da Conceição was an active contributor to the periodical in the early 1870s, publishing sermons.[111] Writers such as Antônio dos Santos Neves and Julio Ribeiro Vaughan also contributed with hymns, poems, and religious controversies.[112] In 1879, Presbyterians decided to move the headquarters of the *Imprensa Evangelica* from Rio de Janeiro to São Paulo, where the editorship of the periodical was placed under the responsibility of the American missionary John Beatty Howell. In the same year, Howell recruited teachers of the São Paulo Presbyterian school to write for the periodical which according to him "increased the popularity of the paper." He also employed students in the work of typesetting, who received financial aid in exchange.[113] Although the editors of the periodical had published mostly anonymous pieces since its foundation in 1864, some of them abandoned this policy in the early 1880s. Brazilian ministers such as the Presbyterians Miguel Torres, Eduardo Carlos Pereira, Antônio de Cerqueira Leite, and the Congregationalist João Manoel dos Santos began to sign their contributions to the *Imprensa Evangelica*, becoming distinctive public agents of the new religion.[114]

Baptist missionaries were also active in the publishing enterprise. Initially they requested their sending bodies in the United States to furnish them with evangelical pamphlets and books.[115] The missionary Zachary Taylor took charge of the publishing business in the 1880s and made it his personal ministry. Denominational differences and religious competition played a significant role in activating the engines of the missionary printing presses. The Baptists' rejection of infant baptism as practiced by Presbyterians, Methodists, Congregationalists, and Catholics prompted the Taylors to produce and circulate tracts and periodicals upholding Baptist doctrines. In January 1883, Taylor wrote to the Foreign Mission Board that baptism meant regeneration in Brazil: "an unbaptized (sprinkled) child or man is called a '*bisho*', or animal: so we judged it of the first importance to put baptism in its proper basis." In reaction to this, Taylor translated and published a set of tracts that formed

---

[110] Ferreira, *História da Igreja Presbiteriana*, 49–50.
[111] Vieira, *O protestantismo*, 145.
[112] Vieira, *O protestantismo*, 149.
[113] BFM-PCUSA Annual Report [1880], 18.
[114] *Imprensa Evangélica*, 1883, numbers 1 to 6.
[115] Quarterly Report by Z. C. Taylor (ending November 30, 1882). IBMB, Zachary Clay Taylor papers.

the earliest body of Baptist literature in Brazil, including a Baptist faith confession and an exegesis of the meaning and practice of baptism in the Bible.[116] Taylor was able to get support from Antônio Teixeira de Albuquerque, a former Catholic priest who initially joined the Methodist Church in Santa Bárbara in 1879. In the following year he was recruited by Baptist missionaries and became the first Brazilian Baptist minister, playing an important role in the expansion of the Bahia mission station.[117] Alburquerque later wrote a pamphlet explaining why he had renounced the Catholic priesthood that the Baptists circulated extensively.[118] Significantly, Baptist missionaries acquired their own printing press and, in connection with the American Bible Society, established a far-reaching operation in the Brazilian northeast. Between 1882 and 1886, colporteurs associated with the Baptist mission sold around 3,500 copies of the Bible and more than sixty thousand books, tracts, and leaflets. From Bahia, Taylor edited and published the periodical *Echo da Verdade* (Echo of the Truth), which sold a thousand copies monthly.[119]

Protestant print furnished missionaries and local converts with an important vehicle for the politicization of dissenting religious identities and their projection into Brazil's public sphere. Evangelicals engaged in political debates and religious controversies through the press. For them, the uneven enforcement of constitutional clauses on religious toleration destabilized the daily lives of Protestant families and congregations. Occasions of public embarrassment motivated by these clauses afforded Protestants some room to forward their political causes. In 1870, the Presbyterian editors of the *Imprensa Evangelica* brought to the spotlight the obscure incidents surrounding the death and burial of the general José Inácio Abreu e Lima in Pernambuco and of the American railroad worker David Samson in Rio de Janeiro. Abreu e Lima had acquired some prestige in Brazil since the wars of independence, but in the last years of his life he endorsed the operations of Protestant Bible societies in Pernambuco and clashed with local priests. Prior to his death in March 1869, Abreu e Lima had severed his ties with the Catholic Church, refusing to confess and to receive extreme unction. The bishop of Olinda denied him a grave in the cemetery of Recife and the deceased general was buried in the British Cemetery of that city, sparking a heated controversy in local newspapers. In October that year, a Protestant

[116] Zachary Taylor to Rev. H. Tupper, Bahia, January 15, 1883. IBMB, Zachary Clay Taylor papers.
[117] Frase, 'A Sociological Analysis', 233–234.
[118] SBC Proceedings [1886], appendix B, xxxi.
[119] Zachary Taylor to T. P. Bell, October 4, 1886. IBMB, Zachary Clay Taylor papers.

railroad worker employed in the construction of the D. Pedro II railway, David Samson, committed suicide and was denied a burial place in the city of Sapucaia. The director of the construction work submitted a petition to the imperial Council of State claiming that such acts could repel non-Catholic engineers and workers.[120]

The imperial minister Paulino Soares de Souza replied in April 1870, instructing ecclesiastical and political authorities to arrange some space in municipal cemeteries for the burial of non-Catholics. The *Imprensa Evangelica* editors wrote a long editorial letter praising the resolution, claiming that it advanced the religious and social wellbeing of the Brazilian people, but lamenting that the whole affair exemplified the inconveniences of the church–state alliance. For the Presbyterians, the imperial decree was a "conclusive proof of the essential antipathy between Romanism and the free institutions of our time and country."[121] In their arguments, juridical reforms, such as the implementation of civil registration of marriages and the secularization of cemeteries, were long overdue and the delay in their implementation risked driving away foreign immigrant workforce, representing a stumbling block on the country's path to modernization.[122]

In mobilizing such arguments, they struck a sensitive chord for the political elites of the era. At least since the beginning of the Brazilian Empire in the 1820s, but especially after the abolition of the African slave trade in 1850, imperial ministers and policymakers were anxious to attract European immigrant workforce to the country. In the racially charged political imagination of the era, besides replacing a moribund system of slave labor with free workers, European immigrants would "whiten" Brazilian society and modernize the nation.[123] The economic and diplomatic pressures implicated in such processes spurred a vigorous public debate about the concession of political rights to non-Catholics and the separation of church and state from the late 1860s onward.[124] In the political fever of the late 1860s and early 1870s,

---

[120] Rodrigues, "Sepulturas e sepultamentos," 26–27; Vieira, *O protestantismo*, 268–271.
[121] *Imprensa Evangelica*, May 28, 1870, n. 11.
[122] *Imprensa Evangelica*, April 21, 1866, n. 8; April 6, 1867, n. 7; December 2, 1871, n. 23.
[123] Viotti da Costa, *The Brazilian Empire*, 94; Luiz Felipe de Alencastro and Maria Luiza Renaux, "Caras e modos dos migrantes e imigrantes," in *História da vida privada no Brasil, vol. 2: Império*, ed. Luiz Felipe de Alencastro (São Paulo: Companhia das Letras, 1997), 291–335, at 292–300.
[124] José Murilo de Carvalho, "Radicalismo e republicanismo," in *Repensando o Brasil dos oitocentos: Cidadania, política e liberdade*, ed. José Murilo de Carvalho and Lúcia M. Bastos P. das Neves (Rio de Janeiro: Civilização Brasileira, 2009), 19–48; Emilia Viotti da Costa, "Brazil: The Age of Reform, 1870–1889," in *The Cambridge History of Latin America, vol. V: c.1870–1930*, ed. Leslie Bethell (Cambridge: Cambridge University Press, 1986), 725–778.

influential politicians and journalists began to openly criticize the papacy of Pius IX and the Vatican's stance against the "errors of modernity." These political transformations and public debates envisioned a future in which the Catholic Church would lose its sway over Brazilian society.

Even though local Protestants and foreign missionaries supported such liberalizing political reforms that extended the limits of religious freedom, their political alliances cut across ideological lines and political parties. The solid and influential work of Swiss historian Jean-Pierre Bastian stressed that Protestant minorities in Latin America established close connections with liberal-radical groups. The dissenting identity of non-Catholic religious minorities resonated with the dissenting politics of liberal minorities, and these similarities brought them together. From the mid-nineteenth century onward, radical political associations upheld a series of reformist agendas including the concession of political rights to non-Catholics and church–state separation that were also a part of the religious aspirations of Protestant converts and ministers. These groups gathered in specific spaces of sociability, such as the "societies of thought," masonic lodges, and circles of mutual aid.[125] Even though this might be the case of Mexico, which Bastian studied with rigor and accuracy, these conclusions cannot be extended to the whole continent.[126]

In Brazil, Presbyterians embraced a conservative view of the Imperial government. This can be captured in the book *Brazil and the Brazilians* by Presbyterian chaplain James C. Fletcher and Methodist missionary Daniel P. Kidder, a best-seller of travel literature in the United States read by the majority of the American missionaries in Brazil. This influential book portrayed Emperor Dom Pedro II as a forward-looking man who appreciated literature, the arts, and modern science; who was conciliatory in his government; and who was tolerant with regard to religion. Above all, Kidder and Fletcher represented Dom Pedro's ascension to the throne in 1840 as the key political move that put an end to the separatist revolts of the 1830s.[127] This depiction

---

[125] Jean-Pierre Bastian, "The Metamorphosis of Latin American Protestant Groups: A Sociohistorical Perspective," *Latin American Research Review* 28 (1993): 33–61; Jean-Pierre Bastian, "Protestantism in Latin America," in *The Church in Latin America, 1492–1992*, ed. Enrique Dussel (Tunbridge Wells: Burns & Oates, 1992); Bastian, *Protestantes, liberales*; Carlos Mondragón, *Like Leaven in the Dough: Protestant Social Thought in Latin America, 1920–1950*, trans. Daniel Miller and Ben Post (Madison, NJ: Fairleigh Dickinson University Press, 2011).

[126] Jean-Pierre Bastian, *Los disidentes: Sociedades protestantes y revolución en México, 1872–1911* (Mexico, DF: Fondo de Cultura Económica, 1989).

[127] James C. Fletcher and Daniel P. Kidder, *Brazil and the Brazilians: Portrayed in Historical and Descriptive Sketches* (Philadelphia: Childs & Peterson, 1857), 223–224.

of the Emperor and the Empire echoed conservative views of the imperial government that represented the Brazilian monarchy as the only institution endowed with sufficient power and prestige to guarantee the political stability of the country and mediate conflicts between political factions.[128] One of the institutions that propagated these views of the Empire was the Brazilian Historical and Geographical Institute (IHGB).[129] Fletcher was appointed to the IHGB in 1862 and was closely associated with members of the imperial political elite.[130] In the last decades of the Empire, Presbyterians and Congregationalists appealed to the Emperor and his ministers when the political rights of missionaries and convert families were endangered or when religious persecution struck. Appropriating the political imagination of the era, they viewed the Empire as a strong and centralized body, the bulwark of national order.

What really troubled Presbyterian missionaries and Brazilian converts in the late 1880s was the succession of the throne. Because imperial laws on religious freedom were unstable and the emperor was growing older, Protestants held political leaders who were devout Catholics under suspicion. That was the case of Princess Isabel, Pedro II's daughter and successor. She embodied this threat. Writing in the last years of the Empire about the flexibility and instability of constitutional clauses on religious freedom, Presbyterian missionaries noted that "there has always been a danger ... that a reactionary Government, such as is feared under the Princess Isabella [sic], heir to the throne, might make serious trouble for infant churches."[131] Whereas Catholic priests considered the possibility of Isabel's reign as an encouraging prospect, Protestants feared that her government would endanger the future of non-Catholic minorities.[132] The moderate enthusiasm with which Protestants celebrated the overthrow of the monarchy in November 1889 was a matter of convenience.

In contrast to Presbyterians and Congregationalists, Baptist missionaries did not uphold a positive view of the Empire. In fact, they emphasized the

---

[128] Marcello Basile, "O laboratório da nação: A Era Regencial (1831–1840)," in *O Brasil Imperial, vol. II: 1831–1870*, ed. Keila Grinberg and Ricardo Salles (Rio de Janeiro: Civilização Brasileira, 2009), 53–119; José Murilo de Carvalho, *A construção da ordem: A elite política imperial/Teatro de sombras: A política imperial*, 3rd ed. (Rio de Janeiro: Civilização Brasileira, 2010).

[129] Manoel L. S. Guimarães, "Nação e civilização nos trópicos: O Instituto Histórico e Geográfico Brasileiro e o projeto de uma história nacional," *Estudos Históricos* 1 (1988): 5–27.

[130] Vieira, *O protestantismo*, 80–81.

[131] *Brazilian Missions*, August 1888, vol. I, n. 8.

[132] George Boehrer, "The Church and the Overthrow of the Brazilian Monarchy," *Hispanic American Historical Review* 48 (1968): 380–401.

intolerance of Brazilian Catholics and the strength of religious persecution in their correspondence with the Southern Baptist Convention. In 1885, Zachary Taylor described some episodes of religious persecution: William Bagby had been arrested for a few days in Rio de Janeiro, Catholics stoned a preaching place in Bahia, and some church members were either arrested or dismissed from their jobs.[133] Edwin Soper, pastor of the Rio de Janeiro Baptist Church, challenged the predominant depiction of the Brazilian Empire, its Emperor, and its people as tolerant and liberal-minded. Instead, Soper wrote, in 1887, that "too many have quite a false idea of Brazil. There is no religious freedom here; we are barely tolerated. Outside our place of worship we have no liberty at all."[134]

Whereas the defense of religious liberty, the creation of civil registration of marriages and births, and the secularization of cemeteries were at the heart of the political aspirations of missionaries in Brazil, the issue of slavery was not. Throughout the nineteenth century, some politicians and intellectuals represented slavery as the foremost problem of the Empire, its "social cancer."[135] Although in sharp decline in the last decades of the Empire, the slave population of Brazil in 1885 surpassed a million people and was mostly concentrated in the center south.[136] The abolitionist movement encompassed a large and structured network of grassroots activists, freed slaves, anti-slavery associations, intellectuals, and political leaders spread at national level and connected to transnational abolitionist organizations.[137] According to historian José Carlos Barbosa, although Presbyterians and Congregationalists supported the abolitionist cause they did not participate actively in the abolitionist struggle in Brazil.[138] Presbyterians, Methodists, and Baptists maintained close ties with the communities of American Confederate immigrants and avoided taking part in political action that could strain their relationship with sending bodies. They did, however, admit slaves and freed slaves in their churches. Since the late 1850s, Robert Kalley organized Bible classes for black people and freed-slaves at the Fluminense Evangelical

---

[133] SBC Proceedings [1885], appendix A, ix.
[134] SBC Proceedings [1887], appendix A, xiii.
[135] José Murilo de Carvalho, *D. Pedro II* (São Paulo: Companhia das Letras, 2007), 130–136.
[136] Costa, "Brazil: The Age of Reform," 763.
[137] Angela Alonso, *The Last Abolition: The Brazilian Antislavery Movement, 1868–1888* (New York: Cambridge University Press, 2022); Leslie Bethell and José Murilo de Carvalho, "Joaquim Nabuco e os abolicionistas britânicos: Correspondência, 1880–1905," *Estudos Avançados* 23 (2009): 207–229.
[138] José Carlos Barbosa, *Slavery and Protestant Missions in Imperial Brazil*, trans. Fraser MacHaffie and Richard Danford (Lanham, MD: University Press of America, 2008), 62.

Church in which they read a tract titled *The African Friend*.[139] Baptists, usually regarded as the most politically conservative of missionaries, did not celebrate the abolition of slavery in their correspondence with the home mission as enthusiastically as the Presbyterians did. However, the pastor Edwin Soper wrote that, in 1887, he was forbidden to visit, at the Rio de Janeiro Hospital, a "negro slave woman, that one of our missionaries bought and freed."[140] And Zachary Taylor depicted the progressive emancipation of slaves in the 1880s that preceded the final abolition as opportune. In his church, a "brother slave" was expecting to obtain his freedom shortly.[141] Missionaries maintained a cautious distance from the abolitionist movement as well as from other forms of organized political engagement in nineteenth-century Brazil, opting instead to attend to the needs of local congregations.

Whereas the foreign missionaries adopted this sort of conciliatory attitude, Brazilian pastors and converts were able to criticize the institution of slavery with impunity through the press. In New York, the Protestant convert and influential journalist José Carlos Rodrigues edited the magazine *O Novo Mundo* (The New World) that circulated widely in Brazil between 1870 and 1879. Rodrigues opened the pages of his magazine to abolitionist leaders, attacked the persistence of slavery in Brazil, and claimed that the emancipation in the United States had been beneficial to the economy.[142] The strongest defense of abolitionism came from the Rev. Eduardo Carlos Pereira. In 1886, he published a tract titled *The Christian Religion in its Relations with Slavery*. Pereira argued that Old Testament servitude differed substantially from contemporary African slavery, and that it was only tolerated, not instituted, by the Mosaic Law. In Pereira's narrative it was the Christian message of deliverance that, emanating from the pulpits of churches, pushed governments in the United States and Britain to pursue abolitionist policies.[143] Addressing Christian audiences regardless of affiliation, Pereira wrote:

> If the religion you profess condemns captivity, it is your duty to *choose* between it and the slaves you own. Either you keep your slaves and continue

---

[139] Joyce E. Clayton, "The Legacy of Robert Reid Kalley," *International Bulletin of Missionary Research* 26 (2002): 123–127, at 126.

[140] SBC Proceedings [1887], appendix A, xiii.

[141] Zachary Taylor to the Foreign Mission Board, October 2, 1884. IBMB, Zachary Clay Taylor papers.

[142] George Boehrer, "José Carlos Rodrigues and *O Novo Mundo*, 1870–1879," *Journal of Inter-American Studies* 9 (1967): 127–144, at 136–137; Barbosa, *Slavery and Protestant Missions*.

[143] Eduardo C. Pereira, *A religião christã em suas relações com a escravidão* (São Paulo: Typographia a vapor de Jorge Seckler & C., 1886), 14, 20, 33–34.

to benefit from the sweat of your neighbor's brow, and, if that is the case, follow the example of the Gadarenes and plead Jesus to leave your home; or, then, restore to your slaves their stolen freedom and declare through this act that you are not a mere hypocrite.[144]

Apart from politics, social transformations also contributed to reshaping the missionary imagination in Brazil and influenced the publishing enterprise. In consequence of the intensification of foreign immigration to Brazil and the growth of cosmopolitan cities, such as Rio de Janeiro and São Paulo, Presbyterian missionaries believed that the country was set to become a melting pot of nationalities. The annual report of 1888 noted that beyond the settlement of Germans, Italians, Portuguese, Poles, and Russians in different parts of the country, one could find seven nationalities represented in the São Paulo Presbyterian Church, among them a Romanian who converted from Judaism and a Lebanese.[145] As missionaries in São Paulo wrote, "'All the world' is coming to Brazil, and our native converts will not have to wait till they can 'go' and preach to the representatives of every nation under the sun."[146] For Presbyterian missionaries the evangelization of Brazil was an introduction to the evangelization of the world.

Despite the grandiose claims of Presbyterians, the missionary work in Brazil was indeed connected to the worldwide evangelical communion. The far-reaching networks of mission and Bible societies linked different religious actors and organizations across territorial and linguistic borders. These transnational links were especially strong throughout the Lusophone Atlantic, as the next chapter will show. Baptist missionaries were well aware of the existence of these networks. In 1883, Kate Taylor wrote a thorough evaluation of the state of evangelical literature in Brazil. She enumerated the different versions of the Bible that circulated in the country, the tracts and books translated into Portuguese, and described how Brazilian and Portuguese ministers actively contributed to the production of evangelical literature in their own language. Interestingly, she did not write about the missionary publishing enterprise in Brazil as self-contained, but explained how Christian books, pamphlets, and periodicals produced in Portugal and Brazil circulated on both sides of the Atlantic.[147]

---

[144] Pereira, *A religião christã*, 36.
[145] BFM-PCUSA Annual Report [1888], 44.
[146] *Brazilian Missions*, March 1888, vol. I, n. 3.
[147] Kate S. Taylor, *The Christian Literature of Brazil*. IBMB, Zachary Clay Taylor Papers.

For Baptist and Presbyterian missionaries, the evangelistic work in Brazil was part of a wider transatlantic missionary endeavor connecting language zones. The first attempt of the Foreign Mission Board of the Southern Baptist Convention to open an evangelistic front in Brazil was established by Thomas Jefferson Bowen in 1860. Bowen had been a missionary in West Africa for nearly a decade and wrote a grammar and dictionary of the Yoruba language. In the late 1850s, he began to suffer from health problems and left West Africa for Brazil. He landed in Rio de Janeiro in May 1860, hoping to recover. Bowen's chief plan was to train Yoruba slaves and prepare them to be missionaries back in West Africa. As Rio was not exactly cooler than his previous post, Bowen's health problems got worse, and he left for his home country nine months later.[148] In a somewhat similar direction, the Presbyterian missionary George Chamberlain believed that the consolidation of the Protestant educational work in São Paulo would reverberate in every place where the Portuguese language was spoken, not only in Brazil.[149] Missionaries and ministers believed that in writing and evangelizing they reached transnational Portuguese-speaking audiences. Their tracts, periodicals, pamphlets, and printed sermons circulated across Lusophone Protestant communities throughout the Atlantic. The addressees they had in mind when writing and preaching were convert men and women in oceanic language zones, instead of citizens of a specific nation state.

Conclusion

The practices, beliefs, expectations, institutions, and ideologies of Protestant missionaries related in multiple ways to the social, political, and religious transformations in Brazilian society in the nineteenth century. The settlement of communities of European and American immigrants and the creation of Protestant schools fulfilled the plans of political and intellectual elites interested in modernization, technical improvement, and the "whitening" of the Brazilian population. Evangelical missionaries arrived when the expansion of coffee production and urbanization were changing the social landscape of the Brazilian center south and shifting the balance of power.

---

[148] Wedemann, "A History of Protestant Missions," 98–99.
[149] Relatório dos trabalhos de G. W. Chamberlain durante o anno Presbyterial de 1874 a 1875. AHP, Coleção Carvalhosa—Relatórios Pastorais (1866–1875).

Evangelical Christianity encountered an important niche amidst the new and mobile social categories arising at this moment of swift social and economic change. Missionaries and local Protestant writers and ministers joined forces with political elites through the press, upholding the cause of church–state separation, enfranchisement of non-Catholic religious minorities, the creation of civil registrations of births and marriages, and the secularization of cemeteries. Even though Protestants and Catholics became rivals in the Brazilian religious landscape, evangelical practices such as lay activism and local fundraising resonated closely with the participatory culture of folk Catholicism.

Missionaries, ministers, and converts encountered multiple opportunities to connect evangelical practices and beliefs to specific transformations arising in such processes of social, political, demographic, and religious change. The religious and social dynamics involved in the diffusion of evangelical Christianity in Brazil shed light on processes of globalization and the localization of religious forces. Ministers and believers moved in different directions throughout migrant and missionary networks; interacted with coreligionists in Europe and the Americas; devoted time, energy, and resources to the worldwide missionary enterprise; and also took part in local religious controversies and social debates and related to the political expectations of the country in multiple ways.

2
Bibles and Tracts in Motion

When the journalist and writer João Paulo Barreto set out to identify the best-selling books in Rio de Janeiro in 1906, he was greatly disappointed. Barreto, better known by the pseudonym João do Rio, discovered that the most popular works were prayer books, the so-called testaments of animals, crime books, and sheets of folk songs. He lamented that these volumes encouraged violence and laziness among "primitive" and idle men. The literary classics spent long periods on the stalls of street libraries, accumulating dust and with their covers scorched by the sun. He was also interested in the booksellers. In Barreto's words, they were "a countless mob that every morning spread itself through the city, enter the commercial houses, go up the hills, run through the suburbs, lurk about the busy places." For him, the most active, astute, and tireless of booksellers were "the vendors of Protestant Bibles," who crisscrossed the Brazilian capital with "the pockets of their old jackets jammed with edifying brochures."[1] João do Rio's remarks closely resemble those of the Methodist minister Hugh Tucker, a longtime agent of the American Bible Society in Rio de Janeiro. In Tucker's words, the American Bible Society had such Bible vendors "constantly at work in the city, going into the markets and through the streets, and all round about the suburbs, seeking in every place and hamlet to offer the inhabitants the written message of salvation."[2]

These itinerant Protestant booksellers were called colporteurs and played an important role in the diffusion of evangelical Christianity in Brazil. They were connected to religious organizations based in the United States and Britain that stretched their networks over the world. Protestant Bible and Tract Societies both benefited from and pushed forward the era of mass publishing and the industrialization of communications.[3] Organizations, such

---

[1] João do Rio, *A alma encantadora das ruas* (São Paulo: Companhia das Letras, 1997 [1906]), 137–138.

[2] Hugh Tucker, *The Bible in Brazil: Colporter Experiences* (New York: Young People's Missionary Movement of the United States and Canada, 1902), 38.

[3] Christopher Bayly, *The Birth of the Modern World, 1780–1914: Global Connections and Comparisons* (Oxford: Blackwell, 2004), ch. 9.

as the American Bible Society and the British and Foreign Bible Society, produced books cheaply and efficiently at an industrial scale, issuing over a hundred million Bibles from their worldwide depositories over the course of the nineteenth century.[4] These societies contributed to the simultaneous globalization and localization of evangelical religion. In West Africa and Kenya, Christianity and literacy were often seen as synonymous and the translation of Christian literature into local vernaculars played an important role in ethnic formation. Translations of Bibles and Christian texts into indigenous languages demanded the input of local converts who drew upon the vocabulary of disparate religious and cultural traditions and indigenized Christianity.[5] Bible Societies began to establish a foothold in Latin America during the wars of independence, meeting widespread demands for education and literacy of the emerging nation states.[6] Schoolteachers hoped to obtain Bibles and evangelical tracts from colporteurs to use them as primers in schools throughout the region. Missionary reports attracted the attention of large audiences of pious believers in Europe and North America, who eagerly contributed to the evangelical publishing enterprise. Yet, despite the scale and cultural impact of their operations, Bible Societies remain under-studied.

This chapter examines the creation of a Portuguese-speaking Protestant public in the nineteenth century through an analysis of the records of two London-based evangelical publishing organizations, the British and Foreign Bible Society (BFBS) and the Religious Tract Society (RTS). It begins by reconstructing some of the experiences of colporteurs. They circulated hundreds of thousands of Bibles, portions of the Bible, books, tracts, and periodicals in Brazil and reported successes and ordeals to their superiors in Rio de Janeiro and London. Although local religious and political dynamics weighed heavily on their work, Bible and Tract Societies consolidated international circuits, connecting religious actors and organizations across national and territorial borders. Paraphrasing Isabel Hofmeyr, these

---

[4] Christopher Clark and Michael Ledger-Lomas, "The Protestant International," in *Religious Internationals in the Modern World: Globalization and Faith Communities since 1750*, ed. Abigail Green and Vincent Viaene (Basingstoke: Palgrave Macmillan, 2012), 23–52, at 30.

[5] David Maxwell, "Historical Perspectives on Christianity Worldwide: Connections, Comparisons and Consciousness," in *Relocating World Christianity: Interdisciplinary Studies in Universal and Local Expressions of the Christian Faith*, ed. Joel Cabrita, David Maxwell, and Emma Wild-Wood (Leiden: Brill, 2017), 47–69, at 58–59.

[6] Ondina González and Justo González, *Christianity in Latin America: A History* (New York: Cambridge University Press, 2008), 209–213.

flows of print matter generated maritime markets of faith, doctrine, and information.[7]

Alongside an array of local and international publishers, these religious organizations contributed to the introduction of new ideas, printing techniques, and reading practices in Brazil.[8] This chapter will look closely at the multiple global and local dynamics at play in the work of Protestant booksellers, paying attention to their interactions on the ground and the materiality of the books. The circulation of religious literature also contributed to the institutionalization and stabilization of ecclesiastical hierarchies, the standardization of beliefs and practices, and the creation of new religious identities.[9] According to historian Heather Sharkey, recent studies on Bible societies and evangelical publishers focus mostly on the commercial and managerial aspects of such organizations, rather than their evangelistic purposes.[10] In some of these studies, the representatives of Protestant publishing societies are cast as "capitalist entrepreneurs" who enthusiastically propagated the values of modern liberalism.[11] The next pages highlight the ambiguous status of evangelical colporteurs in Brazil, examining their double work as booksellers and agents of religious diffusion. They encountered along the way customers interested not so much in the values of free enterprise and capitalist individualism, but especially in sources of spiritual inspiration and personal consolation.

---

[7] Isabel Hofmeyr, *Gandhi's Printing Press: Experiments in Slow Reading* (Cambridge, MA: Harvard University Press, 2013), 33.

[8] On the circulation of books and print matter between Brazil and Europe, see Márcia Abreu and Marisa Deaecto, eds., *A circulação transatlântica dos impressos: Conexões* (Campinas: Unicamp, 2014); Márcia Abreu, "Livros ao mar: Circulação de obras de Belas Artes entre Lisboa e o Rio de Janeiro ao tempo da transferência da corte para o Brasil," *Tempo* 12 (2008): 74–97; Tânia M. Bessone, "Comércio de livros: Livreiros, livrarias e impressos," *Escritos (Fundação Casa de Rui Barbosa)* 5 (2011): 41–52.

[9] Joel Cabrita, *Text and Authority in the South African Nazaretha Church* (New York: Cambridge University Press, 2014); Thomas Kirsch, *Spirits and Letters: Reading, Writing and Charisma in African Christianity* (New York: Berghahn Books, 2008); David Lindenfeld, "Indigenous Encounters with Christian Missionaries in China and West Africa, 1800–1920: A Comparative Study," *Journal of World History* 16 (2005): 327–369, at 365–366; David Maxwell, "'Sacred History, Social History': Traditions and Texts in the Making of a Southern African Transnational Religious Movement," *Comparative Studies in Society and History* 43 (2001): 502–524.

[10] Heather J. Sharkey, "The British and Foreign Society in Port Said and the Suez Canal," *Journal of Imperial and Commonwealth History* 39 (2011): 439–456, at 451.

[11] Karen Racine, "Commercial Christianity: The British and Foreign Bible Society's Interest in Spanish America, 1805–1830," *Bulletin of Latin American Research* 27, supplement 1 (2008): 78–98, at 81.

The British and Foreign Bible Society in Brazil

After a promising start in the 1810s, South America was permanently included into the domains of the BFBS in the mid-1850s, following the temporary pacification of post-independence conflicts in the continent. The initial plan of the Society at that time was to appoint one agent to oversee the work of Bible selling among Spanish-speaking countries and another to Brazil. In 1855, A. Duffield from Birmingham moved to Cartagena, Colombia, as the accredited representative of the BFBS for the Spanish-speaking American world.[12] By that time, the American Presbyterian Rev. James C. Fletcher was based in Rio de Janeiro as the representative of the American Bible Society (ABS), the BFBS's sister organization the United States. Before that post, Fletcher had served as a chaplain of both the American Seamen's Friend Society and the American Legation in Rio between 1851 and 1853, posts that enabled him to become acquainted with members of the political elite and even with the Brazilian emperor, Pedro II.[13] Fletcher was an enthusiast of the operations of Protestant missionary organizations in the country, and wrote to BFBS representatives in 1855 claiming that "a large sphere of operation" awaited the Society.[14] In the following year Richard Corfield from Liverpool was sent to Rio de Janeiro to undertake his post as the BFBS agent in Brazil.[15]

Between 1857 and 1858, Corfield traveled extensively throughout the country trying to create a consistent Bible-selling strategy and to establish partnerships with schoolteachers and religious leaders. But due to financial issues and the scarcity of Corfield's and Duffield's sales in Brazil and Colombia, the BFBS decided to reorganize its operational structure in South America. In 1859, Corfield was sent to Buenos Aires, Argentina, and Duffield went to Lima, Peru. No agent was left in Brazil.[16] Most of the transactions with Brazil after 1860 occurred intermittently, through requests made by Anglican priests or colporteurs from denominational missionary organizations. This situation changed in 1865, when the BFBS appointed the Episcopal Scottish missionary Richard Holden as its superintendent in the Brazilian Empire.

---

[12] *The Fifty-second Report of the British & Foreign Bible Society; M.DCCC.LVI. with an Appendix and a List of Subscribers and Benefactors* (London: F. W. Watkins, 1856), cxci and cxcii. Hereinafter cited as: BFBS Annual Report [year].

[13] David Gueiros Vieira, *O protestantismo, a maçonaria e a Questão Religiosa no Brasil* (Brasília: Editora UnB, 1980), ch. 3.

[14] BFBS Annual Report [1856], cxcii.

[15] BFBS Annual Report [1857], ccxxix and ccxxx.

[16] BFBS Annual Reports [1859], 278; [1861], 214.

Upon his appointment, Holden undertook the responsibility of coordinating the group of colporteurs in Brazil, administering the Bible-depots, and corresponding with the Society's headquarters in London.[17]

By the time of Holden's nomination, the BFBS had been operating at a global level for over sixty years, connecting the British Isles to Asia, Africa, and the Americas. The Society translated, printed, revised, and circulated one single book, the Bible, or portions of it, such as the Old and the New Testaments, the gospels, and the book of Psalms, separately. Because the Society was a non-denominational organization and sought to avoid doctrinal disputes, all prefaces, explanatory notes, or interpretations of biblical texts were strictly forbidden in its books. This was the "fundamental principle."[18] It did not prevent, however, the BFBS from being dragged into theological and denominational conflicts. In 1825, after a bitter reaction from English Puritans and Scottish Presbyterians against the inclusion of Apocryphal books in the scriptures, all deuterocanonical texts were excluded from the Society's versions of the Bible.[19]

Founded in London in 1804 under the spirit of modern evangelicalism, the BFBS acted simultaneously as a publisher, a Christian organization, and a business.[20] As a publisher, the Society carried out from its London base a wide-ranging process that involved the printing, binding, and circulation of books. As a Christian institution, the Society's founders believed that people should have access to the Bible in their own language and that its simple and unaided reading could lead to individual conversions. As a business, the BFBS's main objective was not to accumulate profit, but to coordinate efficient strategies to subsidize the costly work of translation, publication, and dissemination of scriptures. Throughout the nineteenth century the Bible Society developed a complex organizational structure encompassing auxiliary societies at home that collected subscriptions from the ordinary Christians who supported the institution financially, the central committees and sub-committees in London, and the work overseas, carried out by agents and colporteurs.[21] The fact that Bibles should be sold, always at low prices,

---

[17] BFBS Annual Report [1865], 252–253.
[18] Leslie Howsam, *Cheap Bibles: Nineteenth-century Publishing and the British and Foreign Bible Society* (Cambridge: Cambridge University Press, 1991), 6–7.
[19] Howsam, *Cheap Bibles*, 13–5.
[20] Sharkey, "The British," 440–441.
[21] Leslie Howsam, "The Bible Society and the Book Trade," in *Sowing the Word: The Cultural Impact of the British and Foreign Bible Society, 1804–2004*, ed. Stephen Batalden, Kathleen Cann, and John Dean (Sheffield: Sheffield Phoenix, 2004), 24–37. See also Howsam, *Cheap Bibles*, ch. 2.

and not given away reinforced the Society's commercial character. Under these guidelines, BFBS agents and superintendents were, besides good Christians, good businessmen.

That was the case of Richard Holden. He had previously worked as a merchant in Brazil in the northern province of Pará in the early 1850s and, by the time of his appointment to the BFBS in 1865, he was already known in some religious and literary circles in Brazil. In the early 1860s, he engaged in bitter religious controversies with Catholic priests in liberal periodicals in Pará and upheld the legitimacy of the circulation of Bibles in the country against the criticism of the Archbishop of Bahia.[22] During his period as the Society's superintendent in Rio de Janeiro, Holden laid the groundwork of the BFBS transaction in Brazil. Between 1865 and his return to Britain in 1872, Holden hired colporteurs to carry out the work of itinerant Bible-selling in different parts of the country. Colporteurs, who became the most active and distinctive agents of the BFBS in Brazil, were obliged to send Holden, based in Rio, detailed information about their activities, including figures of sales and reports of their travels.[23] Furthermore, Holden and his Brazilian and British contacts engaged in a complicated task: the improvement of a specific translation of the Bible into Portuguese, the Almeida version. Between Holden's retirement in 1872 and the end of the nineteenth century, two other superintendents led the BFBS in Brazil: José Martin de Carvalho (1872–1879) and the Rev. João Manoel Gonçalves dos Santos (1879–1901). Santos had been trained at Spurgeon's College in London and served as successor of Dr. Robert Kalley at the Congregationalist Church of Rio de Janeiro. Throughout this period, the strategy of Bible selling established in the 1860s was maintained with few variations. Table 2.1 shows the figures of Bible sales during this period.

Compared to the wider literary arena in nineteenth-century Brazil, the fact that the BFBS personnel in Brazil managed to put more than 350,000 books in circulation in less than thirty years was a remarkable achievement. The ABS, by its turn, put 283,204 volumes in circulation in the period between 1882 and 1900.[24] The census of 1872 revealed that more than eighty

---

[22] David G. Vieira, *O protestantismo, a maçonaria e a Questão Religiosa no Brasil* (Brasília: Editora UnB, 1980), ch. 8–9.

[23] The first report to mention such method is BFBS Annual Report [1866]. All subsequent reports have a similar structure, including figures and narratives, although varying in the degree of details, such as names of colporteurs and specific strategies of book selling.

[24] Distrubution Abroad, 1861–1900, Summary of ABS Work Abroad and Statistics, by Rebecca Bromley, 1965. ABS, ABS Historical Essay #15, Part V-A&B.

Table 2.1 Sales of the BFBS in Brazil, 1870–1898

Year	Total	Bibles	Testaments	Portions	Grants
1870	7,465	1,611	3,759	2,095	
1871[a]	2,483	787	1,573	123	
1872	4,484	1,329	3,013	142	
1873	5,734	1,349	3,519	866	
1874	10,240	1,286	3,287	5,667	
1875	10,664	1,420	3,428	5,506	310
1876[b]	6,662	533	2,260	3,043	
1877	5,854	904	2,313	2,467	170
1878	6,766	936	2,769	3,061	
1879	4,202	617	1,534	2,051	
1880	8,204	595	1,767	5,842	
1881	12,183	908	2,522	8,753	
1882	17,912	1,190	3,091	13,631	
1883	10,872	1,105	2,737	7,030	
1884	13,879	1,975	4,253	7,651	
1885	12,834	2,524	4,695	5,615	
1886	9,022	1,650	4,311	3,061	
1887	12,058	1,973	2,498	7,587	
1888	8,354	1,459	2,830	4,065	
1889	10,883	1,359	3,294	6,230	
1890	12,756	1,817	2,814	8,125	
1891	21,671	2,260	5,449	13,962	
1892	24,340	2,009	3,748	18,583	
1893	14,658	3,281	4,112	7,265	
1894	19,743	2,967	6,961	9,815	
1895	12,844	2,502	6,059	4,283	
1896	24,043	3,042	2,902	18,099	
1897	23,390	2,596	6,126	14,668	
1898	20,204	2,907	5,220	12,077	
TOTAL:	354,404	48,966	103,164	201,794	480

[a] Figures for the first six months of the year.

[b] There is an amount of 826 books—814 from the depots in Rio de Janeiro and Rio Claro and 12 unlisted—not discriminated in this report.

percent of the Brazilian population was illiterate, which was a constant source of disappointment for men of letters and publishers in the country. Only very successful books were able to reach their second or third editions in this period, usually a couple of decades after the publication of the first thousand volumes.[25] In addition to this, the publishing trade in Brazil was an expensive business. Due to the high cost of living in Rio de Janeiro, the dependence of imported goods, high protective tariffs, and the publishing technologies adopted, books printed in the Brazilian capital were, on average, two or three times more expensive than those printed in European capitals.[26] Partly because of this, the subsidized Bibles of the BFBS were more easily sold than literature printed in Brazil.

One of the most conspicuous features of nineteenth-century evangelicalism and the missionary movement was their reliance on the power of the written word. Missionaries commonly attributed notions of extraordinary textual agency and authority to Bibles and Christian literature in general. For them religious tracts, books, and the scriptures could mesmerize and enchant readers, prompting conversions to Christianity without the aid of evangelists.[27] Texts in these missionary theories of language operated as "noiseless messengers," prosthetic missionaries, non-human agents endowed with mysterious powers that could penetrate regions beyond the reach of missionaries.[28] Evangelical ideas of scriptural power also circulated across the missionary movement in the Lusophone world. A tract printed in Lisbon and sold on both sides of the Atlantic, titled *I Do Not Understand the Bible*, stated the following while discussing the heavenly origins of the Bible:

> the Bible, that comes from God, tells us of a heaven, of a future, of things that, as we have never seen or touched them, might be far more difficult to grasp than any other.... A painter understands very easily a book that deals with painting; a musician, a work about his art; an agriculturist, a treatise on horticulture; if you change [the books], though, little or nothing will the musician understand of painting or the agriculturalist of music.... That is

---

[25] Hélio Guimarães, *Os leitores de Machado de Assis: O romance machadiano e o público de literatura no século 19* (São Paulo: Nankin/EDUSP, 2004), 65–66, 72.

[26] Laurence Hallewell, *Books in Brazil: A History of the Publishing Trade* (Metuchen, NJ: The Scarecrow Press, 1982), 94–95.

[27] Isabel Hofmeyr, "Inventing the World: Transnationalism, Transmission and Christian Textualities," in *Mixed Messages: Materiality, Textuality, Missions*, ed. Jamie Scott and Gareth Griffiths (New York: Palgrave Macmillan, 2005), 19–35, at 21–23.

[28] Hofmeyr, *The Portable*, 19.

what happens with readers of the Bible. The Bible is a heavenly book; we are earthly creatures. It is no wonder, then, that its heavenly language is not always intelligible.[29]

The text recommended that to comprehend such heavenly messages, readers should pray to the Holy Spirit. Only another heavenly agent could help them understand the Bible.

Despite the prevalence of Bible-centric evangelical traditions in Brazil, missionaries and colporteurs did not attribute any supernatural powers to the Bible as a material object. As anthropologist Thomas Kirsch observed in his study of literacy and charisma among evangelicals and Jehovah's Witnesses in southern Zambia, "Christianity as a book religion can be quite a mundane affair." Christians and customers first came into contact with the Bible as a material object, a commodity. Kirsch's Pentecostal informants in Zambia handled their Bibles carelessly and, in period of shortage of paper, used the pages of religious tracts as notebooks, wrapping paper, and toilet paper. It was through the performance of preachers and the inspiration of the Holy Spirit that the Bible and Christian literature gained spiritual significance.[30] In nineteenth-century Brazil, some narratives of colporteurs and missionaries described how the torn pages of evangelical periodicals or Bibles left carelessly aside by uninterested customers initiated processes of religious change. Some of the most illustrative cases in the Brazilian context are those of the conversion of the Portuguese pastor João de Carvalho Braga, and of the layman Joaquim Fernandes de Lima. Braga's process of conversion began after he read pages from a Bible used as packing-paper.[31] And Lima founded the Presbyterian Church of Ubatuba, São Paulo, after reading sermons and articles from the periodical *Imprensa Evangelica* for his congregation. His first contact with the *Imprensa* occurred when he received books and Bibles from the evangelical bookshop of Rio de Janeiro that came to him packed in the pages of the periodical.[32] For missionaries and colporteurs, it was the reflexive act of reading from the Bible and Christian texts that could

---

[29] *Eu não comprehendo a Bíblia* (Lisbon: Typ. De Vicente da Silva & Co., 1897), 4–5.
[30] Kirsch, *Spirits and Letters*, 85–88, 125–127.
[31] Ronald G. Frase, "A Sociological Analysis of the Development of Brazilian Protestantism: A Study of Social Change." (PhD dissertation, Princeton Theological Seminary, 1975), 256.
[32] Primeiro Livro de Actas da Igreja de Ubatuba, 1880, AHP. On the Imprensa Evangelica, see João Leonel, Ivanilson Bezerra da Silva, and Silas Luiz de Souza, eds., *O jornal 'Imprensa Evangelica' e o protestantismo brasileiro* (Votorantim, SP: Linha Fina, 2020).

ignite processes of religious change and assemble religious communities. Their mere physical presence was powerless.

This belief in the power of the written word, however, could become a source of disappointment. The Brazilian staff of the BFBS soon perceived that the widespread circulation of scriptures did not produce the results they expected in the short term. Conversions and the growth of evangelical congregations took longer to become a reality. Writing about the BFBS work in 1870, Holden affirmed that, although almost imperceptible, the progress of the evangelical faith in Brazil could be seen by "the eye of faith."[33] Twenty years later, the Rev. João dos Santos wrote a very pessimistic report asserting that although evangelical expansion was still very slow, "the seed of God's Word is being buried to rise again in the proper season" and his duty was to pursue his work diligently "waiting for the time when God shall give the harvest."[34] The belief in a future plentiful harvest became a commonplace in the correspondence with the BFBS committee in London, and the time lag between the dissemination of Scriptures and the ensuing conversions was a source of frustration for the BFBS personnel in Brazil. Conversion narratives prompted by the simple and unaided individual study of the Bible had the double effect of nurturing evangelical notions of textual agency and relieving the disappointment of the BFBS staff.[35] The longtime agent of the ABS in Brazil, Hugh Tucker, registered specific occasions in which books sold in the first half of the nineteenth century across the Brazilian territory paved the way to evangelical conversion decades later.[36]

Apart from prompting individual conversions, the Bible was also depicted as an instrument of social moralization. In a letter sent to the governor of Córdoba, Argentina, Holden wrote:

> The book, which I have thus the honour to place in your Excellency's hand, is God's book, the book which of all other, has exerted the deepest, most wide spread, and most salutary influence on the character and progress of the human race. Experience has abundantly shown that piety, morality, civilization and liberty attend to its dissemination, and that no greater blessing can be given to a nation than an open Bible as a fountain from

---

[33] BFBS Annual Report [1871], 310.
[34] BFBS Annual Report [1891], 351.
[35] BFBS Annual Reports [1870], 267; and [1885], 251.
[36] Tucker, *The Bible in Brazil*, 45–47, 110–111.

which the national mind may draw healthful instruction and vigorous moral principles.[37]

Similarly, in 1889, João dos Santos corresponded with the Society offering his interpretation of the abolition of slavery and the overthrow of the monarchy. For him, these significant events were signs of a deeper transformation operating beyond the superficiality of politics. Santos associated these events to the circulation of Bibles in Brazil, "which concerns not only the individual, but the character, and therefore the destinies of nations."[38] Protestants advertised the Bible as a source of social improvement, more than only a tool of conversion. In the evangelical imagination, its wide circulation would meet the needs of emerging Latin American nation-states.

Colporteurs: Itinerant Vendors of Christian Literature

Bible Society agents and superintendents such as Holden, Carvalho, Santos, and Tucker had important administrative responsibilities. They corresponded with their organizations' committees in Britain and the United States and coordinated bookselling strategies in different parts of the country. The success of Bible Societies depended to a fair extent on their efficiency and competence. But the agents who worked on the ground on a daily basis advertising and selling Bibles, dealing with customers, and circumventing opposition were the "vendors of Protestant Bibles," as João do Rio called them. In his first year as the BFBS superintendent, Holden employed ten colporteurs to carry out the distribution of Bibles. Five of them were based in Rio de Janeiro while the others were at work in the provinces of Pernambuco, Bahia, Alagoas, and Rio Grande do Sul.[39]

Colporteurs were responsible for selling Bibles and religious books throughout cities and the countryside. They canvassed villages and small farms and advertised their books in public markets and through the streets. Their work was a vital component of the BFBS operations in Brazil and abroad. The methods they used also determined the speed at which Bibles, books, pamphlets, and periodicals circulated throughout the country. All

---

[37] Copy of the Address to the Governor of Cordoba. BSA, BSA/D1/7-123 (Agents Book nº 123, South America).
[38] BFBS Annual Report [1890], 306.
[39] BFBS Annual Report [1866], 230–232.

scriptures published by the Society were shipped to Brazil from England or Portugal, where the BFBS founded a sub-committee. Books took, on average, two months to cross the Atlantic onboard steamships, and then around two or three weeks to be released from the customs houses of the ports of Santos and Rio de Janeiro.[40] Their journeys around the country, however, frequently took longer than the Atlantic crossing. This was due to the vast swathes of land they covered, the poor conditions of roads and tracks connecting cities to the countryside, and the intermittent nature of the mailing systems. Their modes of travel also determined the speed of these transactions. In some cases, colporteurs traveled on horseback from Rio de Janeiro to the far-away provinces of Bahia and Pernambuco.[41] In São Paulo, southern American Presbyterian missionaries hired a colporteur who used a mule to carry the heavy load of books while he traveled on foot.[42] Others combined both methods, traveling themselves on horseback while guiding mules loaded with books.[43] Sometimes colporteurs and agents undertook long expeditions throughout the interior that demanded a larger infrastructure. Tucker and colporteurs of the American Bible Society made one such journey through the state of Minas Gerais that included nine animals, a large tent, cooking utensils, wearing apparel, and, of course, the boxes loaded with Bibles.[44] Figures 2.1 and 2.2, taken by British evangelist Frederick Glass in the early twentieth century, show groups of colporteurs traveling across the Brazilian countryside. The men and women in Figure 2.1 are smartly and respectably dressed, ready for evangelistic work, while in Figure 2.2 colporteur Camillo proudly exhibits a volume of the Bible while guiding the mules carrying the boxes.

Despite being a non-sectarian evangelical organization at home, all BFBS superintendents in Brazil, in the period ranging from 1865 to 1900, were associated with the Fluminense Evangelical Church in Rio de Janeiro. The church's founder and long-time leader was the Scottish Congregationalist Dr. Robert Kalley. He had corresponded and collaborated with the BFBS since the late 1830s, when he opened an evangelistic enterprise in the island

---

[40] Rev. E. Lane to Mr. C. Finch, May 30, 1876. BSA, BSA/D1/7-144 (Agents Book nº 144, South America).
[41] BFBS Annual Report [1883], 225.
[42] E. Lane to the Society, June 4, 1875. BSA, BSA/D1/7-144 (Agents Book nº 144, South America).
[43] Frederick C. Glass, *With the Bible in Brazil: Being the Story of a Few of the Marvellous Incidents arising from Its Circulation There* (London: Morgan & Scott LD., 1914), 77.
[44] Tucker, *The Bible in Brazil*, 162.

Figure 2.1 Group of Brazilian colporteurs in São Paulo. Frederick Glass, *With the Bible in Brazil*.

Figure 2.2 Camillo on a colportage tour. Frederick Glass, *With the Bible in Brazil*.

of Madeira.[45] Richard Holden worked as Kalley's assistant pastor during his tenure as BFBS superintendent. The Rev. João dos Santos became head pastor of the Fluminense Church upon Kalley's return to Scotland in 1876, and he split his work routine between his pastoral duties and the managerial responsibilities of the Bible Society. José Carvalho was also a member of the same church. A good number of colporteurs, too, were recruited from among the ranks of the Congregationalist Church of Rio de Janeiro. Manoel Vianna (Figure 2.3), for instance, was a Portuguese shoemaker who became an active colporteur of the Society in the Brazilian northeast in the late 1860s. While undertaking his duties of colporteur, he also acted as an evangelist of the Fluminense Church in the province of Pernambuco, supporting the foundation of the Congregationalist Church in Recife in 1873.[46] This was at odds with the BFBS policy: the goal of superintendents and colporteurs was to circulate scriptures and support existing evangelistic initiatives, not to conduct missionary work. Vianna's evangelistic efforts caused a brief but stressful conflict of interests involving the missionary couple Robert and Sarah Kalley, the superintendent José Carvalho, and the BFBS committee in London. In undertaking evangelistic trips, Vianna raised the expenses of the BFBS base in Rio de Janeiro and entered into collision with the policy of the superintendent.[47]

Bible societies implemented their worldwide operations upon pre-existing cleavages and conflicts of interest between mission organizations and churches. Bible societies also established closer alliances with certain denominations. Southern American Presbyterian missionaries corresponded frequently with the BFBS, especially Edward Lane, founder of the International School of Campinas. Lane regularly requested Bibles and books for his school and for Presbyterian churches in the province of São Paulo.[48] Few letters were exchanged with northern American Presbyterian, Baptist, and Methodist missionaries, and the German Lutherans. These groups had closer links with the ABS.

A good number of the BFBS colporteurs in Brazil were men of very modest training and from poor backgrounds. The photographs from British colporteur Frederick Glass's book, *With the Bible in Brazil*, also show that some of

---

[45] Robert Reid Kalley, 1839–1877. BSA, BSA/D1/2, Foreign correspondence inwards.
[46] *Imprensa Evangelica*, November 13, 1880, n. 45.
[47] R. R. Kalley to the Igreja Evangélica Pernambucana, Theresópolis, February 25, 1875. BFB-IEF, Correspondência Dr. Kalley.
[48] BFBS Annual Reports [1873, 1876, and 1878].

Figure 2.3 Manoel Vianna. BFBS colporteur and evangelist of the Congregationalist Church. NCL-CSCW51/7/6/5.

them were blacks or mestizos (see Figure 2.1 and Figure 2.4). In an attempt to raise funds among Scottish evangelicals and support his former church in Brazil, Kalley wrote that the Fluminense Evangelical Church of Rio de Janeiro—from where the majority of BFBS colporteurs were recruited—was "composed almost entirely of poor men, shoemakers, tailors, and other of that class."[49] Carvalho wrote to the Society, in 1875, that only one of his

---

[49] R. R. Kalley to unknown. Edinburgh, November 1881. BFB-IEF, Correspondência Dr. Kalley.

Figure 2.4 A Brazilian colporteur at work. Frederick Glass, *With the Bible in Brazil*.

colporteurs could send him detailed written reports of his activities. The others could barely write a report in Portuguese and one of them, Manoel dos Anjos, was unable to write. He also stated that few evangelical converts could write.[50] Both the agents who circulated evangelical Bibles and the publics who purchased them hailed from impoverished and semi-literate backgrounds.

Missionaries, Brazilian ministers, and ordinary believers deployed a range of strategies to overcome these limitations. In various religious communities throughout the country, laypeople usually read the Bible and other Christian texts aloud in religious services and family meetings to illiterate or semi-literate fellow believers. These practices took place in both the domestic privacy of rural and urban families and in public places. Although rates of literacy were very low in the nineteenth and early twentieth centuries, and despite historian José Murilo de Carvalho's accurate assertion that literate elites in nineteenth-century Brazil formed an "island of lettered men" surrounded by an ocean of illiterates, various social categories made use of reading and writing into their everyday lives.[51] Faithful Catholics in the twentieth century held and read prayer cards with images of saints and prayers associated to them seeking protection from illnesses, death, incarceration, and even to prevent women from feeling pains during childbirth.[52] Slaves, too, made use of ink and paper. In the nineteenth century, Muslim slaves from West Africa read the Koran and circulated letters in Arabic in Bahia and Rio de Janeiro. Others acquired literacy by accompanying their masters' children in schools or by getting domestic instruction.[53] Despite the high levels of illiteracy of this era, Brazilian society was "aware of literacy."[54] Print matter had been introduced early in the sixteenth century by Catholic missionaries, metropolitan representatives, and merchants; reading primers and devotional books had achieved some popularity since the colonial era;

---

[50] Carvalho to Finch, Rio de Janeiro, November 15, 1875. BSA, BSA/D1/7-144 (Agents Book n° 144, South America).

[51] José Murilo de Carvalho, *A construção da ordem: A elite política imperial/Teatro de sombras: A política imperial*, 3rd ed. (Rio de Janeiro: Civilização Brasileira, 2010).

[52] Erika Helgen, *Religious Conflict in Brazil: Protestants, Catholics, and the Rise of Religious Pluralism in the Early Twentieth Century* (New Haven, CT: Yale University Press, 2020), 204–205.

[53] Mary C. Karasch, *Slave Life in Rio de Janeiro, 1808–1850* (Princeton, NJ: Princeton University Press, 1987), 214–219; João José Reis, *Slave Rebellion in Brazil: The Muslim Uprising of 1835 in Bahia*, trans. Arthur Brakel (Baltimore: Johns Hopkins University Press, 1993).

[54] I take this expression from Christopher Bayly, *Empire and Information: Intelligence Gathering and Social Communication in India, 1780–1870* (Cambridge: Cambridge University Press, 1996), ch. 1.

and different social groups knew the meaning, power, and prestige associated with reading and writing.[55]

Hugh Tucker of the ABS reported that, on various occasions, he witnessed literate children and young people reading Bibles and Christian literature to their kin and neighbors privately.[56] In an account of his years in Brazil, the British colporteur Frederick Glass encountered in the countryside of Goiás a man, the only literate person of a small village called Gameleira, who read the New Testament to his community in the evenings. In a revealing passage, Glass claimed that "they received the Word as good news from a far country" and that when the colporteurs arrived in the village "the people welcomed them as apostles."[57] Here Glass expressed the evangelical imagination of the era by establishing parallels between the propagation of evangelical religion in Brazil with the age of the apostolic church. But he also shed light on the ways in which ordinary believers deployed and interpreted print matter in rural communities, reading the Bible as a contemporary text.

According to the BFBS superintendent João dos Santos, even illiterate people purchased books, Bibles, and Christian literature.[58] The British colporteur Samuel Elliot reported that on his journeys through the south of Brazil, illiteracy was an obstacle to the selling of scriptures, "but generally there is one in each family who can read and the father is willing to buy one for him, especially if he finds that his neighbour has bought one."[59] Presbyterian missionaries and itinerant preachers encountered similar practices. The Portuguese missionary João Dagama met in the city of Campos, near Rio de Janeiro, a man who purchased the scriptures and paid a small amount of money to have someone read the text for him in the evenings.[60] Bibles and Christian literature were rapidly integrated into the social and liturgical practices prevalent in Brazilian evangelical churches and in the domestic worship of believers. They were read and heard in congregations and

---

[55] Leila Mezan Algranti, *Livros de devoção, atos de censura: Ensaios de história do livro e da leitura na América portuguesa (1750–1821)* (São Paulo: Hucitec, 2004); Stuart Schwartz, *All Can Be Saved: Religious Tolerance and Salvation in Iberian Atlantic World* (New Haven, CT: Yale University Press, 2008), 144–149.

[56] Tucker, *The Bible in Brazil*, 59–60, 69, 89, 91–92, 218.

[57] Glass, *With the Bible in Brazil*, 70–71.

[58] BFBS Annual Report [1882], 279.

[59] Mr. S. Elliot to the Committee, Brazil, May 8, 1875. BSA, BSA/D1/7-144 (Agents Book nº 144, South America).

[60] Relatório Annual, 1872, J. F. Dagama. AHP, Coleção Carvalhosa, Relatórios Pastorais (1866–1875).

houses, and thus had publics and audiences simultaneously.[61] Recitations and public readings of the scriptures and Christian texts interwove print and oral cultures, asserting the authority of print matter and stabilizing doctrinal boundaries.[62]

Additionally, Bible Societies and other Protestant institutions created possibilities of upward social mobility for colporteurs and superintendents. Social scientists have shown how the provision of formal education in mission schools and conversion to evangelical Protestantism, with its consequential behavioral changes, generated new economic cultures among Latin American believers and enabled convert families to accumulate.[63] In a similar manner, the Brazilian branch of the BFBS offered opportunities of income improvement for its staff. By the time of his retirement and return to Britain, Richard Holden appointed the bookkeeper José de Carvalho as his successor. Corresponding with the Society in London, Holden affirmed that "a little gradual social elevation will be desirable in order to strengthen the hands of discipline."[64] Holden suggested that Carvalho's salary should be raised to 100$000 a month, enough to include him in the group of primary electors in Brazil.[65] Carvalho himself tried to negotiate the salaries of his colporteurs with the BFBS. In his first year as superintendent, he managed to increase the salary of Manoel dos Anjos, the semi-literate colporteur whom he described as a "man of little instruction."[66] In the following year, he defended that the salaries of all colporteurs should be updated, arguing that, in contrast to other workers who did not have major personal expenses, such as shoemakers, colporteurs had to walk through the streets clean and well dressed "in order not to be censured." According to Carvalho, shoemakers

---

[61] Robert Darnton, "History of Reading," in *New Perspectives on Historical Writing*, ed. Peter Burke (Cambridge: Polity Press, 1991), 166–167.

[62] Kirsch, *Spirits and Letters*, 145–146.

[63] On this matter, see Antonio Maspoli, *Religião, educação e progresso* (São Paulo: Editora Mackenzie, 2001); David Martin, *Tongues of Fire: The Explosion of Protestantism in Latin America* (Oxford: Basil Blackwell, 1990), 226–229; Elizabeth Brusco, "The Reformation of Machismo: Asceticism and Masculinity among Colombian Evangelicals," in *Rethinking Protestantism in Latin America*, ed. Virginia Garrard-Burnett and David Stoll (Philadelphia: Temple University Press, 1993).

[64] R. Holden to the Rev. Bergne. Homelands, January 22, 1872. BSA, BSA/D1/7-123 (Agents Book nº 123, South America).

[65] R. Holden to the Rev. Bergne. Homelands, January 11, 1872. BSA, BSA/D1/7-123 (Agents Book nº 123, South America).

[66] Report on Bible Distribution in Brazil on Behalf of the British & Foreign Bible Society Under the Supervision of José M. Martin de Carvalho for the Year Ending 31st December 1872. BSA, BSA/D1/7-123 (Agents Book nº 123, South America).

earned better salaries than colporteurs in Brazil and he urged the Society to address this issue.[67]

Epidemics, Economic Crises, and Political Chiefs

Colporteurs faced numerous ordeals on their journeys. Rudimentary modes of travel had a direct impact on their health and mood. Catholic bishops and local priests organized campaigns aimed at discouraging the public form buying the colporteurs' books and to destroy those that were sold. These campaigns, as will be seen ahead, motivated both widespread resistance against and interest in Protestants books and scriptures. Table 2.1 shows the variations in colporteurs' sales. The work of the colporteurs was not easy. Brazil was thinly populated in the nineteenth century and large distances separated cities and provinces from one another, which forced colporteurs to spend months on the road. According to João dos Santos, rough modes of travel, poor accommodation, wretched food, the unhealthy climate, and prolonged periods away from home discouraged potential workers.[68] In 1886, he proposed to divide the large country into ten districts and appoint one colporteur for each of them, a reorganization that would reduce not only the frequency of the costly journeys to the countryside, but also the distance between colporteurs and their families.[69] This strategy, however, was never adopted and, up until the end of the nineteenth century, the Society continued to face problems in the recruitment of personnel.

In most cases, though, the obstacles to Bible-selling were external to the Society. In 1876, José de Carvalho summarized the factors that limited the circulation of books in Rio de Janeiro in four points: heavy rains in the first months of the year, religious indifference, the current economic crisis with its impact on food prices, and outbreaks of yellow fever.[70] This last factor was a source of great anxiety for missionaries and colporteurs. The Brazilian capital became the central stage of widespread outbreaks of yellow fever between the late 1860s and the beginning of the twentieth century.

---

[67] Report of Bible Distribution in Brazil for the year ending 31st December 1873. BSA, BSA/D1/7-144 (Agents Book n° 144, South America).
[68] BFBS Annual Report [1885], 249.
[69] BFBS Annual Report [1886], 298.
[70] J. de Carvalho to Bergne, July 22, 1876. BSA, BSA/D1/7-144 (Agents Book n° 144, South America).

78 PROPAGANDISTS OF THE BOOK

Throughout the latter half of the nineteenth century, epidemics of yellow fever disrupted some centers of missionary work in Brazil. Baptist and Presbyterian missionaries in the city of Campinas, São Paulo, were forced to shut down churches and mission stations because of these outbreaks. And in the northeast the disease also carried off missionary personnel, including an American Baptist schoolteacher.[71] Two serious outbreaks, in 1873 and again in 1876, represented a turning point in the history of yellow fever in Brazil. They pushed state authorities to carry out a series of urban reforms to control the dissemination of the disease.[72] Corresponding with the BFBS committee, Carvalho and Santos explained how these epidemics disrupted the Society's operations. Carvalho's brother died of yellow fever in 1876 and his wife was also infected in the same year. Santos wrote, in 1886, that the fever had carried off some Christian workers in Rio.[73] These outbreaks had a direct impact on the circulation of Bibles: they created difficulties for the shipment of Bibles in Rio de Janeiro and Santos, as all steamships were subjected to quarantine; superintendents found it challenging to recruit colporteurs during epidemics; and they impoverished the Brazilian population.

Economic crises also curtailed the circulation of Bibles. When asked whether he could appoint more colporteurs in 1876, José de Carvalho argued that the agrarian crisis of the 1870s had dramatically raised the cost of living in the country and consequently sales had decreased. In the face of this, it was not economically viable to engage new colporteurs and raise the BFBS expenses.[74] Manoel dos Anjos, working as a colporteur in Rio de Janeiro, told the superintendent that most of his books were sold among fishermen, black sailors, and poor people who could not afford the Bibles printed by the Society in times of scarcity. These customers purchased mostly portions and Testaments instead, but not whole scriptures.[75] One of the guiding principles of the BFBS at home and abroad was that their books should be sold

---

[71] Asa R. Crabtree, *História dos batistas do Brasil até o ano de 1906*, 2nd ed. (Rio de Janeiro: Casa Publicadora Batista, 1962 [1937]), 285; Vicente T. Lessa, *Annaes da 1ª Egreja Presbyteriana de São Paulo (1863–1903): Subsidios para a historia do presbiterianismo brasileiro* (São Paulo: Edição da 1ª Igreja Presbiteriana Independente de São Paulo, 1938), 170; SBC Proceedings [1889], appendix A, xiv.

[72] Sidney Chalhoub, "The Politics of Disease Control: Yellow Fever and Race in Nineteenth-century Rio de Janeiro," *Journal of Latin American Studies* 25 (1993): 441–463, at 455–456.

[73] BFBS Annual Report [1886], 299; Carvalho to Bergne, May 13, 1876. BSA, BSA/D1/7-144 (Agents Book nº 144, South America).

[74] Carvalho to the Rev. C. Jackson, February 8, 1876. BSA, BSA/D1/7-144 (Agents Book nº 144, South America).

[75] Carvalho to the Rev. C. Jackson, February 7, 1873. BSA, BSA/D1/7-123 (Agents Book nº 123, South America).

as cheaply as possible.[76] Prices, though, were subject to variations in inflation rates and fluctuations in the cost of living in mission fields. Despite these challenges, the Brazilian branch of the BFBS remained faithful to the principle that books should not be freely distributed. The saying "*livro dado é livro desprezado*" (a book given away is a book despised) was a commonplace among colporteurs. Some of them alternatively exchanged Bibles for goods, such as black beans or sugar bricks, instead of money, especially on their travels to remote corners of the country or when dealing with poorer families.[77] Colporteurs associated with the ABS, too, only gave away books freely when faced with situations of extreme poverty, and relied on individual donations and local fundraising to compensate and support the Society financially.[78]

The reaction of public authorities against the circulation of evangelical scriptures in Brazil was a source of anxiety for colporteurs. Although Protestant missionaries and foreign visitors in nineteenth-century Brazil acclaimed the liberality of the Empire's Constitution and the qualities of Emperor Dom Pedro II,[79] colporteurs faced different realities in their journeys to small towns and through the Brazilian countryside. Whereas foreign Protestant travelers represented the monarchy as an enlightened institution that enforced order and the "empire of the law" upon its provinces, colporteurs dealt with the peculiarities of local politics. João dos Santos wrote to the Society, in 1882, that to prevent county magistrates from prohibiting the selling of Bibles, each colporteur had been furnished with a "printed copy of the law on the subject, and of the resolution passed by the Brazilian Government in 1868, which authorizes the circulation of the Scriptures as a branch of industry or commerce."[80] In 1885, Santos appealed to the Emperor against a law sanctioned by the Provincial Assembly of Ceará determining that anyone selling non-Catholic books should pay a tax equivalent to fifty-six British pounds.[81] Even after the advent of the republic in 1889 and the

---

[76] Howsam, *Cheap Bibles*, 50.

[77] Glass, *With the Bible*, 42–44. Colporteurs associated with the ABS in Mexico deployed similar strategies, see John Fea, *The Bible Cause: A History of the American Bible Society* (New York: Oxford University Press, 2016), 125.

[78] Tucker, *The Bible in Brazil*, 212–213, 223–224.

[79] James C. Fletcher and Daniel P. Kidder, *Brazil and the Brazilians: Portrayed in Historical and Descriptive Sketches* (Philadelphia: Childs & Peterson, 1857), 229–230; also in Alexander L. Blackford, *Sketch of the Brazil Mission* (Philadelphia, PA: Presbyterian Board of Education, 1886), 3.

[80] BFBS Annual Report [1882], 282.

[81] BFBS Annual Report [1886], 299.

disestablishment of the Catholic Church, these events continued to occur. Describing the campaign a Catholic priest waged against the colporteur Antonio Miranda in Paraíba do Norte in the late 1890s, Santos wrote that "we have a good law, full of liberty, and it is forbidden to persecute any one for the sake of religion, but the law is a dead letter in some places."[82] Hugh Tucker, of the ABS, adopted another strategy. He applied to local authorities, such as delegates, presidents of city councils, and local priests for permission to sell books through the streets, even after the proclamation of the Republic.[83] Interactions involving colporteurs, police delegates, judges of the peace, and other local political chiefs reshaped the missionary imagination of Brazil in the nineteenth century. For Protestant colporteurs and Bible Society superintendents, local political authorities interpreted the Brazilian legislation unevenly and were out of tune with the liberality of Brazilian laws.

Foreign Protestants residing in Brazil, however, were able to appeal to other political authorities. If British missionaries working in the domains of the British Empire could in many cases benefit from their relations with imperial powers,[84] outside the realm of the formal Empire they resorted to diplomats and envoys when their personal safety or properties were under threat. Robert Kalley, for instance, appealed to George Buckley Mathew, a British envoy in Rio de Janeiro, when the police delegate of the capital refused to grant protection for his family and the members of his church who had been threatened by Catholic protesters in 1874. Kalley argued that all his church's meetings and religious services were in accord with the Constitution.[85] In a similar manner, Tucker waived his American passport and threatened to appeal to the American representatives in Rio de Janeiro when an officer of the city of Santa Luzia, Minas Gerais, accused him of doing irregular business and called for his imprisonment in 1888.[86] Throughout the nineteenth century, Catholic periodicals exhibited a particular wariness toward these relations between foreign missionaries, British and American diplomats, and Brazilian authorities. Ultramontane writers associated them with imperialist violations of national sovereignty and wider anti-Catholic

---

[82] BFBS Annual Repors [1897], 267.
[83] Tucker, *The Bible in Brazil*, 101–102, 125, 131, 151, 171, 176.
[84] Andrew Porter, *Religion versus Empire? British Protestant Missionaries and Overseas Expansion, 1700–1914* (Manchester: Manchester University Press, 2004); Jeffrey Cox, *The British Missionary Enterprise since 1700* (New York: Routledge, 2010), ch. 5.
[85] R. R. Kalley to George Buckley Mathew. Theresópolis, February 13, 1874, and R. R. Kalley to George Buckley Mathew. Theresópolis, February 14, 1874. BFB-IEF, Correspondência Dr. Kalley.
[86] Tucker, *The Bible in Brazil*, 101–102.

transnational conspiracies spurred by freemasons, Protestants, and liberal intellectuals aimed at destabilizing the Church.[87]

In the light of these experiences, British missionaries and the Brazilian staff of the BFBS rapidly perceived that local governments did not enforce the Empire's resolutions and laws homogeneously in the country. Instead, the legislation was variously interpreted, negotiated, and, in some cases, rejected by local authorities. This dynamic was, indeed, a component of nineteenth-century Brazilian political life, when landowners and local bosses extended their political influence regionally through informal networks of patron–client relations.[88] Brazilian evangelicals and foreign missionaries quickly noticed that central and local politics lacked synchrony. They also believed that the legal status of dissenting religious minorities in the country was unstable, depending on the interpretation of political bosses and police delegates of constitutional clauses on religious tolerance.

Catholic Reactions

Besides epidemics of yellow fever, economic crises, and the interference of public authorities, Protestant booksellers regarded the reactions of Catholic clerics and believers as the greatest threat to the circulation of Bibles in Brazil. The introduction of Bible Societies and Protestant missions in Brazil coincided with the Romanization of Brazilian Catholicism, a process sometimes referred to as the Ultramontane reform. This movement reasserted the supreme authority of the pope and the Vatican over the worldwide Catholic Church and rejected the "errors of modernity," including nationalist movements, revolutionary mobilizations, and modern liberalism. In the defensive and apologetic rhetoric of Ultramontane clerics and writers, the forces of Protestantism and Positivism challenged deep-seated Catholic traditions and hierarchies. Consequently, they threatened the social stability of the country, its cultural traditions, and the nationalist sentiments of Brazilians.[89] Individual Bible-reading was viewed as particularly disruptive because it undermined notions of priestly mediation and destabilized the institutional solidity of the Church.

---

[87] Vieira, *O protestantismo*, 282–291.
[88] Richard Graham, *Patronage and Politics in Nineteenth-century Brazil* (Stanford, CA: Stanford University Press, 1990).
[89] Riolando Azzi, *A neocristandade: Um projeto restaurador* (São Paulo: Paulus, 1994), 80–82.

When Richard Holden was still associated with the ABS in the cities of Belém and Salvador in 1861–1862, the actions of a colporteur under his charge spurred an intense religious controversy in local periodicals and prompted the reaction of Catholic authorities against Bible Societies.[90] In August 1861, the Bishop of Pará, Dom Antônio de Macedo Costa, issued a pastoral letter warning his flock against the "falsifications of Protestant scriptures." Similarly, the Archbishop of Bahia, Dom Manuel Joaquim da Silveira, used the same strategy and a similar language to condemn the "falsifications and mutilations" of Protestant Bibles. Silveira targeted specifically the João Ferreira de Almeida translation of the Bible into Portuguese. His letter enumerated all the portions in the Old and New Testaments that differed from the authorized Catholic Bible, drawing specific emphasis to the lack of the Apocryphal books, such as the books of Tobit, Judith, and Maccabees. Silveira condemned these "mutilations," and warned Catholics against the "false Bibles and little books against the religion."[91] The letter echoed similar reactions against Protestant propaganda in other parts of Latin America.[92] The content and the language of these pastoral letters had widespread and long-lasting reverberations in Brazil and Portugal in the nineteenth and twentieth centuries.

The BFBS printed and circulated two main versions of the Bible in Portuguese. The first was an eighteenth-century translation from the Latin Vulgate by the Catholic priest Antonio Pereira de Figueiredo. The second was a seventeenth-century version by the reformed minister João Ferreira de Almeida, who translated the whole of the New Testament from the Greek texts and most of the Old Testament from Hebrew.[93] Almeida settled in Batavia after his conversion to Protestantism in 1642 and, upon his ordination in 1656, he served multilingual Portuguese, French, Dutch, and Spanish communities in Java, Ceylon, and southern India. Two Dutch ministers revised his Portuguese translation of the Bible and, in 1683, Almeida delivered to his editors a list of over a thousand grammatical and language mistakes.[94]

---

[90] Vieira, *O protestantismo*, 182–183, 189–192.

[91] Manuel J. da Silveira, *Carta pastoral premunindo os seus diocesanos contra as mutilações, e as adulterações da Bíblia traduzida em português pelo padre João Ferreira D'Almeida; contra os folhetos, e livretos contra a religião, que com a mesma Bíblia se tem espalhado nesta cidade; e contra alguns erros, que se tem publicado no país* (Bahia: Typ. de Camillo de Lellis Masson & Co., 1862).

[92] On Colombia, see BFBS Annual Report [1857], ccxxv.

[93] Innocencio F. Silva, *Diccionario bibliographico portuguez: Estudos de Innocêncio Francisco da Silva*, tome VIII (Lisbon: Imprensa Nacional, 1867), 277; *Dicionário Cronológico de Autores Portugueses*, vol. I (Mem Martins, PT: Publicações Europa-América, 1985), 438.

[94] Thomas Darlow, Horace Moule, and Arthur Jayne, *Historical Catalogue of the Printed Editions of Holy Scripture in the Library of the British and Foreign Bible Society* (London: The Bible House, 1911), 1232.

When the British and American Bible Societies started to circulate their books in Brazil, the public did not appreciate the Almeida version because of its inaccuracies and old-fashioned style. Nevertheless, this was the version Protestant missionaries in Brazil most cherished because it was translated from the Greek and Hebrew texts. The Figueiredo version, on the other hand, was highly appreciated by Brazilian Protestant teachers and grammarians due to its literary style and accurate translation from the Latin. The Figueiredo Bible also bore the seal of approval of the Archbishop of Bahia on its cover, which on many occasions halted opposition.[95] Throughout the nineteenth century, a group of ministers and missionaries connected to the BFBS in Brazil and Portugal joined their efforts to improve the Almeida translation, while colporteurs on both sides of the Atlantic circulated the two versions of the Bible. Most Catholic reactions to the scriptures targeted specifically the Almeida version, although the Figueiredo translation also excluded the Apocryphal texts. Colporteurs met with different echoes of the controversy of the false Bibles in their journeys across the country. In some cases, public authorities intervened in the colporteurs' work deploying the language of the Catholic pastoral letters. This happened to Antonio da Silva in the city of Angra dos Reis, near Rio de Janeiro. The police delegate forbade Silva's sales and alleged his Bibles were false.[96]

In other cases, colporteurs encountered different reverberations of the controversy. Working in the state of São Paulo in 1893, the colporteur Manoel de Souza e Silva reported to the superintendent that he met people who were afraid of the consequences of reading Protestant books.[97] In his first journey to the province of Paraíba in 1874, Manoel Vianna faced strong resistance. Interestingly, it was lay Catholics who objected to the Bibles' grammatical issues and language, not the public authorities or Catholic clerics. For instance, Vianna recalled a conversation with a man who had bought a book from him and burned it after reading passages in which the pronoun *tu* (thou) was used to refer to God. The man argued that it was disrespectful to address a person of rank using the second person singular pronoun. Additionally, people attributed to evangelical Bibles powers of enchantment and possession. In Paraíba, local Catholics brought before Vianna a young man who rode a horse naked through the town and claimed that he had lost

---

[95] Darlow, Moule, and Jayne, *Historical Catalogue*, 1233.
[96] Carvalho to the Rev. Bergne. Rio de Janeiro, August 26, 1876. BSA, BSA/D1/7-144 (Agents Book n° 144, South America).
[97] BFBS Annual Report [1894], 296.

his reason after reading a Protestant Bible.[98] A Catholic periodical in 1873 bemoaned the spread of the "bibliomaniac hysteria" of the Protestants and claimed that a "bibliolater" father decapitated his son in consequence of the "damned interpretation of a biblical text."[99] Once again, on both cases the mere physical presence of the Bible was considered impotent. Bibles as material objects were not endowed with talismanic powers. In the popular imagination, it was through reading that people could be either converted or possessed. Significantly, the controversy of the false Bibles reverberated across time and space. In the late nineteenth and early twentieth centuries, evangelists encountered ordinary Catholics in different parts of the country who resisted being evangelized claiming that Protestant Bibles were false.[100] Moreover, the controversy resonated across the Lusophone world and was deployed by Catholic clerics and laypeople opposing the circulation of Protestant scriptures in Portugal.

As Protestant missions and Bible Societies established a foothold in Brazil and extended their presence to different parts of the country, the public image of Protestants and their religious celebrations became increasingly associated with the Bible. However, this turned out to be a troublesome association. The Rio de Janeiro-based Ultramontane periodical *O Apóstolo* (The Apostle) frequently protested against colporteurs, whom they referred to pejoratively as "Bible dealers," "vendors of false Bibles," or "Bible peddlers."[101] Echoing the controversy of the false Bibles, Catholic editors denounced what they described as the falsifications, adulterations, and mistranslations of the British and American Bible Societies. The periodical referred to colporteurs working in the province of Ceará as "disturbers of the social order and the families' peace" and closed the argument claiming that "Protestantism is disorder, anarchy, and revolution."[102] For them, the lack of explanatory notes and commentaries on the Protestant Bibles had a disruptive potential. Only an authorized body of knowledgeable theologians was entitled to interpret the scriptures and keep the Catholic tradition alive.[103] The periodical popularized a pejorative term to refer to Protestants: they

---

[98] Carvalho to the Rev. Bergne. Rio de Janeiro, May 15, 1874. BSA, BSA/D1/7-144 (Agents Book n° 144, South America).
[99] *O Apóstolo*, September 7, 1873, n. 36.
[100] Maria de Melo Chaves, *Bandeirantes da fé* (Belo Horizonte: Associação Evangélica Beneficente de Minas Gerais, 1947), 22–25, 48.
[101] *O Apóstolo*. Rio de Janeiro, February, 29 1884, N° 24.
[102] *O Apóstolo*. Rio de Janeiro, November 7, 1879, N° 129.
[103] *O Apóstolo*, 31 May 1876, n. 60; October 12, 1877, n. 117.

were called *os bíblias*. In an emphatic article against the idea of individual ownership of scriptures, contributors to *O Apóstolo* affirmed: "All of a sudden, any *carroceiro* [ox-cart driver] or *capinador de quintais* [backyard weeder] becomes a *bíblia* and there they are, preaching and teaching what, according to these Bible *masters*, each one can individually interpret; promoted to the category of Bible minister, they soon attempt to pervert the faith of everyone they encounter."[104] For Ultramontane Catholics, the individual interpretation of the scriptures was destructive, disrupting the wellbeing of families. Worse still, these armies of semi-literate booksellers turned established hierarchies upside down, and undermined the sources of authority of the official religion.

BFBS agents and Protestant missionaries took seriously into account these widespread and grassroots reactions to the Almeida translation and sought to remedy the pejorative meanings attached to the Bible in Brazil. In the 1860s and 1870s, a group of missionaries and evangelists associated with the Society joined their efforts to improve the Almeida translation. In 1869, Robert Kalley wrote to the BFBS that this translation contained "many expressions which appear incorrect to modern Portuguese taste and some which provoke a smile."[105] Richard Holden also warned the Society about the abundance of typographical errors on some of the BFBS editions. He drew attention to the use of accents: the word *mão* (hand) replaced on numerous occasions the word *máo*, which could be read as *evil* at the time. Holden affirmed that it caused major confusion for readers.[106] Lacking a consistent strategy to revise the translation, various people sent to the Society their notes and comments about the text. The Presbyterian missionary Alexander Blackford called it a "patchwork revision" and decried its inefficiency.[107] In 1869, the BFBS published a new edition of the Almeida Old Testament and a revised version of the book of Genesis prepared in Portugal by the translator Manoel Soares. As the new version of Genesis was well received in Portugal and Brazil, the Society commissioned Soares to undertake a complete revision of the Almeida translation, which was published in Lisbon in 1875.[108] This revised version divided opinion among foreign missionaries and Brazilian ministers: Edward Lane and Robert

---

[104] *O Apóstolo*. Rio de Janeiro, May 5, 1882, Nº 51. Italics in the original.
[105] R. Kalley to the Editorial Superintendent. Rothesay, June 12, 1869. BSA, BSA/E3/1/4-7.
[106] R. Holden to the Rev. S. Bergne. Rio de Janeiro, July 6, 1869. BSA, BSA/E3/1/4-7.
[107] A. Blackford to R. Holden. October 2, 1869. BSA, BSA/D1/2, File C.
[108] Darlow, Moule, and Jayne, *Historical Catalogue*, 1248–1249.

Kalley praised, while José Carvalho and João dos Santos disliked the text.[109] This collective translation work involved Portuguese-speaking ministers on both sides of the Atlantic, generating an intense exchange of communication between Portugal, Brazil, and Britain that flowed through the conduits of the BFBS.

Given the widespread popular resistance against the Bible, the Brazilian staff of the BFBS developed an array of strategies related to the advertising and selling of books. Because of the controversy of the false Bibles, the word *Bíblia* was avoided in interactions between colporteurs and potential buyers. Summarizing the reports of Brazilian colporteurs, Kalley informed the BFBS that "the title 'Bíblia' seems to be a hindrance to the sales, especially in Rio, and that 'As Escrituras Sagradas' [The Sacred Scriptures] would probably promote them. The reason is that 'Bíblia' is a term of the greatest scorn, applied to those who read the Word of God, while 'As Escrituras Sagradas' is one of reverence and respect to the book."[110] João dos Santos also observed that having the word "*Bíblia*" printed on the covers of books was a serious obstacle to the circulation of scriptures as the word was loaded with negative associations.[111] Despite these suggestions, the Society never replaced the word "Bible" on its books' covers. From 1868 onward, most of the BFBS Bibles, Testaments, and portions in Portuguese were printed in Portugal and shipped to Brazil from Lisbon, not Britain. According to the American missionary Edward Lane, Presbyterian colporteurs were usually unable to sell Bibles printed in London because they came from a Protestant country, "but they will buy with greatest alacrity the same Bible printed or sent from Lisbon."[112] These were significant details that could either promote sales or shatter the successes of colporteurs.

In the face of these obstacles, the BFBS personnel began to employ new advertising strategies. In 1874, José de Carvalho sent two colporteurs to the streets of Rio de Janeiro during the Holy Week and instructed them to circulate only portions of the Bible. Carvalho also advised them not to hold long conversations with customers to prevent them from learning that their books

---

[109] Kalley to the Rev. Girdlestone. Rio de Janeiro, November 20, 1874; Santos to the Rev. Bergne. Rio de Janeiro, October 7, 1875; and Carvalho to Mr. Frinch. Rio de Janeiro, November 15, 1875. BSA, BSA/E3/1/4-11; E. Lane to Rev. Bergne. Campinas, September 13, 1875. BSA, BSA/D1/7-144 (Agents Book nº 144, South America).

[110] BFBS Annual Report [1881], 187.

[111] BFBS Annual Report [1882], 279.

[112] E. Lane to Rev. Bergne. Campinas, September 13, 1875. BSA, BSA/D1/7-144 (Agents Book nº 144, South America).

were Bibles. As a result, 637 books were sold during Holy Week.[113] In 1880, João dos Santos advised his colporteurs based in Rio de Janeiro to sell books on Good Friday and Christmas, while "being careful not to call the book by the name Bible or Testament, but as one that contained the true account of the birth and death of the Lord Jesus Christ." On November 2, All Souls' Day, colporteurs were able to sell 487 gospels at the Rio de Janeiro cemetery.[114] As the strategy proved successful, the practices of selling portions of the Bible on special dates of the Christian calendar and avoiding the use of the word *Bíblia* in interactions with customers were consistently employed in Brazil. It also explains why sales of portions of the biblical text outnumbered those of Bibles from 1874 onward (see Table 2.1).

A Transatlantic Circulation of Protestant Books

While the BFBS circulated an increasing number of Bibles and portions, another London-based evangelical organization started to operate in Brazil and played an important role in the making of a Brazilian evangelical reading public. This organization was the Religious Tract Society (RTS). Throughout most of the nineteenth century, the RTS operated indirectly in Brazil by sending books and tracts to missionaries and established churches without properly appointing representatives of its own to the country. In the words of Presbyterian missionary Emmanuel Vanorden, the RTS was doing an important service for the Brazilian population, introducing in the country vast amounts of Christian literature that served as a barrier to the immoral influence of the "ungodly" French novels.[115] At that time, pornographic literature and libertine novels had acquired some popularity, forming a collection of licentious works infamously known as the "bachelor's library."[116] Protestant ministers bemoaned such novels and devised Christian literature as a remedy to their "immoral" influences. The RTS was founded in 1799 as

---

[113] Carvalho to the Rev. S. Bergne. Rio de Janeiro, April 21, 1874. BSA, BSA. BSA/D1/7-144 (Agents Book nº 144, South America).
[114] BFBS Annual Report [1881], 186.
[115] *Report of the Centenary Conference on the Protestant Missions to the World, held in Exeter Hall (June 9th–19th), London, 1888, vol. II*, ed. Rev. James Johnston (London: James Nisbet & Co., 1888), 328.
[116] Leonardo Mendes, "The Bachelor's Library: Pornographic Books on the Brazil–Europe Circuit in the Late Nineteenth Century," in *The Transatlantic Circulation of Novels between Europe and Brazil, 1789–1914*, ed. Márcia Abreu (Cham, Switzerland: Palgrave Macmillan, 2017), 79–100.

an interdenominational evangelical society dedicated to the publication and distribution of religious literature. Like the BFBS, the Tract Society also operated at a global level and reached transnational publics and audiences in the nineteenth century. Along with BFBS personnel, RTS administrators and workers regarded religious texts as silent messengers whose presence could be "acceptable where an uninvited missionary would not, and would remain behind after a missionary had departed."[117] According to Vanorden, Brazilian Catholic priests feared the RTS tracts more than BFBS Bibles "for it is these silent preachers which are directing the people to God's Holy Word."[118]

Throughout the nineteenth century, the RTS refrained from developing in Brazil an operational system as consistent and far-reaching as that of the BFBS. The RTS did not employ salaried agents, superintendents, and colporteurs of its own to circulate books and tracts in the country. Instead, it collaborated with established missionaries and evangelical organizations in Brazil. The person who most frequently corresponded with the Society's committee was Vanorden, who had a troubled relationship with his fellow missionaries. By the time Vanorden started to correspond with the RTS, he had severed his bonds with the Presbyterian mission and withdrew to the far south of the country, where he founded a publishing firm of his own and published a Protestant paper titled *O Pregador Cristão* (The Christian Preacher).[119] The RTS supplied him with books, tracts, pamphlets, illustrations, reams of paper, and later with a printing press and electrotypes.[120] The BFBS superintendent João Manoel dos Santos and various agents of the UK-based South American Missionary Society obtained books and tracts, which they circulated in the country along pre-existing routes of colportage.[121] BFBS colporteurs also carried with them RTS books in their journeys across the country.[122] The periodical *Imprensa Evangelica* frequently advertised books and tracts published by the RTS that were sold cheaply in Protestant bookshops in Rio and São Paulo.

---

[117] Aileen Fyfe, "Commerce and Philanthropy: The Religious Tract Society and the Business of Publishing," *Journal of Victorian Culture* 9 (2004): 164–188, at 165, 170.

[118] *The Eighty-ninth Annual Report of the Religious TRACT Society, instituted A.D. M.DCC.XCIX., for Publishing Religious Tracts and Books at Home and Abroad* (London: Pardon & Son Printers, 1888), 195. Hereinafter cited as: RTS Annual Report [year].

[119] Lessa, *Annaes*, 149–150.

[120] For some of the correspondences with E. Vanorden, see RTS Annual Reports [1879], 210–212; [1881], 201–202; and [1889], 205–206.

[121] RTS Annual Reports [1883], 220–221; [1892], 211; [1896], 221–223.

[122] S. P. Kalley to the Rev. Bergne. Petropolis, March 22, 1876. BSA, BSA/D1/7-144 (Agents Book nº 144, South America).

As historian Roger Martin observed, unlike the BFBS, the RTS "did not draft a 'fundamental principle' on the basis of which the various denominations could cooperate. The Society's aim was simply taken for granted."[123] Its objective was to apply the funds collected through subscriptions, donations, and contributions to the production and circulation of Christian literature at home and abroad.[124] As the volume of texts submitted to the Society's committee for approval increased exponentially in the nineteenth century, the RTS hammered out most of its rules relating to the examination and censorship of tracts and books.[125] Devoid of such restrictions, the RTS was more easily adaptable to new circumstances and difficulties arising in Brazil, and its corresponding agents encountered some room for maneuver in their relationship with the Society. This can be seen in a couple of cases. In the 1860s, the RTS withheld support to evangelistic work in Brazil on at least two occasions. The first occurred in 1861, when Richard Holden employed the Society's money to publish Protestant articles in liberal periodicals in the province of Pará in 1861. The RTS committee responded that they could not finance the publication of texts of ephemeral use. The second occasion took place in 1866, when the Presbyterian missionary Ashbel Simonton requested financial support for the periodical *Imprensa Evangelica*. Simonton was informed that the RTS could not fund the publication of texts the London committee could not check.[126] Because of these, it seemed unlikely that the RTS would support the publication of evangelical periodicals in Brazil. In the 1880s, though, they supplied Presbyterian missionaries in Brazil with reams of paper for the publication of the *Imprensa Evangelica*, which the Rev. Edward Lane described as a "little paper" that "reaches places where no missionary has ever been."[127] Vanorden's periodical, *O Pregador Cristão* (The Christian Preacher), also received financial and material support from the RTS.[128]

Because the RTS regarded print matter as a vital evangelistic tool, it also sponsored the publication of Protestant periodicals in Portugal and Brazil. Another occasion that illustrates the RTS's adaptability occurred in 1861,

---

[123] Roger Martin, *Evangelicals United: Ecumenical Stirrings in pre-Victorian Britain, 1795–1830* (Metuchen, NJ: Scarecrow, 1983), 153.
[124] RTS Annual Report [1877], xiii.
[125] Martin, *Evangelicals United*, 154–155.
[126] G. H. Davis to the Rev. Richard Holden, October 22, 1861; Joseph Tara to A. G. Simonton, July 5, 1866. SOAS Library, Special Collections Department, USCL/RTS/03/19-20.
[127] RTS Annual Reports [1888], 194 and [1887], 194–197.
[128] RTS Annual Reports [1879], 210–212; [1881], 201–202; [1882], 228–229.

when Holden warned the committee that images and pictures included in tracts were being used on family altars for "idolatrous purposes," in the same way as Brazilian families revered images of Catholic saints.[129] This warning exerted a lasting influence on the operations of the RTS in the Lusophone Atlantic, which included few images in their tracts and books. In contrast to the BFBS, which tried to accommodate a wide variety of Christian denominations and churches, the RTS considered itself an organization of orthodox Protestant dissenters. Whereas the conflict over the Apocryphal books disturbed the BFBS in the 1820s, the RTS was able to pursue its production of anti-Catholic tracts with impunity.[130]

Significantly, the majority of books and tracts shipped to Brazil were not printed at the Society's headquarters in London. The RTS supplied a broader Lusophone evangelical public through a sub-committee based in Lisbon. The transatlantic exchange of Protestant Lusophone literature between Brazil and Portugal through the conduits of the RTS dated at least from the early 1860s, when this Lisbon committee was formed and decided to publish for circulation in Portugal texts written by Robert Kalley, then based in Rio de Janeiro and already known to Portuguese-speaking audiences across the Atlantic.[131] From then on, an increasing amount of Protestant literature began to circulate both ways in the Lusophone world. In 1882, Santos and Kalley asked the RTS to expand its operations in Brazil, invoking successful examples of colportage overseen by the BFBS and the good prospects that awaited the Tract Society in Brazil. Instead of attending their request, the RTS committee decided to meet the needs of Protestant churches and schools by granting to missionaries established in Brazil discounts of fifty percent on all books and tracts printed in Portugal.[132] The RTS administrators believed that, by giving material support to the Lisbon sub-committee, the Brazilian Protestant reading public would be efficiently supplied.

From the early 1880s, Portugal became one of the main suppliers of Protestant literature to the Lusophone world. In 1882, the Presbyterian Rev. Robert Stewart, who served as the BFBS agent in Portugal, was also appointed as head of the RTS in Lisbon, strengthening the ties between the two

[129] G. H. Davis to the Rev. Richard Holden, July 3, 1861. SOAS Library, Special Collections Department, USCL/RTS/03/19-20. See also Vieira, *O protestantismo*, 170–171.
[130] Martin, *Evangelicals United*, 161.
[131] G. H. Davis to Mrs. Roughton, April 10, 1860. SOAS Library, Special Collections Department, USCL/RTS/03/19-20.
[132] RTS Annual Reports [1883], 221.

organizations.[133] A good number of RTS publications in Portugal defended the circulation of Protestant Bibles against the critiques of Catholic bishops and theologians, and encouraged the individual study of the scriptures.[134] Evangelical tracts flowed from Lisbon and Porto, where these British evangelical organizations were established, to various places in the Iberian Peninsula, the islands of Azores, Madeira, and Cape Verde, where the Lisbon Committee established sub-depots, to African Lusophone communities, and Brazil.[135] Whereas the circulation of literature in Azores and Cape Verde did not meet the expectations of the Lisbon committee, the volume of books sold in Brazil and the resulting financial return drew the favorable attention of RTS agents. In 1890, less than a decade after the arrangements between Lisbon, London, and Rio de Janeiro, the sales of RTS books in Brazil outnumbered those in Portugal and the Atlantic Islands, showing that the Brazilian reading public consumed Christian literature more eagerly than elsewhere in the Portuguese-speaking world.[136] In Brazil, RTS books and tracts were sold at half price compared to those circulated in the Peninsula. Even with reduced prices, Stewart observed that sales in Brazil between 1893 and 1896 accounted for between fifty-six to seventy-seven percent of all the financial return of the Lisbon committee.[137]

Books, people, money, and ideas moved in several directions throughout the conduits of evangelical organizations in the Lusophone Protestant Atlantic. In many cases, theological debates and religious controversies originating in Brazil reverberated in Portugal and prompted the Lisbon committee to respond. For example, upon his return to the United Kingdom in 1872, Holden began to propagate the ideas of the Plymouth Brethren among Portuguese-speaking evangelical communities in Brazil, Portugal, and Illinois. He criticized fiercely the establishment of ecclesiastical hierarchies and the creation of denominational confessions of faith.[138] Kalley responded to Holden's texts from his house in Edinburgh and began to correspond with

---

[133] RTS Annual Report [1883], 54. On Robert Stewart, see *Dicionário de história religiosa de Portugal*, vol. 4 (Lisbon: Círculo de Leitores, 2000), 78–80, 252.
[134] Some of the titles include *A Bíblia e o povo* (Lisbon: Livrarias Evangelicas, 1897), *O estudo devoto da Biblia* (Lisbon: Livrarias Evangelicas, 1899), and E. I. Whately, *Objecções à Biblia e a melhor maneira de lhes responder* (Lisbon: Typ. De Vicente da Silva & Co., 1896).
[135] RTS Annual Reports [1892], 53; [1893], 55.
[136] RTS Annual Report [1891], 61.
[137] RTS Annual Reports [1894], 55–56; [1895], 56; [1896], 54; [1897], 62.
[138] Émile G. Léonard, *O protestantismo brasileiro: estudo de eclesiologia e história social*, 3rd ed. (São Paulo: ASTE, 2002 [1963]), 82–83. The impact and reach of the Brethren's ideas in Brazil are discussed in the next chapter.

his old friends and pastors in Rio de Janeiro, Recife, and Illinois, instructing them against the radical egalitarianism of the Brethren. This theological controversy conveyed through private communications was later compiled, published in Lisbon in 1891, and circulated on both sides of the Atlantic.[139] Also in the 1890s, the Lisbon committee decided to publish one of Brazil's most widely circulated Protestant tracts. *The Future of the Catholic Peoples* was written by the Belgian economist Émile de Laveleye and translated into Portuguese by the republican leader and evangelical preacher Miguel Vieira Ferreira in Rio de Janeiro in 1875. The tract was later republished by the RTS in Lisbon in 1891.[140] This short but influential tract affirmed that Protestantism nurtured the values of democracy, liberty, and modernity, whereas European Catholic societies, notably the "despotic" models of the Iberian Peninsula, were in steady decay.[141] RTS agents claimed the tract exerted a strong influence in Portugal.[142] The RTS Lisbon committee also reacted to the controversy of the false Bibles and its reverberations across the Lusophone Atlantic. In response to a pastoral letter written by the Bishop of Porto condemning Protestant missions in Portugal, Kalley criticized anti-Protestant publications in Brazil and Portugal that stigmatized the BFBS scriptures as false and adulterated.[143] Theological debates, religious controversies, and evangelistic strategies connected Portuguese-speaking audiences in multiple locations, bringing together religious specialists and ordinary believers around common causes and creating a transatlantic evangelical public sphere.

Protestant missionaries, evangelical publishers, and Portuguese-speaking ministers adapted the literary forms, textual genres, and physical features of books as these evangelical tracts crossed the Atlantic. In this process, Christian texts conformed to the literary customs and editorial cultures prevailing in each society. The Protestant classic *The Pilgrim's Progress*, for instance, translated into Portuguese by Kalley, was serialized and published over thirty-five volumes of the secular periodical *Correio Mercantil* of Rio

---

[139] *O Darbysmo, cartas do Dr. Robert R. Kalley* (Lisbon: Adolpho, Modesto & C. Impressores, 1891). Robert Kalley passed away in Edinburgh in 1888.

[140] RTS Annual Report [1893], 56.

[141] Émile de Laveleye, *Do futuro dos povos catholicos: Estudo de economia social*, trans. Miguel Vieira Ferreira (Rio de Janeiro: Typographia Universal de E. & H. Laemmert, 1875), 27.

[142] *Abstract of the Ninety-third Annual Report of the Religious Tract Society* (London: n/p., 1892), 18.

[143] Robert R. Kalley, *Observações á instrucção pastoral do Exc.mo. Bispo do Porto, D. Americo sobre o protestantismo* (Porto: Imprensa Civilisação de Santos & Lemos, 1879), 25–28.

de Janeiro in the 1850s. These articles were later assembled and published again in the form of books in Scotland and Lisbon, and then put into circulation in the Lusophone world.[144] These adaptations of print matter show how different textual genres and literary forms permeated each other in the Lusophone Atlantic and influenced the transnational circulation of Christian literature.[145]

Conclusion

Organizations such as the BFBS and the RTS played important roles in the making of Brazilian evangelicalism and in shaping the evangelical imagination. Colporteurs and agents reported to Protestant audiences, at home and abroad, the "spontaneous" conversions spurred by the circulation of Bibles. Hugh Tucker of the ABS argued that, on many occasions, Protestant missionaries followed at the heels of colporteurs: they catered to congregations which had been already assembled by the circulation of Bibles and opened new mission stations in communities first canvassed by the Bible Societies.[146] The imagined communities which Protestant missionaries and publishing societies had in mind differed significantly from Benedict Anderson's discussion of the origins of nationalism. In Anderson's influential account, the consolidation of print laid the basis of national consciousness by stabilizing print-languages and creating "unified fields of exchange and communication below Latin and above the spoken vernaculars."[147] The newspaper and the novel, disseminated throughout a market, addressed these emergent national communities of readers. Anderson also emphasized the secularized time at the basis of this modern conception of the nation. The newspaper addressed its readers simultaneously as a collective, replacing older Christian temporalities by the "homogeneous, empty time" of the calendar.[148]

---

[144] João Leonel, *História da leitura e protestantismo brasileiro* (São Paulo: Editora Mackenzie, 2010), 56–57.
[145] Lucy Delap and Maria DiCenzo, "Transatlantic Print Culture: The Anglo-American Feminist Press and Emerging 'Modernities,'" in *Transatlantic Print Culture, 1880–1940: Emerging Media, Emerging Modernisms*, ed. Ann Ardis and Patrick Collier (Basingstoke: Palgrave Macmillan, 2008), 56.
[146] Tucker, *The Bible in Brazil*, 156, 199, 214.
[147] Benedict Anderson, *Imagined Communities: Reflections on the Origin and Spread of Nationalism*, revised ed. (London: Verso, 2006 [1991]), 44.
[148] Anderson, *Imagined Communities*, 22–36.

94 PROPAGANDISTS OF THE BOOK

Bible and Tract Societies, in contrast, operated in broader oceanic language zones and addressed communities of readers in multiple locations. The networks connecting Portuguese-speaking evangelical communities across the Atlantic thickened and deepened in the first decades of the twentieth century.[149] Calling attention to these links, the Brazilian Presbyterian minister Erasmo Braga advocated the "unity of Luso-Brazilian evangelicalism" in the 1920s. Braga claimed that missionary organizations should consider Lusophone communities spread across the Atlantic, Indian, and Pacific oceans as an ethnic and linguistic unity, taking into account "their continental scale, or their cosmic grandeur."[150] The imagined community conjured up by missionaries, colporteurs, and local pastors far surpassed the boundaries of the nation. Their conception of time also differed from Anderson's account. Missionaries and booksellers were animated by eschatological expectations. BFBS superintendent João dos Santos claimed that he kept working to circulate the Bible against the tribulations of his age patiently "waiting for the coming of Lord."[151] Inspired by millenarian expectations Protestant missionaries and pastors believed that their worldly efforts to preach the Christian message and disseminate Bibles would hasten the return of Christ and the final judgment. Evidence also indicates that believers bound together Protestant newspapers, periodicals, and tracts to keep them in order and organize serialized publications.[152] Readers did not envisage Protestant periodicals as texts of ephemeral use, but expected to consult them at different times, seeking religious instruction and spiritual inspiration. Multiple temporalities were at play in the imagination of booksellers, missionaries, pastors, and evangelical readers.

A close look at the BFBS and RTS agents also draws attention to the important "grassroots dynamics of Christianization" in Brazil.[153] Itinerant booksellers and preachers recruited from among the local churches played a key role in the diffusion of evangelical religion throughout the country. Animated by the evangelical confidence in the power and agency of the

---

[149] Pedro Feitoza, "Immigrants, Missionary Networks, and the Rise of a Luso-Brazilian Evangelical Movement, 1850–1900." Paper given at the Christian Missions in Global History Seminar, Institute of Historical Research, University of London, February 2021.

[150] Erasmo Braga, *Religião e cultura* (São Paulo: União Editora Cultura, n/d), 109–110.

[151] BFBS Annual Report [1892], 301.

[152] RTS Annual Report [1900], 207–208; Pedro Feitoza, "Experiments in Missionary Writing: Protestant Missions and the *Imprensa Evangelica* in Brazil, 1864–1892," *Journal of Ecclesiastical History* 69 (2018): 585–605.

[153] Peggy Brock, "New Christians as Evangelists," in *Missions and Empire*, ed. Norman Etherington (Oxford and New York: Oxford University Press, 2005), 132–152, at 132.

Bible, they ventured out into the interior dealing with customers, local political bosses, police delegates, and Catholic priests in their efforts to circulate Christian print. Ultimately, these agents contributed to linking evangelical religion to literacy in Brazil, as the public image of converts became increasingly associated to their texts. The records of Bible and Tract Societies illuminate the reading practices that emerged from below in a country with high rates of illiteracy. Urban artisans, shoemakers, small farmers, female instructors, and slaves read and listened to the Bible in houses, religious services, family meetings, and in private encounters with neighbors and friends. The public sphere of social communication and exchange in nineteenth-century Brazil interwove together literate and oral cultures, and it involved social categories beyond the communities of lettered elites. The operations of the BFBS and the RTS in Brazil and the Lusophone Atlantic gave way to deep-seated missionary aspirations and reaffirmed the universal sense of belonging that characterized worldwide expressions of Christian movements in the nineteenth and twentieth centuries.

3
Doctrines in Motion

For evangelical converts and foreign missionaries in late nineteenth-century Brazil, saints and devils inhabited the realm of the printed word. In a missionary conference held in London in 1888, the long-time Presbyterian missionary Emmanuel Vanorden referred to a famous Reformation scene to illustrate the wickedness of the Brazilian press: "When Luther threw the inkstand at the devil's head the devil did not get offended, but he said to himself, 'Master Luther, you will find out what use I am going to make of that ink.'" In Vanorden's words, "the devil [was] busy in Brazil," as numerous Brazilian presses published translations of libertine French novels.[1] A few years later, the Brazilian engineer Miguel Vieira Ferreira, founder of the Brazilian Evangelical Church and of the Republican Party of Rio de Janeiro, issued a different opinion about the press in 1891: "Lately I read in the daily press that if St Paul lived in this century, he would have been a journalist: —Yes; I believe it, for the press is a very big mouth, a veritable trumpet to spread the word, which must be of the truth."[2] Vanorden and Ferreira believed that evangelicals should take to the press to spread the Christian message to broader audiences and Christianize society through the publication of godly tracts, books, and periodicals. They envisioned the circulation of Christian literature as a moral barrier to the "immoral" influence of French literature and as a tool to publicize the gospel truth.

The evangelical publishing enterprise projected the doctrines and ideologies of missionaries and ministers into public debates on religious difference, church–state relations, and sociopolitical change. This chapter looks at an array of tracts, short books, and periodicals published between the late nineteenth and early twentieth centuries and examines the ideas and arguments of Protestant ministers and writers in Brazil. Special attention will be given

---

[1] *Report of the Centenary Conference on the Protestant Missions to the World, held in Exeter Hall (June 9th–19th), London, 1888*, vol. II, ed. Rev. James Johnston (London: James Nisbet & Co., 1888), 328.

[2] Miguel Vieira Ferreira, *O Cristo no júri* (São Paulo: Oficinas Gráficas de Saraiva, 1957 [1891]), 216.

to the endeavors of Presbyterian ministers and missionaries and to the ideas of the Plymouth Brethren in Brazil and the Lusophone Atlantic. The texts they produced deployed different strategies to engage with multiple publics. Foreign missionaries and local ministers translated and produced both argumentative tracts aimed at lettered elites and aspiring middle classes as well as sermons and short stories with evocative images and metaphors that communicated effectively with semi-literate audiences. They also touched upon a wide variety of religious and sociopolitical issues. Protestants objected to the revival of Romanized Catholicism, argued that church–state conflicts in Brazil in the 1870s would hasten the disestablishment of the Catholic Church, criticized prevailing notions of racial determinism, called for the abolition of slavery, and maintained an ambiguous relationship with the republican regime installed in 1889. Despite this, analysts have usually deployed bipolar categories of political and ideological analysis to categorize Protestant thought. Social scientists and theologians depicted evangelical thought in modern Brazil and Latin America as conservative and imitative: missionaries and ministers are seen as inspired by a defensive and fundamentalist Protestant theology, which widened the gap between themselves and the sociopolitical concerns of the secular intelligentsia.[3] Alternatively, the robust scholarly works of Jean-Pierre Bastian and David Gueiros Vieira identified connections between Protestant religious minorities and radical liberal minorities in Mexico and Brazil in the nineteenth and early twentieth centuries. The reformist agendas of Protestants and the liberal elites gathered in Masonic lodges and societies of thought converged on many issues, especially their defense of church–state separation, the concession of political rights to non-Catholics, and the diffusion of basic schooling.[4]

Instead of locating the ideas of Brazilian Protestants into fixed positions in the ideological and theological spectrums, this chapter examines their specific responses to the religious and sociopolitical transformations of their time. It offers a nuanced understanding of the ideas created and appropriated

---

[3] Antonio G. Mendonça, *O celeste porvir: A inserção do protestantismo no Brasil*, 3rd ed. (São Paulo: Ed. USP, 2008); Antonio G. Mendonça and Prócoro Velasques Filho, *Introdução ao protestantismo no Brasil* (São Paulo: Edições Loyola, 1990); Ronald G. Frase, "A Sociological Analysis of the Development of Brazilian Protestantism: A Study of Social Change." (PhD dissertation, Princeton Theological Seminary, 1975).

[4] Jean-Pierre Bastian, "The Metamorphosis of Latin American Protestant Groups: A Sociohistorical Perspective," *Latin American Research Review* 28 (1993): 33–61; David G. Vieira, "Liberalismo, masonería y protestantismo en Brasil, siglo XIX," in *Protestantes, liberales y francmasones: Sociedades de ideas y modernidad en América Latina, siglo XIX*, ed. Jean-Pierre Bastian (Mexico, DF: Fondo de Cultura Económica, 1990), 39–66.

by Portuguese-speaking ministers and foreign missionaries in the context of the worldwide renewal of Catholicism and of conflicts between the Catholic Church and the Brazilian Empire. These identities shifted over time in response to political and religious transformations, including the proclamation of the Republic in 1889, the subsequent disestablishment of Catholicism, the institutional reconstruction of the Catholic Church, and the increasing diversification of the Brazilian religious landscape. Amid turbulent political and intellectual contexts, Protestants employed concepts and ideas from a wide range of ideological and religious traditions and assembled their own, new sets of doctrinal bodies and teachings, instead of just reproducing theological conservatism or liberal discourse.

The Catholic Revival, the Religious Question, and Evangelical Responses

The 1860s and 1870s were decades of hopes and turbulence for Catholics and Protestants in Brazil. Evangelical missions gained some traction and began to set a foothold in the southeast. Foreign missionaries and local converts envisioned a future of solid and continuous evangelical diffusion. The Catholic Church by its turn experienced both enthusiasm and defeat at the national and international levels. Clerics, bureaucrats, and ordinary Catholics alike served as protagonists in a worldwide movement of hierarchical reconstruction, institutional expansion, and devotional revitalization in the nineteenth and twentieth centuries. This vigorous movement challenged the secularizing aspirations of nationalist movements and liberal revolutions. The experience of disestablishment and revolution in late eighteenth-century Europe exerted a profound impact on the reorganization of international Catholicism, pushing lay and clerical agents to reaffirm the centrality of the Vatican and the pope in the Church's bureaucracy. The long papacy of Pius IX (1846–1878) embodied the reformist impetus of this era. It was he who declared the dogma of the Immaculate Conception of Mary in 1854, with its important impact on the spread of Marian pietism; issued controversial decrees condemning ideological liberalism; presided over the First Vatican Council (1869–1870); and declared the dogma of Papal Infallibility in 1870. Despite Pius IX's crusade against the "errors of the modern age," his papacy contributed to the rejuvenation of the Church. He surrounded himself with able propagandists, made extensive use of modern means of communication, encouraged the mobilization of the faithful, and became the first pope known as a personality to Catholics.[5]

At the same time, lay associations such as brotherhoods and confraternities became the main propagators of the modern Catholic devotions. Marian piety, with its rosaries and daily recitations of the Angelus, and the cult of the Sacred Heart of Jesus reinvigorated religious services, the domestic worship, and the dedication of ordinary believers to religious causes.[6] These cults standardized popular Catholic devotion across national borders by rooting individual faith in intimate and romantic experiences. They also brought the world of the Church and the world of the faithful together, energizing Catholic worship and mobilization.[7] Modern devotional practices gave rise to a "borderless economy of salvation" that helped Catholics to imagine themselves as a transnational community of committed believers.[8] In its efforts to engage the laity, spread the renewed devotions, and reassert the authority of Rome and the Pope, the Catholic Church deployed modern methods of communication and mobilization. Despite the Ultramontane rhetoric against the disaggregating effects of liberal and nationalist movements, Ultramontanism "was more than just defiance of modernity, it was itself created by modernity and it promoted modernity."[9] Conservative Catholics created a sophisticated institutional apparatus to consolidate this program: they founded schools and seminaries, opened new voluntary associations, engaged in demonstrative mass actions, and made extensive use of mass-circulation media.[10]

These reforms had lasting and profound effects in Latin America. Regional cults dating from the colonial era, such as the worship of Our Lady of Guadalupe in Mexico and the devotion to America's first saint, the Peruvian

---

[5] Sheridan Gilley, "The Papacy," in *The Cambridge History of Christianity: World Christianities, c. 1815–c. 1914*, ed. Sheridan Gilley and Brian Stanley (New York: Cambridge University Press, 2006), 13–29.

[6] Mary Heimann, "Catholic Revivalism in Worship and Devotion," in *The Cambridge History of Christianity: World Christianities, c. 1815–c. 1914*, ed. Sheridan Gilley and Brian Stanley (New York: Cambridge University Press, 2006), 70–83.

[7] Ruth Harris, *Lourdes: Body and Spirit in the Secular Age* (London: Penguin, 1999), 14.

[8] Vincent Viaene, "Nineteenth-century Catholic Internationalism and Its Predecessors," in *Religious Internationals in the Modern World: Globalization and Faith Communities since 1750*, ed. Abigail Green and Vincent Viaene (Basingstoke: Palgrave Macmillan, 2012), 82–110, at 87–89.

[9] C. F. G. De Groot, *Brazilian Catholicism and the Ultramontane Reform* (Amsterdam: CEDLA, 1996), 6.

[10] Christopher Clark, "From 1848 to Christian Democracy," in *Religion and the Political Imagination*, ed. Ira Katznelson and Gareth Stedman Jones (Cambridge: Cambridge University Press, 2010), 190–213, at 195–196, 201–202.

Rosa de Lima, were revitalized in the nineteenth and twentieth centuries, when independence movements and revolutionary processes threatened the cultural and political power of the Church.[11] In contrast to the predominantly male, white, and urban bourgeoisie that upheld the values of liberalism across the continent, the Church furnished frameworks of identity and ritual that cut across barriers of class and gender through its manifold organizations.[12]

In nineteenth-century Brazil, the reformation of the Catholic clergy and the rise of new religious devotions went hand-in-hand, and they were in many ways linked to the worldwide renewal of Ultramontane Catholicism. The process of Romanization of the Brazilian clergy began in the 1840s, when Emperor Dom Pedro II, in his attempts to fill the Catholic bureaucracy with morally irreproachable clergymen, appointed Antônio Ferreira Viçoso as bishop of the diocese of Mariana, Minas Gerais. Upon finding that, apart from a few respectable exceptions, the majority of priests in his diocese were publicly keeping women, Dom Viçoso proceeded immediately with the reform of the bishopric. This process was twofold, involving, on the one hand, the imposition of strict moral standards upon the members of his diocese and, on the other, sending the most promising seminarians to prestigious Ultramontane schools in Rome and Paris.[13] This initiative was strengthened in 1858, when Pope Pius IX and the Chilean priest José Eyzaguirre Portales, lamenting the immorality and debility of the clergy in the Americas, created a school in Rome aimed at training Latin American priests. This institution evolved into the prestigious seminary *Pontificio Collegio Pio Latino Americano* in 1867, arguably the first institution to use the expression "Latin America" in its name.[14] In 1870, there were fifty Brazilians studying at the *Collegio Pio*.

---

[11] Douglass Sullivan-González, "Religious Devotion, Rebellion, and Messianic Movements: Popular Catholicism in the Nineteenth Century," in *The Cambridge History of Religions in Latin America*, ed. Virginia Garrard-Burnett, Paul Freston, and Stephen Dove (New York: Cambridge University Press, 2016), 269–285.

[12] Austen Ivereigh, "Introduction," in *The Politics of Religion in an Age of Revival: Studies in Nineteenth-century Europe and Latin America*, ed. Austen Ivereigh (London: Institute of Latin American Studies, 2000), 8.

[13] George Boehrer, "The Church in the Second Reign, 1840–1889," in *Conflict and Continuity in Brazilian Society*, ed. Henry H. Keith and S. F. Edwards (Columbia: University of South Carolina Press, 1969), 124.

[14] Enrique Ayala Mora, "El origen del nombre América Latina y la tradición católica del siglo XIX," *Anuario Colombiano de Historia Social y de la Cultura* 40 (2013): 213–241; Francisco Javier Ramón Solans, "The Creation of a Latin American Catholic Church: Vatican Authority and Political Imagination, 1854–1899," *The Journal of Ecclesiastical History* 71 (2020): 316–336.

It was these orthodox, well-educated, and stern clergymen who became the vanguard of Romanization in Brazil.[15] They were appointed to influential seminaries and bishoprics and exerted some control over the appointment of parish priests.[16] Their attempts to bring the Brazilian Church closer to Rome and to assert the authority of the pope over the worldwide Catholic communion led them into a serious conflict with the Brazilian Monarchy. In 1872, the French-educated Bishop of Olinda-Recife, Dom Vital Oliveira, and the Bishop of Belém, Dom Antonio Macedo Costa, following the advice of papal bulls that had not been approved by the imperial government, ordered the expulsion of all freemasons from lay brotherhoods under their dioceses. Conservative Party ministers of the Brazilian Empire reacted by bringing the bishops on trial in 1874 and condemning them to four years of imprisonment with hard labor.[17] This conflict was known as the Religious Question, and it exerted a lasting impact over church–state relations in Brazil.

At the same time, a revival of Catholic worship and spiritual life sprung up in Brazil, especially in the northeast. Clergymen trained in the seminaries of Bahia and Ceará appropriated Rome's apologetic and defensive discourse and began to combat three forces they viewed as threatening and disruptive to the traditional social order: freemasonry, Positivism, and Protestantism.[18] In doing so, the Church promoted the engagement of the laity, who, under renewed and intensified connection with the clergy, opened charity houses, orphanages, and schools that created new channels of upward social mobility for men and women of the northeastern backlands.[19]

It was in this period that Brazilian converts and foreign Protestant ministers began to formulate a more systematic critique to the worldwide reform of Ultramontane Catholicism. Variations of this critique sat at the heart of Brazilian evangelical identities up until the mid-twentieth century. In 1870, Protestants responded quickly when the Vatican Council promulgated the dogma of Papal Infallibility. The Presbyterian periodical *Imprensa Evangelica* (Evangelical Press) published a series of articles titled "Is the Papal System a Divine Institution?" The periodical's editors criticized the

---

[15] Kenneth Serbin, *Needs of the Heart: A Social and Cultural History of Brazil's Clergy and Seminaries* (Notre Dame, IN: University of Notre Dame Press, 2006), 56.
[16] Boehrer, "The Church in the Second Reign," 128.
[17] Mary C. Thornton, *The Church and Freemasonry in Brazil, 1872–1875: A Study in Regalism* (Washington: Catholic University of America Press, 1948).
[18] Ralph Della Cava, "Brazilian Messianism and National Institutions: A Reappraisal of Canudos and Joaseiro," *The Hispanic American Historical Review* 48 (1968): 402–420, at 406, 408, 410.
[19] Della Cava, "Brazilian Messianism," 405.

dogma arguing that the primacy of the pope had neither been instituted by the scriptures, nor was it a practice of the early church. They claimed instead that the papacy emerged only in the fourth century when Roman bishops usurped the power of various Christian councils.[20] Reinterpreting the biblical verse of St. Matthew 16:18, "Thou art Peter, and upon this rock I will build my church" against the traditional Catholic exegesis, Protestant writers argued that in this verse Jesus had not established the primacy of Peter over the apostles. Instead, the text reasserted the centrality of Peter's confession two verses earlier: "Thou art the Christ, the Son of the living God."[21] According to Brazilian Protestants, the verse was all about the supremacy of Christ, not of Peter. Jesus had instituted a regime of complete equality among the apostles, combating "several times the anti-Christian inclinations that his disciples manifested on this matter."[22] In their interpretation, the Catholic dogma ascribed to a sinful man the very attributes of God and thus revitalized old pagan practices.

Interestingly, these articles did not quote a single Reformation figure directly, such as Luther, Calvin, or Melanchthon. Instead, references to Church Fathers abounded, especially to Origen, Tertullian, Cyprian, Augustine, and Jerome. These articles argued that, according to the book of Acts, all the apostles had been equally endowed by the Holy Spirit to evangelize and lead the church. And it quoted Origen's interpretation of the verse of St. Matthew, stating that every disciple of Christ was the "rock" to which Jesus had referred.[23] The year 1870 had been, to Brazilian evangelicals, a particular reminder of how biblical prophecies were unfolding and that "the day of Christ" was at hand. They viewed the dogma of Papal Infallibility as the "great apostasy," depicted Pius IX as the "son of perdition" of 2 Thessalonians, and portrayed the Franco–Prussian war as a sign of the end of times. Regarding the war, the *Imprensa Evangelica* stated: "For us, Christians, who see in everything the accomplishment of the infallible promises of the Scripture, such a fact is all but odd: it is the punishment of the pride and impiety of the France of Napoleons; it is the decay of modern Babylon's arrogance, of selfish Paris."[24]

---

[20] *Imprensa Evangelica*, January 7, 1871, n. 1.
[21] *Imprensa Evangelica*, September 17, 1870, n. 19.
[22] *Imprensa Evangelica*, October 1, 1870, n. 19.
[23] *Imprensa Evangelica*, October 15, 1870, n. 21; November 5, 1870, n. 22; November 19, 1870, n. 23.
[24] *Imprensa Evangelica*, January 28, 1871, n. 2.

In the context of the Religious Question, editors of the *Imprensa Evangelica* harshly decried the reverberations of the Ultramontane renewal in Brazil as well as the church–state alliance. According to them, state patronage threatened the principles of religious liberty and tolerance written in the imperial Constitution and tied Brazilian society to permanent backwardness. Unexpectedly, when imperial ministers condemned bishop Dom Vital to imprisonment at the height of the Religious Question, the *Imprensa Evangelica* editors praised the bishop's courage and religious zeal in his choice to remain faithful to his Church. According to the Presbyterian periodical, the key issue at the heart of this problem was the church–state alliance. This forced faithful Catholic clergymen like Dom Vital into embarrassing situations. The Religious Question showed that at the crossroads of irreconcilable interests, priests were forced to declare their loyalty either to the Empire, and its national sets of rules, or to the Church and its global aspirations. However, in choosing to keep the latter, the editors wrote, Dom Vital decided to "obey submissively to a foreign potentate, a declared enemy of ... the free institutions that govern his country, but that he acknowledged as his spiritual guide."[25] In praising the bishop's courage but condemning his supra-national loyalties, the Presbyterian journal was in tune with a widely circulated secular periodical, *O Novo Mundo* (The New World), edited in New York by the influential journalist and Protestant convert José Carlos Rodrigues.[26] A petition titled "freedom of worship" accompanied the article on Dom Vital in the *Imprensa Evangelica*. Its authors were Miguel Vieira Ferreira, then an elder of the Presbyterian Church of Rio de Janeiro, and one of the founders of the Republican Party in the capital, Aureliano Tavares Bastos, a prominent leader of the Liberal Party, amongst others. The petition upheld the principle of *free churches in a free state*, demanded the enforcement of full religious liberty and equality of worship, the abolition of all privileges granted to the official church, the emancipation of the state from the church, the secularization of public schools and cemeteries, and the creation of civil registration of births and marriages.[27]

Instead of viewing the church–state clash as something that conformed itself to the existing political divides, or the defense of religious freedom and laicization as an agenda that belonged to liberals, Brazilian evangelicals

---

[25] *Imprensa Evangelica*, March 7, 1874, n. 5.
[26] George Boehrer, "José Carlos Rodrigues and *O Novo Mundo*, 1870–1879," *Journal of Inter-American Studies* 9 (1967): 127–144.
[27] *Imprensa Evangelica*, March 7, 1874, n. 5.

believed that reactions to the Religious Question cut across ideological lines. It was the Conservative Party that enforced the legislation of the Empire and brought the bishops on trial, and it was the mighty figure of the Liberal Party, Zacarias de Góes e Vasconcellos, who defended Dom Vital in the court.[28] This became a distinctive feature of Brazilian evangelical politics in this period. Protestants associated themselves with various political and intellectual actors in the country who defended principles of religious liberty and church–state separation regardless of their political affiliation.

Evangelical Critique of Catholic Politics and Ethics

In the heat of the Religious Question, when the official status of the Catholic Church was hotly debated in the press, Brazilian evangelicals and foreign missionaries published important tracts that helped advance their political agendas. The arrest of Dom Vital and Dom Antonio Costa generated a considerable stir within the Brazilian public sphere. The Catholic press reacted promptly to the dramatic events of 1874–1875 by praising the bishops' virtues and courage. Some papers also claimed that freemasons, liberals, republicans, and Protestants took part in an international network aimed at undermining the foundations of the Catholic Church, its traditions, and institutions.[29] An article published by the Rio de Janeiro-based Catholic journal *O Apóstolo* (The Apostle) in 1874 argued that the evangelical dogma of free examination of the scriptures led Protestants to a life of wandering, disquiet, and anxiety in their endless search for a doctrine that could ultimately respond to their doubts.[30] *Imprensa Evangelica* editors responded, affirming that the general public could not get reliable information about evangelical doctrines and practices through this Catholic publication. Instead, a recently published tract could furnish them with an appropriate analysis of the differences between Catholics and Protestants.[31]

This tract was titled *Historical Traces and Main Points of Divergence of the Evangelical Protestant and Roman Catholic Churches*, and its author was the German pastor and theologian Erich Stiller. The preface, written by the

---

[28] *Imprensa Evangelica*, June 7, 1873, n. 11.
[29] David G. Vieira, *O protestantismo, a maçonaria e a Questão Religiosa no Brasil* (Brasília: Editora UnB, 1980), ch. 11.
[30] *O Apóstolo*, April 5, 1874, n. 40.
[31] *Imprensa Evangelica*, April 18, 1874, n. 8.

tract's translator, lamented that the Religious Question and its unpredictable consequences were incompatible with the "enlightenment of the modern world." And considering the inability of the imperial state to solve the conflict peacefully, this publication was a timely evangelical contribution aimed at accelerating "the emancipation of Brazil from the roman curia."[32] The tract's first part outlined a brief history of Christianity up to the Reformation, claiming that it was only from the third and fourth centuries onward that Christians began to divide themselves into different factions. One of these claimed to be the true universal church and transformed Christian humility into pride, "fraternal love into thirst for persecution, and devotion soon enough limited itself to exterior practices."[33] Stiller portrayed the Catholic Church as a tyrannical, degenerate, and corrupt institution that disfigured the Christian faith through the centuries and transformed heresies into dogmas. The history of the Christian church was, for Stiller, a history of degeneration mixed with glimpses of evangelical purity and religious zeal. His tract included short biographies of reformers, such as Peter Waldo, John Wycliffe, Jan Huss, Martin Luther, Zwingli, and John Calvin, who "preached the pure Gospel to the people."[34] He affirmed that Protestants were labeled as such because they protested the decisions of the Diet of Speyer and the Edict of Worms to interdict the propagation of evangelical Christianity. Therefore, the evangelical church could also be called Protestant:

> for it continually protests (as S. John in Revelations 22. 18), or enlightens itself and shields itself against all human authority in matter of faith, and against everything that is contrary or does not conform to the Gospel in matter of doctrine, of practice, and of religious constitution. It is best, therefore, to unite these designations and call *Protestant evangelical* the church that is founded on the Gospel.[35]

This way of conjoining the labels "evangelical" and "Protestant" and of defining as evangelicals all those who protested the "degeneration" of the practices and doctrines of the early church continued to characterize evangelical identities in Brazil for decades to come.

---

[32] Erich Stiller, *Traços historicos e pontos principaes de divergencia das igrejas evangelica protestante e catholica romana* (Rio de Janeiro: E. & H. Laemmert, 1874), iv.
[33] Stiller, *Traços*, 13.
[34] Stiller, *Traços*, 14–19.
[35] Stiller, *Traços*, 19. Emphases in the original.

Stiller claimed that two principles defined the evangelical church: that the Bible was the only rule of faith of Christians and that men and women were saved by grace alone.[36] He then enumerated the key differences between Protestants and Catholics. These included the centrality of the pope, indulgences, the veneration of saints, the auricular confession, and Purgatory. For Stiller, all mediating figures that obfuscated the centrality of Jesus Christ as the "supreme leader" of the Christian church were illegitimate. This is clear in his rejection of the pope as head of the church because Christ was the only authority over the spiritual body of the church; in his criticism of the veneration of saints, which displaced Christ as the only mediator between God and humanity; and in his denial of Purgatory, whose doctrine undermined the significance of Christ's sacrifice.[37] The result was that, along these lines, no single temporal power could claim permanent or uncontested authority over the Christian communion. Also, the Christian church was conceived as an invisible, spiritual entity and the primary allegiance of evangelical Protestants was to this imagined community of believers connected through time and space by means of their doctrines, worship, and liturgical practices.

Whereas Stiller's tract explored the doctrinal and historical differences distinguishing Catholics and Protestants, a tract published in 1875 focused on moral, social, and political differences. This was Émile de Laveleye's *The Future of the Catholic Peoples: A Study of Social Economy*, translated into Portuguese by Miguel Vieira Ferreira. This text exerted a formative and longlasting impact on the ideologies of Brazilian evangelicals. It popularized the idea that instead of racial difference, religious practice and belief underpinned the progress of German, Slavic, and Anglo-Saxon countries in Europe and the Americas, and the decay of Latin societies.[38] The author affirmed that England began to surpass France in terms of economic power and social progress from the sixteenth century onward, after the Puritans defeated the Stuarts in England and French Emperor Louis XIV suppressed Protestant worship.[39] Picking examples from Switzerland, Laveleye argued that the Latin cantons of Neuchâtel, Vaud, and Geneva made greater progress in their literary, artistic, industrial, and commercial achievements than the German

---

[36] Stiller, *Traços*, 20.
[37] Stiller, *Traços*, 26–29, 38–39, 52–53.
[38] Émile de Laveleye, *Do futuro dos povos catholicos: Estudo de economia social*, trans. Miguel Vieira Ferreira (Rio de Janeiro: Typographia Universal de E. & H. Laemmert, 1875), 7.
[39] Laveleye, *Do futuro*, 9.

cantons of Lucerne and Valois: "the first are Latin, but Protestants; the latter are Germans, but subject to Rome. Worship and not race is, therefore, the cause of the first's superiority."[40] For Laveleye, the primitive Christian church was the supreme example of freedom and egalitarian democracy, whereas the Catholic Church showed a historical inclination to assert the absolute authority of kings and priests. To exemplify this, he referred to Jacques-Bénigne Bossuet's theology in seventeenth-century Europe and the dogma of Papal Infallibility in the nineteenth century.[41] According to Laveleye, ideas of liberty, autonomy, and sovereignty, as well as the "principles of 1789," had been first upheld by the Puritans and the Quakers, not by the "immoral" eighteenth-century French philosophers. These principles, he affirmed, had been successfully implemented in the Netherlands and England two hundred years before the French Revolution.[42] Laveleye's tract preceded Max Weber's influential study of the relation between the Protestant ethic and the rationalization of capitalist economy by three decades and the reception of Weberian thought in Brazil in the 1930s by more than half a century.[43]

The Catholic press promptly repudiated this tract. *O Apóstolo* published a series of articles claiming that Laveleye's examples and arguments were based on inaccurate and manipulated data and utterly misrepresented the relationship between religion and social progress. The Catholic periodical also claimed that Laveleye ignored the promotion of primary instruction in Catholic countries such as Italy and Spain, the overwhelming impoverishment of the British working class, and the economic might of Austria and France.[44] Obviously, in all such cases Protestants and Catholics manipulated historical facts and interpretations and made use of grand, sweeping generalizations about religion and national history to validate their arguments. These exchanges, however, generated a vigorous flow of print matter, information, and opinion involving multiple actors in the context of the Religious Question.

Once disseminated in the country, Laveleye's ideas made their way into the transnational networks that connected Brazilian Protestants with other

---

[40] Laveleye, *Do futuro*, 10.
[41] Laveleye, *Do futuro*, 27, 29–30.
[42] Laveleye, *Do futuro*, 34–36. On the immorality of French philosophers see pp. 22–23.
[43] Max Weber, *The Protestant Ethic and the Spirit of Capitalism*, trans. Talcott Parsons (New York: Routledge, 2001 [1905]); Sérgio Buarque de Holanda, *Raízes do Brasil* (São Paulo: Companhia das Letras, 2009 [1936]).
[44] *O Apóstolo*, October 3, 1875, n. 152; October 13, 1875, n. 156; October 27, 1875, n. 162; October 31, 1875, n. 164.

missionary enterprises in the Atlantic Ocean. In 1892, for instance, a subcommittee of the Religious Tract Society based in Lisbon, Portugal, decided to publish his tract and make it available to the Lusophone Protestant public on both sides of the Atlantic.[45] The American Presbyterian missionary Alexander Blackford also echoed Laveleye's ideas corresponding with his home mission. In a brief history of the Brazil Mission published for circulation in the United States, he affirmed that Catholicism cast its shadow upon the mental and social culture of Brazil and constituted the main cause of the country's moral "debasement" and material "backwardness." Blackford argued that the superiority of Protestant nations in educational attainment and industrial development did not "result from the difference of race, but from the difference in their religion; it is the effect of the power of the truth of God's Word on the intellects and hearts of men."[46]

Brazilian evangelicals developed a complex relationship with the concept of race in this context, when the secular intelligentsia began to appropriate theories of scientific racism, and on account of the country's long history of slave trade and labor. Although few Brazilian scholars believed in theories of absolute biological differences in the nineteenth and early twentieth centuries, the vast majority of intellectuals did embrace elements of pseudo racial science to explain the economic and social situation of the country. Even staunch abolitionists, such as José do Patrocínio and Joaquim Nabuco, believed that the "whitening" of the Brazilian population would "upgrade" the nation.[47] For the majority of men of letters, the superiority of whites and the inferiority of black and indigenous populations were self-evident. These notions of racial difference and their bearing upon "progress" came from various intellectual sources. Brazilian thinkers found inspiration in the American school of ethnology, social Darwinism, and the historical school of Arthur de Gobineau.[48] Few of them went as far as Raimundo Nina Rodrigues, the influential chair of legal medicine at the Bahia Medical Faculty between 1891 and 1905, to whom inherited racial characteristics affected social behavior. For Nina Rodrigues, penal responsibility applied differently between

---

[45] RTS Annual Report [1893], 56. On the Religious Tract Society and its work in Brazil, see the previous chapter.

[46] Alexander L. Blackford, *Sketch of the Brazil Mission* (Philadelphia: Presbyterian Board of Education, 1886), 5.

[47] Thomas Skidmore, "Racial Ideas and Social Policy in Brazil, 1870–1940," in *The Idea of Race in Latin America, 1870–1940*, ed. Richard Graham (Austin: University of Texas Press, 1990), 7–36, at 8–11.

[48] Thomas Skidmore, *Black into White: Race and Nationality in Brazilian Thought* (New York: Oxford University Press, 1974), 48–53.

blacks and indigenous people on one side and the "superior races" on the other, for the first were naturally inclined toward criminal behavior.[49] Despite Rodrigues's prestige in Brazilian academic circles, and despite his negative views of miscegenation as a possible solution to Brazil's "racial problem," early twentieth-century intellectuals began to counter this pessimism. They firmly believed that blood mixture and European immigration would, in the end, "whiten" the Brazilian population and put the country on the road to social and economic progress.[50] Interestingly, these debates circulated in literature, journalism, and museum exhibitions, not only in scientific compendia of the time.[51] The idea of degeneration, associated with racial mixtures and "vicious" human behavior, such as alcoholism, consanguineous marriages, and laziness, was a central theme in the books of prestigious writers, such as Machado de Assis, Aluísio de Azevedo, and Monteiro Lobato.[52] The multiple forms in which the concept of degeneration and scientific racism circulated in the country gave these ideas a wider social resonance.

Brazilian evangelicals, however, held such racial theories under suspicion. They emphasized the regenerative capacity of knowledge and the belief that a "lost" humanity could be redeemed through faith in Christ. Protestant mission theorists insisted on the fundamental unity of humanity as a foundational biblical principle in contrast to the polygenism of physical anthropologists, the belief that races had different origins.[53] Of course, theologians and biblical scholars in Europe and North America encountered a plethora of biblical counterarguments to justify slavery and question the foundations of monogenism, the principle of the original unity of humankind.[54] But Brazilian Protestants rejected the fatalism of racial theories, claiming that conversion and education were the two leading forces that fostered individual improvement and social uplift. After the abolition of slavery in the late 1880s, Protestant missions and Bible Societies expanded westward.

---

[49] Skidmore, *Black into White*, 57–60.

[50] Charles Hale, "Political and Social Ideas in Latin America, 1870–1930," in *The Cambridge History of Latin America. Vol. IV: c. 1870–1930*, ed. Leslie Bethell (Cambridge: Cambridge University Press, 1986), 367–441, at 402–403.

[51] Lilia Moritz Schwarcz, *The Spectacle of the Races: Scientists, Institutions, and the Race Question in Brazil, 1870–1930*, trans. Leland Guyer (New York: Hill and Wang, 1999).

[52] Dain Borges, "'Puffy, Ugly, Slothful and Inert': Degeneration in Brazilian Social Thought, 1880–1940," *Journal of Latin American Studies* 25 (1993): 235–256.

[53] Brian Stanley, "Christian Missions and the Enlightenment: A Reevaluation," in *Christian Missions and the Enlightenment*, ed. Brian Stanley (Grand Rapids, MI: W. B. Eerdmans Publishing Co., 2001), 1–21, at 11–12.

[54] Colin Kidd, *The Forging of Races: Race and Scripture in the Protestant Atlantic World, 1600–2000* (New York: Cambridge University Press, 2006).

Foreign and Brazilian evangelical missionaries encountered the country's indigenous populations and defended their inclusion in the scope of the Protestant missionary endeavor. The journals *Revista de Missões Nacionais* (Review of National Missions), edited in São Paulo by the Rev. Eduardo Carlos Pereira, and *Brazilian Missions*, edited in São Paulo by Presbyterian missionaries and circulated in the United States, affirmed that there were probably one million people within these indigenous communities who were completely neglected by the state and violently exploited by landowners.[55] These journals invited missionaries, educators, and evangelists to "Christianize and civilize" the indigenous people.[56] The same principle was applied to freed slaves, to whom missionaries were called upon to "provide for their social, moral, and spiritual regeneration."[57] Brazilian evangelicals did not naturalize notions of racial difference in their writings and were wary of theories of scientific racism. But they did replace such explanations for the social and economic situation of the country with the idea that religious difference produced different civilizing impulses, advocating that evangelical Christianity was the main driver of social progress, democracy, and morality.

Besides Stiller's and Laveleye's texts, two other tracts published in the context of the Religious Question influenced the ideologies of Brazilian evangelicals. The first was the translation of a pamphlet written, in 1874, by the British politician William Gladstone and published in Rio de Janeiro in the following year. In it, Gladstone harshly criticized the universalist ambitions of the Vatican and the decrees of Pope Pius IX. The papal documents issued during Pius IX's papacy, he claimed, extended the temporal power of the Catholic Church indefinitely and raised questions about the relationship between religious communities and civil power. For the British Prime Minister, documents such as the *Syllabus* and the dogmas of the Immaculate Conception of Mary and the Papal Infallibility repudiated the foundations of modern science and civilization and put the civil loyalty of Catholics in check because they owed allegiance to both Rome and their home nations.[58] The other tract was written by the German Catholic bishop Joseph Reinkens. After the proclamation of the dogma of Papal Infallibility, Reinkens joined a group of dissident priests who objected to the reforms of

---

[55] *Brazilian Missions*, June 1888, vol. I, n. 6, 43–44.
[56] *Brazilian Missions*, September 1888, vol. I, n. 9, 72.
[57] *Brazilian Missions*, May 1888, vol. I, n. 5, 33.
[58] William Gladstone, *Os decretos do Vaticano em suas relações com a lealdade civil: Discussão política* (Rio de Janeiro: Typographia Universal de Laemmert, 1875).

Pius IX and called themselves the "Old Catholics." The tract deployed the concept of degeneration and claimed that the papacy of Pius IX had perverted the original rites of the Christian church into a "spiritual despotism that strips the pastoral craft of all reason, all freedom, and all joy, paralyzing the most noble drivers of the human spirit, and suffocating the consciousness of free will and of personal responsibility."[59]

All these four tracts were published in Rio de Janeiro at the Laemmert Brothers' publishing house, one of Brazil's leading printing firms at that time. Established in the Brazilian capital in the late 1820s by Eduard and Heinrich Laemmert, the sons of a German Protestant minister, the firm published on a variety of topics, from cookery books to manuals of agriculture. This contrasted with the operations of their main rival in Rio, the French publisher Baptiste Louis Garnier, who printed only pure literature.[60] The Presbyterian missionary Emmanuel Vanorden arranged for their publication with the Laemmerts. Some of the tracts achieved a considerably high circulation for the period. Laveleye's tract on the decadence of Catholic societies sold 4,500 copies upon publication and William Gladstone's pamphlet on the decrees of the Vatican sold 1,500.[61]

The tracts by Stiller, Laveleye, Gladstone, and Reinkens were fairly highbrow. They were argumentative texts, ranging between fifty to sixty pages, with complex historical and theological interpretations that were most likely unappealing to the modestly educated and semiliterate first generations of Brazilian converts. Their ideas, however, were reworked in popular publications, sermons, and short tracts and informed much of the evangelical critique of Catholic hierarchy and devotions in the following decades. One such text was a short tract titled *Differences Between Catholics and Protestants*, first published over three issues of the *Imprensa Evangelica* in 1877 and later assembled as a pamphlet by the Evangelical Bookshop of Rio de Janeiro.[62] This piece unpacked the arguments of Stiller in the form of a simple and straightforward dialogue between a Catholic and a Protestant. In it, the evangelical believer argued that his religion was a divine creation entirely devoted to the Trinity while Catholicism was anthropocentric. Whereas Protestants read God's word, were guided by God's Holy Spirit,

---

[59] Joseph H. Reinkens, *Profissão de fé dos Velhos-Catholicos na Allemanha*, trans. Miguel Vieira Ferreira (Rio de Janeiro: E. & H. Laemmert, 1874), 10.

[60] Laurence Hallewell, *Books in Brazil: A History of the Publishing Trade* (Metuchen, NJ: The Scarecrow Press, 1982), ch. 9.

[61] *Brazilian Missions*, November 1891, vol. IV, n. 11, 86.

[62] *Imprensa Evangelica*, October 6, 1877, n. 20; November 3, 1877, n. 22; November 17, 1877, n. 23.

belonged to a church created by Jesus Christ, confessed their sins to God alone, and were saved by God's grace, Catholics followed in the opposite direction. They did not read the scriptures, their doctrines were taught by the priest, they belonged to a church whose head was the Pope, they confessed their sins to a vicar, and believed they were saved by the intercessions of Mary and the saints or their own good deeds.[63] Another tract published in Lisbon, titled *The Priest and the Protestant*, had a similar format and arguments. Conceived as a dialogue between an unfriendly Catholic priest and an unabashed evangelical believer called Domingos, this tract portrayed an ordinary and unschooled Protestant man responding with biblical quotations, simple theological arguments, and constitutional laws to the incitements and provocations raised by a clergyman.[64]

Protestants, along the lines of these arguments, were not under the unchallenged authority of religious leaders, belonged to a horizontal fellowship in which members could not claim any inherent spiritual prominence, and participated in an invisible community of faithful believers spread across time and space. In a sermon delivered to the Presbyterian Church of Rio de Janeiro in 1874, the American missionary Francis Schneider deployed Stiller's distinction between the visible church, materialized in local communities of believers, and the invisible church. To the latter belonged all those who were "called by the divine grace to participate in the blessings of the same Gospel, saved by the same Savior, sanctified by the same Spirit and the same truth, and even though they are spread all over the world and belong to different communions, they are nevertheless united by spiritual bonds more intimate and stronger than those of the external communion."[65] Gladstone's verdict on the incompatibility between the reforms of Pope Pius IX and the values of modern civilization continued to inform the evangelical objection to Romanized Catholicism in the early twentieth century.[66] And the Old Catholics' attempts to restore the traditions of the Church and oppose the reforms of Pius IX were praised even amongst staunch critics of the Catholic Church, such as the Rev. Eduardo Carlos Pereira.[67] The most

---

[63] *Differença entre catholico e protestante* (Rio de Janeiro: Livraria Evangelica, 1889).

[64] *O cura e o protestante* (Lisbon: Livrarias Evangelicas, 1903).

[65] Francis J. Schneider, "O governo da igreja," in *O Pulpito Evangelico: Volume primeiro, 1874* (Rio de Janeiro: Livraria Evangelica, 1874), 4.

[66] Eduardo C. Pereira, *Nossa attitude para com a Egreja Romana* (Rio de Janeiro: Casa Publicadora Baptista, 1916).

[67] Eduardo C. Pereira, *O problema religioso da America Latina: Estudo dogmatico-historico* (São Paulo: Imprensa Methodista, 1920), 377, 387.

influential tract, however, was Laveleye's. By positing that the diffusion of Protestantism could pave the way to economic modernity and social progress and by sidelining racial theories, Protestants made a strong case in favor of religious change that resonated with the modernizing aspirations of political and intellectual elites. Laveleye's thesis on the decay of Catholic societies was reworked in numerous other texts, both high and low literature.[68]

Evangelical Ideas in a Changing World

For missionaries and converts, the last decades of the nineteenth century were a period of profound agitation. Presbyterian missionaries cheerfully celebrated the abolition of slavery in 1888, which invigorated their missionary zeal with the challenge of evangelizing the freed slaves.[69] A military coup overthrew Emperor Pedro II in 1889 and inaugurated a republican government that pursued some of the political reforms to which Protestants had long aspired, including the disestablishment of Catholicism, the creation of civil registrations of marriages and births, the secularization of cemeteries, and full liberty of worship. Congregationalists, Presbyterians, and Baptists depicted the proclamation of the Republic as a bloodless and peaceful revolution. They commemorated its immediate aftermath and urged their sending bodies in the United States and Britain to recruit more missionaries to Brazil.[70]

All these significant transformations, however, carried certain ambiguities within themselves and, to evangelicals, the twilight of the nineteenth century could be the best of times and the worst of times. In the words of historian Jacqueline Hermann, the Catholic clergy viewed the overthrow of the monarchy with mixed feelings of relief and apprehension. They were uneasy with the loss of temporal power imposed by the new republican government, which limited the Church's scope of action, severed its ties with the state, and barred clerics and monks from being elected to the parliament. But on the other hand, disestablishment meant deliverance from the burdensome state patronage that submitted the ecclesiastical hierarchy to the imperial

---

[68] An example is Eduardo C. Pereira, *O protestantismo é uma nullidade: polêmica religiosa* (São Paulo: Typographia Aurora, 1896).
[69] *Brazilian Missions*, June 1888, vol. I, n. 6, 41.
[70] BFBS Annual Report [1890], 306–307; SBC Proceedings [1890], appendix B, xxvii; BFM-PCUSA Annual Report [1890], 22–23.

government.[71] Released from the control of the state and still resentful about the assault of the Religious Question, Brazilian clerics sought to regain terrain lost since the 1870s. The Church strengthened its connections with the Vatican; sent numerous priests to pursue their studies in prestigious schools in Italy, France, and Belgium; created new seminaries, dioceses and bishoprics; reinforced ecclesiastical control over brotherhoods and lay associations; and expanded the church's bureaucracy to counter the expansion of Protestantism.[72] Despite the lay character of the Republican Constitution of 1891, the Church managed to retain some privileges, such as permission to receive public funds destined to charity work.[73]

The 1880s and 1890s were also a fruitful period for Brazilian Positivists, who managed to expand their intellectual influence in the country. Its leading disseminators were professors of the Military School of Rio de Janeiro, law school graduates, and the Positivist Church of Rio de Janeiro. The latter was founded in 1881 by influential intellectuals such as Teixeira Mendes and Miguel Lemos.[74] Positivists gave significant support to the republican movement in Brazil, especially through Benjamin Constant de Magalhães, the popular professor at the Military School who helped to orchestrate the movement in Rio de Janeiro and mobilized Positivist cadets during the 1889 coup. Positivist intellectuals also played a central role in shaping social and economic policies in the first decades of the Republic, emphasizing the relevance of education, national integration, and industrialization in their modernizing agenda.[75] Latin American Positivists departed from their French founding fathers' ideas, especially Auguste Comte, in various ways. If Comte began to hold more sympathetic views of the Catholic Church from 1848 onward and defended the disestablishment of public schools from state control, Latin American Positivists usually showed anticlerical inclinations and campaigned in favor of state-controlled public education.[76] Also, whereas

---

[71] Jacqueline Hermann, "Religião e política no alvorecer da República: Os movimentos de Juazeiro, Canudos e Contestado," in *O tempo do liberalismo oligárquico: Da Proclamação da República à Revolução de 1930*, 10th ed., ed. Jorge Ferreira and Lucilia de A. Neves Delgado (Rio de Janeiro: Civilização Brasileira, 2018), 111–152, at 111–112; Serbin, *Needs of the Heart*, 74–75.

[72] Sérgio Miceli, *A elite eclesiástica brasileira: 1890–1930*, 2nd ed. (São Paulo: Companhia das Letras, 2009), 60–66, 141–145, 154–155, 161.

[73] Sérgio Moura and José M. G. Almeida, "A Igreja na Primeira República," in *História Geral da Civilização Brasileira, vol. 2, tomo III*, ed. Boris Fausto (Rio de Janeiro and São Paulo: DIFEL, 1977), 327–328.

[74] João Cruz Costa, *A History of Ideas in Brazil: The Development of Philosophy and the Evolution of National History*, trans. Suzette Macedo (Berkeley: University of California Press, 1964), 107.

[75] Robert Nachman, "Positivism, Modernization, and the Middle Class in Brazil," *The Hispanic American Historical Review* 57 (1977): 1–23, at 10–12.

[76] Hale, "Political and Social Ideas," 386.

Comte blamed Protestantism and its individualistic ethic for the lack of a universalist approach to men, Brazilian Positivists, such as Luis Pereira Barreto, argued that Protestantism was the most evolved form of religion, the fittest to create the conditions necessary for the advent of the Positivist stage.[77] Despite this, the majority of Brazilian Positivists continued to believe that Christianity belonged to the infancy of human history. In the same period, Spiritist doctrines began to penetrate the country via religious literature disseminated in the largest cities of Brazil, and it found adepts among the same social classes as Positivism: well-educated urban middle classes, especially civil servants and low-rank military officers.[78]

For evangelicals, these transformations, along with the emergence of liberal theologies in Europe and North America, challenged the credibility of their fundamental doctrines. Lamenting the dissemination of these intellectual and religious trends among urban elites, Eduardo Carlos Pereira wrote, in a dramatic article published in 1882, that the only remedy strong enough to counter this "cancer that erodes the entrails of our nation" was Christianity. For Pereira, the origins of the present moral and intellectual crisis could be traced back to eighteenth-century French philosophers: "When in modern times, the atheism of Helvetius and the impiety of Voltaire, Diderot, d'Alembert, J. J. Rousseau, was transmitted to the popular spirit, the people became a monster and its excesses terrified humanity."[79] In January 1883, Pereira advertised in the *Imprensa Evangelica* a project for the creation of a society of evangelical tracts. In his words, such an endeavor could counter the corruptive effects of such contemporary intellectual trends, "preach the gospel to the poor," and bring Brazilian evangelical churches into maturity by encouraging emancipation from foreign mission societies. Pereira's plan included raising funds among Brazilian evangelicals: two hundred subscribers contributing a modest two hundred *réis* per month would suffice to publish two or more short tracts a year.[80] His effort can be viewed as an attempt to Christianize culture via the production and circulation of evangelical literature.

As a result of Pereira's efforts, the Brazilian Society of Evangelical Tracts (BSET) was created on September 17, 1883, at the Presbyterian School of São

---

[77] Isabel DiVanna, "Reading Comte across the Atlantic: Intellectual Exchanges between France and Brazil and the Question of Slavery," *History of European Ideas* 38 (2012): 452–466, at 454, 460.
[78] Diana Brown, *Umbanda: Religion and Politics in Urban Brazil* (New York: UMI Research Press, 1994), ch. 2.
[79] *Imprensa Evangelica*, September 15, 1882, n. 17.
[80] *Imprensa Evangelica*, January 25, 1883, n. 2.

Paulo. On that occasion the attendees also elected an administrative board composed mostly of Brazilian ministers and laypeople. The board included Pereira as president of the Society; the teacher and elder of the Presbyterian Church of São Paulo, Remigio de Cerqueira Leite, as treasurer; and the Revs. Miguel Torres, José Zacarias de Miranda, and Robert Lenington.[81] Individual subscribers had their names and contributions published in the *Imprensa Evangelica*, a common practice among evangelical and missionary organizations in the United States and Europe. Between 1884, when the first tract was published, and 1892, the Society managed to put around ninety thousand volumes of its first fifteen titles in circulation, a substantial achievement for such a small religious minority. The first tracts were printed by private publishing houses in São Paulo. In 1889, the BSET purchased its own press. Out of this enterprise the Presbyterians of São Paulo created the small publishing house *Typographia Aurora*, located near the church in the city center.[82] Tracts were inexpensive, made of cheap material, and did not include any drawings or images. By means of the BSET, Protestant leaders translated some of the basic concepts and practices of modern evangelicalism to the Brazilian public. The BSET encouraged churches and believers to contribute to the evangelistic endeavor. Its tracts made ample use of parables and comparisons to convey their message and opposed both the worldwide renewal of Catholicism and the anticlerical leanings of intellectual elites.

It is possible to identify some trends in the first seventeen publications of the BSET between 1883 and 1897. A good number of titles attacked the very heart of the nineteenth-century Catholic revival: the renewed popular devotions and the centrality of Rome and the pope. The BSET's first tract was titled *The Worship of Saints and Angels*. It was entirely dedicated to showing that the idea of spiritual intermediation between men and God through Mary, saints, angels, and godfathers was a rejection of one of the foremost Christian values: the sufficiency of Christ's sacrifice. Its author was Pereira, who claimed that in resorting to such spiritual mediators, men committed "the heinous crime of high treason, in the sacrilegious attempt to elevate creatures to the throne that can only be occupied by the eternal Son of God."[83] For Pereira, in associating specific saints with specific actions,

---

[81] *Imprensa Evangelica*, September 29, 1883, n. 18.

[82] Vicente T. Lessa, *Annaes da 1ª Egreja Presbyteriana de São Paulo (1863–1903): Subsidios para a historia do presbiterianismo brasileiro* (São Paulo: Edição da 1ª Igreja Presbiteriana de São Paulo, 1938), 231–232.

[83] Eduardo C. Pereira, *O culto dos sanctos e dos anjos* (São Paulo: Typ. de Leroy King Bookwalter & Co., 1884), 17–18, 20.

such as protecting from epidemics, healing sore throats, and soothing toothaches, Brazilian Catholic devotions revived ancient pagan practices.[84] The Rev. José Zacarias de Miranda explained more specifically the reasons underlying evangelicals' opposition to the veneration of saints in a tract titled *The Worship of Images*. Addressing Catholic readers, he asserted that the veneration of icons and statues degenerated and materialized the true spiritual Christian worship.[85] In Miranda's explanation, Rachel, the wife of the Hebrew patriarch Jacob, took some of her father Laban's idols with her upon leaving the house of her parents. It was telling that Laban, who tricked Jacob into fourteen years of servitude and did not "prize either piety or morality," cultivated these idols: his was a "formalist religion, all material, as were the gods he worshipped."[86] And it was only in the eighth century that veneration came to be practiced among Christians. Before that, the practice was absent in the early church and condemned in the theology of Church Fathers. Miranda argued that these practices created a "deplorable state of affairs," substituting the "spiritual worship to a spiritual God by the material worship paid to the *gods* of wood, rock, clay, etc. *fabricated by the hands of sinners*."[87]

Pereira echoed Miranda's argument in his tract *The Blessed Virgin Mary*, published in 1887. Written in the form of a dialogue involving himself, a man called Aristides, his mother Maria, and his grandmother Francisca, this text encapsulates the attitudes of Brazilian evangelicals toward Marian devotions. Upon being asked if Protestants did not believe in the Virgin, Pereira answered that they believed she was Christ's mother, blessed among women, and "surrounded by glory in the Heavens, praising and glorifying the eternal God in the company of saints and angels."[88] However, evangelicals refused to attribute to her the title "Mother of God" for Christ the man, was Mary's son, but God was eternal.[89] Citing the gospel of Matthew (12:48–50), Pereira argued that as head of the Christian church and mediator of his people, the persona of Christ did not fit squarely into worldly family relations. As God incarnate, Christ did not have mother or brothers and in the spiritual kingdom of God, whoever did God's will belonged to Christ's family.

---

[84] Pereira, *O culto*, 28–32.
[85] José Zacarias Miranda, *O culto das imagens* (São Paulo: Typ. a vapor de Jorge Seckler & Co., 1885), 6–8.
[86] Miranda, *O culto*, 9–10.
[87] Miranda, *O culto*, 9, 11–14. Italics in the original.
[88] Eduardo C. Pereira, *A bemaventurada Virgem Maria* (São Paulo: Typ. King Leroy King Bookwalter, 1887), 4.
[89] Pereira, *A bemaventurada*, 22–23.

Criticizing a declaration attributed to the bishop of Rio de Janeiro, who supposedly argued that Saint Joseph was twice as omnipotent for he governed over his wife Mary and his son Christ, Pereira wrote that this idea showed how far could go the "impious and fatal tendency of the roman church in materializing the spiritual Kingdom of God, seizing upon the rough ideas of the people, to conceive of the Heaven in the image and likeness of earthly society, with all its blood relations, hierarchies, subordinations, contingencies, and petty passions!"[90] The idea of materiality assumed a central place in the evangelical critique of Catholic worship. It is likely that Pereira and Miranda took this concept from Reinkens's tract. The German bishop depicted ecclesiastical materialism as a brutalizing force that emerges in separation from the scriptures and "transforms religion into an emotion of the senses, reduces it to the mechanism of the administration and the ritual, binds the Holy Spirit to specific places, specific individuals, and transforms them into an object of worship."[91] But whereas Reinkens linked religious materialism to Vatican I and the dogma of Papal Infallibility, Pereira and Miranda built upon the concept and channeled it into the devotional renewal of the Catholic Church in its local incarnations. Evangelicals insisted upon the idea that the kingdom of God was a spiritual realm without any resemblance to earthly power hierarchies or family relations, and that the real worship resulted from a spiritual devotion.

Such a straightforward repudiation of priestly and saintly mediation, insistence on the spiritual dimension of faith, and defense of the dogmas of the sufficiency of Christ's atonement were sifted down into the daily lives of Brazilian evangelicals in multiple ways. The rejection of the mediation of saints, angels, and Mary in heavenly affairs altered the way believers viewed similar mediations in a worldly perspective. Protestant converts initially showed an inclination to dismiss the intermediation of godfathers and patronage in human associations.[92] The belief in individual salvation strengthened notions of individual self-improvement and social mobility among Brazilian Protestants. Converts broke away with traditional links of patronage and rejected the mediation of godfathers and godmothers in human affairs.[93] Later, the expansion of religious organizations enabled

---

[90] Pereira, *A bemaventurada*, 29–30.
[91] Reinkens, *Profissão de fé*, 25.
[92] Pereira, *O culto dos sanctos*, 17–18; Eduardo C. Pereira, *Nosso Pae que está nos céos* (São Paulo: Livraria Evangélica—M. Flexa & C., 1903), 11.
[93] Richard Graham, *Britain and the Onset of Modernization in Brazil, 1850–1914* (Cambridge: Cambridge University Press, 1968), 284, 288–289.

the re-introduction of clientelist relations in evangelical communities.[94] However, the first generations of foreign missionaries and Brazilian believers in the late nineteenth and early twentieth centuries held these practices under suspicion.[95] Moreover, in envisioning the Christian church as a spiritual reality, Protestants opposed the traditional Brazilian Catholic devotions, which they deemed as materialistic and anthropomorphized, and facilitated a reimagining of the worldwide Christian communion. Brazilian Protestants imagined themselves as active participants in a spiritual church, connected across space and time in their attachment to the Bible and their endless "protest" against the beliefs and practices they viewed as a distortion of primitive Christianity.

This was how Brazilian Protestants defined their religious identities. Attempting to offer the Brazilian public opinion an image of the Protestant worship different from that offered by the Catholic press, Pereira wrote: "we follow the holy religion of God's Son, and *protest* against all impiety, as well as against the doctrines condemned by the Holy Scriptures."[96] For him, Protestantism's fundamental principles could be summarized in three doctrines. The first was the doctrine of atonement: evangelicals believed that the power of Christ's death and resurrection could deliver men and women from the consequences of sin, eternal condemnation, and the power of sin, the human inclination to do evil.[97] The second was the doctrine of justification by faith, but "not the *blind faith* or the *dead faith*, nor the faith in the wood or the stone; but the *living faith* in Jesus Christ."[98] In Pereira's argument, good deeds and works of charity were the noble fruits of this living faith, not the causes of salvation.[99] The third fundamental principle was the centrality of the Bible in Christian worship and doctrines. And he suggested to his non-Protestant readers:

> Seek, therefore, the Testament of your Heavenly Father, of which no *tutor* can rightly deprive you of, and you will see that the teachings of [this tract's]

---

[94] Ronald C. Frase, "The Subversion of Missionary Intentions by Cultural Values: The Brazilian Case," *Review of Religious Research* 23 (1981): 180–194.
[95] David Martin, *Tongues of Fire: The Explosion of Protestantism in Latin America* (Oxford: Basil Blackwell, 1990), 64; Frase, "A Sociological Analysis," 431–432.
[96] Eduardo C. Pereira, *Vem e vê!* (São Paulo: n/p, 1891), 2. A very similar argument can be found in Eduardo C. Pereira, *Trabalho e economia ou A fidelidade de Deus manifestada na vida de um discipulo* (São Paulo: Typ. a vapor de Jorge Seckler & C., 1885), 11.
[97] Pereira, *Vem*, 3–5.
[98] Pereira, *Vem*, 5.
[99] Pereira, *Vem*, 6–8.

pages are in conformity with what *is written*. Read the admirable book of Christians, read the Bible, the Sacred Scriptures, and you will see that the religion followed by the various Protestant denominations is the old, pure, and holy religion taught by Christ and his Apostles.[100]

For Brazilian evangelicals, modern Protestantism was more than a late fruit of the European Reformation. They were animated by an impetus to recover the doctrinal purity, spiritual energy, and evangelistic fervor of the early Christian church. Once again, there are few references to Reformation figures in the BSET publications, whereas quotations of Church Fathers abound, especially to Augustine and Origen. Authors frequently cited patristic literature to object to the worship of images and the authority of the pope.[101] One of the tracts dealt specifically with the papacy. The BSET editors translated into Portuguese a discourse given by the Croatian Catholic Bishop Josip Strossmayer at the First Vatican Council attacking the dogma of Papal Infallibility. In it, the bishop argued that the golden age of the Christian church preceded the rise of the papacy. Quoting Augustine's, Gregory's, Cyril's, Jerome's, and Chrysostom's exegeses of Matthew 16:16–18, Strossmayer stated that Jesus did not establish the primacy of Peter over the apostles or the church in these verses.[102] Of course, this return *ad fontes* Brazilian Protestants advocated was mediated by the specific challenges they faced, contingent upon the theological and intellectual climate of their time, and that they quoted selectively from the patristic texts in response to contemporary impulses, both national and international. Nevertheless, this was the argument they presented to the Brazilian public, representing Romanized Catholicism in its universal and local embodiments as a degeneration of the early church.

Brazilian evangelicals believed, however, that yet another specter haunted the country. Whereas Catholicism was portrayed as a "mixture of paganism, Judaism, and empty formalities"[103] administered by a class of fanatical and superstitious clergymen, the "enlightened spirits" of the intellectual elites shifted to the opposite side of the spectrum in reaction to this, "preaching

---

[100] Pereira, *Vem*, 9.
[101] As in Miranda, *O culto*, 38–40, and Miguel G. Torres, *Pela graça é que somos salvos mediante a fé* (São Paulo: Typ da Sociedade Brasileira de Tractados Evangélicos, 1894), 13–15.
[102] Josip Strossmayer, *O papado e a infallibilidade* (São Paulo: Typ. Aurora da Sociedade Brazileira de Tractados Evangélicos, 1897), 8, 12–19.
[103] *O cura e o protestante*, 16.

irreligion and materialism."[104] In the nineteenth and early twentieth centuries, Brazilian Protestant ministers believed that their country was caught up in the midst of centrifugal spiritual forces. On one pole, Catholic priests and lay associations propagated an array of "religious superstitions," while, on the other, the secular intellectual elites, in reaction to these religious "absurdities," strayed further away from forms of organized religion.[105] In a tract intended to oppose the anticlerical inclinations of Brazil's liberal intellectuals, Pereira argued that religion was the soul of all peoples, the moral foundation of humanity. The abandonment of religion had terrible consequences, such as the "heinous depravation of customs" in the end of the Roman Empire, and the "bloodthirsty ferocity" of the revolutionaries of 1793.[106] Disbelief led societies to moral decadence and anarchy. Pereira depicted Brazilian intellectual elites as a "reactionary, disbelieving, mocking class, whose revolted reason ... impels it, naturally, beyond the middle line where the truth is."[107] Arguing that the immortality of the soul was a universal truth, Pereira invited readers to imagine the "dark despair of impious Voltaire in his last moments."[108]

Brazilian evangelicals decried the incredulity of Enlightenment and Positivist French philosophers, the radicalism of the French Revolution, and the arrogance of French elites. In fact, they viewed Rome and Paris as the two Babylons of the modern world: Rome stood for the corrupting religious power of the Vatican, while Paris embodied the social and moral anarchy of irreligious secularism. They did not, however, reject the ideas and principles of Enlightenment and modern liberalism altogether. In a stark abolitionist tract published by the BSET in 1886, Pereira affirmed that, in being enslaved, Africans were violently deprived of their natural rights, and that "slavery [was] the violation of a natural right, a crime against humanity, a sacrilegious attack against the Creator's work."[109] He deployed Enlightenment and liberal concepts of natural rights to uphold the abolitionist cause. In this sense, Pereira's arguments against slavery resembled those of John Wesley about a century earlier, who also deployed Enlightenment concepts in his defense

---

[104] Eduardo C. Pereira, *Um brado de alarma* (São Paulo: Typ. a vapor de Jorge Seckler & C., 1885), 7.
[105] Pedro Feitoza, "The Middle Line of Truth: Religious and Secular Ideologies in the Making of Brazilian Evangelical Thought, 1870–1930," *Modern Intellectual History* 19 (2022): 1033–1057.
[106] Pereira, *Um brado*, 3, 4, 8.
[107] Pereira, *Um brado*, 22.
[108] Pereira, *Um brado*, 5–6, 31.
[109] Eduardo C. Pereira, *A religião christã em suas relações com a escravidão* (São Paulo: Typ. a vapor de Jorge Seckler & C., 1886), 6, 30.

of abolitionism.[110] Brazilian Protestants did advocate self-improvement and social progress, they did promote values of religious tolerance and state laicization, and they did believe in human progress and liberty. For Brazilian Presbyterians, every single act of religious intolerance was an "iniquitous attack against the inalienable rights with which the Creator has endowed men."[111] However, they viewed the fundamental concepts of modern liberalism and the Enlightenment as grounded on the scriptures and Christian traditions, not on secular philosophies. Brazilian Protestants encompassed modern conceptions of natural rights, human progress, and freedom under their evangelical doctrines, disconnecting these concepts from their original intellectual sources. As Pereira wrote, "liberty and fraternity, sublime utopias of the human spirit, are the universal fruits of true Christianity."[112] Laveleye made similar statements. He affirmed that the French philosophers who preached liberty, such as Rabelais, Voltaire, and Rousseau, also scandalized the youth, whereas one could find the best examples of respect for human liberty, morality, and religion among American and British Protestant writers, especially John Milton.[113] It was in this way that Pereira constructed his political theology and declared the social and political relevance of Protestantism. He stated that it was from the pulpits of evangelical churches in Britain and the United States that the principles of liberty and justice emanated, stirring the national conscience and the public opinion, and fulminating with the fire of "justice and charity the heinous traffic of Africans."[114]

In an attempt to familiarize their reading public with Protestant values and doctrines, a good number of tracts published by the BSET addressed evangelical audiences. They carried moral teachings on deportment, manners, and personal conduct. As Zacarias de Miranda wrote, both converts and potential believers should bear in mind the existence of a wicked trinity whose influence was virtually inescapable, except for those under Christ's protection. This trinity was formed by the *world*, with its temptations and attractions; the *devil*, with his fury and astuteness; and men's own *flesh*, with its sinful inclinations.[115] Brazilian evangelicals believed that these three

---

[110] David Hempton, *Methodism: Empire of the Spirit* (New Haven, CT: Yale University Press, 2005), 42.
[111] *Imprensa Evangelica*, February 2, 1870, n. 14.
[112] Pereira, *A religião christã*, 20.
[113] Laveleye, *Do futuro*, 22–23.
[114] Pereira, *A religião christã*, 33–34.
[115] José Zacarias de Miranda, *Procrastinação ou O perigo de adiar a salvação* (São Paulo: Typ. a vapor de Jorge Seckler & C., 1886), 12–13.

forces tempted men and women in various ways and contributed to deflect them from the path of righteousness. Pereira warned converts against gossip, described as a wicked disposition to criticize and scrutinize the lives of others.[116] Protestants also bemoaned indolence and laziness. BSET tracts encouraged believers to be hard workers six days a week, to pay all their debts, and to live a life of temperance and parsimony. The cultivation of these virtues would attract divine providence and aid.[117] All kind of work, however, should be suspended on Sundays, the Sabbath of Brazilian evangelicals. The Rev. Guilherme da Costa advised believers to abstain from mundane business and diversions, reading secular books, talking about petty matters, and gambling on Sundays. They should, instead, dedicate themselves to the public and private worship, read the Bible and other religious books, and pray.[118]

Conversion to Protestantism was, therefore, associated with a profound and extensive reformation of believers' conduct. This kind of ascetic message and its consequential impact over a convert's behavior refashioned individual subjectivities and social relations.[119] Miranda argued that such an internalization of Protestantism's values and ethic had alienating effects, as believers became increasingly wary of traditional social norms.[120] For social scientists and theologians, the combination of these ascetic values and the missionaries' staunch opposition to Catholicism widened the gap between the values of evangelical Protestantism and traditional Brazilian culture. For such scholars, Protestantism acted as an alienating force that detached converts and churches from their cultural surroundings.[121] Brazilian evangelicals and foreign missionaries, however, developed a selective response to culture and custom.[122] For instance, according to the American Episcopal Bishop of Brazil, Lucien Kinsolving, it was in the modern and fast growing cities of the country that young people, attracted by opportunities of study and employment, were exposed to the three main temptations of the day: pornographic

[116] Eduardo C. Pereira, *A lingua* (São Paulo: n/p, 1890).
[117] Pereira, *Trabalho e economia*.
[118] Guilherme A. Costa, *A sanctificação do domingo* (São Paulo: n/p, 1891).
[119] The social and cultural implications of conversion are examined in the next chapter.
[120] Miranda, *Procrastinação*, 17–18.
[121] Antonio G. Mendonça and Prócoro Velasques Filho, *Introdução ao protestantismo no Brasil* (São Paulo: Edições Loyola, 1990); Zwinglio M. Dias, "A larva e a borboleta: Notas sobre as [im]possibilidades do protestantismo no interior da cultura brasileira," in *Diálogos cruzados: Religião, história e construção social*, ed. Mauro Passos (Belo Horizonte: Argumentum, 2010), 133–147.
[122] On selectivity, see David Lindenfeld and Miles Richardson, "Introduction," in *Beyond Conversion and Syncretism: Indigenous Encounters with Missionary Christianity, 1800–2000*, ed. David Lindenfeld and Miles Richardson (New York: Berghahn Books, 2012), 1–23, at 6.

literature, gambling, and vulgarity. In the bishop's argument, traditional family relations and religious life in the countryside shielded young people from these immoral influences.[123] Missionaries also stressed the importance of training and ordaining local clergy, making local churches self-supporting and self-governing, and they depicted Protestantism as a truly patriotic force in its endeavor to modernize the nation. In the beginning of the twentieth century, when numerous Catholic priests from Belgium, France, and Italy migrated to Brazil and rode the Brazilian countryside extending the Catholic sacraments and church doctrines to larger publics, evangelicals tried to show how nationalist and republican Protestant churches and values really were. Whereas they represented the Brazilian Catholic church as a monarchical institution, subject to supra national powers and governed by foreign priests, evangelical churches were depicted as truly republican in their governance and controlled by native pastors.[124]

The Lusophone Brethren

The tracts and books published by the BSET in the late nineteenth century touched upon various religious, social, and political issues. They objected to the devotional rejuvenation of the Catholic Church, opposed the ecclesiastical reforms of Pope Pius IX, translated the practices and beliefs of evangelical religion into local idioms, and sought to inspire processes of religious change. Tracts deployed a clear and simple language, making use of dialogues, powerful contrasts, and evocative images to persuade readers. Although the authors were mostly Presbyterian, the messages and texts persuaded missionaries and believers across a broad range of Protestant denominations.[125] But other publications had a strong denominational flavor. Missionaries and Brazilian ministers translated into Portuguese the Westminster Confession of Faith and published it, in 1876, alongside a declaration of the ecclesiastical forms of government adopted by the Presbyterian Church of Brazil. These documents regulated matters of doctrine and

---

[123] Lucien L. Kinsolving, *A razão de ser da Associação Christã de Moços* (Rio de Janeiro: Casa Publicadora Baptista, 1903), 9–15.

[124] Frase, "A Sociological Analysis," 313. See also Erika Helgen, *Religious Conflict in Brazil: Protestants, Catholics, and the Rise of Religious Pluralism in the Early Twentieth Century* (New Haven, CT: Yale University Press, 2020).

[125] For Baptists, see Kate Taylor, "The Christian Literature of Brazil," *Bahia*, February 1, 1883. IBMB, Zachary Clay Taylor papers.

practice such as the administration of sacraments and the hierarchy of the church.[126] In the earliest decades of the Protestant missionary enterprise in Brazil, Presbyterians and Baptists took to their printing presses to either uphold or condemn infant baptism.[127] The need to secure the self-government of local churches and the institutional reproduction of denominations set Protestants in motion. Congregationalists sent local leaders to undertake theological and pastoral training abroad, while Presbyterians developed an array of initiatives to train Portuguese-speaking ministers locally.

A somewhat discreet group of evangelical converts opposed these attempts at denominational differentiation and ecclesiastical organization in late nineteenth-century Brazil. They were called the Plymouth Brethren. Originated in Ireland and south-west England during the first half of the nineteenth century, the Brethren asserted the supreme authority of the Bible in worship and conversion, believed that the second coming of Christ was imminent, and disapproved of denominational divisions and ecclesiastical hierarchies. John Nelson Darby, one the Brethren's leading thinkers and founders, believed that the Christian church had eroded its own foundations by casting aside the expectation of Christ's immediate return and accommodating itself to life in the world. The "ruin of the church" was visible in the importance Protestant denominations attributed to the "clerical principle," by which only official appointees could exert leadership. For the earliest Brethren, this principle expressed mistrust in the Holy Spirit and the sufficiency of Christ's sacrifice.[128] The British Christian Brethren stressed the centrality of the Holy Spirit in the direction of the worship and the church, dispensed ordination and training as prerequisites for the establishment of leadership, and centered their religious celebrations on the "breaking of bread," the holy communion.[129] One of the movement's earliest leaders, Anthony Groves, objected to the mechanisms of fundraising created by missionary societies and called missionaries and evangelists to rely solely on God's providence, adopting a simpler lifestyle and assimilating native ways of living as far as possible. Groves and the Brethren influenced the idea of

---

[126] *A confissão de fé da Igreja Presbyteriana do Brazil* (Rio de Janeiro: Livraria Evangelica, 1876), 63–68, 82–87.

[127] Eduardo Carlos Pereira, *A divina instituição do baptismo de crianças* (São Paulo: Typographia Commercial de H. Rossi, 1905); W. E. Entzminger. *Fiat Lux ou Resultado do meu exame do "exame" do Snr. Juvêncio Marinho sobre "O Modo do Baptismo"* (Rio de Janeiro: Casa Editora Baptista, 1902).

[128] Tim Grass, *Gathering to His Name: The Story of Open Brethren in Britain and Ireland* (Milton Keynes: Paternoster, 2006), 95–96. See also Donald Lewis, ed., *The Blackwell Dictionary of Evangelical Biography: 1730–1860*, 2 vols (Oxford: Blackwell, 1995), 290–291.

[129] Grass, *Gathering to His Name*, 97–98.

"living by faith" adopted by missionaries such as George Müller and Henry Craik, and in the development of faith missions, such as Hudson Taylor's China Inland Mission (1865).[130]

Plymouth Brethren ideas were introduced in Brazil via the Luso-Atlantic Protestant networks examined in the previous chapter. Since the early 1870s, small groups of Brazilian converts showed some antipathy to ecclesiastical hierarchies and an inclination to disassociate from the organized bodies of denominations. These included the journalist José Carlos Rodrigues and the shopkeeper José Maria Barbosa, a member of the São Paulo Presbyterian Church who refused to be appointed elder of his church despite being elected by the congregation.[131] It was Richard Holden, superintendent of the British and Foreign Bible Society (BFBS) and assistant pastor of the Fluminense Evangelical Church in Rio de Janeiro, who began to introduce Brethren's ideas in the Lusophone Protestant public sphere.[132] He came into contact with the Christian Brethren in Britain upon his retirement from the BFBS in the early 1870s. Persuaded by their doctrines, Holden began to correspond with Portuguese-speaking evangelicals in Illinois and Rio de Janeiro near the end of the decade, fomenting the circulation of Brethren literature across Lusophone networks.

Holden showed special contempt for denominational divisions among Brazilian and Portuguese churches. In a letter originally written in Lisbon in 1879 and circulated across Lusophone evangelical networks, Holden claimed that the publication of confessions of faith and denominational creeds exemplified Darby's idea of "the ruin of the church." In Holden's argument, such documents expressed a sectarian suspicion in the sufficiency of the scriptures and the authority of the Holy Spirit over the church.[133] As long as these confessions continued to exist, he argued, the unification of the Christian church was virtually impossible. Through such statements, Holden claimed, denominations and their committees expressed their sectarian arrogance by attempting to circumscribe the meanings of the Bible and limit the action of the Spirit, just like Catholic popes.[134] The Congregationalist missionary

---

[130] Andrew Porter, *Religion versus Empire?: British Protestant Missionaries and Overseas Expansion, 1700-1914* (Manchester: Manchester University Press, 2004), 191-197; Lewis, *The Blackwell Dictionary*, 485-486; Grass, *Gathering to His Name*, 110-111.
[131] Boehrer, "José Carlos Rodrigues," 128; Lessa, *Annaes*, 191-195.
[132] Émile G. Léonard, *O protestantismo brasileiro: Estudo de eclesiologia e história social*, 3rd ed. (São Paulo: ASTE, 2002), 82-83.
[133] Richard Holden, *Confissões de fé* (Rio de Janeiro: Ladeira do Barroso, 1906), 1-5.
[134] Holden, *Confissões de fé*, 7-8, 10-13.

Robert Kalley, writing from Edinburgh upon retirement, responded quickly to Holden's tracts corresponding with colleagues in Illinois, Lisbon, and Rio de Janeiro, where Holden's writings circulated. Kalley sought to reassert the authority of church leadership by leaning on the text of I Corinthians 12. He argued that, in line with the biblical teaching, God gave different gifts and skills to believers.[135]

The most active disseminator of the Christian Brethren's ideas in Brazil was the British engineer and missionary Stuart McNair (1867–1959). In the early 1890s, McNair moved to Lisbon and came into contact with Caterina Holden, Richard Holden's widow, from whom he received news of non-denominational evangelical gatherings in Rio de Janeiro. In 1896, he settled in Rio. Alongside a Brazilian convert, Daniel Faria, they established the headquarters of the Brethren movement in a shanty at the Livramento Hill, one of Rio de Janeiro's earliest *favelas*. There they set up a printing business with branches in Lisbon and Madeira.[136] McNair made lengthy journeys across South America, supporting non-denominational evangelistic work and gathering information about the growth of evangelical Christianity in the continent. He also wrote and published extensively, circulating evangelical literature in Brazil and Portugal, and trying to connect the Lusophone Brethren across the Atlantic.

For McNair, non-denominational evangelical churches were fully compatible with the biblical model. In letting denominations impose their rules and discipline over believers and by choosing specific men to direct worship and liturgy, Christians attempted to control the Holy Spirit and gave room to "iniquitous" doctrines.[137] McNair believed that religious services should not be confounded with evangelistic meetings, which gathered believers and non-believers. He conceived an ideal religious service as "a meeting of believers, in which there is liberty and opportunity for them to exercise their spiritual priesthood in worship to God, and to admonish one another, according to the Spirit's direction."[138] McNair also introduced ideas that inspired faith missions in the Lusophone world. He affirmed that as representatives of God's work in the world, ministers received their financial

---

[135] *O Darbysmo, cartas do Dr. Robert R. Kalley* (Lisbon: Adolfo, Modesto & C—Impressores, 1891), 7–8, 15–16.

[136] Stuart McNair, *Round South America on the King's Business* (London: Marshall Brothers, 1913), 125–126.

[137] Stuart McNair, *Que devemos fazer?* (Lisbon: Calçada dos Mestres, 1906), 4, 9.

[138] McNair, *Que devemos*, 5; Stuart McNair, *O culto* (Lisbon: Calçada dos Mestres, 1906), 6–8.

support from God: "Everyone believes in this theoretically, but how feeble proofs many give of their faith! ... And this incredulity, which can be seen in individuals, is also manifest in the complex organizations that Christians have been instituting to guarantee the provision of necessary means."[139] In journeys around South America, McNair claimed he was entirely dependent on divine providence and proudly emphasized his independence from mission societies.[140]

Despite their energetic dedication to evangelistic work and the circulation of evangelical literature in Brazil and Portugal, the Lusophone Brethren lagged behind mainline Protestant and Pentecostal denominations in Brazil. Unlike Presbyterians and Methodists, who created a complex institutional apparatus encompassing schools and seminaries, the Brethren developed assertive methods of direct evangelization that further extended the reach of evangelical Christianity in Brazil. Their suspicion of ecclesiastical institutionalism prevented them from developing cohesive mechanisms of institutional reproduction. Despite this, the Lusophone Christian Brethren left a lasting mark in the making of Brazilian Protestantism. Some evangelists associated with them were prolific hymn-writers, and their music was introduced in the hymnals of all Brazilian denominations. The most active songwriter was Henry Maxwell Wright (1849–1931), a Lisbon-born Briton who, during his adolescence, took part in Dwight Moody's and Ira Shankey's evangelistic campaigns in Britain. Wright spent most of his missionary life in Portugal and made four evangelistic trips to Brazil, in 1881, 1890–1891, 1893, and 1914, working alongside different denominations and in association with McNair.[141] He composed and translated several evangelical songs into Portuguese, which formed the basis of Protestant hymnals. There are 104 of Wright's hymns in the *Psalms and Hymns*, adopted by Congregationalists and Presbyterians, and he also contributed with the Baptist pastor and hymn-writer Solomon Ginsburg.[142] Following his energetic style, some of his songs were full of evangelistic appeals to believers: "Behold the millions, who in fearsome darkness/Lay lost without the Savior!/Who will unto them proclaim the news/That God, in Christ, saves the sinner?/All the authority

---

[139] Stuart McNair, *Os ministros de Deus: Seu Senhor, seu serviço e seu sustento* (Lisbon: Calçada dos Mestres, 1903), 4–5.
[140] McNair, *Round South America*, 114–116.
[141] Douglas N. Cardoso, "Henry Maxwell Wright (1849–1931): O poeta do amor que salva," *Revista Caminhando* 19 (2014): 61–70.
[142] Henriqueta F. Braga, *Salmos e hinos: Sua origem e desenvolvimento* (Rio de Janeiro: Igreja Evangélica Fluminense, 1983), 42, 54–55.

my Father gave me/On earth as in heaven/Go ye therefore and preach the Gospel/And, lo, I am with you always."[143]

The ideas of Holden, McNair, and the Brazilian Brethren carried some of the Protestant doctrines expressed in the BSET tracts to their ultimate consequences. The principle of the priesthood of all believers was reenacted with such a force that shunned ecclesiastical hierarchies. The Christian Brethren attempted to relive the experiences of the apostolic church through a wholesale rejection of ecclesiastical institutionalism. These principles gave way to a radical egalitarianism that accentuated the individualizing implications of evangelical Christianity in Brazil.[144] Furthermore, despite the British Brethren's suspicion of religious enthusiasm and McNair's negative views of Pentecostalism, which he pejoratively labeled "the tongues movement," it was the Assemblies of God that recovered the Brethren tradition in Brazil.[145] In the 1980s, the Publishing House of the Assembly of God, founded in 1940, republished and commercialized some of McNair's texts, especially his extensive biblical dictionary. Indeed, the doctrine of dispensational premillennialism, which postulated that an imminent and secrete rapture of believers would be followed by seven years of tribulation of earth, was initially articulated by the Plymouth Brethren. As historian Grant Wacker has shown, this doctrine exerted a decisive intellectual influence on the early Pentecostal movement.[146]

Conclusion

Brazilian Protestant ministers and writers accommodated an array of unexpected and contrasting intellectual and theological traditions into their tracts and periodicals. In the context of the Religious Question, they bemoaned the universal and local embodiments of Ultramontane Catholicism and the First Vatican Council. Their objections to Catholic faith, morals, and politics were extended into public arguments on racial difference, national identity, political change, and religious diversification. Protestants equated conversion to social and economic progress and claimed that a general religious

---

[143] *Collecção de hymnos escolhidos* (Recife: n/p, 1895), 15.
[144] Graham, *Britain and the Onset*, 285–289.
[145] Grass, *Gathering to His Name*, 86–90; McNair, *Round South America*, 47, 66, 113, 124.
[146] Grant Wacker, *Heaven Below: Early Pentecostals and American Culture* (Cambridge, MA: Harvard University Press, 2001), introduction.

reformation would moralize and modernize the nation. In mobilizing all these arguments and debates, evangelicals engaged closely with the specific religious, social, and political ideologies of their age. Interestingly, Protestant writers like Pereira, Zacarias de Miranda, and McNair portrayed evangelical religion as the recovery of the pristine purity of the early Christian church against the "degenerate" innovations of Catholicism, most notably of Vatican I and Pius IX. They romanticized the church of the apostolic era as the ultimate model for Christian thought and practice in the modern world. But this "primitivist impulse" exceeded the confines of evangelical religion, also serving as a model for social formations and modern democracy. For the earliest generations of Brazilian evangelicals, the egalitarian experiences of the apostolic community should inspire and Christianize the modern democratic spirit, delivering men and women from despotic forms of government in church and society while simultaneously serving as a barrier to violent revolutionary upheaval. Their attempts to restore pristine, age-old religion were filtered through the political and intellectual vocabularies of their age, creating opportunities for startling religious innovations.[147]

Instead of situating Brazilian evangelical thought in specific positions of the political and theological spectrums, this chapter has shown how Protestant ministers and writers responded to a wide range of ideologies and religious movements. They disaggregated, unpacked, and dismembered modern intellectual traditions, combining them again in different ways. They embraced concepts of human freedom and natural rights, but they objected to the anticlerical leanings of Enlightenment French philosophers; they embraced tenets of classical liberal thought but decried revolutionary change and the effects of liberal revolutions. The ideas that circulated in evangelical periodicals, such as the *Imprensa Evangelica* and the texts of the BSET, were by no means simple imitations or rote translations of conservative American theology, isolated from the intellectual contexts and transformations of Brazilian society. They engaged very closely with the religious and political debates in the context of the Religious Question, shared in the hopes and anxieties in the context of the overthrow of the Empire, replaced the dictates of racial determinism by a loosely defined religious determinism, and sought to demarcate the specific status of evangelicals within a Catholic majority society. Evangelical ministers and writers became active and engaged participants in the heated debates circulating in the Brazilian public sphere.

---

[147] Charles Taylor, "Religious Mobilizations," *Public Culture* 18 (2006): 281–300.

4
The Dynamics of Religious Change

In the early twentieth century, the British engineer-turned-missionary Frederick Glass encountered a man called Pedro in a prison in the state of Goiás. The convict had been sentenced to thirty years of imprisonment for robbery and complicity in a murder. According to Glass's helpers, Pedro had converted to evangelical Christianity while reading alone a Bible he had purchased from colporteurs. The Bible came into Pedro's hands halfway through the sentence when he completed fifteen years at the insalubrious prison. In Glass's flamboyant narrative, the convict had taught himself to read from the Bible "and then God's Holy Spirit unfolded to his mind and heart the wonderful truth as it is in Jesus, with its healing and transforming power." The new convert insisted on being baptized. He evangelized his fellow prisoners and achieved some success. Through his work as a shoemaker, Pedro raised funds for Glass's mission organization. The two men started a lasting friendship. When Glass's daughter was first presented to the church of Goiás, Pedro held the girl in his arms and offered the dedicatory prayer, and when the missionary undertook an expedition among the Carajá Indians near the Araguaia River, Pedro was one of the main individual contributors to Glass's long trip.[1] The photograph of "Pedro Feliz" (Happy Pedro) features the former convict smartly attired with a clear shirt and blazer, proudly holding a thick volume of the Bible in his right hand (see Figure 4.1).

Glass himself experienced a somewhat Pauline conversion experience. He embarked for Brazil in 1892 to work at a railway company but was later employed by a gold-mining establishment in the state of Minas Gerais. In Glass's words, although he believed in God, abstained from alcohol and gambling, and even prayed, he was not a Christian, for he "knew absolutely nothing of conversion or the need of it." Glass became acquainted with Reginald Young, a Canadian Congregationalist evangelist, who worked as a typist at the mining company. One day, while riding past a mountain stream, Glass's horse stumbled and fell, throwing the engineer through the air while he noted,

---

[1] Frederick Glass, *Adventures with the Bible in Brazil* (London: Pickering & Inglis, 1923), 64–71.

Figure 4.1 Pedro Feliz and his Bible. Frederick Glass, *With the Bible in Brazil.*

with despair, that one foot was fast held in the stirrup iron. Surprisingly, the wild horse lay quietly after the incident, giving Glass some time to release his foot and escape unscathed. Glass believed that divine providence had spared him from a violent death, and this set him thinking about the destiny of his soul. Led by Young, Glass professed his faith in 1897.[2]

The stories of Pedro Feliz and Frederick Glass encapsulate some stereotypes associated with evangelical conversion. Pedro's solitary encounter with the Bible turned a criminal into a joyful Christian and, in the evangelical imagination of the era, demonstrated the extraordinary power of the printed word. The results of his labor were deployed in favor of the evangelizing

[2] Glass, *Adventures*, 9–13.

enterprise. The two men became active members of the same religious community and entered into a lasting relation of friendship. The providential encounter of the promising British engineer with the humble Canadian typist in the interior of Minas Gerais prompted a radical turn in Glass's career, whose sudden conversion transformed a nominal Christian into an active evangelist.

Conversion is the theme of this chapter. It examines a set of shifting religious, social, and cultural dynamics related to religious change in nineteenth- and early twentieth-century Brazil. The analysis concentrates on the region where Protestantism first took off through the labors of foreign missionaries, local pastors, and evangelists: the Brazilian center south, more specifically the states of Rio de Janeiro, Minas Gerais, São Paulo, and some adjoining areas. Throughout, the chapter analyzes the media, interactions, and objects that brought about religious change; the ways in which converts made sense of it; and its embodiment in forms of dress, behavior, and vocabulary. The academic study of conversion has long sparked a lively debate between historians and social scientists.[3] In the past two decades, anthropologist Joel Robbins has made important contributions to the debate on Christian conversion. He objected to the approach of cultural anthropologists who conceptualize culture as a long-standing tradition that is continually passed on by calling it "continuity thinking." Such an approach, Robbins claims, fails to capture the Christian conception of time as a dimension in which radical change is possible, casting a shadow of suspicion on the claims of converts to have radically transformed their lives.[4] In short, while conversion narratives focus on discontinuity, scholarly analysis of conversion emphasizes continuity. Robbins and his collaborators have challenged anthropologists to come to terms with Christian religion as an ethnographic object of analysis, thinking comparatively about the various shapes and histories of Christianity across the world, and considering its changing social and cultural formations.[5]

However, when scholars examine religious change over different generations, the rhythms of social change and cultural discontinuity reveal more

---

[3] Robin Horton, "African conversion," *Africa* 41 (1971): 85–108; John D. Y. Peel, "Conversion and Tradition in Two African Societies: Ijebu and Buganda," *Past & Present* 77 (1977): 108–141.

[4] Joel Robbins, "Continuity Thinking and the Problem of Christian Culture: Belief, Time, and the Anthropology of Christianity," *Current Anthropology* 48 (2007): 5–17.

[5] Jon Bialecki, Naomi Haynes, and Joel Robbins, "The Anthropology of Christianity," *Religion Compass* 2 (2008): 1139–1158.

complex patterns. First-generation converts experience religious change as a severe rupture with their cultural and social surroundings. Their rigor and zeal often appear excessive to outsiders. But their offspring do not undergo this experience of rupture, and they re-introduce as nostalgia what their parents cast aside as improper or demonic. It is, therefore, necessary to study how religious change evolved amidst a dynamic of change and continuity, and to examine precisely how Christian converts produce new syntheses of old and new customs.[6]

In the Brazilian case, missionaries and evangelists joined forces in a global struggle against another variant of the Christian faith. They sought to eliminate what they viewed as "degenerate" Catholic traditions and superstitions. The earliest Protestant believers often depicted conversion to Protestantism as a break with family heritage, which they referred to as "the religion of my parents." In the process, long-held Catholic devotions yielded to a new religious subjectivity that conceived the veneration of the Virgin, saints, and religious icons as the fruits of spiritual corruption. One of the most dramatic stages of this process occurred when converts got rid of their statues and images of saints by either burning them or throwing them into a river. After conversion, believers found the Catholic festivals and processions they previously cherished to be utterly repugnant. But believers did not depict conversion as the embrace of a new religion. Instead, they claimed to recover the gospel in its pristine purity. They broke away from the religion of their worldly parents to embrace the religion of their spiritual parents: the apostolic community of the New Testament. In this sense, Brazilian believers conceptualized conversion not as a movement of rupture, but of renewal. Not innovation, but purification. Not departure, but recovery. In the early 1890s, the evangelical convert and republican leader Miguel Vieira Ferreira expressed this ideal by claiming he indeed preached the religion of his spiritual forefathers, that of Jesus Christ and the apostles, not his earthly parents.[7] Clearly, this turn to the early Christian past was mediated through the specific religious, social, and cultural vocabularies of their own age, and the chapter will examine this interplay.

---

[6] David Maxwell, "Continuity and Change in the Luba Christian Movement, Katanga, Belgian Congo, c. 1915–50," *Journal of Ecclesiastical History* 69 (2018): 326–344.

[7] Miguel Vieira Ferreira, *O Cristo no júri* (São Paulo: Oficinas Gráficas de Saraiva, 1957 [1891]), 217.

The Social and Political Contexts of Conversion

The religion of foreign missionaries and Portuguese-speaking evangelical pastors found acceptance amongst certain social categories and in specific places. In the far south of the country, it was not the evangelistic zeal of missionaries and local preachers that drove religious diffusion, but the settlement of communities of German Lutheran immigrants. Evangelical expansion was slower in the north and northeast of the country. Although the policies of the Empire thwarted the recruitment of Catholic novices and the institutional reproduction of the Church, in the provinces of Ceará, Pernambuco, and Bahia a group of influential and charismatic priests managed to revive local devotions and mobilize the faithful around religious causes.[8] Their rhetoric was zealously anti-Protestant, and the missionaries who worked in such fields found it difficult to make headway.[9] It was in the growing cities and the vast countryside of Rio de Janeiro, São Paulo, and Minas Gerais that Protestants established flourishing Congregationalist, Presbyterian, Methodist, and Baptist congregations in the nineteenth and early twentieth centuries.[10] And in such places, a diverse social compound including *sitiantes* (small farmers), free peasants, shopkeepers, artisans, the urban middle classes, and decadent elites joined the emerging churches. For social scientists Ronald Frase and Antonio Gouvêa Mendonça, it was the relative marginality and mobility of these social groups that created a climate favorable to conversion. Estranged from mechanisms of political participation, the emerging middle classes and small landowners encountered, in Protestant congregations and schools, channels of institutional representation. Along with this, the expansion of coffee plantations of the agricultural frontiers created a class of mobile and impoverished small farmers that were more susceptible to the new religion in the countryside of São Paulo and Minas Gerais.[11]

---

[8] Ralph Della Cava, "Brazilian Messianism and National Institutions: A Reappraisal of Canudos and Joaseiro," *Hispanic American Historical Review* 48 (1968): 402–420.

[9] For an excellent treatment of Catholic–Protestant interactions in the Brazilian northeast in the twentieth century, see Erika Helgen, *Religious Conflict in Brazil: Protestants, Catholics, and the Rise of Religious Pluralism in the Early Twentieth Century* (New Haven, CT: Yale University Press, 2020).

[10] Émile G. Léonard, *O protestantismo brasileiro: Estudo de eclesiologia e história social*, 3rd ed. (São Paulo: ASTE, 2002 [1963]).

[11] Ronald G. Frase, "A Sociological Analysis of the Development of Brazilian Protestantism: A Study of Social Change." (PhD diss., Princeton Theological Seminary, 1975), 248–274, 330–331; Antonio G. Mendonça, *O celeste porvir: A inserção do protestantismo no Brasil* (São Paulo: Editora da Universidade de São Paulo, 2008 [1984]), 197, 203–209, 220–224.

Conversion to evangelical Christianity in nineteenth-century Brazil also carried political consequences for believers. Up until the overthrow of the Brazilian Empire in 1889, non-Catholic religious minorities in the country encountered a series of juridical and political constraints imposed by the law. The imperial constitution of 1824 acknowledged the official status of the Catholic Church in Brazil, but at the same time granted some measure of religious liberty to dissenting minorities. Non-Catholics were allowed to celebrate their religious services, but only in private houses that could not resemble religious buildings.[12] Primary electors who voted in the national and provincial polls were not required to profess the official religion, but deputies and senators had to be, at least nominally, Catholics.[13] In addition to this, up until 1881 elections for the parliament and provincial assemblies took place in parish churches.[14] These constitutional prescriptions did not preclude the rise of an anticlerical political elite in the Empire, deeply suspicious of the universalist aspirations of the Vatican.[15] Nevertheless, the avenues that gave access to the legislative chambers of the Empire were closed to Protestants.

At that time, however, evangelicals did not hold serious political aspirations, and hence these clauses did not represent a major burden. The laws that exerted a direct impact on the daily lives of foreign immigrants and Brazilian Protestants related to civil registrations and to burial. A law approved in 1828 resolved that it was the responsibility of local religious authorities and political bosses to determine the places in which public municipal cemeteries would be established. The blessing of the land with holy water was part of the ritual involved in the creation of cemeteries, which put the land under the control of the Catholic Church.[16] Another legislative decree of 1827 recognized eighteenth-century ecclesiastical regulations on marriage, granting civil effects to marriages celebrated by Catholic priests. Although some political reforms in the 1860s recognized the legal effects of

---

[12] Alexander L. Blackford, *Sketch of the Brazil Mission* (Philadelphia: Presbyterian Board of Education, 1886), 3.

[13] *Collecção das leis do Imperio do Brazil, 1824, parte 1ª* (Rio de Janeiro: Imprensa Nacional, 1886), 2, 19–20.

[14] Richard Graham, *Patronage and Politics in Nineteenth-century Brazil* (Stanford, CA: Stanford University Press, 1990), 114–115.

[15] José Murilo de Carvalho, *A construção da ordem: a elite política imperial/Teatro de sombras: a política imperial* (Rio de Janeiro: Civilização Brasileira, 2010), 56.

[16] Claudia Rodrigues, "Sepulturas e sepultamentos de protestantes como uma questão de cidadania na crise do Império (1869–1889)," *Revista de História Regional* 13 (2008): 23–38; *Collecção das leis do Imperio do Brazil, 1828, parte 1ª* (Rio de Janeiro: Typographia Nacional, 1878), 83.

non-Catholic marriages, these laws were only fully implemented decades later.[17]

In this context, Protestants believed that the laws of the Empire contained both protective devices against religious persecution and repressive means of regulation against dissenting minorities, with disruptive consequences at a private level. They claimed that the imperial legislation on marriage forced them into illegitimate marital relations, creating problems for the transfer of family property and inheritance.[18] Additionally, throughout the late 1860s, non-Catholics were denied a burial place in public municipal cemeteries in the provinces of Pernambuco, São Paulo, and Rio de Janeiro, adding to the anxieties of religious minorities in Brazil. The establishment of burial sites for non-Catholic immigrants, such as the Gamboa Cemetery in Rio de Janeiro, the British Cemetery in Recife and Salvador, and the Protestants' Cemetery in São Paulo, enabled evangelicals to bypass such limitations.[19] But even in the decades following the overthrow of the Empire, Protestants continued to encounter resistance when trying to bury their dead in public cemeteries.[20] Becoming a Protestant in nineteenth-century Brazil entailed living on the margins of the juridical and political arrangements of the time.

Although these social and political factors contributed to either facilitate or constrain processes of religious change, they by no means suffice to explain how conversion was brought about or account for its implications. Functionalist explanations for religious change see "religious transformation as mere reflections of more quantifiable ... forms of interest such as class or politics rather than as a creative force for change in its own right."[21] Such accounts run the risk of portraying conversion simply as a response to asymmetrical power relations and changing social and economic landscapes, not paying attention to the psychocultural and intellectual realities of religious change.[22] Whereas functionalist studies situate the diffusion of evangelical

---

[17] Boanerges Ribeiro, *Protestantismo no Brasil monárquico (1822–1888): Aspectos culturais da aceitação do protestantismo no Brasil* (São Paulo: Pioneira, 1973), 111–116. See also Mercedes G. Kothe, "O Brasil no século XIX: Restrições aos grupos não católicos," in *História em movimento: Temas e perguntas*, ed. Albene Menezes (Brasília: Thesaurus, 1999), 92–103.

[18] Pedro Feitoza, "Experiments in Missionary Writing: Protestant Missions and the *Imprensa Evangelica* in Brazil, 1864–1892," *Journal of Ecclesiastical History* 69 (2018): 585–605, at 595–596.

[19] Rodrigues, "Sepulturas s sepultamentos."

[20] Vicente Themudo Lessa, *Annaes da 1ª Egreja Presbyteriana de São Paulo: Subsidios para a historia do presbiterianismo brasileiro* (São Paulo: Edição da 1ª Egreja Presbyteriana Independente de São Paulo, 1938), 359–360, 594–595.

[21] Joseph Florez, *Lived Religion, Pentecostalism, and Social Activism in Authoritarian Chile: Giving Life to the Faith* (Leiden: Brill, 2021), 14.

[22] Gabriela Ramos, "Conversion of Indigenous People in the Peruvian Andes: Politics and Historical Understanding," *History Compass* 14 (2016): 359–369; Robert Hefner, "Introduction: World Building

Christianity firmly into its relevant sociopolitical dynamics, it is equally crucial to ask who transported the new religion to new places and to examine its novel social and cultural configurations.

The Dissolution and Reconstitution of Social Bonds

To a certain extent, the missionary emphasis on the conversion of the individual resonated with the modernizing aims of the country's elites. In sermons and tracts, foreign missionaries and local pastors stressed the importance of sobriety, thrift, decency, and diligence, encouraging believers to shun the consumption of alcohol and to lead exemplary lives as industrious, law-abiding citizens.[23] Evangelical hymns invited believers to envision both their worldly labor and evangelistic responsibilities as part of a same divine calling. A popular, slightly upbeat hymn of this period sang, "To the work! To the work! Let the hungry be fed/To the fountain of life let the thirsty be led/ In the cross of the Lord our glory shall be/For Christ brings the tidings: salvation is free/To labor, with fervor/Let us serve our Lord/With hope and faith and with steadfast prayer/Let's labor 'till the Lord returns."[24] Moreover, the Protestant attachment to the Bible and the transformative capacities of religious literature drew converts and their offspring to the parish and secondary missionary schools established across the country. The orderly prescriptions of the Protestant ethic were in tune with the desires of both imperial and republican rulers for political order, stability, and progress.

But the ideal of individual salvation espoused by Protestants stood in contrast with another set of traditional customs in Brazil. According to Peter van der Veer, conversion shares with modernity a positive view of change that transforms the self in its relations with the past and with others.[25] The intricacies involved in such transformation were played out in various ways in Brazil, destabilizing the position of individuals within their communities.

---

and the Rationality of Conversion," in *Conversion to Christianity: Historical and Anthropological Perspectives on a Great Transformation*, ed. Robert Hefner (Berkeley, CA: University of California Press, 1993), 3–44.

[23] Eduardo C. Pereira, *Trabalho e economia ou a fidelidade de Deus manifestada na vida de um discipulo* (São Paulo: Typographia a vapor de Jorge Seckler & Comp., 1885).
[24] *Collecção de hymnos escolhidos* (Recife: n/p, 1895), 31–32.
[25] Peter van der Veer, "Introduction," in *Conversion to Modernities: The Globalization of Christianity*, ed. Peter van der Veer (New York: Routledge, 1996), 1–21, at 18–20.

For historian Richard Graham, one of the main contributions of foreign missionaries to the modernization of Brazil was the emphasis they placed upon the individual: "Once people began to think of themselves as independent units rather than as parts of a larger whole in which their place was permanently fixed, the breakdown of traditional society was imminent."[26] This evangelical conception of the self dissolved the vertical social bonds that characterized relations of patronage, with significant consequences for believers. In Brazil, customary obligations of protection and sponsorship contracted in baptisms and marriages created vast networks of co-parenthood (*compadrio*) that were decisive for the making or breaking of an individual's life. These widespread practices enabled people to extend kinship voluntarily, cemented the authority of the older and the male in the Brazilian countryside, and ascribed sacred status to established worldly hierarchies.[27]

First-generation converts, however, eschewed such practices. They did not accept the idea of godfathers or godmothers.[28] Inspired by the doctrines of the sufficiency of Christ's sacrifice and of individual salvation, evangelical pastors urged believers to reject the notion that saints and godfathers served as their spiritual and social intermediaries and encouraged them to address God directly in their prayers. The Presbyterian schoolteacher Maria de Melo Chaves, writing about the conversion of her family in the countryside of Minas Gerais, recorded the perplexity of her kin and neighbors with this. Her uncle David Melo was the first convert in the village of Carmo da Bagagem. When his brother Manuel de Melo invited David to be the best man (*padrinho*) in his wedding in 1897, David accepted it only partially, saying he would happily stand by his brother's side in the civil ceremony but not at a Catholic parish, to Manuel's shock. When Maria was born a few years later into a convert family, a Brazilian Presbyterian pastor celebrated her baptism and the Catholic neighbors who attended the ceremony quickly noted the absence of godparents (*padrinhos*).[29] Amongst Presbyterians, the baptism of infants implicated the nuclear family into a commitment to instruct the

---

[26] Richard Graham, *Britain and the Onset of Modernization of Brazil, 1850–1914* (Cambridge: Cambridge University Press, 1968), 284.

[27] Duglas Teixeira Monteiro, *Errantes do novo século: Um estudo sobre o surto milenarista do Contestado* (São Paulo: Duas Cidades, 1974), 57–80; Dain Borges, *The Family in Bahia, Brazil, 1870–1945* (Stanford, CA: Stanford University Press, 1992), 222–224; Maria Sylvia de Carvalho Franco, *Homens livres na ordem escravocrata*, 4ª ed. (São Paulo: Editora UNESP, 1997), 86–94.

[28] Graham, *Britain and the Onset*, 288–289.

[29] Maria de Melo Chaves, *Bandeirantes da fé* (Belo Horizonte: Associação Evangélica Beneficente de Minas Gerais, 1947), 47, 81.

children into the basic principles of Christian religion and to teach them to read the Bible, but left the extended family out of such obligations.[30] Baptist missionaries and pastors went further. In contrast to the Presbyterians, they staunchly opposed the public baptism of infants, claiming that this sacrament should be administered to an individual and mature conscience regenerated by God. Whereas the Presbyterian baptism of children entailed some demands from the nuclear family, Baptists rejected this practice altogether. Their conception of baptism accentuated the individualizing implications of religious change.[31] Conversion had the potential to isolate converts from their extended kin and the communal obligations implicated in networks of patronage. Aware of these alienating consequences, ministers and missionaries urged believers to remain steadfast to their religious commitments and resist the temptation of coming to terms with the "social prejudices or familial conveniences" of their age.[32]

Religious change, however, did not trigger a complete break with established customs. Mendonça, in his influential account of the expansion of Protestantism in late nineteenth-century rural Brazil, stressed the ways in which converts distanced themselves from the festive culture of the Brazilian countryside. The strictures of the Protestant ethic led converts to disapprove of community festivals and their rejection of Catholicism entailed a repudiation of the celebration of days of patron saints.[33] But evangelicals developed a selective response to custom. Their selectivity can be illustrated in the involvement of converts with *mutirões*, a constitutive part of the forms of sociability in the Brazilian countryside. A *mutirão* was a collective mobilization of family members and neighbors that involved clearing, working, and planting on the land of a small farmer. The beneficiary usually offered the day's meals to his helpers and threw a party in recognition, becoming morally obliged to help his neighbors in the next *mutirão*.[34] Converts usually took part in these events, supporting *sitiantes* and rural workers in such acts of collective labor. Maria Chaves remembered the occasions when her father and first-generation convert, Manuel de Melo, recruited neighbors,

---

[30] *Imprensa Evangelica*, n. 9, September 1881.

[31] Israel Belo de Azevedo, *A celebração do indivíduo: A formação do pensamento batista brasileiro*, 2nd ed. (São Paulo: Edições Vida Nova, 2004).

[32] José Zacarias de Miranda, *Procrastinação ou o perigo de adiar a salvação* (São Paulo: Typographia a Vapor de Jorge Seckler & C., 1886), 14.

[33] Mendonça, *O celeste porvir*, 225–230.

[34] Antônio Candido, *Os parceiros do Rio Bonito: Estudo sobre o caipira paulista e a transformação dos seus meios de vida*, 11th ed. (Rio de Janeiro: Ouro Sobre Azul, 2010), 81–82.

camaradas (comrades), family members, and hired workers, including former slaves, to help him set up his small farm by the Perdizes River in the countryside of Minas Gerais.[35] What converts could not tolerate were the excessive drinking and violence in the parties that followed.

In this respect, the elder of the Presbyterian Church of Boa Vista do Jacaré, São Paulo, Francisco Lopes Ribeiro, was the embodiment of Protestant rigor. His biographer, the Rev. Herculano de Gouvêa, claimed that Ribeiro was an overzealous, impertinent believer. For him, converts did not need the "*pagodes do século*" (revelries of the world) to amuse their spirits: "Entertainments such as—balls, *cateretês*, horse races and the excesses of *mutirões* soaked in alcohol, greatly horrified Francisco Lopes."[36] Converts did take part in other rural festivities, though. A colleague of Ribeiro in the Presbyterian congregation of Boa Vista do Jacaré, the elder Henrique Gomes, was regarded as a highly respectable and amiable man in his community. One of the indicators of Gomes's social standing were the frequent invitations he received to the "intimate parties" of his neighbors and to village marriages.[37] In the countryside of Minas Gerais, too, converts participated in the wedding ceremonies of their communities and invited non-convert neighbors to those of their family members. As the extended kin of the married couple traveled to the villages where the weddings took place, convert villagers who hosted the visitors believed such occasions of intimate sociability afforded them an opportunity to evangelize their guests.[38]

Whereas the evangelical message of individual conversion severed some of the bonds that kept converts tied to their communities and into networks of co-parenthood, they established new social links within the religious congregations they joined. In churches, believers imagined themselves as members of a common spiritual family, forging relations of kin "in God" and recreating notions of belonging.[39] In the countryside of São Paulo and Minas Gerais, as well as in the northeastern states of Pernambuco and Piauí, extended families joined Protestant congregations together in the nineteenth and early twentieth centuries, which alleviated the individuating

---

[35] Melo Chaves, *Bandeirantes da fé*, 39–46, 76–77.

[36] Herculano de Gouvêa, *Francisco Lopes Ribeiro* (Rio Claro: Typographia Brasil, 1922), 9. The *cateretê* is a folkloric dance in which pairs of men choreograph the rhythm of the music by clapping hands and stomping their feet in specific patterns.

[37] Herculano de Gouvêa, *Notas biographicas de Henrique Gomes de Oliveira*, 2nd ed. (Jaú: Typographia da Casa Mascote, 1911), 9, 13–17.

[38] Melo Chaves, *Bandeirantes da fé*, 53, 72, 172–174.

[39] David Martin, *Tongues of Fire: The Explosion of Protestantism in Latin America* (Oxford: Basil Blackwell, 1990), 203.

implications of religious change.⁴⁰ First-generation converts indeed broke away from networks of patronage and the sponsorship of godfathers, which undermined opportunities of social and material improvement for some. But, in the first decades of the twentieth century, evangelical converts were able to benefit from the expansion of religious bureaucracies in Brazil. The consolidation of Protestant organizations such as schools, seminaries, Bible-training institutes, publishing houses, and bookshops opened opportunities of employment for believers, who under these circumstances recreated clientelist relations with pastors and missionaries.⁴¹

Even the simple, small-scale religious bureaucracies created in the nineteenth century enabled believers to compensate for the loss of a protective social network involved in conversion experiences. Local congregations engaged in fundraising and benefited from the flow of missionary funds, which enabled believers to share in the distribution of missionary resources.⁴² In 1875, congregants of the Presbyterian Church of Palmeiras, São Paulo, purchased a piece of land upon which they expected to build a church, a cemetery, and a house for an impoverished member of the congregation who would serve as the church's custodian.⁴³ Local churches and missionary schools also offered basic instruction to illiterate adults and converts' children. In the 1870s, dozens of parish schools scattered across the countryside of Rio de Janeiro and São Paulo offered elementary education to over two hundred pupils.⁴⁴ Convert parents often sent their children to missionary and parish schools. Maria de Melo Chaves and her sister Marta, for instance, studied at the boarding school of the Presbyterian Church of Araguari and later at the prestigious Evangelical College of Lavras, directed by the American missionary and educator Samuel Gammon, both in Minas Gerais. When Maria and Marta returned to their parents' small farm in Perdizes for holidays in 1917, they were welcomed as religious and educational specialists, who delivered sermons in the local congregation, taught in the parish school, and could count quickly how many days their neighbors and family members had lived so far, to the astonishment of the community.⁴⁵ In their case, the rejection of the established religion and adoption of

---

⁴⁰ Mendonça, *O celeste*, 234; Léonard, *O protestantismo*, 66–67, 105–110.
⁴¹ Ronald Frase, "The Subversion of Missionary Intentions by Cultural Values: The Brazilian Case," *Review of Religious Research* 23 (1981): 180–194.
⁴² For further details on these practices and their meaning, see Chapter 1 of this text.
⁴³ Relação de meus breves trabalhos na pregação do Evangelho desde Agosto do anno pp. até o presente (J. F. Dagama), AHP, Coleção Carvalhosa—Relatórios Pastorais (1866–1875).
⁴⁴ BFM-PCUSA Annual Report, 1878, 24.
⁴⁵ Melo Chaves, *Bandeirantes*, 12–14, 101–102, 107–118.

the Protestant faith did not prevent them from acquiring some social prestige through formal education.

It is important to note, however, that the interest of converts in literacy and the religious community was by no means purely instrumental, an expression of their desire to come to terms with the tools of modernity. By acquiring formal education, believers did not simply expect to harness the power and prestige associated with literacy or the opportunities of social uplift afforded by schooling. Converts longed to approach God through the medium of the written word. They were animated by a desire to enter in a relationship with the Trinity through prayer, worship, and the devoted study of the Bible. They also held an everyday sense of the divine. This is captured in a story written by Maria Chaves. On a certain occasion her father employed a fair share of his savings in a crop of rice, which was followed by a severe drought that threatened to ruin his business. Her anguished and pious mother went to the field and uttered an "ardent prayer." In Maria's narrative, the skies darkened immediately, and a copious rain spared the crop. In a revealing sentence, Maria claimed that "this rain covered such a small area that it seemed to have been sent only for us."[46] Their religion was neither the disenchanted Protestantism of learned elites nor the world of signs and wonders of the Pentecostals. By that time, missionaries, local ministers, and converts viewed expressions of religious enthusiasm and mysticism with suspicion, but they nevertheless believed that divine providence and aid manifested in their daily lives. Converts experienced the divine presence as an everyday reality. Evangelical Christianity addressed the "existential passions" of converts, fulfilling their search for purity and security through community life and worship.[47] In reading the Bible, praying, singing, and attending religious services, believers sought to draw near to their God and to encounter comfort, consolation, and inspiration.

Conversion, Conversation, and Literacy

In their influential study of the encounter of non-conformist British missionaries with the Tswana of southern Africa, the anthropologists Jean and John Comaroff depicted the conversion of the latter to Christianity as

---

[46] Chaves, *Bandeirantes*, 99–100.
[47] I take the expression "existential passions" from Harri Englund and James Leach, "Ethnography and the Meta-narratives of Modernity," *Current Anthropology* 41 (2000): 225–248, at 234.

a "long conversation." The Christian missionaries sought to incorporate the Tswana into the Western language of ethical and cultural universalism extending "the European system of distinction over Africa, drawing its peoples into a single scale of social, spiritual, and material inequality."[48] For the Comaroffs, the Tswana were dragged into the unfamiliar terrain of Western conceptions of modernity, progress, and the self in the process, surrendering to European forms of scientific discourse. Despite the enormous influence of the Comaroffs's compelling account of the religious encounter in southern Africa, historians and anthropologists have contested some of their claims. One of the most conspicuous charges against the Comaroffs is that although they describe the "long conversation" as a dialectical process, Tswana narratives are largely ignored, which obfuscates indigenous agency and fails to account for their creative appropriation of Christian religion.[49]

The anthropologist John Peel has, in contrast, examined religious conversion as the result of actual conversations, lively exchanges between Christian evangelists and their interlocutors. In studies of the encounter of Christian missionaries with the Yoruba of West Africa, Peel has considered the mechanisms that brought about religious change. For him, conversion was above all a process of "impassioned communication" whose outcome, although conditioned by an array of social and religious forces, ultimately emerged out of the interaction between preachers and their publics.[50] Historian David Killingray has referred to similar processes in his studies of the expansion of Christianity in southern Africa. Highlighting the role of local agency in the missionary enterprise, Killingray claimed indigenous evangelists "gossiped the gospel" at the local level.[51] These emphases on the actual interaction between evangelists in mission fields help calibrate scholarly accounts of the worldwide diffusion of Christianity. Although foreign missionaries controlled most of the missionary funds and mediated between their sending agencies and the mission stations, armies of indigenous

---

[48] Jean Comaroff and John Comaroff, *Of Revelation and Revolution: Christianity, Colonialism, and Consciousness in South Africa*, vol. 1 (Chicago: University of Chicago Press, 1991), 198–199, 206–213, 244–245.

[49] See for instance, J. D. Y. Peel, "For Who Hath Despised the Day of Small Things? Missionary Narratives and Historical Anthropology," *Comparative Studies in Society and History* 37 (1995): 581–607; Elizabeth Elbourne, "Word Made Flesh: Christianity, Modernity, and Cultural Colonialism in the Work of Jean and John Comaroff," *American Historical Review* 108 (2003): 435–459.

[50] J. D. Y. Peel, "The Pastor and the *Babalawo*: The Interaction of Religions in Nineteenth-century Yorubaland," *Africa* 60 (1990): 338–369, at 339.

[51] David Killingray, "Passing on the Gospel: Indigenous Mission in Africa," *Transformation* 28 (2011): 93–102, at 95.

evangelists played a key role in expanding religious frontiers through face-to-face interactions and translating Christian religion into local idioms. In a similar way, conversion to Protestantism in Brazil was a process of persuasion, a transformation that emerged out of the interaction between Protestant agents and their (mostly) Catholic interlocutors.

Throughout the *caipira* zone of the countryside of São Paulo and Minas Gerais, as well as in urban settings, the process of religious change evolved amidst traditional forms of sociability. In this rural world, mixed-race small farmers and rural workers, frequently regarded as Brazil's "hillbillies," gathered in the properties of neighbors and family members on occasions of collective labor and leisure.[52] Protestant writers recorded, with a hint of nostalgia, that an informal conversational climate predominated in such gatherings, in which *caipira* men and women exchanged stories and information around the table over meals or by the fire. In 1921, the then-Presbyterian folklorist and writer Cornélio Pires wrote that the "fire was the meeting point, the club" of the *caipiras*.[53] On numerous accounts, conversion processes started around such interactions. The Rev. Eduardo Carlos Pereira wrote a series of tracts in the 1880s exemplifying the ways in which local evangelists preached the beliefs and doctrines of evangelical Christianity to rural families. In these tracts, itinerant preachers traveling across southern Minas Gerais engaged in a close and friendly conversation over dinner with the families who welcomed the evangelists in their huts. A tract titled *Our Father in Heaven* started with a preacher asking to stay overnight at the house of a woman called Amelia, whose grieving countenance set the conversation in motion. Amelia told the evangelist how she fled her parents' house to marry a wealthy but troubled man who abandoned Amelia and their children a few years later. Amelia's parents died sometime later, disheartened by their daughter's disgrace. In the story, the evangelist picked examples from the Lord's Prayer and the parable of the prodigal son instructing Amelia to confess her sins to God alone, instead of confessing to the priest, and to seek the consolation of God directly, not offering prayers and promises to the saints.[54] Another tract portrayed an itinerant evangelist engaging in a friendly conversation with a respectable and hospitable old

---

[52] Cândido, *Os parceiros*, 131–146.
[53] Cornélio Pires, *Conversas ao pé-do-fogo* (Itu: Ottoni Editora, 2002 [1921]), 32. See also Otoniel Mota, *Selvas e choças* (São Paulo: Imprensa Methodista, 1922), 53–65.
[54] Eduardo C. Pereira, *Nosso pae que está nos céos* (São Paulo: Edição da Aliança Evangelica de S. Paulo, 1903 [1886]), 3–5, 10–17.

sitiante who offered the preacher a shelter. Throughout the conversation, the evangelist explained the doctrines of atonement and the sufficiency of grace by drawing examples from a court case. He ended up persuading the old farmer that only the sacrifice of Christ could reconcile men with God, challenging the notion of saintly mediation.[55]

In a similar way, networks of kin and co-parenthood (*compadrio*) facilitated the diffusion of evangelical Christianity throughout the rural interior of São Paulo and Minas Gerais. The aforementioned Henrique Gomes Oliveira, for instance, was first introduced to Protestantism through his "old buddies" (*compadres*) José Castilho and Antonio Francisco de Gouvêa. At first, Henrique refused, in his *caipira* language, to listen to the *regilion* (*regelião*) of his old friends, but he agreed to attend a domestic religious service at Antonio's to "listen to the Word of God." Deeply impressed with the biblical explanations, Henrique went back home and instructed his son to dump their family oratory and images of saints into "the deepest pit" of the Jacaré River. Once a convert, Oliveira helped bring friends, family members, and acquaintances into the evangelical fold.[56] Maria de Melo Chaves wrote that her uncle David Melo was introduced to the Bible by his "old buddy" (*compadre*) José Quirino. Prior to his first encounter with a Protestant missionary, David spent a period reading the Bible in the company of his friend José Dornelas at Dornelas's small farm.[57] Although conversion processes had individuating consequences and liberated men and women from the communal obligations implicated in relations of kin and co-parenthood, religious change started around long-standing forms of sociability, in the domestic intimacy of rural and urban families and through the interaction of family members, neighbors, and friends.

The powers of persuasion and rhetoric were deeply enmeshed in these exchanges. Preaching individual adherence to a new religion involved familiarizing the Catholic interlocutors of Protestant evangelists with a set of religious practices and beliefs with which they were only vaguely acquainted. Missionaries, pastors, and ordinary believers drew images from the natural world and everyday life to anchor tenets and practices of evangelical Christianity into Brazilian culture. For instance, whereas the biblical imagery against idleness deployed the figure of the laborious ant to call people

---

[55] Eduardo C. Pereira, *O unico advogado dos peccadores* (São Paulo: Typographia a Vapor de Jorge Seckler & Comp., 1884).
[56] Gouvêa, *Notas biographicas*, 7–9.
[57] Melo Chaves, *Bandeirantes*, 22–27.

to work, Brazilian missionaries and pastors found a promising correlate in the *joão de barro* (red ovenbird). This bird labored tirelessly to build its oven-shaped clay nest. But another set of moral teachings accompanied the *joão de barro*. The bird was known for its monogamous instincts, forming a lasting bond with its pair, and in the local imagination rested on the seventh day of the week. The *joão de barro* was set as an example of industry, but also of religious observance and stable marital relationship.[58] The world of work and leisure also offered opportunities for evangelical preachers. Maria de Melo Chaves wrote about her encounters with the American missionary Robert Daffin at her parents' *sítio* in Minas Gerais. Daffin's temperament, according to Chaves, was very "pleasing to our *sertanejo* [backlander]." He was a friendly and approachable man, who enjoyed telling anecdotes and tales about his homeland. During a *mutirão*, Daffin seized a gourd with corn seeds and began teaching the parable of the sower while planting the seeds in the furrows, readily captivating the attention of the rural workers around him, some of whom became Protestant converts.[59] These associations with nature and custom helped missionaries and preachers to communicate with their publics more effectively and to locate evangelical religion into the ebb and flow of everyday life.

Print was another important driver of religious change, furnishing missionaries and evangelists with a "vital technology of conversion."[60] Believers depicted their encounter with God as the outcome of their encounter with the word of God. Along with the scriptures, religious tracts and books featured prominently in conversion stories. Conversion narratives themselves were amongst the most circulated genres of evangelical propaganda in nineteenth-century Brazil. They were important devices for the consolidation of religious change. Writing about the self produces a separation between the self as a subject and the self as an object, enabling the writers of spiritual autobiographies to integrate their "memories, experiences, and aspirations in a schema of long-term action."[61] Through narration, believers

---

[58] *Brazil: The Quarterly Record of the "Help for Brazil" Mission*, n. 54, July 1908, 4. See also Otoniel Mota, *A filosofia do joão-de-barro* (São Paulo: Estab. Graphico Cruzeiro do Sul, 1935).

[59] Melo Chaves, *Bandeirantes*, 76.

[60] Christopher Clark and Michael Ledger-Lomas, "The Protestant International," in *Religious Internationals in the Modern World: Globalization and Faith Communities since 1750*, ed. Abigail Green and Vincent Viaene (Basingstoke: Palgrave Macmillan, 2012), 23–52, at 30.

[61] Karin Barber, "Hidden Innovators in Africa," in *Africa's Hidden Histories: Everyday Literacy and Making the Self*, ed. Karin Barber (Bloomington: Indiana University Press, 2006), 8; Peel, "For Who Hath Despised," 581–607, at 587.

made sense of conversion and its implications, weaving their personal stories into a broader providential history. These stories, often narrated in the first person, illustrate the relevance of print matter to conversion processes.

Two texts published in the 1880s are particularly revealing. The first was titled *The Reverend and Evangelical Pastor José Manoel da Conceição*, published in 1884 as a literary supplement of the *Imprensa Evangelica*. This fifty-page tract recorded the trajectory of the former Catholic priest Conceição, the first Brazilian Presbyterian minister, ordained in 1865. The text examined his long process of conversion, his trajectory in the Presbyterian Church of Brazil, and the controversies that surrounded his premature death during the Christmas of 1873. The author of the pamphlet collected and organized a set of texts written by Conceição, the medical reports of his death, and wrote some observations about his career as an evangelical pastor. The former priest described his conversion as a long process that lasted for fourteen years between his first contact with the Bible and his renunciation of the Catholic priesthood. The reading of the scriptures produced some spiritual discomfort: "I was eighteen when I started to read the Bible. I had barely read the first three chapters of the Genesis when I noticed that the practice and doctrine of the Roman Church stood in irreconcilable opposition to the Word of God."[62] In a text published in 1867, Conceição explained that his renunciation of the priesthood was not an impetuous decision taken in the heat of the moment, but that "for years the reading of the Bible, of the history of the Reformation, and of other religious and literary books had provided me ideas that did not harmonize with the dogmas I professed [as a priest]."[63] Conceição wrote that he felt deeply disturbed when he compared the teachings of the Bible with his own life, ministry, and the Catholic traditions of penitence and indulgences. All these beliefs made him an undesirable Catholic minister whose nickname was *padre protestante* (Protestant priest).[64] Indeed, his biographers usually note that he was trained in the reformist tradition of the Jansenists, a Catholic movement that preached the need for an austere personal piety, independence from Rome, and fostered an almost ecumenical conviviality between Protestants and Catholics in Brazil in the first decades of the nineteenth century. Conceição's godfather and seminary tutors introduced him

---

[62] *O Reverendo pastor evangélico José Manoel da Conceição (supplemento aos mezes de janeiro e fevereiro de 1884)* (Rio de Janeiro: Typ. a vapor de Leroy King Bookwalter & Comp, 1884), 4.
[63] *O Reverendo*, 11.
[64] *O Reverendo*, 5, 12–13.

into the Jansenist literature from an early age, which facilitated his conversion to Protestantism.[65] His rupture with Catholicism was prefigured in his long-lasting unease with the Catholic dogmas and the isolated, reflexive reading of the scripture.

The other conversion narrative, published in 1885 as a literary supplement of the *Imprensa Evangelica*, enjoyed great prestige among the missionaries and pastors of the Rio de Janeiro mission station. This highly readable tract was titled *My Conversion: Revelations of a Lady to her Catholic Friend* and was published in the form of a collection of letters sent from a woman named Ausonia to a friend. Little is known about the author, but missionary correspondence informed that Ausonia was an Italian immigrant residing in Rio de Janeiro.[66] In the tract's narrative, Ausonia was first introduced to evangelical ideas through a friend—Mr. M—who, in a domestic gathering, tried to persuade some friends of the illegitimacy of the veneration of images. He declared emphatically that the "Roman Church and the Christian Church are divorced for ever!"[67] After a couple of additional conversations between the two characters, Ausonia felt deeply uneasy. M lent her a copy of the Figueiredo version of the Bible, an eighteenth-century translation from the Vulgate, and another book titled *History of the Popes*. Ausonia spent a week eagerly reading these books, along with a dictionary, and wrote to the addressee of her letters: "If you could make an idea of the terrible trances I went through, the perplexity, the anguish in which I lived during that week! I viewed all my beliefs profaned by myself, rolling in the dust as the petals of a withered flower, and I insisted in keeping my eyes opened to witness their fall."[68] As Ausonia read this material, she became convinced of the "errors of Romanism" and learned how several Catholic customs, such as the sign of the cross and the clerical celibacy, had been instituted by the medieval Church, not the Bible or the apostles.[69] On the following Sunday, Ausonia attended mass in Rio de Janeiro and felt repugnance for the symbols and practices she had previously cherished.[70] Upon arriving back home, she

---

[65] Boanerges Ribeiro, *José Manoel da Conceição e a reforma evangélica* (São Paulo: Livraria O Semeador, 1995), 12–20. On Brazilian Jansenism, see David Gueiros Vieira, *O protestantismo, a maçonaria e a Questão Religiosa no Brasil* (Brasília: Editora UnB, 1980), 29–32.
[66] BFM-PCUSA Annual Report [1885], 48.
[67] *A minha conversão: Revelações de uma senhora à sua amiga catholica* (Rio de Janeiro: Typographia Universal de Laemmert, 1885), 6–8; 13–20.
[68] *A minha*, 29.
[69] *A minha*, 30–35.
[70] *A minha*, 53–55.

gathered her religious icons and statues, opened her Figueiredo Bible, read several texts of the Pentateuch condemning the worship of sculptures, and burned her images.[71]

In both narratives, the long process of the protagonist's rupture with Catholicism and conversion to evangelical Christianity was the result of their individual and isolated reading of the Bible and religious books. The attentive and careful examination of written texts was viewed as powerful enough to initiate processes of religious change and transform the consciousness of the individual. In the Brazilian context, missionaries and pastors linked processes of conversion and religious change to reading and writing, conceiving evangelical literature and the Bible as powerful technologies that gave rise to new individual subjectivities. The unmediated and reflexive interactions of the individual with the printed word were considered tools of self-improvement.

The Reformation of Manners and Morals

The process of religious change encompassed a set of moral norms and behavioral codes that characterized the Protestant persona. Some of the embodiments of the evangelical self were related to deportment, dress, and language, and they played a key role in shaping evangelical identities. The Presbyterian folklorist, comedian, and writer Cornélio Pires illustrated the behavioral demands implicated in conversion experiences with an anecdote. During a preaching tour through the interior of São Paulo, a pastor named Odilon spent a week in a certain town. Odilon quickly noticed the close interest of a *caipira* in his sermons: the man attended several meetings and asked for additional explanations after services. Believing this was heading toward a conversion, the pastor asked whether the *caipira* wanted to make his profession of faith, to which he replied: "Why, reverend... to be quit'honest, for t'while, no. Let's leave it for the end of t'year... I still have some naughty stuff [*safadage*] to do in t'meantime and wanna enjoy 'em."[72] The *caipira* was fully aware that professing the new faith entailed leaving his shenanigans and sexual adventures behind.

The reformation of morals and manners was at the very heart of the conversionist message of evangelical missionaries in Brazil. It demarcated

---

[71] *A minha*, 55–56.
[72] Cornélio Pires, *Patacoadas* (Itu: Ottoni Editora, 2002 [1927]), 34–35.

their respectable status. Personal cleanliness, neat dress, a moderate language, and a methodical organization of life were the visible signs of religious change and paths to self-improvement and social mobility. A healthy body, an alert mind, and a sincere heart were closely connected in the modern evangelical notion of personhood.[73] The Scottish missionary Sarah Kalley, one of the most active evangelical hymn-writers in the Lusophone world, captured this notion in *The Joy of the House*, first published in Brazil in 1866. This volume taught generations of Brazilian and Portuguese Protestant women that a neat and methodical organization of the house were entwined with an inner transformation of the spirit and helped convert women to channel their intellectual abilities. Stressing the importance of having a clean and well-organized kitchen to avoid waste of time, Kalley wrote: "It is not, perhaps, out of the purpose to remind you, my ladies, that the *habit of exterior order* greatly helps us in acquiring habits of order in the regulation of our ideas, thoughts, and intellectual customs." And Kalley closed the advice reminding her readers what came first in the arrangement of spiritual life: "*Seek first* the kingdom of God and his righteousness."[74] The outer shell of the individual and its inner, spiritual, and intellectual core were closely connected in the evangelical conception of personhood.

In some manifestations, the evangelical reformation of mores was expressed through a set of behavioral prohibitions and counsels. Converts were instructed to refrain from alcohol, tobacco, and gambling; to keep an orderly organization of their houses; to dress modestly; to be zealously dedicated to their work; and to keep the Sabbath, usually the Sunday. These sets of behavioral instructions can be seen clearly in the "rules of conduct" written by the founder of the evangelical congregation of Perdizes, Minas Gerais, Manuel de Melo. Manuel was an archetypical *caipira* convert: a man of unsophisticated manners and ungrammatical language whose "zeal towards the sacred things" bespoke of his religious sincerity amidst his rusticity.[75] Manuel's rules of conduct contained a set of general prohibitions against lying, idleness, and fanaticism, including some specific warnings against bearing arms or sleeping during religious services. One of the rules read: "The believer must have his house well cleaned, even if it is a hut.

---

[73] Comaroff and Comaroff, *Of Revelation*, 60–63.
[74] Sarah P. Kalley, *A alegria da casa ou Raios de luz sobre a vida familiar* (Lisbon: Tipografia Eduardo Rosa, 1916 [Rio de Janeiro, 1866]), 10–11. Italics in the original.
[75] Chaves, *Bandeirantes*, 191.

He himself must walk around clean, even though his clothes may be very humble, because Jesus loves poverty but condemns laziness."[76]

Local churches carefully guarded their own set of doctrinal boundaries and behavioral demands. Pastors and church leaders enforced these moral codes at the local level. Presbyterian and Congregationalist pastors, for instance, closely observed the customs of the men and women who wished to join their flocks, evaluating the sincerity of their conversion. For instance, the Scottish medical-missionary Robert Kalley, founder of the Congregationalist Church of Rio de Janeiro, had a troubled correspondence with another doctor, Emilio Castro, who wanted to join the church and become a pastor. Upon observing Castro's conduct, Kalley wrote to the man informing him that he would not be welcomed at the Congregationalist Church, even less appointed as an evangelical pastor, because Kalley had not seen the signs of a sincere conversion in Castro, the "fruits of the Spirit." Instead, he had viewed "too much vanity and pride along with other things that are not the fruits of the Spirit, but of corruption."[77] In the late 1880s, the Presbyterian Church of Faxina in the countryside of São Paulo suspended the membership of two congregants who engaged in extra-marital affairs and violated the Sabbath by working on Sundays.[78] In his first year as pastor of the Presbyterian Church of Bahia the American missionary, Alexander Blackford dismissed his colporteur for drunkenness, suspended the membership of three believers for "living an impure life," and three others for openly violating the Sabbath.[79] However, small farmers and merchants obtained a significant part of their sustenance trading in city markets on Sundays, the busiest and most profitable day of the week. For these people, conversion came at a higher personal cost.

But the external markers of conversion did not come only through moral prohibitions. There were assertive ways of embodying and enacting the new faith. Dress and body language were closely enmeshed in conversion processes and the making of the evangelical persona. This imagery abounds in Frederick Glass's stories about the rural interior of southeastern and central Brazil. Although some of his narratives are clearly exaggerated, they exhibit a before-and-after pattern, depicting the converts' life prior to their encounter

---

[76] Chaves, *Bandeirantes*, 191.
[77] R. R. Kalley to E. Castro, Petrópolis, January 25, 1876. BFB-IEF, Correspondência Dr. Kalley.
[78] Mendonça, *O celeste porvir*, 225–226.
[79] A. L. Blackford to D. Irving, Bahia, May 6, 1881. PHS, BFM-PCUSA, Mission Correspondence, South American Letters.

with the Bible as tainted with religious superstitions and personal vices, especially drinking, smoking, and gambling, followed by conversion and self-improvement. One of the stories that encapsulate this pattern is the conversion of Maria, who was an old woman in Goiás. Glass described her house as a "veritable den of evil": a place completely covered with relics, crucifixes, and rosaries, where chickens moved around with liberty. Maria was addicted to *cachaça* (distilled sugarcane spirit) and tobacco.[80] After preaching and exchanging a Bible with the elderly woman, Glass did not believe it would have any impact on her. But to his surprise the ninety-year-old woman converted: "it came about very slowly, and nobody was more surprised than myself when I saw her at a meeting one night, and with a decent, clean dress on, too. She abandoned her rum and tobacco in a very short time, cleared all her idols from her walls, and relegated the chickens to the back-yard."[81] It is telling that the first element that caught Glass's attention and pointed to Maria's conversion was her orderly attire. Itinerant Bible-sellers like Glass were similarly expected to express their respectable selves through neat and tidy dress. In 1874, the agent of the British and Foreign Bible Society based in Rio de Janeiro, José Martin de Carvalho, asked the organization to update its workers' salaries. In Carvalho's words, colporteurs earned as much as any other laborers, such as artisans and shoemakers, but unlike these, who could work "at home with old clothes," the Bible vendors were required to look neat and clean "in order not to be censured."[82]

Such Protestant prescriptions related to body language and dress, along with its array of behavioral codes, set converts apart from the forms of sociability associated with the urban and rural working classes. Prohibitions against alcohol and gambling drew converts away from socialization in bars and clubs.[83] In the countryside, these behavioral pressures detached believers from the large parties and festivals of saints' days, which furnished occasions of excessive drinking and violence across *caipira* rural communities.[84] First-generation converts expressed their disgust at such festivals with

---

[80] Frederick C. Glass, *With the Bible in Brazil: Being the Story of a Few of the Marvellous Incidents Arising From Its Circulation There* (London: Morgan & Scott LD., 1914), 118–119.

[81] Glass, *With the Bible*, 120.

[82] J. M. de Carvalho to Rev. S. B. Bergne, Rio de Janeiro, March 3, 1874. *Report of Bible Distribution in Brazil for the Year Ending 31st December 1873*. BSA, BSA/D1/7-144 (Agents Book nº 144, South America).

[83] On working class sociability, see Sidney Chalhoub, *Trabalho, lar e botequim: O cotidiano dos trabalhadores do Rio de Janeiro na belle époque*, 3rd ed. (Campinas: Editora Unicamp, 2012).

[84] Candido, *Os parceiros*, 155; Carvalho Franco, *Homens livres*; Mendonça, *O celeste*, 227–228.

strong words, even deploying racialized stereotypes to bemoan the "blackened Carnival."[85] But evangelical claims of modesty and moderation were also at odds with the customs of the salons and clubs of the urban elites.[86] Evangelical writers and church leaders warned believers against conspicuous consumption, claiming it was inappropriate for believers to spend their wages on luxurious clothes and extravagant lifestyles. In their view, this expressed a misleading, even sinful ambition to conforming to worldly values and social practices.[87]

Scholars have too easily dismissed the evangelical reformation of manners as indicators of moral conservatism and individualism. The zealous religious piety, observance of behavioral sanctions, and concern with personal salvation of converts were viewed as symptoms of their lack of a broader social ethic that legitimized existing social and political formations.[88] But these facile assumptions are misleading. In the late nineteenth and early twentieth centuries, intellectual and political elites held the mixed-race populations of the Brazilian backlands in contempt. Pseudo-scientific racial theories and popular literary works depicted the *sertanejos* of the northeast and the *caipiras* of the center-south as degenerate populations, constituting a stumbling stone on Brazil's road to progress. The more fatalistic indictments claimed there was no space in the modern world for these social categories, which were doomed to disappear.[89] In the face of such stereotypes, *caipira* converts sought to demonstrate that they were both able and eager to harness the means of improvement available as a way of expressing their self-reliance and respectability. Their behavioral norms; strict body language; claims to honesty, honor, and industry; and search for formal education expressed a broader desire for self-improvement and recognition against the antipathy of the educated elites.

---

[85] Gouvêa, *Francisco Lopes*, 9–10.

[86] On urban elite culture, see Jeffrey Needell, *A Tropical Belle Époque: Elite Culture and Society in Turn-of-the-century Rio de Janeiro* (Cambridge: Cambridge University Press, 1987).

[87] Sarah P. Kalley, *A alegria da casa ou raios de luz sobre a vida familiar* (Lisbon: Tipografia Eduardo Rosa, 1916 [Rio de Janeiro, 1866]), 48–52.

[88] Pablo A. Deiros, "Protestant Fundamentalism in Latin America," in *Fundamentalisms Observed*, ed. Martin E. Marty and R. Scott Appleby (Chicago: University of Chicago Press, 1991), 142–196, at 151–152, 171–173; Rubem Alves, *Protestantism and Repression: A Brazilian Case Study*, trans. John Drury (London: SCM Press, 1985), 152–170; Prócoro Velasques Filho, "'Sim' a Deus e 'não' à vida: Conversão e disciplina no protestantismo brasileiro," in *Introdução ao protestantismo no Brasil*, ed. Antonio Gouvêa Mendonça and Prócoro Velasques Filho (São Paulo: Edições Loyola, 1990), 205–232.

[89] Lilia Moritz Schwarcz, *The Spectacle of the Races: Scientists, Institutions, and the Race Question in Brazil, 1870–1930*, trans. Leland Guyer (New York: Hill and Wang, 1999); Dain Borges, "'Puffy, Ugly, Slothful and Inert": Degeneration in Brazilian Social Thought, 1880–1940," *Journal of Latin American Studies* 25 (1993), 235–256.

The behavioral transformations Protestant notions of personhood brought about were not solely confined to the individual. Family configurations and notions of community life, too, received the impact of religious change. Research on Christianity in Latin America and Africa has shown how the evangelical emphasis on monogamy, marital fidelity, and family harmony, along with its prohibitions on alcohol and gambling "domesticate men" by reforming the aggressive male psyche.[90] Emilio Willems's research amongst evangelical communities in twentieth-century Brazil has encountered similar dynamics. Gendered notions of masculinity and femininity, as well as ideals of familial harmony, were reshaped amongst Protestant communities in the Brazilian interior. The Protestant defense of sexual purity undermined the indulgence of male infidelity, regarded as a marker of manhood. In congregations, spouses denounced the sexual misbehavior of their husbands to ecclesiastical authorities, sometimes motivating the suspension and excommunication of male church members. For Willems, the behavioral sanctions of the Protestant ethic validated more egalitarian family structures in Brazilian society.[91]

For the first generations of evangelical converts, these changes in gender roles and family structure manifested themselves in specific ways. Missionaries and local pastors condemned what the Presbyterian Rev. Erasmo Braga called the double standards of sexual morality, which viewed adultery as necessary to the constitution of the male self, while castigating female adultery. Braga claimed that one of the greatest contributions of evangelical religion to the moral life of Latin America was the "unification of the moral standards for the two sexes."[92] Foreign missionaries and local evangelists stressed the virtues of domesticity. The Christian household aptly captured the reformation of the self: it was a neat and hierarchical space, characterized by order, cleanliness, and hygiene, where husbands and wives engaged in a respectful relationship with their offspring by taking on different responsibilities in child-rearing, and where literacy and Christian virtues were cultivated through Bible study and the domestic

---

[90] Martin, *Tongues*, 181–184, 197–202; Elizabeth Brusco, *The Reformation of Machismo: Evangelical Conversion and Gender in Colombia* (Austin: University of Texas Press, 1995); David Maxwell, "Historicizing Christian Independency: The Southern African Pentecostal Movement, c. 1908–60," *Journal of African History* 40 (1999): 243–264, at 246.

[91] Emilio Willems, *Followers of the New Faith: Culture Change and the Rise of Protestantism in Brazil and Chile* (Nashville, TN: Vanderbilt University Press, 1967), 169–173.

[92] Erasmo Braga, *Pan-Americanismo: Aspecto religioso* (New York: Sociedade de Preparo Missionário, 1916), 55.

worship.[93] Protestants also romanticized a specific representation of the honored and respectful *caipira* man, who engaged in an equitable relation with his family as a remedy to the hardened manners of *caipiras*, who treated their children harshly and overburdened their wives with domestic chores.[94]

It is important to note, however, that notions of individual improvement, personal purification, and rupture with established traditions were not uniquely propagated by Protestants. Catholic priests and missionaries were equally concerned with the customs and habits of believers. Vincentian priests from Italy, Belgium, and France rode the Brazilian interior in search of a lost flock combating the vices of gambling and drinking, and exposing larger publics to the sacraments of the Church.[95] Catholic brotherhoods played an important role in revitalizing the Church in the last decades of the Empire by bringing the laity into the fold and engaging ordinary Catholics in the reconstruction of an institution in need of resources.[96] In a process reminiscent of the early modern European religious reformations, in which religious reformers attempted to eliminate ungodly cultural customs and disseminate the virtues of sobriety and decency,[97] Catholics priests and evangelical missionaries aimed to reform popular culture and extirpate popular vices.

Generation Change and the Evangelical Imagination

The rhythms and outcomes of religious change played an important part in shaping the imagination of Brazilian evangelicals. For the first generation of local converts and foreign missionaries, the evangelistic endeavors of Protestant preachers seemed to mirror the experience of the early Christian church. The laws of the Brazilian empire confined non-Catholic

---

[93] Sarah P. Kalley, *O casamento e a vida domestica: seus deveres e suas provas de alegria*, 2nd ed. (Lisbon: Typ. e Lith. de Adolpho Modesto & Cª, 1887). On Protestant missionary conceptions of domesticity, see Dana Robert, "The 'Christian Home' as a Cornerstone of Anglo-American Missionary Thought and Practice," in *Converting Colonialism: Visions and Realities in Mission History, 1706–1914*, ed. Dana Robert (Grand Rapids, MI: William B. Eerdmans Publishing Co., 2008), 134–165.

[94] Mota, *Selvas*, 111–127.

[95] Kenneth Serbin, *Needs of the Heart: A Social and Cultural History of Brazil's Clergy and Seminaries* (Notre Dame, IN: University of Notre Dame Press, 2006), 70–72.

[96] Ralph Della Cava, "Brazilian Messianism and National Institutions: A Reappraisal of Canudos and Joaseiro," *Hispanic American Historical Review* 48 (1968): 402–420.

[97] Peter Burke, *Popular Culture in Early Modern Europe*, 3rd ed. (Farnham: Ashgate, 2009), 289–300.

religious services to private houses of worship. Before the opening of the first Protestant church buildings in the growing cities of Rio de Janeiro and São Paulo, the vast majority of local congregations spread across the Brazilian center-south, gathered in the houses or *sítios* of believers.[98] For missionaries, pastors, and converts, it was as if their generation was re-living the experiences of the Christian church in the apostolic age, when the first religious communities also met in houses. In sermons and historical accounts, missionaries and pastors drew parallels between the expansion of evangelical Christianity in modern Brazil and the histories described in the biblical book of the Acts of the Apostles.[99] Moreover, in synod and presbytery meetings, unschooled *caipira* converts, like Henrique Gomes, gathered with foreign missionaries and the seminary-trained Protestant elites to deliberate on ecclesiastical matters. Such occasions fostered the idea that these men were re-enacting the egalitarian experiences of the early Christian church as active and committed members of a common religious fraternity.[100]

These metaphors and associations with the apostolic age energized the religious zeal of evangelical converts. They disdained the modern devotions to Mary and the saints and the local reverberations of the ecclesiastical reforms of the First Vatican Council.[101] But besides this, Protestant converts also held heterodox religious ideas in contempt. Historian Stuart Schwartz has shown that a broader culture of religious dissidence that conceived the possibility of universal salvation outside the limits of Catholic dogma circulated widely in the early modern Iberian Peninsula and the American colonies. The proposition that "each one can be saved in his own law" encapsulated these attitudes of religious relativism and tolerance, encouraging Christians, Jews, and Muslims to remain faithful to the religion in which they were raised.[102] On the one hand, these long held cultural traditions laid the groundwork for the diffusion of Protestantism. For some, these attitudes of lenience may have softened the shock of conversion. When Manuel de Melo decided to break

---

[98] Léonard, *O protestantismo*, 90–104.

[99] Antonio Trajano, *Quadragesimo anniversario da Egreja Evangelica Presbyteriana do Rio de Janeiro, 1862–1902* (Rio de Janeiro: Casa Editora Presbyteriana, 1902), 1–5; Alexander Blackford, "Cultos e casas de culto," in *O pulpito evangelico: Volume primeiro, 1874* (Rio de Janeiro: Livraria Evangelica, 1874), 4–17.

[100] Vicente Themudo Lessa, *Annaes da 1ª Egreja Presbyteriana de São Paulo (1863–1903): Subsidios para a historia do presbiterianismo brasileiro* (São Paulo: Edição da 1ª Igreja Presbiteriana Independente de São Paulo, 1938), 176–177, 199–200, 235–237.

[101] Protestant criticism to Catholic devotions and cults were examined in the previous chapter of this text.

[102] Stuart Schwartz, *All Can Be Saved: Religious Tolerance and Salvation in the Iberian Atlantic World* (New Haven, CT: Yale University Press, 2008).

with the Catholic Church, some of his family members mobilized a religious campaign aimed at bringing him back to the fold. One of his uncles, however, refused to join the campaign saying: "I don't want [Manuel's] religion for me, but if he thinks this is good for him, may he follow it and be happy."[103] In the countryside, evangelical Christianity was regarded as another "law" and local religious leaders as its main bearers. According to the Portuguese Presbyterian minister Modesto P. Carvalhosa, the congregation of Pouso Alegre, southern Minas Gerais, was referred to by the village's inhabitants in the early 1870s as "the law of Antonio Joaquim," who was the church's "patriarch" and in whose house the congregation gathered.[104] On the other hand, Protestants disapproved of religious relativism. They broke with Catholic faith and practice with a rigor and sense of urgency that left little room for compromise. In Ausonia's conversion story, her friend M expressed this zeal during an informal conversation:

> You gentlemen are saying that men should remain faithful to the religion in which they were raised, be it Muslim or Greek, Protestant or Catholic ... That it suffices to follow the religion of our parents. I am sorry ... this is wrong! or then you would believe that intelligence and free-will are not only useless gifts, but also impossible to attain. You add that the truth is difficult to find and that it belongs to God only. All right! why don't you study the Sacred Scriptures, which are God's word and, consequently, the truth?

M added that only in the "gospel in its primitive purity" could his friends find the way to God and salvation.[105] For converts, ministers, and missionaries, the only valid law was "the *old law* of the Holy Scripture, the religion of Christ in its purity and simplicity."[106] Long held attitudes of religious relativism and conceptions of universal salvation were at odds with the conversionist ethos of evangelicals.

We have seen the religious and social formations entailed by the rupture of first-generation evangelicals against the "religion of their parents." Conversion isolated believers from established networks of patronage and extended kin, but their participation in the institutional frameworks

---

[103] Chaves, *Bandeirantes*, 57.
[104] *Thirty-Fifth Annual Report of the Board of Foreign Missions of the Presbyterian Church of the United States* (New York: Mission House, 1872), 32; Themudo Lessa, *Annaes*, 36, 70.
[105] *A minha*, pp. 6, 8–9.
[106] Eduardo C. Pereira, *Trabalho e economia ou A fidelidade de Deus manifestada na vida de um discipulo* (São Paulo: Typographia a Vapor de Jorge Seckler & Comp., 1885), 11.

of churches and denominations socialized them again in a new religious community. The moral and behavioral demands implicated in conversion experiences drew them away from socialization in bars, religious festivals, and elite clubs, with important consequences for class formation. Their offspring, however, did not experience conversion as a rupture and were able to benefit from the institutional apparatus of mission societies and churches.

Some of these second-generation believers became increasingly detached from the social and cultural world of their parents. The majority of the earliest *caipira* converts mentioned above, including Manuel de Melo, Henrique Gomes, and Francisco Lopes, were unschooled believers who, up until the end of their lives, struggled to read the Bible and relied on friends and family members for religious instruction.[107] Their biographers recorded how they continued to use regional slangs and to speak ungrammatical *caipira* variations of the Portuguese language.[108] Their children, however, acquired formal instruction in parish and mission schools from an early age. Maria de Melo Chaves, daughter of Manuel de Melo, studied first at the boarding school of the Independent Presbyterian School in Araguari and later at the Gammon Institute in Lavras, both in Minas Gerais.[109] Erasmo Braga, the son of the Portuguese shoemaker turned evangelical minister João de Carvalho Braga, began his studies at a parish school in Rio Claro before enrolling at the American School of São Paulo.[110] Herculano de Gouvêa's trajectory was similar. A son of Severino de Gouvêa, an early leader and elder at the Presbyterian Church of Brotas, Herculano began his studies at the same parish school and was sent to the same American School.[111] Through the acquisition of formal education, they gradually adopted the formal rules of Portuguese language. Maria Chaves even mentioned the specific moments in which she slipped back into *caipira* Portuguese on occasions of astonishment.[112]

Once again, the Presbyterian folklorist and comedian Cornélio Pires captured the cultural estrangement prompted by the acquisition of formal education with an anecdote. In the story, two *caipira* infants, Durvalino and Maria, grew up together in the countryside and fell in love with one another.

---

[107] Chaves, *Bandeirantes*, 53, 116–117; Gouvêa, *Notas biographicas*, 10–11; Gouvêa, *Francisco*, 8–9.
[108] Most notably, Gouvêa, *Notas biographicas*, 13–17.
[109] Chaves, *Bandeirantes*, 100–105, 107–113.
[110] Paul Pierson, *A Younger Church in Search of Maturity: Presbyterianism in Brazil from 1910 to 1959* (San Antonio, TX: Trinity University Press, 1974), 153.
[111] Themudo Lessa, *Annaes*, 363.
[112] Chaves, *Bandeirantes*, 163.

When Maria's parents sent the girl to an elementary school in São Paulo, the boy was left disheartened. Durvalino paid a visit to his girlfriend two years later and upon arriving at the school he encountered a different, elegant girl. Maria greeted Durvalino politely:

- Oh... What a surprise! How are you doing, Durvalino? And how is the family?
- Ya look so dif'rent! Was all the astonished *caipira* was able to say, eyes wide open, shocked.
- Did you come for a tour?
- Well... Marica... lady... I brought ya some fruit...

At the end of the awkward conversation, the ashamed *caipira* bade farewell and said to himself: "Goddamn school."[113] As in the anecdote, formal schooling opened a rift between the first rural converts and their increasingly educated, cosmopolitan children.

The educational mobility of this generation fed into geographical and social mobility. Upon graduating from the Presbyterian school of Lavras, Maria Chaves served as a schoolteacher in different cities across the state of Minas Gerais, including Perdizes, Doradoquara, Patrocínio, and Patos.[114] Herculano de Gouvêa and Erasmo Braga became Presbyterian ministers, which led them to various places. Herculano pastored congregations in the cities of Itatiba, Rio Claro, Brotas, Campinas, and Araraquara, all in the state of São Paulo.[115] Braga's career as a minister and professor took him further away. His first pastoral post was in Niterói, near Rio de Janeiro, but he soon moved on and taught at different Protestant schools and seminaries in São Paulo, Campinas, and Rio de Janeiro, also undertaking international trips to Panama, the United States, Europe, and Palestine.[116] Acting as teachers and ministers, second-generation evangelicals found opportunities of employment and stable remuneration in the growing cities of the Brazilian center south. By acquiring formal education and undergoing physical dislocation, they became further detached from the social and cultural background of their parents.

---

[113] Cornélio Pires, *Conversas ao pé-do-fogo* (Itu: Ottoni Editora, 2002 [1921]), 59.
[114] Chaves, *Bandeirantes*, passim.
[115] Themudo Lessa, *Annaes*, 363.
[116] Erasmo Braga, *Religião e cultura* (São Paulo: União Cultural Editora, n/d), 9–12.

Alienation became a source of nostalgia. Removed from their geographical and cultural origins, Protestants set out to idealize the virtues, bravery, and strength of the first rural converts. The Rev. Herculano de Gouvêa depicted early *caipira* believers, such as Henrique Gomes and Francisco Lopes, as pure, unpolished gems: men of little instruction and rough manners whose piety, rectitude, and sincerity demonstrated their moral reputation.[117] In a similar way, Maria de Melo Chaves romanticized the rural congregation founded by her father and her uncle in the countryside of Minas Gerais and portrayed this first generation of believers as humble but honored, who preached the evangelical message "in a rough language, though anointed by the Holy Spirit."[118] The idealization of rural converts, however, extrapolated religious boundaries and was extended to all *caipiras*. Opposing representations of the *sertanejos* (backlanders) as backward, Chaves wrote:

> The man of the backlands is ... quick, dedicated, and smart. ... If our scholars, rulers, and politicians had lived there where the *caboclo* lives, experiencing the limitations of the environment, the lack of instruction, without assistance of any kind, neither material nor spiritual, completely abandoned, yes, if the great men who are surrounded by fame and name in the high administrative posts and in higher social spheres had experienced the same suffering, the same environment, and had the lack of instruction of the *caboclo*, would they be, by any chance, better than the *sertanejo*? I doubt it. On the moral and spiritual level we can scarcely compare the *sertanejo* to the townsfolk. Apart from a few exceptions the peasant cultivates a respect for his commitments, is punctual, does not take up responsibilities beyond those he can accomplish, respects his family, and holds the social moral in high esteem.[119]

Turning social hierarchies upside down, Maria Chaves portrayed the *caipiras* as valuable counterpoints to the corrupted vices of urban elites. It was their isolation and lack of education that toughened their manners. For her, education, disciplined labor, and conversion were key drivers of self and social improvement.[120] Chaves also stressed the authenticity of her family's

---

[117] Gouvêa, *Notas biographicas*, 4, 10–11; Gouvêa, *Francisco*, 8–9.
[118] Chaves, *Bandeirantes*, 26, 86.
[119] Chaves, *Bandeirantes*, 122.
[120] Chaves, *Bandeirantes*, 13–14, 99–106.

rural congregation, whose bamboo pews and roof thatched with babassu leaves attested to the rusticity and originality of the church.[121]

Along with this romanticization of the populations of the backlands ran a broader impetus to recover the image of the *bandeirantes*. These seventeenth-century prospectors, pathfinders, and slavers of mixed Portuguese and Amerindian descent were unlikely candidates to stand as a myth of origin in Brazil. They were depicted in early modern accounts as vulgar and self-interested characters, whose profitable and violent slaving expeditions against indigenous populations put them in conflict with Jesuit missionaries.[122] But in the late nineteenth and early twentieth centuries, with the economic and demographic boom experienced by the state of São Paulo, *paulista* folklorists, historians, and writers recast the *bandeirantes* in a new light, depicting them as heroic pioneer entrepreneurs.[123]

Evangelicals engaged with and modified this regionalist tradition. For them, the foreign missionaries and local evangelists who traveled across the countryside on the backs of mules and horses tending to remote congregations and evangelizing far off communities bore some resemblance to the path-finding expeditions of the *bandeirantes*. Maria Chaves referred to American missionaries, Brazilian pastors, and local converts as "*bandeirantes* of the Christian faith" who "leaving the comfort and welfare of the civilized centers ... , threaded their way through the jungles, crossed the fields in search of souls for the Savior, undertaking all those losses for the love of Jesus Christ!"[124] Indeed, echoing regionalist motifs, she projected the evangelical values of honesty, thrift, and deportment into the *bandeirante* past, portraying the earliest generations of *caipira* converts in western Minas Gerais as descendants of the *bandeirantes*.[125] In this regard, Protestant responses to erudite representations of popular culture and the national past projected by the national intelligentsia differed significantly from those of Pentecostals worldwide. Whereas Pentecostals in Latin America

---

[121] Chaves, *Bandeirantes*, 188.

[122] John Monteiro, *Blacks of the Land: Indian Slavery, Settler Society, and the Portuguese Colonial Enterprise in South America*, trans. James Woodard and Barbara Weinstein (New York: Cambridge University Press, 2018 [1994]), ch. 2; Richard Morse, *The Bandeirantes: The Historical Role of the Brazilian Pathfinders* (New York: Alfred A. Knopf, 1965).

[123] Mônica Pimenta Velloso, *A brasilidade verde-amarela: Nacionalismo e regionalismo paulista* (Rio de Janeiro: CPDOC, 1990); Barbara Weinstein, *The Color of Modernity: São Paulo and the Making of Race and Nation in Brazil* (Durham, NC: Duke University Press, 2015), ch. 1.

[124] Chaves, *Bandeirantes*, 27–28.

[125] Chaves, *Bandeirantes*, 26, 88–89, and passim; Velloso, *A brasilidade*, 15. The evangelical idealization of *caipiras* and *bandeirantes* will be resumed in Chapter 6 of this text.

and Africa have shown an inclination to reject cultural policies aimed at restoring national pride and the historical rootedness of popular culture,[126] the protagonists of this chapter positively embraced and modified cultural and historical representations emerging from the national intelligentsia, channeling such representations into idealized depictions of Protestant evangelists.

Conclusion

This chapter has examined the complex and ambiguous religious, social, and cultural dynamics implicated in processes of religious change in Brazil. For believers, conversion was conceptualized as the recovery of the spiritual energy, evangelistic zeal, and steadfast religious commitment of the early Christian church. The radical turn that gives the concept of conversion its meaning was experienced as a return to age-old religion. Converts indeed imagined their religious communities and missionary efforts as tributaries and continuators of the work of the apostles. Interestingly, these attempts to recover purer forms of spiritual and doctrinal inspiration are usually the sites of profound religious innovations, producing new syntheses of old and new. Whereas the Protestant repudiation of social and spiritual mediators led converts to break away from systems of co-parenthood, evangelical religion spread along networks of kin and neighborhood, usually through the evangelistic efforts of convert *compadres*. Even though conversion was closely linked to changing forms of sociality and introduced converts into new social and institutional settings, religious change was carried out amidst established forms of socialization, through informal conversations in the domestic intimacy of rural and urban families. First-generation believers displayed a fairly radical iconoclastic impulse, seeking spiritual cleansing through the repudiation of images of saints, relics, rosaries, and the Marian devotions. At the same time, they engaged closely with local imagery and idioms, locating the values and practices of evangelical religion into multiple historical, natural, and linguistic landscapes. Converts maintained an ambiguous relation with long established heterodox ideas of universal salvation, building upon

---

[126] David Lehman, *Struggle for the Spirit: Religious Transformation and Popular Culture in Brazil and Latin America* (Cambridge: Polity Press, 1996), 168; Birgit Meyer, "'Make a Complete Break with the Past': Memory and Post-colonial Modernity in Ghanaian Pentecostalist Discourse," *The Journal of Religion in Africa* 28 (1998): 316–349.

widespread attitudes of religious toleration while simultaneously rejecting the idea that all could be saved in their own "law."

All these religious and cultural ambiguities involved in processes of conversion enabled evangelical religion to take local color and move again through the agency of ordinary believers. Religious change took different forms as religious communities and institutions developed and consolidated, enabling believers to slowly ascend through the social ladder. At the same time, evangelicals developed a variegated repertoire of forms of rupture and reconciliation with established customs and cultural traditions that enabled evangelical religion to create local roots while also becoming a powerful force for religious, social, and cultural change.

5
The Idea of Christian Cooperation

In April 1916, Brazil's largest periodical, *Jornal do Commercio*, published amongst news of the First World War and of the Pan-American Financial Conference of Buenos Aires, a long report on the Congress on Christian Work in Latin America, gathered in Panama City in February. The periodical's owner and editor was the influential journalist José Carlos Rodrigues, a Protestant convert involved with evangelical organizations in Brazil, such as the Young Men's Christian Association (YMCA) and the American Bible Society (ABS). The report highlighted some of the goals of the Panama Congress. Its central tasks were to examine the religious, social, economic, and educational situation of Latin America and strengthen the ties of cooperation between the missionary organizations operating in the continent. The article also echoed some of the concerns surrounding the missionary imagination at that time, which the Congress addressed: the relationship between evangelical Christianity and social change, the promotion of education from primary to university levels, the need to reconcile Christianity with modern science, and the social position of women in Latin America. The most difficult issue faced by the Congress' participants, though, was to determine the boundaries of such an ambitious endeavor enveloping a wide range of Christian groups. This thorny discussion revolved around the possibility of cooperation with the Catholic Church, a fact that many of the Congress' participants viewed with suspicion. According to the report, the solution encountered at the Panama Congress involved promoting cross-denominational cooperation between evangelical churches to devise solutions to the "moral and religious problems" of Latin America.[1]

The Panama Congress of 1916 was a direct tributary of the momentous World Missionary Conference of Edinburgh in 1910. In Edinburgh, representatives of a wide range of missionary societies and Christian organizations examined the challenges and limitations of the missionary endeavor in the modern world and developed strategies to overcome them.

---

[1] *Jornal do Commercio*, April 6, 1916, n. 96.

But because the conference considered Latin America as a Christianized territory, on account of the historical presence of the Catholic Church, Protestant missionaries and ministers in the region were left disappointed and the Panama Congress was conceived as a remedy to that. As scholars interested in the history of Christianity in Latin America have shown, the Panama Congress of 1916 inaugurated a new era of missionary practice and thought in the continent. It fostered movements toward Christian unity and enabled Latin American Protestant leaders to redefine evangelical identities in a context of accelerated social change.[2] Theologians situate the Congress in a long line of Christian meetings in the continent that shaped modern notions of ecumenism.[3] However, as Argentinian theologian José Míguez Bonino and Costa Rican historian Arturo Piedra Solano have shown, the Panama Congress of 1916 produced ambiguous theological and missionary legacies. For Piedra Solano, in setting their goals of religious cooperation under the banner of the principle of Pan-Americanism, which sought to intensify diplomatic interactions and commercial exchanges in the Americas, missionaries promoted veiled forms of North American expansionism in the continent.[4] Míguez Bonino's critique is more penetrating. For him, Protestant missionaries and Latin American evangelicals embraced two conflicting theological traditions in the wake of the Panama Congress of 1916. On the one hand, they promoted liberal notions of individual freedom and responsibility and promoted the principles of the Social Gospel in the continent. On the other, they inherited otherworldly millenialist theologies that prevented evangelicals from developing a "socially committed" missionary model. In his analysis, participants at Panama in 1916 and the evangelical missionaries who supported the cause of Christian cooperation across the Americas ultimately promoted the penetration of North American capitalist economic rationality in Latin America.[5]

---

[2] Jean-Pierre Bastian, *Le protestantisme en Amérique latine: Une approche socio-historique* (Geneva: Labor et Fides, 1994), ch. 4.

[3] See, for instance, Dafne S. Plou, "Ecumenical History of Latin America," in *A History of the Ecumenical Movement: Volume 3, 1968–2000*, ed. John Briggs, Mercy A. Oduyoye, and Georges Tsetsis (Geneva: World Council of Churches, 2004); William R. Hogg, *Ecumenical Foundations: A History of the International Missionary Council and its Nineteenth-century Background* (Eugene, OR: Wipf and Stock, 2002 [1952]).

[4] Arturo Piedra Solano, *Evangelização protestante na américa latina: Análise das razões que justificaram e promoveram a expansão protestante, vol. 2* (São Leopoldo: Sinodal, 2008), 11–76.

[5] José Míguez Bonino, *Rostros del protestantismo latinoamericano* (Buenos Aires: Nueva Creación, 1995), ch. 1.

Despite the importance of these scholars' contributions, their analyses of the Panama Congress of 1916 only make full sense when one looks at the congress and its significance in retrospect. The association of the Pan-American aspirations of the congress' participants with the emergence of American-style capitalism in the region comes full circle when the evangelical discourse of the early twentieth century is seen in the light of the neoliberal reforms of the 1980s and 1990s. By the time of the congress, Brazilian and Latin American Protestants shared in their age's utopias of American unity and integration in the context of the Great War, rather than uniquely embracing capitalist modernity and American imperialism. Furthermore, the call to cooperation launched at Panama was overtly critical of the Catholic Church and its social effects in Latin America, differing significantly from the modern concept of ecumenism.

This chapter examines the appropriations of the idea of Christian cooperation in Latin America. The following discussion examines the agents who domesticated this concept in Brazil and how they modified them. Since the late nineteenth century, various denominational missionary enterprises in Brazil began to negotiate the terms of religious collaboration to avoid conflicts in the occupation of the territory. At various times negotiation gave way to sectarian competition, and the first part of the chapter discusses them. The second part examines how the idea of Christian cooperation underwent multiple adaptations as it traveled through a series of missionary meetings in Edinburgh in 1910, New York in 1913, Panama in 1916, and finally to Brazil. The last part looks at the writings of two participants at Panama 1916, the pastors Erasmo Braga and Eduardo Carlos Pereira, and to how they translated the principles of Pan-Americanism and the goals of the Panama Congress to their Brazilian audiences.

Collaboration and Competition in the Brazilian Religious Arena

The arrival of American missionaries of the Southern Baptist Convention and of American Episcopalians in Brazil in the 1880s completed the occupation of mainline missionary societies in the country. Alongside Presbyterian, Methodist, and Congregationalist missions, as well as with German and Swiss Lutheran immigrants, these mainline denominations at times negotiated and at times competed for space and souls. There were instances of collaboration and mutual help among the various denominations on account of both the policies of mission boards and interactions in the field. But doctrinal singularities and differences in ritual, sacramental practice, and ecclesiastical governance also drove evangelical churches apart. Catholic writers frequently criticized the fissiparous feature of evangelical religion and discredited Protestants as sectarian and insincere, whose divisiveness undermined hierarchical order and social cohesion.[6]

Interdenominational interactions in the field were key drivers of evangelical collaboration in the late nineteenth century. In this period, missionaries avoided competition with other evangelistic enterprises for space and resources. So, when the Baptist missionary couple William and Anne Bagby arrived in Santa Bárbara, countryside of São Paulo in 1881, to work among Southern American immigrants they quickly perceived that the province was already extensively occupied. Presbyterians had opened numerous congregations and schools across the region. In the following year, the Bagbys moved the Baptist mission station to Bahia alongside the newly arrived couple Zachary and Kate Taylor. They argued that, among several reasons, Bahia's densely populated capital was nearly unoccupied by missionaries.[7] Shortly after that, in 1884, the Baptist mission began to spread nationwide, opening new stations in Maceió, São Paulo, and Rio de Janeiro. From then on, more explicit competition took place. In the south of Brazil, however, exchanges between Presbyterian, Methodist, and Episcopal missionaries were friendlier, anticipating the emphasis placed on missionary cooperation by the World Missionary Conference of Edinburgh in 1910 and the Panama Congress of 1916.

It was a Brazilian Methodist physician, João da Costa Corrêa, who began his denomination's missionary work in Rio Grande do Sul, in 1875, in association with the Uruguay-based *La Plata Mission*, managed by the northern American Methodists.[8] Dr. Corrêa expanded the Methodist front by distributing Bibles and evangelical literature in the eastern part of Rio Grande and two years later the missionary Rev. John James Ransom, from the southern American Methodist Episcopal Church, joined him. Northern and southern American Methodists cooperated in Rio Grande up until 1896, when

---

[6] Leonel Franca, *A Igreja, a Reforma e a civilização*, 5th ed. (Rio de Janeiro: Ed. Agir, 1948 [1922]), 237–249.
[7] SBC Proceedings [1883], appendix A, ix–x.
[8] Walter Wedemann, "A History of Protestant Missions to Brazil, 1850–1914," (unpublished PhD dissertation, Southern Baptist Theological Seminary, 1977), 143.

Dr. Corrêa retired and the field was transferred to the southern Methodists.[9] American Presbyterians had a mission station in the same province since 1877, under the leadership of the Rev. Emmanuel Vanorden, in the small city of Bagé, on the border with Uruguay.[10] Later, in 1888, this mission station was transferred to the responsibility of the Portuguese minister and former Catholic priest Rev. Manoel Antônio de Menezes. Due to his bad health and the poor prospects of Bagé, Menezes ended up being obliged, albeit reluctantly, to turn the missionary field over to the newly arrived American Episcopalians two years later.[11] The American Episcopalians arrived in Rio Grande do Sul in 1890, accompanied by Presbyterian converts from Minas Gerais, and they soon began to work alongside the Methodists, whose educational legacy they appreciated.[12] Apart from this experience, Presbyterians, Methodists, and Baptists negotiated the occupation of other important fields, such as Minas Gerais and Bahia, in the 1880s and 1890s.[13]

In consequence of these interactions, Presbyterian missionaries created a committee in 1897 aimed at establishing the basis of an alliance among missionary societies and negotiate the occupation of territory. In 1900, they were joined by the Methodists and negotiated the terms of this agreement with other missionary societies.[14] This committee agreed on a few points based on a pact of missionary cooperation signed by North American missionary societies in Mexico in 1888. First, no city of less than 25,000 inhabitants should be occupied by more than one denomination. Second, a city would be considered as duly occupied if Protestant religious services were held regularly. Third, churches should not offer advantages or employment to believers of other denominations to attract membership. And finally, denominations should respect forms of government and discipline of the other churches.[15]

Christian literacy and missionary print demonstrated both how missionaries collaborated in Brazil prior to the Edinburgh and Panama conferences, and the limits of such collaboration. Theological similarities, institutional partnerships, and ritual differences accounted for that. In the early

---

[9] James L. Kennedy, *Cincoenta annos de methodismo no Brasil* (São Paulo: Imprensa Methodista, 1928), 173–185.
[10] Júlio A. Ferreira, *História da Igreja Presbiteriana do Brasil, vol. I*, 2nd ed. (São Paulo: Casa Editora Presbiteriana, 1992), 266–268; *Brazilian Missions* IV, no. 11 (November 1891): 86–88.
[11] *Brazilian Missions* IV, no. 7 (July 1891): 51; BFM-PCUSA Annual Report [1890], 30.
[12] *Brazilian Missions* IV, no. 7 (July 1891): 53.
[13] Wedemann, "A History of Protestant Missions," 181–182.
[14] *Regional Conferences in Latin America* (New York: The Missionary Education Movement, 1917), 243–244.
[15] *Regional Conferences*, 244.

1880s, for instance, Presbyterian missionaries granted space in their periodical, *Imprensa Evangelica*, to the Rev. João Manoel Gonçalves dos Santos of the Congregationalist Church of Rio de Janeiro and superintendent of the Brazilian branch of the British and Foreign Bible Society. Santos objected to the accusations of Catholic periodicals against the circulation of Bibles and published a series of sermons and articles in *Imprensa Evangelica* explaining the meanings of fundamental evangelical creeds, such as the doctrine of atonement, the effects of spiritual worship, and the sufficiency of the Bible.[16] Later, in the beginning of the twentieth century, denominations began to collaborate with one another by publishing tracts and books of other groups.[17]

Doctrinal and ritual differences, on the other hand, split evangelical denominations across multiple lines. In the late nineteenth and early twentieth centuries, Baptist missionaries were more prone to factional divisions in the Brazilian religious landscape, especially on account of their resolute opposition to infant baptism and defense of baptism by immersion. These doctrinal stances even weighed upon the Baptist missionaries' choice of Bible version. In 1882, soon after the Baptists started their activities in Bahia, the American missionary Zachary Taylor found out that the Almeida translation of the Bible used the words "with water" instead of "in water" to describe baptismal scenes. Because prepositions mattered, the Baptist mission decided not to use the Almeida version, but the Figueiredo translation circulated by the BFBS.[18] The problem was that António Figueiredo was a Portuguese Catholic priest who translated the Latin Vulgate into Portuguese in the eighteenth century and his version bore the seal of approval of the Catholic archbishops in Lisbon and Bahia. Echoing anti-Catholic sentiments, Zachary Taylor and his fellow Baptist ministers of Bahia decided not to use the BFBS Figueiredo translation, too, "on account of its great

---

[16] *Imprensa Evangelica*, January 31, 1882, vol. XVIII, n. 17; March 15, 1882, vol. XVIII, n. 5; March 30, 1882, vol. XVIII, n. 6; January 15, 1883, vol. XIX, n. 1; February 28, 1883, vol. XIX, n. 4; July 15, 1883, vol. XIX. n. 13. Santos also published a series of short exegetical analyses of biblical texts: September 15, 1883, vol. XIX, n. 17; October 15, 1883, vol. XIX, n. 19; November 30, 1883, vol. XIX, n. 22.

[17] For instance, Methodist presses in Rio and São Paulo printed anti-Catholic controversies, critiques of Freemasonry, and books of historical grammar of Presbyterian ministers and writers: Nicolau S. C. Esher, *Religião do estado: Propaganda pela igualdade de cultos* (Rio de Janeiro: Casa Publicadora Methodista, 1900); Eduardo C. Pereira, *Balanço historico da Egreja Presbyteriana Independente Brasileira* (São Paulo: Imprensa Methodista, 1921); Lauresto (Nicolau S. C. Esher pseudonym). *I—A Maçonaria como Religião, pelo Rev. J. D. Brownlee; II—A Maçonaria perante o Christianismo, pelo Rev. W. Foster; III—"As Sociedades Secretas", uma resolução synodal* (Rio de Janeiro: Casa Publicadora Methodista, 1900).

[18] Duncan A. Reily, *História documental do protestantismo no Brasil*, 3rd ed. (São Paulo: ASTE, 2003), 149.

corruption made by the Romanists." Instead, they opted for another version of the Trinitarian Bible Society of London.[19]

The clearest expressions of evangelical sectarianism, however, did not come from the Taylors or the Bagbys in Bahia. In fact, they maintained friendly connections with other churches and viewed young Brazilian Presbyterian ministers with optimism.[20] It was the influential Baptist missionary and polemicist Solomon Ginsburg who most frequently unnerved other evangelical missionaries. Ginsburg had an international career. He was a Polish Jew raised in Germany, who converted to Christianity in London. There, he studied at the Regions Beyond Missionary Training School, prepared for work as an evangelist under the Congregationalists in Portugal, and had a long and accomplished missionary career in Brazil.[21] Ginsburg was a talented writer and a persuasive speaker, who produced a good number of hymns, tracts, and publications for Portuguese-speaking evangelical audiences. He landed in Rio de Janeiro in June 1890, where he quickly objected to the caution of his fellow Congregationalists and began to do street preaching in the public squares of Niteroi.[22] He joined the Southern Baptist Convention (SBC) in 1891 and moved to Bahia. Ginsburg's methods of direct evangelization and stubborn insistence on the "real baptism" soon attracted the opposition of other missionaries in the field. In 1892, Ginsburg traveled to Pernambuco to hold a series of meetings at the local church and visited the believers he had previously "sprinkled" as a Congregationalist minister, re-baptizing some and attracting them to the Baptist church.[23] In his correspondence with the SBC, Ginsburg frequently equated the opposition of Presbyterians, Methodists, and Congregationalists to his methods with that of Catholics, and commemorated the re-baptism of ministers and believers of other denominations.[24] In a letter commemorating the building of a new Baptist temple in Campos, he wrote: "Let other Missions dream of great succes [sic] while their Missionaries try to hide themselves from the

---

[19] Incidents in Bahia. IBMB, Zachary Clay Taylor papers.
[20] "The Christian Literature of Brazil," by Mrs Kate Taylor. IBMB, Zachary Taylor papers. The report makes particularly positive remarks about the Presbyterian Revs. José Manoel da Conceição and Miguel Torres.
[21] Solomon Ginsburg, *A Wandering Jew in Brazil: An Autobiography of Solomon L. Ginsburg* (Nashville: Sunday School Board, 1922).
[22] Ginsburg, *A Wandering Jew*, 44–46.
[23] Ginsburg, *A Wandering Jew*, 67.
[24] S. Ginsburg to H. A. Tupper, Rio de Janeiro, February 16, 1893; S. Ginsburg to H. A. Tupper, Rio de Janeiro, April 4,. 1893; Progress in Brazil, 1896. IBMB, Solomon Ginsburg papers. Ginsburg referred to Presbyterians, Congregationalists, and Methodists as "pedo-baptists" in his letters.

heat of the day and the fevers of the night, it belongs to us Baptists the conversion of the World."[25]

Other missionaries strongly opposed Ginsburg's methods, his poaching from other flocks, and Baptist sectarianism more broadly. Instances of religious competition and dispute in Brazil reached as far as Presbyterian and Baptist mission societies in the American south in the early twentieth century. According to Presbyterian missionaries, Ginsburg attempted to persuade Brazilian evangelists in Pernambuco to abandon their denomination by offering incentives and directed his work to places that had already been occupied by other missions.[26] These actions violated the terms of evangelical cooperation of Mexico 1888 and Brazil 1897. Sectarian differences multiplied in different directions in the early twentieth century and, of course, Baptist missionaries were not fully responsible for it. Although some scholars stated that foreign missionaries and Brazilian ministers lacked intellectual sophistication,[27] Baptist defense of immersion baptism and opposition to infant baptism had solid theological grounds. According to the contributors to *O Jornal Baptista* (The Baptist Journal), the act of being submersed in the waters and taken back to the surface symbolized Christ's sacrificial death and resurrection.[28] The American missionary William Edwin Entzminger, founder of the Baptist Publishing House of Rio de Janeiro and an active writer, used his denomination's publishing machine to respond to the criticism of Baptist practices and rites. In Entzminger's argument, symbolic acts bridged the gap between spiritual realities and the materiality of rites: "Baptism and Communion are symbols, and the symbol's purpose is to teach spiritual truths that are only understood by reference to the material. The symbol of baptism, therefore, is destined to show in a visible manner the effects of Christ's redemption, the effects of Christ's blood when applied to the heart and to the spirit of man."[29] Quoting Reformed theologian Phillip Schaff, he stated that the acts of immersion and emersion symbolized the burial of the old man and the resurrection of the new.[30]

---

[25] S. Ginsburg to R. J. Willingham, Campos, July 29, 1898. IBMB, Solomon Ginsburg papers.

[26] W. M. Anderson to R. J. Willingham, Nashville, TN, September 17, 1903. IBMB, Solomon Ginsburg papers.

[27] Ronald Frase, "A Sociological Analysis of the Development of Brazilian Protestantism: A Study of Social Change." (unpublished PhD dissertation, Princeton Theological Seminary, 1975), 347.

[28] Anna Lúcia Adamovicz, "Imprensa protestante na Primeira República: Evangelismo, informação e produção cultural. O Jornal Batista (1901–1922)." (unpublished PhD dissertation, Universidade de São Paulo, 2008), 72–73.

[29] W. E. Entzminger, *Fiat lux ou Resultado do meu "exame" do Snr. Juvêncio Marinho sobre "O modo do baptismo"* (Rio de Janeiro: Casa Editora Baptista, 1902), 50.

[30] Entzminger, *Fiat lux*, 60.

Baptist defense of their rituals and practices drew from different intellectual traditions, such as biblical narratives and modern Protestant theology. However, Presbyterian ministers and writers dismissed these deeper grounds to legitimize their criticism of Baptist doctrines, drawing disdainful caricatures of Baptist practices. In 1911, Brazilian Presbyterian pastor Mattathias Gomes dos Santos published a series of articles in the Presbyterian periodical *O Puritano* (The Puritan) criticizing the rites of what he labeled "the immersionist church." Although he stated that there were sincere and zealous Christians in Baptist churches, Santos also observed that one could find a group of blind "coryphaeus of sectarianism" within the movement. According to Santos's articles, a materialist and destructive tendency was flourishing among Brazilian Baptists, "taking the threatening proportions of a pagan worship: the *hydrolatry*."[31] For Baptists, he claimed, Christian truth and salvation were all about the amount of water with which one was baptized, and with little water it was impossible to please God.[32] His article series on *hydrolatry* called the attention of *O Jornal Baptista* in Rio, generating a heated debate between the Presbyterian and the Baptist presses on national level.

At the time of Santos's *hydrolatry* controversy in the 1910s, the Baptist church in Brazil was growing at a faster rate compared to the other denominations. Whereas the Presbyterian Church developed a more centralized bureaucratic structure that subjected local congregations, seminaries, and publishing houses to the control of regional Presbyteries and a national synod, Baptists adopted the congregational system, ensuring the independence of local churches. Moreover, while training to the Presbyterian pastorate was a long process that required the acquisition of deeper knowledge of church doctrine, church history, and systematic theology, Baptist instruction was simpler and faster, enabling its ministers to identify more closely with the realities of their flocks.[33] Since the late nineteenth century, Baptist evangelists, pastors, and missionaries employed methods of direct evangelism that were later expanded and fully developed by the Pentecostals, such as street preaching, open-air meetings, ordination of pastors and leaders with little formal theological training, and evangelization of black and poor

---

[31] *O Puritano*, July 6, 1911, n. 603.
[32] *O Puritano*, August 17, 1911, n. 609; September 21, 1911, n. 614.
[33] H. B. Cavalcanti, "The Right Faith at the Right Time? Determinants of Protestant Mission Success in the 19th-century Brazilian Religious Market," *Journal for the Scientific Study of Religion* 41 (2002): 423–438.

people in impoverished neighborhoods and slums.[34] By 1930, Baptists were the largest Protestant denomination in the country, comprising thirty percent of the overall Brazilian evangelical population, whereas Presbyterians lagged behind, representing twenty-four percent.[35]

Baptist growth presaged that of Pentecostalism a few decades later, and it is not surprising that the first group of believers and missionaries who founded Brazil's Assemblies of God came from a Baptist church in the Amazon region. The founders of the Assemblies of God in Brazil were two Swedish missionaries who had a history of involvement with Baptist churches in their homeland: Gunnar Vingren and Daniel Berg. They migrated to the United States in the early twentieth century and soon joined the emerging Pentecostal movement. By entering existing missionary networks, they moved to Brazil in 1910 and served as evangelists in the Baptist Church of Belém, in the Amazon rainforest. After a few months doing manual labor in the iron industry, selling Bibles, and practicing street evangelism, Vingren and Berg began to preach the doctrines of the gifts of the spirit to the Baptist church of Belém, from where they were quickly dismissed alongside nineteen congregants. This group formed a church called "Apostolic Faith Mission," changing its name to Assemblies of God in 1917.[36] Disputes with Baptist leaders in the north of Brazil followed shortly, with Baptists complaining that the "Holy Rollers" were poaching from their flock and adding complexity to the existing religious competition in the country.[37]

Anti-Protestant Rhetoric and Mobilization

Despite these interdenominational divisions and sectarian disputes, the Protestant churches of Brazil shared a loose set of characteristics. They belonged to a non-Catholic Christian minority that idealized the experiences and inspiration of the early Christian church and opposed the modern reforms of the Vatican. This sense of besiegement and competition

---

[34] Paul Freston, "Protestantes e política no Brasil: Da Constituinte ao impeachment." (unpublished PhD dissertation, Universidade Estadual de Campinas, 1993), 61.

[35] Erasmo Braga and Kenneth Grubb, *The Republic of Brazil: A Survey of the Religious Situation* (London: World Dominion Press, 1932), 68–71.

[36] Paul Freston, "Breve história do pentecostalismo brasileiro," in *Nem anjos nem demônios: Interpretações sociológicas do pentecostalismo*, ed. Alberto Antoniazzi et al. (Petrópolis: Vozes, 1994), 80–81.

[37] Laura Premack, "'The Holy Rollers are Invading our Territory': Southern Baptist Missionaries and the Early Years of Pentecostalism in Brazil," *Journal of Religious History* 35 (2011): 1–23.

with the institutional power and historical rootedness of Catholicism contributed to bringing evangelicals together. The complex dynamic of the modern Catholic revival and its local incarnations were already discussed in previous chapters. However, the eruption of Catholic popular messianic movements in the late nineteenth and early twentieth centuries, especially in the backlands of the Brazilian northeast, agitated and further fragmented the religious landscape.

Since the late nineteenth century, lay and ordained Catholic leaders articulated new forms of religious activism in Brazil's religious arena. The creation of Spiritist federations, the expansion of evangelical religion, and the influence of Positivism among urban intellectual elites gave a new impetus to faithful Catholics.[38] A missionary, José Maria Ibiapina, known as Padre Ibiapina, inaugurated new forms of religious mobilization in the northeast. Between 1862 and 1883, Ibiapina created twenty-two so-called *Casas de Caridade* (Houses of Charity) in the provinces of the Brazilian northeast, the seedbed of these messianic movements. These institutions served as orphanages for abandoned girls and schools for the daughters of local elites. Besides altering the social stratification in the northeast, by providing new channels of social mobility for rural men and women, Ibiapina staffed these houses with pious Catholics who took on vows and lived according to a sort of rule, entering a quasi-religious order.[39] These laypeople, called *beatas* and *beatos*, were known for their religious zeal and activism and organized collective mobilizations called *mutirões* to repair rundown church property such as old shrines and cemeteries.

Some of these *beatos* gained broad support and recognition for their work, such as the mystic Antônio Mendes Maciel. Like Ibiapina, Maciel was also born in Ceará to a middle-class family in 1830, and after a series of misfortunes became a *beato* in the backlands of Brazil's northeast, a region stricken by severe cyclical droughts. Following the model set by Ibiapina, Maciel also organized lay mobilizations. He reconstructed old chapels, repaired walls of abandoned cemeteries, held prayer meetings and preached sermons in public squares, exhorted his listeners against the threats of Protestantism, secularism, and Freemasonry, and attracted a

---

[38] Dain Borges, "Catholic Vanguard in Brazil," in *Local Church, Global Church: Catholic Activism in Latin America from Rerum Novarum to Vatican II*, ed. Stephen Andes and Julia Young (Washington: Catholic University of America, 2016), 21–49.

[39] Ralph Della Cava, "Brazilian Messianism and National Institutions: A Reappraisal of Canudos and Joaseiro," *Hispanic American Historical Review* 48 (1968): 402–420.

large and socially heterogeneous group of followers.[40] In 1893, Maciel, then known as Antônio Conselheiro (the Counselor) and his followers settled the valley of the river Vaza-Barris, adding dramatically to the population of a small settlement called Canudos that, at its peak, had around fifteen thousand to twenty thousand inhabitants.[41] Although local priests in Bahia supported Conselheiro, especially on account of his efforts to repair church property, the settlement was seen as a challenge to the orthodoxy of the Ultramontane reform, and clergymen in the northeast attempted to regain control of their flock by disciplining the folk at Canudos. While the settlement was connected to regional commercial networks in Bahia, the local landed elite disliked the popularity of Canudos. Also, the infant Republican government held the settlement and its leader in low esteem. Conselheiro was accused of attempting to restore the monarchy and his followers were dismissed as a bunch of religious fanatics, whose activities were rooted in madness and criminal behavior.[42] Between 1896 to 1897, four military expeditions dismantled the settlement, massacred its population, and killed Conselheiro.[43]

Another messianic movement of this era revolved around a Catholic priest known as Cícero Romão Batista, the Padre Cícero. Like Ibiapina and Conselheiro, Cícero was also born in Ceará, in 1844. He was one of the first graduates of the seminary of Fortaleza, the capital of Ceará, whose foundation was closely connected to the Ultramontane renewal and its "unflagging hostility towards Masonry, positivism, and Protestantism."[44] Shortly after ordination in 1870, Cícero was sent to the chaplaincy of a hamlet near Crato called Joaseiro, where he remained an orthodox priest faithful to the Catholic hierarchy. On the first morning of March 1889, he administered communion to a group of pious *beatas* in Joaseiro, and in the mouth of one of them the white host was transformed into blood, thought to be the blood of Christ. This extraordinary event was subsequently repeated every Wednesday and Friday of Lent. News of the alleged miracle ran fast and Joaseiro began to attract large hosts of pilgrims and settlers, projecting the now overcrowded

---

[40] Robert Levine, "'Mud-Hut Jerusalem': Canudos Revisited," in *The Abolition of Slavery and the Aftermath of Emancipation in Brazil*, ed. Rebecca Scott (Durham, NC: Duke University Press, 1988), 119–166.
[41] On Canudos, see Robert Levine, *Vale of Tears: Revisiting the Canudos Massacre in Northeastern Brazil, 1893–1897* (Berkeley: University of California Press, 1992).
[42] Levine, "Mud-Hut Jerusalem," 122, 129, 144, 152.
[43] Levine, *Vale of Tears*, 206–208.
[44] Della Cava, "Brazilian Messianism," 406–409.

hamlet into the political and ecclesiastical conflicts of the region. Later, it also projected Padre Cícero into the regional political arena of the northeast.[45]

In the early years of the Republic, when civil rights were equally granted to non-Catholics and relations between the Brazilian state and the Catholic Church were severed, Protestants clung to these achievements and reacted promptly when such conquests were under apparent threat. So, when evangelical missionaries viewed such expressions of popular religiosity seeking to reassert the centrality of Catholicism to the life of the nation they feared that a potential Catholic re-conquest of its official status would undermine the principle of religious freedom.[46] In the beginning of the twentieth century, after the massacre of Canudos, Presbyterian editors of *O Puritano* embraced the then prevailing interpretation of the messianic movement and referred to Conselheiro and his followers as a group of monarchist fanatics who threatened the foundations of the Republic.[47] From then on, Brazilian Protestants began to add yet another set of critiques to the Catholic Church and its legacy in Brazil. Whereas in the aftermath of Vatican I and the Religious Question of 1872–1875 Protestants produced literature attacking the effects of the Ultramontane reform and the papacy of Pius IX, after Canudos and Joaseiro they began to argue that Catholicism was a medieval, syncretistic form of Christianity interwoven with pagan practices and beliefs.

It was in this context of religious competition and dispute that Brazilian evangelicals encountered the idea of Christian cooperation as conceived at the World Missionary Conference of Edinburgh in 1910. This concept undertook a long journey before arriving in Brazil. As it often happens with concepts disseminated on worldwide level, multiple mediations and modifications reconfigure their original meanings.[48] Here, an "upward hermeneutic" that draws attention to the local dynamics and internal struggles that informed the reception of global arguments and debates, aptly captures these conceptual reconfigurations.[49] The idea of cooperation was modified in a series of conferences in the Americas in the context of the Great War, and

---

[45] On Padre Cícero and Joaseiro, see Ralph Della Cava, *Miracle at Joaseiro* (New York: Columbia University Press, 1970).

[46] BFM-PCUSA [1897], 189.

[47] *O Puritano*, February 19, 1903, n. 189; January 16, 1913, n. 683.

[48] Christopher L. Hill, "Conceptual Universalization in the Transnational Nineteenth Century," in *Global Intellectual History*, ed. Samuel Moyn and Andrew Sartori (New York: Columbia University Press, 2013), 134–158.

[49] Christopher Bayly, *Recovering Liberties: Indian Thought in the Age of Liberalism and Empire* (Cambridge: Cambridge University Press, 2012), 28.

the next section will investigate how this concept traveled throughout the global circuits of the early twentieth-century evangelical world.

From Edinburgh to New York, Panama, and Rio de Janeiro: The Idea of Christian Cooperation

It is widely acknowledged that the World Missionary Conference of Edinburgh in 1910 was a landmark in the development of the modern concept of ecumenism. In bringing together representatives of various Protestant bodies to consider the practice and prospects of missionary work, and excluding from its purview the situation of Protestant missions in societies of Catholic and Orthodox majority, the conference is viewed as an introduction to the mid-twentieth-century ecumenical movement.[50] Brian Stanley's authoritative account of the Edinburgh Conference in 1910, however, shows how the leaders of the conference redefined the boundaries of Christendom in order to appreciate the challenges and promise of the missionary movement.[51] The World Missionary Conference was predominantly an evangelical event that gathered delegates and participants recruited mostly from the Anglophone Atlantic. However, to get the important support from the Anglo-Catholics and their missionary organizations, such as the Society for Propagating Christian Knowledge (SCPK), the American and British organizers carefully negotiated the terms of the conference. John Mott, the influential American Methodist layman who presided at the sessions of Edinburgh in 1910, took part in consultations on both sides of the Atlantic, and after much negotiation, it was decided that the Edinburgh Conference should only consider the missionary endeavors to the non-Christian world. Because the Catholic societies of Europe, South and Central America, and the Caribbean were regarded as Christianized lands, the conference did not consider the situation of Protestant missions in these places.[52]

For missionaries and ministers at work in Latin America, this was inadequate. The Rev. Álvaro Reis, head pastor of the Presbyterian Church of Rio de

---

[50] See, for instance, Ruth Rouse and Stephen Neill, eds., *A history of the ecumenical movement, 1517–1948* (London: SPCK, 1954), especially K. S. Latourette's chapter, "Ecumenical Bearings of the Missionary Movement and the International Missionary Council"; Hogg, *Ecumenical Foundations*.

[51] Brian Stanley, *The World Missionary Conference, Edinburgh 1910* (Grand Rapids, MI: Eerdmans, 2009), ch. 3.

[52] Stanley, *The World Missionary*, 64.

Janeiro and a delegate at the World Missionary Conference, bemoaned the decision. Writing from Edinburgh to the Rio de Janeiro-based periodical *O Puritano*, Reis claimed that the exclusion of southern and central American countries from the missionary atlas of Edinburgh created a "stupid gap," for modern Romanism was "theoretically and practically—anti-Christian."[53] An influential participant in the event was the American Presbyterian minister Robert Speer, the executive secretary of the Board of Foreign Missions of the Presbyterian Church of the United States. During the conference, Speer held two unofficial meetings to consider the missionary work in Latin America, and began to make the first arrangements for a small consultation aimed at studying the missionary situation in this vast field.[54] One of the conference's eight commissions, in charge of discussing missionary cooperation and the promotion of Christian unity, eventually organized a "continuation committee," an international and interdenominational missionary body that sought to encourage Christian collaboration in missionary fields.[55] These two fruits of the World Missionary Conference in 1910 were of particular relevance for the development of the missionary work in Brazil and Latin America.

In 1912–1913, Speer convened a series of gatherings in the United States alongside various mission boards in America and Canada to consider the prospects and difficulties of missions in Japan, China, and "the Moslem World." This committee, formed by representatives of Baptist, Episcopal, Methodist, and Presbyterian mission boards in the United States, as well as the ABS, also began preparations for another conference dedicated to Latin America. For Speer, this conference was of vital importance "in view of the omission of the work in Latin America from the consideration of the Conference in Edinburgh, and in view of the increased attention which the building of the Panama Canal is attracting to South America."[56] He sent letters inviting representatives of missionary bodies for a conference that took place in New York on March 12–13, 1913.

This was a small, though representative, meeting. It brought together missionaries who had been active in the field and leaders of various American mission bodies, alongside a couple of organizations from Canada and Britain

---

[53] *O Puritano*, July 21, 1910, n. 553.
[54] Stanley, *The World Missionary*, 303–304.
[55] Stanley, *The World Missionary*, 277–302.
[56] R. Speer's model letter, New York, January 23, 1913. PHS, RG81-34-21, Latin America Conference, 1912–1914.

that had been operating for some time in Latin America. Speer presided at the New York conference and, in tune with the spirit of the ecumenical conferences of the age, opened the first session with a survey of the situation of Protestant missionary work in the continent displaying statistics, figures, and geographical data.[57] Other guest speakers discussed various topics with the audience, such as the educational situation of Latin American countries, the role of missionary women in the field, and the issue of training and ordination of local ministers. However, the topic that attracted most attention, and that showed more clearly the objections of these representatives with the World Missionary Conference, was the attitude of Protestant missionaries toward the Catholic Church.

This issue emerged before the conference took place when Speer started corresponding with the delegates. John Kyle, a long-time Presbyterian missionary in Brazil who spent a considerable part of his career in Petrópolis near Rio de Janeiro, recommended Speer *The Arrested Reformation*, a book by the Rev. William Muir. In Kyle's words, Muir's argument was "that the Reformation movement which was 'arrested' by the Counter-Reformation should now be taken up by the Evangelical Churches and carried forward to completion.... He [Muir] shows how impossible is any union or co-operation with Rome and that the only solution is the elimination of the Papacy by the conversion of all Romanists to the Gospel."[58] During the New York Conference, some speakers and participants took this discussion forward, showing little agreement with how the organizers of the Edinburgh Conference had drawn the boundaries of Christendom.

Henry Carroll of the Methodist Episcopal Church, in an address on church–state relations, painted a bleak picture of the moral state of the Catholic Church in Latin America and its influence on politics. For him, the reason underlying the scant intellectual and cultural progress of these countries after their hard-won independence, was "the permanent influence of the Church." And whereas the constitutions of countries such as Mexico and Brazil granted freedom of worship to citizens, old customs and old prejudices kept alive "the old spirit of intolerance."[59] Even more emphatic were George Smith's remarks on the condition of the Catholic Church as compared to

---

[57] *Conference on Missions in Latin America, March 12 and 13, 1913* (Lebanon, PA: Sowers Printing Co., 1913), 9–17.

[58] J. M. Kyle to R. Speer, Lowell, MA, February 17, 1913. PHS, RG81-34-21, Latin America Conference, 1912–1914.

[59] *Conference on Missions*, 50–51.

twenty-five years before the New York meeting. Smith, a missionary of the United Presbyterian Church, focused on Brazil, Uruguay, Argentina, and Peru, and he stated that in looking at the situation of the Church in these countries, "no true Bible Christian would dare to say that South America has a Christian church in the Church of Rome."[60] In his words, the Catholic Church "will always remain the greatest enemy of true Evangelical teaching." Instead of making compromises, evangelical Christians should "recognize the fact that there must be a great fight—we, using spiritual weapons, and Rome will use anything that comes along. We simply can't be friendly with that that is opposed to God and his Word."[61] In another address, the Methodist Episcopal Bishop Eugene Hendrix resumed the issue of the social and political impact of the Catholic Church. For Hendrix, "absolutism in religion leads to absolutism in government" and in his opinion Catholicism should be held accountable for the political instability of Latin America.[62] Unlike Smith, Hendrix adopted a more conciliatory stance, affirming that the right attitude of Protestant missions toward the Catholic Church should be the same of Christ toward Judaism: "We should not come to destroy, but to fulfill."[63] At the end of his address, Hendrix summoned Protestant missions to heal the wounds of sectarianism and denominationalism opened by the Reformation and organize a united front against "the most centralized organization the world has ever seen."[64]

Although the prevailing climate at New York was one of disapproval of the Catholic Church in Latin America and its bearings upon politics and culture, the final statement adopted by the conference was milder and conciliatory. The statement affirmed that whereas in Africa and Asia, Protestant missionaries encountered "ethnic faiths entrenched behind the sanctions of many centuries of national thought and practice," in Latin America they found "no great non-Christian religious system," but "representatives of the Roman Communion." The field was peculiar because "the vast majority of the people of Latin America, especially the men, claim no vital relation, and acknowledge no allegiance to, the Roman Communion." And in a passage that provoked mixed reactions among the audience, the statement affirmed: "We acknowledge gladly that the Roman Communion has

---

[60] *Conference on Missions*, 62.
[61] *Conference on Missions*, 66.
[62] *Conference on Missions*, 81–82.
[63] *Conference on Missions*, 87.
[64] *Conference on Missions*, 89.

done useful work among these varied peoples. We would do nothing to detach sincere Christians from their allegiance."[65] For the statement's authors, Protestant missions should unite their forces to, on the one hand, combat social and intellectual ills, such as widespread illiteracy and the prevalence of agnosticism in universities. On the other hand, mission societies should provide education from elementary to higher levels, circulate Bibles and high-quality Christian literature, and promote the evangelization of women. Some participants at the conference showed certain unease with the statement, especially those with long missionary careers in Latin America, such as John Kyle and Sylvester Jones.[66]

The New York Conference was a small meeting that did not include Latin American delegates. However, it had a lasting significance for the missionary work in the continent for three reasons. First, delegates created the Committee on Cooperation in Latin America (CCLA). Throughout the first half of the twentieth century, the CCLA represented Latin American Protestant bodies in international ecumenical meetings and gathered a group of distinguished Protestant intellectuals in the region.[67] It was the CCLA that planned and organized the Panama Congress in 1916. Second, the records of the conference reveal the extent to which participants reconfigured some ideas of the Edinburgh Conference of 1910, though remaining faithful to the principle of Christian cooperation. While the leaders of the Edinburgh Conference proclaimed the unity of Christendom and divided the world religious atlas along imaginary lines between the Christian west and the pagan east,[68] participants of the New York Conference in 1913 were reluctant to acknowledge the Catholic Church as a part of it. For some of them, Christian cooperation involved the congregation of various Protestant mission bodies in the continent to Christianize culture via promotion of basic education, production of Christian literature, and intensified presence in universities. Collaboration with the Catholic Church was not on the horizon. Third, during both the preparation and the conference itself, Speer and the other participants had to clarify constantly what the expression "Latin America" really meant. In his advertisement of the conference's printed volume to

---

[65] Statement Adopted by Conference on Latin America, March 12–13, 1913. PHS, RG81-34-21, Latin America Conference, 1912–1914.
[66] *Conference on Missions*, 185–188.
[67] On the CCLA and its relevance see Piedra, *Evangelização protestante*, and Carlos Mondragón, *Like Leaven in the Dough: Protestant Social Thought in Latin America, 1920–1950*, trans. Daniel Miller and Ben Post (Madison, NJ: Fairleigh Dickinson University Press, 2011).
[68] Stanley, *The World Missionary Conference*, 64, 72.

THE IDEA OF CHRISTIAN COOPERATION   183

American missionary societies, Speer defined Latin America in geographical terms, as comprising Mexico, Central America, Cuba, Porto Rico, South America, and the Philippines.[69] And the conference statement asserted a similar geographical division: "By Latin-America we mean Mexico, the countries of South America and Central America, Cuba, Porto Rico and the Philippine Islands."[70] This was something new for missionary societies. In the nineteenth century, they operated in the continent employing basic geographical units to divide their work (e.g. South America, Brazil, the Caribbean, etc.).

The idea of Latin America was not new by the time of the New York Conference. According to historian John Phelan, it emerged among French Pan-Latinist intellectuals in the mid-nineteenth century, who claimed that Latin peoples shared linguistic and cultural affinities. For them, France was the natural leader and inspiration of the Latin world. According to Phelan, this principle legitimized French intervention in Mexico in the 1860s when the idea of Latin America was finally conceived.[71] However, at least since the 1850s, South American writers and intellectuals, such as Chilean socialist Francisco Bilbao and Colombian journalist José María Torres Caicedo, had already articulated the idea that there was a "Latin" America in contrast and opposition to an "Anglo-Saxon" America. While the continent's "liberators" in the aftermath of independence were chiefly concerned with threats to American sovereignty posed by European colonialism, Caicedo and Bilbao in the mid-nineteenth century were concerned with North American intervention. For both of them, the antagonism between the south and the north of the American continent stemmed from racial differences, not mere geographical divisions.[72] With the strengthening of US expansionism toward Central and South America and the proliferation of American filibuster expeditions in the Caribbean in the mid-nineteenth century, Spanish American intellectuals and diplomats began to "view their relations with

---

[69] R. Speer, New York, May 28, 1913; May 15, 1913. PHS, RG81-34-21, Latin America Conference, 1912–1914.

[70] *Conference on Missions*, 183.

[71] John L. Phelan, "Pan-Latinism, French Intervention in Mexico (1861-7) and the Genesis of the Idea of Latin America," in *Conciencia y autenticidad históricas: escritas en homenaje a Edmundo O'Gorman*, ed. Juan A. Ortega y Medina (Mexico City: UNAM, 1968), 279-298.

[72] Aims McGuinness, "Searching for 'Latin America': Race and Sovereignty in the Americas in the 1850s," in *Race and Nation in Modern Latin America*, ed. Nancy Appelbaum, Anne Macpherson, and Karin A. Rosemblatt (Chapel Hill, NC: University of North Carolina Press, 2003), 87-107, at 99. See also Leslie Bethell, "Brazil and 'Latin America,'" *Journal of Latin American Studies* 42 (2010): 457-485.

the United States in terms of a race war."[73] Throughout the nineteenth century, the concept of Latin America that crystalized among Spanish American elites was defined, amongst other characteristics, by their opposition to the expansionist impulses of a Protestant Anglo-Saxon America, the exaltation of a noble Latin spiritualism against Anglo-Saxon materialism, and the democratic republicanism prevailing in the American continent that viewed the imperialism of European monarchies as a threat.[74]

Racial divides were of central importance to the making of the idea of Latin America, but so were religious boundaries. Catholic priests and intellectuals built upon this racialized idea of Latin America to elaborate their own "unified reactionary front against the secular and liberal temptations" posed by nationalist movements and liberal revolutions.[75] Indeed, the first institution to use the expression *Latin America* in its name was the *Collegio Pío Latino Americano*, founded in Rome in the second half of the nineteenth century by Chilean priest José Eyzaguirre Portales under the auspices of Pope Pius IX. The school trained a generation of influential priests who defined their Latin and Catholic identities against the schismatic Protestants and a heretic Europe.[76] Therefore, the idea of Latin America carried various linguistic, historical, religious, and racial connotations that opened much room for multiple appropriations. As will be seen in the last part of this chapter, Brazilian evangelical ministers modified this conceptual repertoire.

After the New York Conference in 1913, members of the newly founded CCLA spent the next three years planning and organizing a larger congress. Preparations, format, methodology, and logistics followed closely the model of the Edinburgh Conference.[77] Like Edinburgh, the Latin American congress had eight commissions, some of them even had the same names used in the World Missionary Conference, questionnaires were sent beforehand to the various delegates who attended the meeting, and an advisory committee prepared reports in advance. This advisory committee included, among others, influential figures such as John Mott, Josiah Strong, and the Brazilian

---

[73] Michel Gobat, "The Invention of Latin America: A Transnational History of Anti-imperialism, Democracy, and Race," *American Historical Review* 118 (2013): 1345–1375, at 1352.

[74] Gobat, "The Invention of Latin America," 1367. See also James Sanders, *The Vanguard of the Atlantic World: Creating Modernity, Nation, and Democracy in Nineteenth-century Latin America* (Durham, NC, and London: Duke University Press, 2014).

[75] Mauricio Tenorio-Trillo, *Latin America: The Allure and Power of an Idea* (Chicago: University of Chicago Press, 2017), 51.

[76] Enrique Ayala Mora, "El origen del nombre América Latina y la tradición católica del siglo XIX," *Anuario Colombiano de Historia Social y de la Cultura* 40 (2013): 213–241.

[77] Hogg, *Ecumenical Foundations*, 173.

journalist José Carlos Rodrigues.[78] The meeting was named the Congress on Christian Work in Latin America and, upon deliberation, the committee decided to hold the congress in Panama City because, for the organizers, that symbolized the pan-American ideal and the integration of the Latin and Anglo-Saxon Americas.[79] The congress took place between February 10–20, 1916. Two hundred and thirty-five delegates representing forty-four American missionary societies, one Canadian, and one British, participated. Only twenty-seven delegates were Latin Americans. The official language was English, but participants often spoke Spanish and Portuguese in between plenary meetings.[80] A Uruguayan Methodist university professor, Eduardo Monteverde, was elected president of the congress; Speer became chairman of the conference's sessions; Samuel Inman, who had been a missionary in Mexico, was elected executive secretary; and Mott was appointed chairman of the business committee.[81]

From the outset, the congress adopted a geographical definition of Latin America that differed from that of the New York Conference in 1913.[82] Although style and structure bore remarkable resemblance to that of Edinburgh in 1910, participants of the Panama Congress reworked the notion of Christian cooperation and unity in important ways. The central point of disagreement was collaboration and unity with the Catholic Church. The report of Commission II on "Message and Method," for instance, made an extensive analysis of the influence of Catholic missions in Latin America quoting from colonial laws, history books, and primary sources to provide a "just and adequate" portrait. And although they praised the courage, religious zeal, and enthusiasm of the first missionary orders in the colonial period, especially Franciscans and Jesuits, the report also observed that these missionaries left much room for the incorporation of "Indian paganism" into Christianity.[83] According to the report, while one could find good, noble examples in Catholic history of "peaceable evangelism," such as the

---

[78] *Christian Work in Latin America: Survey and Occupation, Message and Method, Education, Tome I* (New York: The Missionary Education Movement, 1917), 4–17.
[79] *Christian Work in Latin America, Tome I*, 16–17, 24–25.
[80] Bastian, *Le protestantisme*, 143.
[81] *Christian Work in Latin America, Tome I*, 28.
[82] *Christian Work in Latin America, Tome I*, 47. In Panama it was extended to include Cuba, Haiti, Santo Domingo, Porto Rico, the other islands of the West Indies, Mexico, British Honduras, Guatemala, Honduras, Salvador, Nicaragua, Costa Rica, Panama, Venezuela, Colombia, Ecuador, Peru, Bolivia, Chile, Argentina, Uruguay, Paraguay, Brazil, and the three Guianas: French, Dutch, and British.
[83] *Christian Work in Latin America, Tome I*, 253–254, 258–259.

medieval missions to northern and central Europe, it was the aggressive, intrusive, and colonialist evangelistic model of early modern Spain that took root in Latin America. And if medieval Spanish Catholic orthodoxy set noble examples of Christian theology and practice, it was the militant and hierarchical missionary movement inspired in the Counter-Reformation that prevailed, bringing to the Iberian colonies the Inquisition and "fanaticism."[84] So, whereas the Catholic Church could be proud of its heroic examples of Christian orthodoxy and positive social influence in other parts of the world, in South America the institution "proved an almost complete failure."[85]

Commission VIII on "Cooperation and the Promotion of Unity" made a plainer assertion regarding collaboration with the Catholic Church: "When the inevitable question is raised, whether at any point or in any form we may expect cooperation with the Roman Catholic Church, the usual reply is that such an expectation is hopeless." For this commission's delegates, due to the long-lasting competition between Protestants and Catholics in Latin America and to the suspicions on both sides of the Christian divide, cooperation with the Catholic Church as an institution was undesirable.[86] However, the report stated that cooperation with specific Catholic individuals was bearing good fruits in many parts of the continent.[87]

The Panama Congress conceived the idea of Christian cooperation as the unity and collaboration of evangelical missions and non-denominational organizations in the field, working together around common goals such as provision of formal education, circulation of Bibles and Christian literature, and evangelization of women. The Congress was particularly concerned with the "social effects of the gospel" in societies where the Industrial Revolution was being quickly introduced, mobilizing international capital, restructuring work relations, and attracting migrant workers.[88] Delegates turned their attention not only to direct evangelization or purely religious matters, but also to the social and political implications of the missionary enterprise. And along these lines Catholicism was viewed as a branch of Christianity that did not nurture a strong sense of individual responsibility and intellectual reasoning.

---

[84] *Christian Work in Latin America*, Tome I, 255–256, 261.
[85] *Christian Work in Latin America*, Tome I, 265.
[86] *Christian Work in Latin America: Cooperation and the Promotion of Unity, the Training and Efficiency of Missionaries, the Devotional Addresses, the Popular Addresses*, Tome III (New York: The Missionary Education Movement, 1917), 12–13, 52.
[87] *Christian Work in Latin America*, Tome III, 53–54.
[88] *Christian Work in Latin America*, Tome I, 283–300; Bastian, *Le protestantisme*, 141–142.

At the end of the Panama Congress, a group of delegates embarked on a series of meetings across Latin America aimed at disseminating the findings and strategies of the congress. Disagreements between Latin American participants at Panama and the American members of the organizing committee gained momentum during these regional conferences of Lima, Santiago, Buenos Aires, and Rio de Janeiro.[89] The divisive issue revolved around the attitude of evangelical missions toward the Catholic Church in the continent. Whereas Latin American delegates and missionaries in the continent wanted to issue a clear statement on this matter, the central committee at Panama was wary of it. Brazilian delegates, such as the Rev. Eduardo Carlos Pereira, were suspicious of North American patronage.[90] In the Rio de Janeiro Conference, presided over by the American Episcopal bishop Lucien Kinsolving, Pereira presented a statement titled *Our Attitude Towards the Roman Church* that, in his words, summarized the opinion of many Brazilians and Latin Americans on the matter. Although this statement clearly diverged from the decisions taken in Panama, Pereira insisted on the relevance of his work, arguing that the prevailing atmosphere in Rio was in significant ways different from that of Panama City. Even though his statement did not receive full approbation from the conference's participants, it was unanimously decided that Pereira's document should be sent to Brazilian evangelical churches for deliberation.[91]

Pereira's ten-page statement was carefully worded, retaining some of the spirit of the Edinburgh Conference of 1910 and the Panama Congress of 1916 while also displaying the result of decades of Protestant–Catholic rivalry in Brazil. The statement, printed by the Baptist Publishing House of Rio de Janeiro, dedicated one page to acknowledging that the Catholic Church was a part of Christendom. It declared that the Catholic Church had preserved in its central doctrines and practices all the fundamental dogmas of Christianity, such as the centrality of the Bible, the dogma of the Holy Trinity, and the principle of the divine institution of the church.[92] It also stated that throughout history the Church had acted as a positive force to keep alive the "Christian idea" in the world. However, Pereira argued, the Catholic Church

---

[89] *Regional Conferences in Latin America* (New York: Missionary Education Movement, 1917).
[90] John Sinclair and Arturo Piedra Solano, "The Dawn of Ecumenism in Latin America: Robert Speer, Presbyterians, and the Panama Conference of 1916," *Journal of Presbyterian History* 77 (1999): 1–11.
[91] *Regional Conferences*, 219–221.
[92] Eduardo C. Pereira, *Nossa attitude para com a Egreja Romana* (Rio de Janeiro: Casa Publicadora Baptista, 1916), 1–2.

prevented believers from having direct access to the Bible and replaced it with a host of traditions. In his words, Catholics recognized the existence of an even more popular trinity composed by Jesus, Mary, and Joseph, whose central figure "absorbs the filial affection of the people."[93] The Catholic Church was represented in his statement as a mundane institution, "a kingdom of this world" whose centralized hierarchy, governed by a group of omnipotent priests, replaced Christ as sole mediator between mankind and God and was thus in constant conflict with political and national sovereignties.[94] More explicitly, Pereira attacked three nineteenth-century Catholic dogmas promulgated by pope Pius IX and the Vatican. First, the dogma of the Immaculate Conception, that consolidated "the divinization of the Virgin;" second, the dogma of Papal Infallibility, that complemented the divinization of a woman with the deification of a man; and third, the promulgation of the *Syllabus*, described as declaration of war against modern civilization in its condemnation of civil and religious liberties.[95] In the conclusion, Pereira translated into Portuguese lengthy passages from the documents of the Panama Congress dedicated to inspiring the attitudes of Protestant missions toward the Roman Church. First, he described it as twofold involving intimate sympathy and solidarity toward "the Christian element" and the repudiation of the elements they considered anti-Christian. Second, to assert the Protestant roots of Latin American evangelical churches, he repeated words uttered in Panama: "Heirs of the noble religious impulse of the sixteenth century, we will endeavor, in the bosom of Christendom, to be faithful witnesses: a) of the supremacy of the Word of God over the traditions of men, b) of the supremacy of faith over works, c) of the supremacy of God's people over the clergy."[96]

In fact, most of the Brazilian Protestant ministers and intellectuals at that time believed that a general Christian reunion with the Catholic Church four hundred years after the Reformation was an impossible task, especially in the face of both the Ultramontane revival and the eruption of popular messianic movements. In the early twentieth century, the Catholic Church was experiencing a process of institutional reconstruction and expansion, seeking to regain some of the terrain lost to Protestant evangelization and

---

[93] Pereira, *Nossa attitude*, 3.
[94] Pereira, *Nossa attitude*, 4–5.
[95] Pereira, *Nossa attitude*, 8–9.
[96] Pereira, *Nossa attitude*, 9–10. On the principles defined at the Panama Congress, see Daniel Salinas, *Taking Up the Mantle: Latin American Evangelical Theology in the 20th Century* (Carlisle: Langham Global Library, 2017), 14.

religious competition during the last decades of the Empire.[97] However, if Pereira's statement of 1916 made substantial changes to the idea of Christian cooperation since the World Missionary Conference of 1910, it was two books written in the wake of the Panama congress, one by Pereira and another by the Presbyterian minister Erasmo Braga, that modified the idea of cooperation more substantially.

Braga and Pereira: Pan-American Integration and Missionary Views of Science and Race

Among the twenty-seven Latin American delegates at the Panama Congress of 1916 there were three Brazilians, all of them Presbyterian ministers: the Rev. Álvaro Reis, pastor of the Presbyterian Church of Rio de Janeiro who attended the World Missionary Conference in 1910; the Rev. Eduardo Carlos Pereira, who was at that time an influential grammarian and polemicist; and the Rev. Erasmo Braga, a pastor, educator, writer, and theology professor. They were all active and engaged participants in the congress and the regional meetings. Braga and Pereira wrote important accounts, although of a very different nature, of the Panama Congress that translated and modified the idea of Christian cooperation to their Brazilian and Latin American publics. Braga's two-hundred-page book, *Pan-Americanism: Religious Aspect*, became a sort of official account of the Panama Congress. Both its original publication in Portuguese and translation into Spanish were sponsored by the Missionary Education Movement of the United States and Canada.[98] More than simply describing the Congress, Braga's book was an interpretation of the significance and impact of the Panama Congress of 1916. Pereira's book, in contrast, was much longer, with nearly 450 pages, and of a very different sort. Entitled *The Religious Problem of Latin America: A Dogmatic-Historical Study* and published in 1920 by the Methodist Press of São Paulo, this book was Pereira's masterpiece of religious controversy.[99] Here he expanded Émile de Laveleye's arguments in *The Future of the Catholic Peoples*, published in Brazil in 1875. Pereira's central argument was that the solution to Latin

---

[97] Sérgio Miceli, *A elite eclesiástica brasileira: 1890–1930*, 2nd ed. (São Paulo: Companhia das Letras, 2009).
[98] Erasmo Braga, *Pan-Americanismo: Aspecto religioso* (New York: Missionary Education Movement, 1916).
[99] Eduardo C. Pereira, *O problema religioso da America Latina: Estudo dogmatico-historico* (São Paulo: Imprensa Methodista, 1920).

America's political instability, social unrest, and economic inferiority was a general Christian reformation that substituted the influence of Roman Catholicism with the values, practices, and egalitarian experience of the early Christian church. In these books, Braga and Pereira reworked the idea of Christian cooperation in significant ways, channeling them into the sociopolitical debates that surfaced in the Brazilian and Latin American public spheres in the early twentieth century.

In this period, conservative Catholics and nationalist intellectuals held Protestant missionaries in contempt. In many cases they were seen as strangers backed by powerful international bureaucracies who acted on behalf of North American interests and favored foreign intrusion in the continent.[100] In addition to this, leading Brazilian scholars and diplomats in this period were suspicious of Pan-Americanism, the intensification of commercial and diplomatic exchange among the various countries of the American continent. This policy was frequently equated with North American imperialism. For diplomat and historian Manoel de Oliveira Lima, the principle of Pan-Americanism and the emergence of an American conscience were at odds with the establishment of a North American protectorate over the continent.[101] Physician and sociologist Manoel Bomfim contested the legitimacy of the Monroe Doctrine, by which the United States would collaborate with the rest of the Americas to combat attempts of European empires to re-conquer the continent. In Bomfim's words, the Monroe Doctrine would ultimately dissolve the sovereignty of Latin America, absorbing the region into the expansionist policy of the United States.[102] Even Sérgio Buarque de Holanda showed suspicion toward the diplomatic and commercial interests of the United States in Latin America when he began to publish his very first pieces in Brazilian periodicals in the 1920s. For Holanda, the Monroe Doctrine was not a show of American goodwill in the face of European imperialism. Rather, it was an expression of American imperialism and it was an attempt to promote the "Americanization of the world."[103] On the other

---

[100] Virginia Garrard-Burnett, *Protestantism in Guatemala: Living in the New Jerusalem* (Austin: University of Texas Press, 1998), 68–69; Piedra, *Evangelização protestante*, ch. 1; Paul Freston, "Pentecostalism in Latin America: Characteristics and Controversies," *Social Compass* 45 (1998): 335–358.

[101] Manuel de Oliveira Lima, *The Evolution of Brazil Compared with that of Spanish and Anglo-Saxon America* (Stanford, CA: Stanford University Press, 1914), 128–129; Manuel de Oliveira Lima, *Pan-Americanismo (Monroe-Bolivar-Roosevelt)* (Rio de Janeiro: H. Garnier, 1907).

[102] Manoel Bomfim, *A América Latina: Males de origem* (Rio de Janeiro: Topbooks, 2005 [1905]), 48–49.

[103] *A Cigarra*, São Paulo, July 1920.

hand, there was yet another group of influential intellectuals and politicians, such as Joaquim Nabuco, Sílvio Romero, and Ruy Barbosa, who believed that Pan-American integration would exert a positive economic and political impact in the country.[104]

It was in this context, and responding to both Catholic and nationalist intellectuals, that Braga and Pereira highlighted the relevance of Pan-American cooperation and sought to restore the public image of Protestantism and Protestant missionaries. More specifically, they brought together the ideas of Christian cooperation and Pan-Americanism, conceptualizing the former as a driver of transnational fellowship. The two authors employed racial categories to account for the difference between Latins and Anglo-Saxons in the American continent. But they also contested the legitimacy of racial theories as appropriate explanations for the social problems of the continent.

Braga, for instance, in an attempt to enumerate the factors that set apart Anglo-Saxon and Latin peoples in the continent, argued that any explanation relying solely on ethnic factors would not capture these differences. Instead, any such analysis of the "components of our social mass, must attend much more to the value of the intellectual tendencies, to the spiritual content of the two great elements that form the bulk of the population of the Americas, than to the other ethnic factors."[105] Braga began his account of the Panama Congress of 1916 by singling out the historical and religious differences between the Anglo-Saxon and the Latin races resorting to powerful contrasts. In his words, whereas the Pilgrim Fathers who settled the north of the continent were an austere people who had fled religious persecution in their homeland seeking religious liberty, the Iberian *conquistadores* came from societies dominated by the bonfires of the Inquisition. While Anglo-Americans managed to remain throughout history as a racially homogeneous people, Iberian colonists cultivated violent relationships with indigenous women, generating a mestizo race. Furthermore, while those who settled the north founded communities based on the principles of liberty of conscience, democracy, and modern individualism, the Latin colonizers imposed absolutist forms of government

---

[104] Bethell, "Brazil and 'Latin America,'" 470–474. For a comprehensive study of the reception of Pan-Americanism in Brazil, see Kátia Gerab Baggio, "A 'outra' América: A América Latina na visão dos intelectuais brasileiros das primeiras décadas republicanas." (unpublished PhD dissertation, University of São Paulo, 1998).

[105] Braga, *Pan-Americanismo*, 3–4.

in the Americas through the force of the military and the hierarchy of the Catholic Church.[106] Braga's description drew upon some of the origin myths that had been surfacing in the Brazilian evangelical imaginary since at least the 1870s. However, he did not explain racial difference in rigid, inflexible terms. In fact, he viewed a series of complex and long-standing interactions and exchanges that mutually shaped the Latin and the Anglo-Saxon races since the first century AD. And in this trajectory the central driver of change was Christian religion, shaping both cultures through its apologists, poets, and theologians.[107]

Pereira built his argument about racial difference in another way. Like Braga, he explained the differences between the Anglo-Saxon and Latin peoples deploying racial categories, without yielding to racial determinism. In Pereira's words, it was not the cephalic index, widely used by early twentieth-century Brazilian physicians to identify traces of racial degeneration, that differentiated the "dolichocephalic" of northern or southern Europe, where these races emerged. Instead, it was "specific affinities" that distinguished them.[108] In contrast to Braga, who thought that the distinctive traces that shaped each race were fluid, Pereira described the differences between Anglo-Saxons and Latins using stable characteristics and marked contrasts. Anglo-Saxons were an individualistic and pragmatic people, who sacrificed aesthetics in favor of safety and comfort; a people of analytical aptitudes, who did not appreciate abstract theories but were attached to facts. Latin peoples, on the other hand, were inclined toward collectivist forms of social organization. They were sympathetic, communicative, and social; a people of synthetic intellectual aptitudes, prone to making generalizations.[109] Although Pereira described these traces in a positive light, his racial typology also pointed to some shortcomings: "The degeneration of Anglo-Saxon individualism is insolence and selfishness, and the degeneration of Iberian-American collectivism is indolence and parasitism."[110] And, formulating his argument in favor of Pan-American integration, he wrote that "the ideal of a perfect civilization is neither, manifestly, in the exclusivist individualism of

---

[106] Braga, *Pan-Americanismo*, 5–8.
[107] Braga, *Pan-Americanismo*, 193–195.
[108] Pereira, *O problema religioso*, 147. On the uses of the cephalic index in Brazil, see Lilia M. Schwarcz, *The Spectacle of the Races: Scientists, Institutions, and the Race Question in Brazil, 1870–1930*, trans. Leland Guyer (New York: Hill and Wang, 1999), 260–262; Levine, *Vale of Tears*, 207–208.
[109] Pereira, *O problema religioso*, 149–153.
[110] Pereira, *O problema religioso*, 151.

the Anglo-Saxon race, nor in the exclusive mutualist collectivism of the Latin race; but in the combination of the two races."[111]

The two Presbyterian intellectuals portrayed the encounters between Latin and North Americans in the Panama Congress as a friendly and fraternal gathering of the two dominant races of the continent along the racial typologies established. Braga and Pereira depicted the Panama Congress as an expression of Christian fellowship and communion, a major contrast to the on-going war in Europe. In fact, one of the effects of the twentieth-century ecumenical conferences was that they encouraged Christians throughout the world to reimagine their affiliation and belonging to the "Universal Church." African participants at the Tambaram Conference in India in 1938 described how Christian communion displaced racial differences.[112]

Braga's memories of the Panama Congress of 1916 displayed similar sentiments. Enumerating the characteristics that defined Latin America's evangelical churches, he affirmed that all its quarter-million communicant members were connected in one spirit by the strength of their religious belonging. And he observed: "the spiritual bond that connects them is stronger than the sentiment of race."[113] The Panama Congress was, in his words, a fraternal and amiable meeting of some of the most distinguished men and women in the Americas interested in the unification of the religious and moral forces of the continent in a place where American unity was previously dreamt.[114] Here he was referring to the Panama Congress of 1826, idealized by Simón Bolívar, that first propounded the unity of the Americas. On describing the outcomes of the congress, Braga observed that the most sensible and immediate effect of the meeting was "the occasion for individuals committed to the same work and who did not even know each other by name, to meet each other, engage in friendship, and feel stronger through their unity and solidarity—this was the particular effect that the Congress had on the Latin delegates."[115] For him, Christian unity and cooperation across national borders should offer a corrective to the Monroe Doctrine and

---

[111] Pereira, *O problema religioso*, 154.
[112] This was the case of Thompson Samkange, Terence Ranger, *Are We Not Also Men? The Samkange Family & African Politics in Zimbabwe, 1920-64* (Harare: Baobab; London: James Currey, 1995), 70–74. On the universalist appeal of Christianity, see Joel Cabrita and David Maxwell, "Introduction: Relocating World Christianity," in *Relocating World Christianity: Interdisciplinary Studies in Universal and Local Expressions of the Christian Faith*, ed. Joel Cabrita, David Maxwell, and Emma Wild-Wood (Leiden: Brill, 2017), 1–44.
[113] Braga, *Pan-Americanismo*, 50.
[114] Braga, *Pan-Americanismo*, 62, 87–88, 92–94.
[115] Braga, *Pan-Americanismo*, 181–182.

exert a decisive influence on the principle of Pan-Americanism. Cooperation and unity meant for him more than only the promotion of Protestant missionary work in Latin America, the union of denominations and churches in favor of the missionary enterprise, and the autonomy of national churches.[116] It should also awaken in the United States the interest in Latin American affairs, history, and prospects. And that was one of the contributions of the Panama Congress of 1916 to the remaking of Pan-Americanism. Braga affirmed that in the wake of the congress, schools, churches, and public opinion in the United States were taking a closer interest in the commercial, cultural, and religious situation of Latin America, as well as producing secondary school textbooks sympathetic to Latin American issues. For him, such a wide dissemination of knowledge of the region among the North American public would help dissolve old rivalries and misconceptions about Latin America.[117]

Pereira made even stronger connections between the Panama Congress, the idea of Christian cooperation, and the principle of Pan-Americanism. He defined Pan-Americanism as "the affirmation of the continental conscience, that brightens itself in the light of liberty and progress; it is the noble sentiment of solidarity of the peoples of the Western hemisphere, who utter peace and love, in this distressing moment, in which an entire continent drowns itself in the blood of a barbarian and fratricidal war."[118] Pereira linked the unifying tendencies of Pan-Americanism to the actions of America's most famous liberators: San Martín, Simón Bolívar, and Thomas Jefferson. More significantly, whereas organizers of the Panama Congress of 1916 and Braga situated the congress on a succession of earlier ecumenical missionary meetings that could be traced back to the mid-nineteenth century,[119] Pereira located the meeting in a succession of Pan-American congresses since 1824.[120] For Pereira, the Panama Congress expressed the dream of religious cooperation across the Americas while the other congresses developed the commercial, diplomatic, and scientific aspects of Pan-Americanism. In accordance with Braga, Pereira believed that one of the most distinctive aspects of the Panama Congress was the "spirit of confraternity" that brought the assembly together. In his words, both the Edinburgh Conference of 1910 and the Panama

[116] Braga, *Pan-Americanismo*, 24, 38, 44–45, 73–74.
[117] Braga, *Pan-Americanismo*, 185–187.
[118] Pereira, *O problema religioso*, 143.
[119] *Christian Work in Latin America, Tome I*, 4–6; Braga, *Pan-Americanismo*, 72, 80–82.
[120] Pereira, *O problema religioso*, 144.

Congress of 1916 were significant demonstrations of the contemporary movement toward cohesion among the various Protestant denominations, manifest in "fraternal love, dogmatic and moral unity."[121] Unlike Braga, Pereira wrote about the occasions of disagreement between the Congress delegates. In his analysis, these conflicts conformed to the racial lines he had previously drawn. The contentious issue was how the congress would define the attitude of evangelical churches toward the Catholic Church. In Pereira's narrative, the loquaciousness of Latin Americans clashed with the taciturn nature of the Anglo-Saxons: the former demanding from the assembly a firm and marked declaration of principles, and the latter avoiding any form of direct confrontation.[122] His ten-page statement, presented to the delegates in the Rio de Janeiro Regional Conference, was an attempt to combine the impulsive and vehement mood of Latin Americans with the tolerant and inoffensive character of Anglo-Saxons.[123] Pereira believed there was space for amicable negotiation and accord in the midst of the encounter between two different races with their distinctive traces.

Braga's and Pereira's reflections on the Panama Congress of 1916 built upon an earlier set of ideas and values that informed much of the nineteenth-century missionary and political imagination in Brazil. At least since the publication of the book *Brazil and the Brazilians*, written by Methodist missionary Daniel P. Kidder and Presbyterian chaplain James C. Fletcher in the United States, missionaries believed that Brazil held a distinguished position among South American countries. This book was a nineteenth-century best-seller among English-speaking audiences. Brazil was depicted in the missionary imagination as a vast country, larger than the contiguous United States, with abundant natural resources, governed by an enlightened political elite who did not yield to the tyrannical impositions of the army and the Catholic Church. The country, however lacked technical and economic progress, and needed the appropriate impulses to prosper.[124] This notion of the exceptionality of Brazil among South American countries had been first articulated by members of the conservative imperial intelligentsia in the nineteenth century. In their view, the independence of the solitary Portuguese-speaking monarchy continued the civilizing traditions of the

---

[121] Pereira, *O problema religioso*, 175.
[122] Pereira, *O problema religioso*, 176–177.
[123] Pereira, *O problema religioso*, 200–201.
[124] James C. Fletcher and Daniel P. Kidder, *Brazil and the Brazilians: Portrayed in Historical and Descriptive Sketches* (Philadelphia: Childs & Peterson, 1857).

Portuguese Empire, rather than breaking away from it. And for them, this unique feature of Brazilian society contrasted with the surrounding Spanish-speaking republics, whose violent conflicts against Spain resulted in political instability.[125]

Decades later, in an address given to the Geographical Society of New York in December 1889, the Presbyterian missionary George Chamberlain echoed similar notions of Brazilian exceptionalism. He affirmed that Brazil was, "by eternal determination," to be one and undivided. Its geographical unity was inscribed in the foreordained laws of nature, rendering secession a rebellion against divine law. Additionally, Chamberlain argued, physical geographers had shown how the "old hemisphere" tended to divide and scatter the families of the earth, whereas the American continent favored the congregation of the peoples. The long-time missionary in Brazil asserted that all measures taken by politicians to "close the 'Golden Gate'" to immigrants in the United States would be vain, for "the blessings of our civilization belong to the nations of the earth." And he declared that "a similar theatre has been prepared on the southern half of this continent in what we now know as the United States of Brazil. Vast area, healthfulness and indivisibility all point to a congregating of the families of man and a development in the near future."[126]

When the Brazilian delegates of the Panama Congress of 1916 began to uphold the ideas of Christian cooperation and unity in Brazil there was already an older intellectual tradition that conceived the giant of the north and the giant of the south as the greatest lighthouses of modern civilization in the New World. For Braga and Pereira, Christian cooperation would reshape and modify the principle and practice of American integration by attaching the values of Christian fraternity and transnational fellowship to Pan-Americanism. At the same time, these principles would offer a corrective to the problem of American imperialism. In Pereira's words, the Panama Congress of 1916 sought to avoid both a "unilateral interpretation" of the Monroe Doctrine on the part of the United States, and the "red flag of an exclusivist Latinism" on the part of Latin Americans. Instead, the goal was

---

[125] Luís Cláudio V. G. Santos, *O Brasil entre a América e a Europa: O império e o interamericanismo (do Congresso do Panamá à Conferência de Washington)* (São Paulo: Editora UNESP, 2004); Manoel L. S. Guimarães, "Nação e civilização nos trópicos: O Instituto Histórico e Geográfico Brasileiro e o projeto de uma história nacional," *Estudos Históricos* 1 (1988): 5–27. See also Tenorio-Trillo, *Latin America*, ch. 3.

[126] *Brazilian Missions* IV, no. 3 (March 1891): 23–24.

to construct a bilateral interpretation of the Monroe Doctrine via the tightening of "the current ties of friendship."[127]

The evangelical enthusiasm with the destinies of the American continent resonated with broader utopian expectations in Brazil in the context of the Great War. Journalists and writers in the aftermath of the conflict compared the modernity and openness of the city of São Paulo to the collapse of the Old World. Whereas Europe had revived old divisions in a destructive and fratricidal war, the New World and its modern epitome, São Paulo, were inversions of Babel, accommodating the displaced and despised peoples of the earth.[128] For some observers, the Great War shattered the image of Europe as the embodiment of Christian civilization.[129] For delegates at Panama, the New World offered promising prospects. The ideals of American integration proclaimed by missionaries and ministers like Braga and Pereira did not simply derive from idealized views of North American civilization or served to legitimize US imperialism. They drew upon local utopias about the flourishing of American societies in the early twentieth century, their place in the world, and the century-old dreams of American unity.[130]

At this point, it may be clear that the ideas that circulated in the early twentieth-century evangelical public sphere were situated in at least two different contexts that inform much of their meaning and the expectations surrounding them. The first is the vibrant intellectual landscape of nineteenth- and twentieth-century Brazil, in which notions of race, nationality, and modernity mobilized the national intelligentsia. Second, the transnational networks generated by the worldwide expansion of missionary Protestantism, that enabled people, ideas, and books to move in different directions.

The Panama Congress of 1916 reinforced yet another set of ideas and theologies that circulated in Brazil and throughout the worldwide circuits of global Protestantism in the early twentieth century. According to historian Brian Stanley, the World Missionary Conference of 1910 consolidated a new "science of missions," the rigorous application of modern scientific methods

---

[127] Pereira, *O problema religioso*, 162–163.
[128] Nicolau Sevcenko, *Orfeu extático na metrópole: São Paulo, sociedade e cultura nos frementes anos 20* (São Paulo: Companhia das Letras, 1992), 37–38.
[129] Brian Stanley, *Christianity in the Twentieth Century: A World History* (Princeton, NJ: Princeton University Press, 2018), 17.
[130] On the Pan-American utopias of the twentieth century, see Richard Cándida Smith, *Improvised Continent: Pan-Americanism and Cultural Exchange* (Philadelphia: University of Pennsylvania Press, 2017); Maria Ligia Prado, *Utopias latino-americanas: Política, sociedade, cultura* (São Paulo: Contexto, 2021).

to the understanding of the missionary challenges of the day, a trend promoted by advocates of the evangelical missionary movement since the late nineteenth century.[131] As historians and anthropologists have shown, missionaries made important contributions to scientific and anthropological research before the specialization of academic disciplines in the nineteenth and twentieth centuries.[132] Braga and Pereira, in the wake of the Edinburgh Conference of 1910 and the Panama Congress of 1916, shared in the scientific enthusiasm of their age. They portrayed the Panama Congress as a meeting that excited both the spiritual sensibilities and the scientific rigor of participants. In Braga's words, the "atmosphere of the Congress was intensely spiritual," as all sessions included hymn singing, Bible reading, and prayers.[133] Pereira claimed that the religious services at the end of each session, comprising prayers, singing, and a sermon, instilled a spirit of fraternity in the assembly.[134] However, the Congress' organizers tightly controlled the timetables and chronograms, trying to keep in time the religious services, presentations of the reports of each commission, and the following discussion.[135]

The two Brazilian delegates highlighted the interplay between the spiritual and the scientific aspects of the Panama Congress. According to Braga, all reports prepared for the congress drew upon data on the physical, moral, social, and religious situation of Latin American countries collected from reliable and unbiased sources. These included official documents; information provided by consulates and embassies; books written by respectable travelers, scientists, and Latin American intellectuals; along with data taken from works of reference such as the Statesman's Year Book.[136] Fieldwork was regarded as a "sociological work" of vital importance, because it charted Latin America's most pressing social and moral issues, and one of the missionaries' central task was to address these social ills through energetic Christian action.[137] In one of the regional meetings following the Panama Congress,

[131] Stanley, *The World Missionary*, 4–5.
[132] Patrick Harries and David Maxwell, "Introduction: The Spiritual in the Secular," in *The Spiritual in the Secular: Missionaries and Knowledge about Africa*, ed. Patrick Harries and David Maxwell (Grand Rapids, MI: W. B. Eerdmans Publishing Co., 2012), 1–29; Sujit Sivasundaram, *Nature and the Godly Empire: Science and Evangelical Mission in the Pacific, 1795–1850* (Cambridge: Cambridge University Press, 2005).
[133] Braga, *Pan-Americanismo*, 90, 96–97.
[134] Pereira, *O problema religioso*, 167.
[135] Braga, *Pan-Americanismo*, 96.
[136] Braga, *Pan-Americanismo*, 119.
[137] Braga, *Pan-Americanismo*, 131–133, 174.

Braga gave an address at the University of Santiago, Chile, claiming that the values of Christianity nourished a spirit of scientific inquiry that dispelled the skepticism of intellectual elites. Upon quoting from the biblical passage in which the resurrected Christ invited Thomas to touch his scars, Braga asked: "What does it mean?—It is the real expression of Christ's desire to submitting himself to proof, to require from his disciples an intelligent, experimental, and affectionate faith."[138]

Pereira took this idea of the scientific dimension of Christianity even further, channeling it into his work of religious controversy. He believed that the social, political, and moral inferiority of Catholicism could be assessed scientifically, via the application of "rigorous scientific methods" and "unbiased observations."[139] In the last part of his book, Pereira proceeded to a historical and dogmatic study of Roman Catholicism, producing a bleak portrait of its history and moral consequences. Pereira made extensive reference to Apostolic and Church Fathers, such as Irenaeus, Origen, and Polycarp, along with modern theologians, such as Joseph Lightfoot, William Smith, George Salmon, Peter Schaff, and Ferdinand Baur, to validate his criticism of Catholic theology and his argument that the papacy was a late-Roman invention.[140] He cited William Gladstone to endorse his views on the incompatibility between the modern idea of liberty and the reforms of Pius IX, and referred to the writings of Catholic priests Père Hyacinthe Loyson and Josip Strossmayer to demonstrate how authoritarian the proclamation of the dogma of papal infallibility had been.[141] Pereira wanted to show that his work drew from reliable and balanced intellectual sources, the cornerstones of any rigorous scientific analysis.

However, Brazilian evangelical intellectuals fought on different fronts. Besides combating the modern Catholic renewal, they also stood against the secularist leanings of Brazil's intellectual elites, especially Positivist intellectuals and radical liberals. In the light of the Panama Congress of 1916, Pereira argued that, in the beginning of the twentieth century, the culture wars characteristic of the last decades of the previous century had given way to new forms of reconciliation between Christianity and science. Citing a lecture given at the Panama Congress by Francis J. McConnell, a bishop of the Methodist Episcopal Church, Pereira affirmed that whereas

---

[138] Erasmo Braga, *Religião e cultura* (São Paulo: União Editora Cultura, n/d), 42.
[139] Pereira, *O problema religioso*, 51, 119.
[140] Pereira, *O problema religioso*, 256–271, 295–301, 309–326.
[141] Pereira, *O problema religioso*, 355–360.

modern scientists showed certain inclination to materialism and agnosticism in the late-nineteenth century, especially after the publication of Charles Darwin's *The Origin of Species*, in the present day they were reconciling with Christianity. In his view, this was due to increasing pressures from Christian intellectuals. On the other hand, modern science had inflected on Christianity by stimulating new forms of theological inquiry, such as modern biblical criticism. For Pereira, the historical-critical method did not undermine Christ's spiritual supremacy, but it played a key role in the reconciliation between Christianity and science.[142] In making such assertions, Pereira was not alone. At the same time, José Carlos Rodrigues was preparing a major work of biblical theology aimed at showing that the so-called higher criticism, instead of undermining the evangelical emphasis on the centrality of the Bible, actually reasserted the spiritual authority of the scriptures.[143]

Moreover, in his attempts to dismiss polygenist interpretations of the origins of human races, Pereira connected modern science with Christianity once again. In the light of Darwinist notions of human evolution, which he referred to as "transformism," Pereira claimed that no one could reject the idea that all human races were varieties of a primitive family. On this matter, modern science and the biblical cosmogony showed that humankind descended from a common denominator. This is close to what historian Jane Samson has called "a theological anthropology that stressed human universality," which also inspired evangelical missionaries in the Pacific.[144] This convergence between evolutionism and the Christian narrative of creation was, for Pereira, a conclusive proof of the falseness of polygenism:

> At this time, the polygenism of human races must have entered into a coma, and contemporary science, hand in hand with Christian religion, was proclaiming the fraternity of all races, the original equality of all the branches of the human family (...). In fact, there is no absolute physiological and psychological distinction among the various ethnic groups that we call races. In the individuals of all of them, there are the same organs

---

[142] Pereira, *O problema religioso*, 168–169.
[143] Bloco de notas de José Carlos Rodrigues com estudos sobre alfabeto e religiões. BN, Correspondência de José Carlos Rodrigues, Caixa 003, 32,04,03 n 001. This issue will be examined in the next chapter.
[144] Jane Samson, *Race and Redemption: British Missionaries Encounter Pacific Peoples, 1797–1920* (Grand Rapids, MI: William B. Eerdmans Publishing Company, 2017), 52–53.

and functions, the same intellectual and moral faculties, the same essential thoughts and sentiments.[145]

For Pereira, given the contemporary reciprocity between the "religious and the scientific spirit," Christianity and science should join their forces to dominate physical nature and "solve the urgent problems of health and pauperism, as well as the social problems of organization and morality."[146] And here lies yet another contribution of the Panama Congress of 1916.

As social scientists and theologians have shown, Protestant intellectuals associated with the CCLA and the Panama Congress introduced the principles of social Christianity in Latin America.[147] Braga's book provides the clearest evidence of this in the Brazilian context. Building upon an earlier evangelical literature that had been circulating in the country, Braga affirmed that any careful observer who traveled across Latin America would find it easy to establish a connection between the expansion of evangelical Protestantism and the flourishing of civil liberties, social organization, happiness, and education.[148] In a remarkable passage, he argued that one could best see the effects of evangelical Christianity by looking at its moral and social impact. The force of evangelical religion was best noticed in the domestic intimacy of rural families, whose morality was reshaped by the regular and rigorous examination of evangelical literature, or in the big cities, where evangelical teachings on purity and equality had been exerting powerful influence on the "sexual hygiene" of the youth and fostering movements for fairer work relations.[149] One of the central tasks of missionary Christianity was to promote the common good: disseminate public instruction, combat infections, reorganize work relations so that each worker received the real value they produced, and fight social vices.[150] Braga proudly emphasized that, for the first time in the history of ecumenical missionary conferences, the Panama Congress dedicated a whole commission to studying the role of female missionaries in the evangelization of the world. In his narrative, the address given by Mrs. Anita de Monteverde from Uruguay was a landmark,

---

[145] Pereira, *O problema religioso*, 148–149.
[146] Pereira, *O problema religioso*, 168–169.
[147] Bastian, *Le protestantisme*; Bonino, *Rostros del protestantismo*, 26–27; Mondragón, *Like Leaven*, ch. 3.
[148] Braga, *Pan-Americanismo*, 48. On this page Braga refers to Émile de Laveleye's tract as "*a lei de Laveleye*" (Laveleye's law).
[149] Braga, *Pan-Americanismo*, 52–54.
[150] Braga, *Pan-Americanismo*, 75–77.

showing how evangelical women were raising funds to combat tuberculosis and promote temperance campaigns. For Braga, evangelical schools and women's associations should help women who were now entering the job market, a process he considered positive, to keep their prudence and sexual purity in such transformative processes.[151]

Through their texts and books, Braga and Pereira navigated across a wide range of theological and intellectual traditions. They appropriated the missionary defense of interdenominational and international cooperation and applied them to deep-seated Pan-American utopias. They drew upon the evangelical suspicion of racial theories and reframed the differences between the Anglo-Saxon and the Latin races in the American continent. And for both men, the expansion and strengthening of the evangelical missionary enterprise in Brazil and Latin America touched upon a wide range of social, intellectual, and moral issues that resonated with diplomatic and political interests in the integration of the Americas.

Conclusion

In light of this chapter, it might be useful to situate the rise of social theologies in Brazil and Latin America into an older intellectual lineage, punctuated by continuities and ruptures that can be traced back to the early twentieth century. Scholarly studies on Latin American public theologies, especially those on theologies of liberation and integral mission, have emphasized the role of post-WWII Catholic and Protestant responses to the radical left and receptions of Vatican II in shaping new forms of theological reflection and social action.[152] Few of them trace the older intellectual influences and social contexts of public theologies in the continent.[153] What this chapter has

---

[151] Braga, *Pan-Americanismo*, 150–154.

[152] Daniel Salinas, *Latin American Evangelical Theology in the 1970s: The Golden Decade* (Leiden: Brill, 2009); Todd Hartch, *The Rebirth of Latin American Christianity* (New York: Oxford University Press, 2014); David C. Kirkpatrick, *A Gospel for the Poor: Global Social Christianity and the Latin American Evangelical Left* (Philadelphia: University of Pennsylvania Press, 2019); David C. Kirkpatrick, "C. René Padilla and the Origins of Integral Mission in Post-war Latin America," *Journal of Ecclesiastical History* 67 (2016): 351–371; Ivan Petrella, "The Intellectual Roots of Liberation Theology," in *The Cambridge History of Religions in Latin America*, ed. Virginia Garrard-Burnett, Paul Freston, and Stephen Dove (New York: Cambridge University Press, 2016), 359–371; Paul Sigmund, *Liberation Theology at the Crossroads: Democracy or Revolution?* (New York: Oxford University Press, 1990).

[153] Mondragón, *Like Leaven*; Raimundo Barreto Jr, "The Church and Society Movement and the Roots of Public Theology in Brazilian Protestantism," *International Journal of Public Theology* 6 (2012): 70–98.

shown is that there was a slow but multifaceted process of intellectual reconstruction and modification integrating, on the one hand, ideas and concepts that circulated in the transnational circuits of global Protestantism and, on the other hand, the Brazilian public sphere. Brazilian evangelical ministers and intellectuals, such as Braga and Pereira, were the key agents who mediated between these distinct domains.

As Jean-Pierre Bastian rightly observed, the Latin American evangelical congresses of the early twentieth century gave way to a Latin American evangelical conscience responsive to the pressing social issues of the region.[154] And as Carlos Mondragón has shown, the CCLA, through its magazine *La Nueva Democracia* (The New Democracy), provided Latin American evangelical intellectuals with an efficient platform from which they articulated their distinct social and political agendas, connecting notions of Protestant individualism to liberal democratic values. By means of these vehicles, evangelical intellectuals crafted new religious identities in Catholic-majority societies.[155] Evangelical agents associated with the CCLA, such as Braga, consolidated pan-evangelical organizations in twentieth-century Latin America that encompassed a range of denominations and, to a certain extent, fulfilled the ideal of Christian cooperation.[156] All these transformations, however, were implemented in a context riven by factional divisions and sectarianism that further fragmented the Brazilian religious arena. Responding to the call for unity launched at the Panama Congress of 1916, the Brazilian Baptist Convention in 1918 re-affirmed its attachment to its own denominational principles, asserting that Baptist autonomy should be safeguarded in spite of the climate of Protestant cooperation.[157] In addition to this, mainline Protestants looked down on the emerging Pentecostal churches in the early twentieth century. Pentecostals were usually underrepresented in most of the interdenominational organizations of Brazil. So, from the outset, the movement of evangelical convergence launched at the Panama Congress was deprived of the participation of the two fastest growing evangelical groups in the country. For decades to come, the ecumenical movement attracted mostly the new evangelical intellectual elites of Brazil, especially those coming from among Presbyterian, Methodist, Congregationalist, and Anglican ranks.

---

[154] Bastian, *Le protestantisme*, 141.
[155] Mondragón, *Like Leaven*, chs. 6 and 7.
[156] Barreto Jr, "The Church and Society Movement," 73–77.
[157] *Atas da Convenção Batista, 1918*, apud Duncan A. Reily, *História Documental do Protestantismo no Brasil*, 3rd ed. (São Paulo: ASTE, 2003), 239–242.

Pereira's book of 1920 generated a considerable stir in the Brazilian religious arena. In 1922, the influential priest Leonel Franca, a distinguished Catholic intellectual and polemicist in Brazil, published a book in response to Pereira's work entitled *The Church, the Reformation, and Civilization*. Displaying vast erudition and solid persuasion, Franca's apologetic defense sought to redeem the prestige of the Vatican and the Catholic bureaucracy after the Protestant critique by arguing that hierarchical order and chains of command had been organically instituted by God and inscribed in the natural world.[158] Pereira did not live long enough to keep the debate alive; he passed away in the following year at the age of sixty-seven. Catholic–Protestant disputes became even more intense after Getúlio Vargas's rise to power in 1930. After decades of ecclesiastical reorganization and expansion since the overthrow of the Empire in 1889, the Catholic Church was able to reconnect with a government in need of legitimacy. The Church backed the actions of Vargas's corporatist state by providing corporatist models of social discipline, engaging with trade unions, and fostering cooperation among social classes. At the same time, the government made a series of political concessions to organized Catholic movements.[159] This quasi reestablishment of Catholicism provoked strong reactions on the Protestant side. Braga qualified it as a "reactionary movement" that hastened the evangelical movement toward unity.[160] The Brazilian Evangelical Confederation was created in this context in 1934, two years after Braga's premature death, but a clear outcome of his efforts with the CCLA. Also, this prompted Brazilian Protestants to launch the campaign of the Methodist Rev. Guaracy Silveira for the Parliament, who was elected in 1934 and took part in the Constitutional Assembly.[161] So, whereas Braga and Pereira imagined that Christian cooperation across national borders would improve diplomatic relations and intensify north–south exchanges in the American continent, at home the movement for Christian unity was still deficient and unable to persuade the vast majority of Brazil's Christian leadership.

---

[158] Franca, *A Igreja*.

[159] Ralph Della Cava, "Catholicism and Society in Twentieth-century Brazil," *Latin American Research Review* 11 (1976): 7–50; Serbin, "Church and State Reciprocity," 728.

[160] Braga and Grubb, *The Republic of Brazil*, 93. Again, this movement in the direction of Christian unity excluded the Catholic Church.

[161] Freston, "Protestantes e Política no Brasil," 154–157.

6
The Rise of an Evangelical Intelligentsia

At the dawn of the twentieth century the Protestant churches of Brazil entered a new era. Local fundraising campaigns, the training of a body of Portuguese-speaking pastors, and the consolidation of ecclesiastical institutions seemed to fulfill missionary hopes in the transformation of local churches into self-sustaining and self-governing bodies. The independence of the Presbyterian Church of São Paulo from the Board of Foreign Missions of the Presbyterian Church of the United States in 1903, while certainly a traumatic event for missionaries and pastors, signaled to a bright future. Mission organizations, congregations, and Bible societies expanded nationwide, reaching the states of central and western Brazil. The small Protestant organizations of the 1860s and 1870s evolved into a large institutional machinery comprising schools, publishing houses, seminaries, and Bible institutes. Local ministers and lay leaders were able to connect with their counterparts around the world through networks of missionary conferences and organizations since the foundation of the Committee on Cooperation in Latin America in 1913 and the meeting of the Panama Congress of 1916. For the Presbyterian pastor Erasmo Braga, the participation of Brazilian ministers in these international evangelical networks overcame the isolation that characterized much of the religious experience of previous generations of converts.[1] The pastors educated locally were now viewed as more than just religious dissidents. Seminary training projected them into the intellectual and literary life of the country. The evangelical intelligentsia that emerged in early twentieth-century Brazil was simultaneously indigenized and cosmopolitan, and their theological and academic production mixed together local and global ideologies.

Although the protagonists of this chapter appear here and there in studies of the cultural and political history of Brazil, their religious affiliations are

---

[1] Erasmo Braga, "Following Up the Jerusalem Meeting in Brazil," *International Review of Missions* 28 (1929): 261–265.

largely overlooked, if not ignored.[2] Their backgrounds and careers differed significantly from the Catholic and secular intelligentsia. These came from both decadent and emergent rural and urban elites; were educated in established schools of law, medicine, engineering, and arts; and were loosely connected to political and literary circles through networks of kin and patronage.[3] Protestant ministers, on the other hand, hailed from families of small farmers, immigrants, and urban professionals in the states of São Paulo, Minas Gerais, and Rio de Janeiro. They were educated in provisional Presbyterian seminaries and trained both in mission schools as educators and local congregations as ministers. Their trajectories are somewhat akin to the processes sociologist David Martin has identified in Pentecostal niches in Latin America and Eastern Europe. In these places, young people and second-generation believers read and study together the Bible and Christian literature, through evangelism and sermonizing they develop rhetorical and argumentative skills, congregational music introduces them to a larger musical culture, and this sort of socialization throws to the surface a "buried intelligentsia" that has long remained underground.[4] This book's final chapter examines some dynamics related to the rise of a Brazilian Protestant intelligentsia. It begins by tracing the unlikely educational and professional trajectories of these agents. The demanding language requirements of the existing seminaries and the Protestant interest in the original languages of the biblical world, especially Greek, Hebrew, and Latin, created a generation of ministers who straddled the fields of theology and philology. Evangelical ministers and writers published widely on a broad array of topics. The chapter analyzes their body of work and reconstructs the multiple intellectual contexts and mediations that shaped Brazilian evangelical thought. The final section examines how these ministers drew upon local traditions, language variations, and historical accounts to locate evangelical religion into Brazilian culture and history.

---

[2] Nicolau Sevcenko, *Orfeu extático na metrópole: São Paulo, sociedade e cultura nos frementes anos 20* (São Paulo: Companhia das Letras, 1992), 247; James Woodard, *A Place in Politics: São Paulo, Brazil, from Seigneurial Republicanism to Regionalist Revolt* (Durham, NC: Duke University Press, 2009), 113, 149, 177; Gilberto Freyre, *Order and Progress: Brazil from Monarchy to Republic*, trans. Rod W. Horton (New York: Knopf, 1970), 117–118.

[3] Sérgio Miceli, *Intelectuais e classe dirigente no Brasil (1920–1945)* (São Paulo e Rio de Janeiro: DIFEL, 1979).

[4] David Martin, *Forbidden Revolutions: Pentecostalism in Latin America and Catholicism in Eastern Europe* (London: SPCK, 1996), 32–33.

The Education of Protestant Ministers

In the nineteenth and early twentieth centuries the acquisition of higher education in Brazil was an elite affair. Faculties and other specialized educational institutions were scarce. The law schools of São Paulo and Recife played a key role in the formation of modern Brazil's political elite. Recruited from among the same social ranks, trained in the same schools, socialized in the same political associations and cultural institutions, and following similar careers in the Empire's high-ranking political and diplomatic offices, this homogeneous political elite was the "midwife of Brazilian unity" in the nineteenth century.[5] From the 1870s onward, broader movements of sociopolitical change diversified processes of intellectual formation in Brazil. Liberal Party dissidents, Positivists, and republicans marginalized from the traditional power structures of the Empire circulated proposals for political reform, appropriated liberal and republican thought in multiple ways, and further accelerated the crisis of the Brazilian Empire.[6] The groups that disseminated Positivism in Brazil were socially and intellectually heterogeneous, too, encompassing old-guard law school graduates from São Paulo, leaders of the Positivist Church of Rio de Janeiro, and republican professors of military schools in Rio and the Brazilian south.[7] Catholic seminaries and other ecclesiastical institutions also offered opportunities for long-term schooling and trained its own specialized personnel who, unlike the magistrates and other political elites, had closer contact with the people.[8] In the first decades of the republican era seminarians were able to study in prestigious European Catholic schools, becoming the vanguard of the process of Romanization of the Brazilian Church.[9]

---

[5] Eul-Soo Pang and Ron Seckinger, "The Mandarins of Imperial Brazil," *Comparative Studies in Society and History* 14 (1972): 215–244, at 217; José Murilo de Carvalho, *A construção da ordem: A elite política imperial/Teatro de sombras: A política imperial*, 3rd ed. (Rio de Janeiro: Civilização Brasileira, 2010); Andrew Kirkendall, *Class mates: Male Student Culture and the Making of a Political Class in Nineteenth-Century Brazil* (Lincoln: University of Nebraska Press, 2002).

[6] Angela Alonso, *Idéias em movimento: A geração de 1870 na crise do Brasil-império* (São Paulo: Paz e Terra, 2002).

[7] Robert Nachman, "Positivism, Modernization, and the Middle Class in Brazil," *Hispanic American Historical Review* 57 (1977): 1–23.

[8] Kenneth Serbin, *Needs of the Heart: A Social and Cultural History of Brazil's Clergy and Seminaries* (Notre Dame: University of Notre Dame Press, 2006), 97; Carvalho, *A construção da ordem*, 181–187.

[9] Sérgio Miceli, *A elite eclesiástica brasileira: 1890–1930*, 2nd ed. (São Paulo: Companhia das Letras, 2009); George Boehrer, "The Church in the Second Reign, 1840–1889," in *Conflict and Continuity in Brazilian Society*, ed. Henry Keith and S. F. Edwards (Columbia: University of South Carolina Press, 1969).

Although lacking the historical depth of Catholic institutions and the social prestige of Brazil's schools of law and medicine, Protestant schools and seminaries also offered opportunities of long-term and specialized schooling to converts. The first generations of prospective ministers were usually recruited from among evangelical families in the countryside of the states of São Paulo and Minas Gerais. Seminary training transformed them into religious specialists and enabled them to take a place among Brazil's lettered elites. Presbyterian missionaries began to offer seminary education to young church leaders from the 1860s.[10] From 1876 onward, they took concrete steps to open a theological institute with a solid teaching staff and broad curriculum. The American missionary George Chamberlain was the main impetus behind this initiative, persuading his fellow missionaries to open a literary institute and a normal school in São Paulo, aimed at training schoolteachers and Bible-readers.[11] Chamberlain also organized fundraising campaigns in the United States and Britain. He requested donations among British churches to construct a building to host a theological institute in São Paulo, to endow a professorship, and to create five scholarships. For the missionary, such a plan would form a "native Christian Ministry of pastors and teachers" able to carry out the evangelical work "in the Empire of Brazil, and in other parts where the Portuguese tongue is spoken."[12]

A series of internal disagreements among the Presbyterians postponed the opening of the seminary in São Paulo, which began to operate only in 1893 in a context of expansion of private higher education in Brazil.[13] Despite these challenges, the Brazil Mission prepared its national leaders in various other ways. In 1878, the missionary Robert Lenington presented to the other Presbyterian missionaries a plan of a regular seminary course. The whole program comprised six years of study. In the first two years, prospective ministers were obliged to study a diverse range of subjects aimed at complementing their secondary education including Portuguese grammar and writing, studies on the Shorter Catechism, geography, history, music,

---

[10] On the Primitive Seminary of Rio de Janeiro and the education of Brazil's first Presbyterian ministers, see Julio A. Ferreira, *História da Igreja Presbiteriana do Brasil*, vol. I, 2nd ed. (São Paulo: Casa Editora Presbiteriana, 1992), 85–88.

[11] Relatório dos trabalhos de G. W. Chamberlain durante o anno Presbyterial de 1874 a 1875. AHP, São Paulo. Coleção Carvalhosa, Relatórios Pastorais (1866–1875).

[12] *Institution for the Training of Native Preachers and Teachers in the Empire of Brazil*, Glasgow, November 1876. PHS, Philadelphia. Mission Correspondence, South American Letters.

[13] Miceli, *Intelectuais e classe dirigente*, 36–37.

English, arithmetic, Latin, and natural sciences. Advanced subjects from the third year onward included a heavy emphasis on languages (Greek, Hebrew, Latin, and French), theology (the compendia of Princeton theologians Alexander and Charles Hodge), ecclesiastical history (the books of James Wharey, Johann L. von Mosheim, and Johann Kurtz), mental and moral philosophy (Francis Wayland and Thomas Upham), exegesis, homiletics, sacred eloquence, and religious polemic.[14] A few years later, it was the missionaries George Chamberlain and John Beatty Howell who were in charge of training the candidates for the Presbyterian pastorate. Under their guidance, classes lasted from two to three-and-a-half hours per day and encompassed English, Greek, geometry, arithmetic, Brazilian history, church history, mental and moral philosophy, theology, and the Shorter Catechism.[15] Eduardo Carlos Pereira and José Zacarias de Miranda prepared for the pastorate under this system and shortly after ordination in 1881 became distinguished ministers, writers, and religious polemists.

After passing through Campinas and Nova Friburgo, near Rio de Janeiro, the Theological Institute of the Presbyterian Mission was finally installed in São Paulo in 1893. Fundraising campaigns in churches enabled the institute to acquire the furniture necessary for the seminary classes, given at the back of the Presbyterian Church in the 24 de Maio Street, and to refurbish the pastoral house, creating two dormitories for students (Figure 6.1).[16] Throughout the early twentieth century, Protestant seminaries and schools continued to depend on the contributions and donations of churches and believers. The various associations of women played a crucial role in this. Their members sewed clothes, sold foodstuffs, administered small cafés, organized fundraising campaigns, and sent their collections to evangelical orphanages, schools, seminaries, and hospitals.[17]

A good number of distinguished Protestant intellectuals prepared for the ministry at the Theological Institute of São Paulo, including Erasmo Braga, Otoniel Mota, and Vicente Themudo Lessa. Prospective ministers studied theology and philosophy with American missionaries and Brazilian pastors, including Eduardo Carlos Pereira and John Rockwell Smith. Other professors were in charge of teaching arithmetic, universal history, Greek,

---

[14] *Imprensa Evangelica*, January 17, 1878, n. 3.
[15] Annual Report of J. B. Howell, São Paulo, Brazil, for the year 1880. PHS, Philadelphia. Mission Correspondence, South American Letters.
[16] Ferreira, *História da Igreja Presbiteriana*, 381–384.
[17] *O Puritano*, February 10, 1910, n. 530; February 17, 1910, n. 531.

Figure 6.1 The Presbyterian Church of São Paulo, 24 de Maio Street. CDH-VTL, Pasta de Fotos.

Latin, and French. Professors included Remigio Braga, an elder of the São Paulo Presbyterian Church and director of the Mackenzie College; Augusto Baillot, chair of arithmetic at the Gymnasium of São Paulo; Oskar Nobiling, a German philologist; Canuto Thorman, an enthusiast of the Volapük, an international constructed language; and Luiza Magalhães, a French teacher and Eduardo Pereira's Swiss wife.[18] As Otoniel Mota wrote in a memoir of his seminary years, students lived together in the dormitories at the Presbyterian Church of São Paulo for the duration of their studies. They were trained under Pereira and gave mock sermons from his pulpit. The general climate was of companionship but also of intellectual rigor. There, students debated "philosophical, moral, and sociological" topics and exposed the arguments and performance of their fellow seminarians to frank criticism, "like an animal that falls in a river of piranhas."[19]

---

[18] Vicente Themudo Lessa, *Annaes da 1ª Egreja Presbyteriana de São Paulo (1863–1903): Subsidios para a historia do presbiterianismo brasileiro* (São Paulo: Edição da 1ª Igreja Presbiteriana Independente de São Paulo, 1938), 478–479.

[19] Otoniel Mota, *Historietas* (São Paulo: Livraria Técnica, 1946), 141–143.

In undertaking seminary training, which usually lasted for a minimum of four years, Protestant pastors attained higher educational level, becoming part of Brazil's intellectual elite. Throughout the first half of the twentieth century some Brazilian ministers sat in influential literary academies and were elected to prestigious university chairs in São Paulo. Erasmo Braga was one of the founders of the influential *Paulista Academy of Letters*, occupying chair number 13.[20] Otoniel Mota was also elected to the academy, occupying chair 17, and edited the Academy's journal for a long time. Apart from that, Mota also served as director of the Public Library of the State of São Paulo and became the first chair of philology in the department of languages of the University of São Paulo in 1936.[21]

Although women took part in the evangelical publishing enterprise writing conversion narratives and textbooks, and some became influential educators,[22] seminary training was closed to them in this period. In contrast to the education of boys, with its strong emphasis on foreign languages and scientific subjects, in Protestant schools female students were mostly trained to be homemakers, taking classes of domestic work, needlework, and music.[23] Evangelical women also trained in the Presbyterian normal school of São Paulo and found employment in Protestant schools across the country.[24] Even though they were able to attain elementary and secondary education in Protestant and Catholic schools in the late nineteenth and early twentieth centuries, institutions of higher education remained male-dominated.

Although seminaries were the key institutions that formed Brazil's evangelical ministers, some individuals who took part in the Protestant intelligentsia did not undertake seminary training. Miguel Vieira Ferreira, founder of the Brazilian Evangelical Church and of the Republican Party of Rio de Janeiro, was an engineer and was awarded a doctorate in mathematical and physical sciences from the Polytechnic School of Rio de Janeiro.[25] Nicolau

---

[20] *Revista da Academia Paulista de Letras*, vol. 13 (1941), 131–132.

[21] *Revista da Academia Paulista de Letras*, vol. 17 (1942), 118–119; Theodoro H. Maurer Jr., "Professor Otoniel Mota (1878–1951),"*Revista de História* 3 (1951): 478–479.

[22] Such as the Methodist Martha Watts, founder of the *Colégio Piracicabano*, and the Presbyterian Marcia Brown, who was invited by the educationalist Caetano Campos in 1890 to support a general educational reform in São Paulo.

[23] *Programma e Regulamento do Instituto de S. Paulo, Escola Americana* (São Paulo: Typ. de Leroy King Bookwalter, 1885), 14–18.

[24] Antônio G. Mendonça, *O celeste porvir: A inserção do protestantismo no Brasil*, 3rd ed. (São Paulo: Ed. USP, 2008), 150–151.

[25] Miguel V. Ferreira, *Liberdade de consciência: O Cristo no júri* (São Paulo: Oficinas Gráficas de Saraiva, 1957 [1891]), 286.

Soares do Couto, one of the founders of the Independent Presbyterian Church of São Paulo, got a degree in medicine in Rio de Janeiro in 1894. Couto descended from an aristocratic family of the Empire and was a third-generation Protestant.[26] The most influential lay Protestant writer and intellectual was José Carlos Rodrigues. Raised in Rio de Janeiro in a large coffee plantation by his wealthy aunt, Rodrigues graduated from the Law School of São Paulo in 1864. It was in São Paulo that Rodrigues became a Protestant, while taking English lessons with the American missionary George Chamberlain.[27] Although he never joined a church, Rodrigues actively supported the American and the British and Foreign Bible Societies, the YMCA, as well as Presbyterian and Methodist churches in Brazil, donating books from his vast private library, money, and properties. He also took part in the steering committee of the Panama Congress of 1916, supported a new translation of the Bible into Portuguese, and published influential studies of Christian theology.[28]

What brought these evangelical intellectuals together were not their social origins, training, or careers. They shared the experience of being a dissenting Christian religious minority in a context of increasing religious diversification, intense Catholic reformism, as well as rapid political and social change.[29] Moreover, this heterogeneous group of individuals was connected to each other through denominational institutions, and national and transnational missionary networks. They did not always embrace the ideas of their peers and frequently disagreed, but nevertheless engaged with each other within the boundaries of a somewhat loose, yet recognizable, religious milieu.[30]

Social and Political Theologies in the Interwar Era

For an influential group of commentators, theological conservatism was the intellectual hallmark of Latin American evangelicalism until the 1960s. In a

---

[26] *Semana Evangélica*, August 8, 1928. I am thankful to Sônia Mabel for this information.
[27] Charles Gaud on Rodrigues's life and career. BN, Rio de Janeiro. 32,04,01 n 020.
[28] Hugh C. Tucker, *Dr José Carlos Rodrigues [1844–1923]: A Brief Sketch of His Life* (New York: American Bible Society, n/d).
[29] On the relationship between shared social experiences and intellectual formation in Brazil, see Alonso, *Idéias em movimento*, 42–43, 100–101, 124–125.
[30] Carlos Mondragón, *Like Leaven in the Dough: Protestant Social Thought in Latin America, 1920–1950*, trans. Daniel Miller and Ben Post (Madison, NJ: Fairleigh Dickinson University Press 2011), 51–52.

contribution to *The Fundamentalism Project*, Paraguayan historian and theologian Pablo A. Deiros affirmed categorically that in Latin America "evangelical Protestantism is fundamentally conservative in doctrine and firmly committed to zealous proselytism in the name of the gospel." And this reactionary fundamentalism, that in Deiros's analysis circulated in both evangelical and Pentecostal churches, manifested itself in an emphasis on the centrality and inerrancy of the Bible; the belief in premillennial dispensationalism; and a pietistic, individualist emphasis on personal moral reform. These last two aspects of the "fundamentalist impulse" resulted in a vertical spirituality that, for Deiros, focused on inward personal transformation and alienated believers from their social surroundings, legitimizing the "status quo."[31] In a similar way, Brazilian sociologist Antonio Gouvêa Mendonça affirmed that Protestant individualism, pietism, and theological rigidity isolated believers and church leaders from Brazil's movements of social change, which accounted for their distance from processes of political and cultural renewal.[32] For the American theologian Paul Pierson, what characterized the thinking of Brazilian Presbyterians was the influence of conservative "Old School" American Presbyterianism, an emphasis of personal morality and cleanliness, and a strong pietism that prevented Presbyterians from developing a political and social ethic.[33]

Even though these jargons may apply in some circumstances, such a procession of big concepts obscures the various ways in which religious specialists appropriated and modified concepts and ideas deriving from a global theological arena. Locally specific public debates and religious dynamics informed the selective and adaptive reception of the fundamental tenets of Protestant theology in Latin America. So, if evangelical individualism may appear as a source of political quietism and social alienation, in the early twentieth century the American Argentinian Methodist minister Jorge P. Howard affirmed that a personal religious experience was a prerequisite for understanding the true spirit of democracy. Because democratic life required responsible and participatory individuals, the evangelical idea that men and women face God alone and alone take the ultimate decision to live according to the principles of the gospel served as a "pedagogical

---

[31] Pablo A. Deiros, "Protestant Fundamentalism in Latin America," in *Fundamentalisms Observed*, Martin Marty and R. Scott Appleby (Chicago: University of Chicago Press, 1991), 142–196, at 149, 151–152, 171–173.
[32] Mendonça, *O celeste porvir*, 362.
[33] Paul E. Pierson, *A Younger Church in Search of Maturity: Presbyterianism in Brazil from 1910 to 1959* (San Antonio: Trinity University Press, 1974), 94–98, 102–103.

experience" that prepared believers for active citizenship.[34] Also, in societies with overwhelming levels of illiteracy, the evangelical emphasis on the centrality of the Bible encouraged converts to promote educational campaigns. In Guatemala, Protestant teachers and mission schools became the vanguard of campaigns for universal literacy in the 1940s after they codified indigenous languages and established a wide network of educational institutions.[35]

Evangelical ministers in Brazil were not isolated from international movements of theological renewal. From the 1930s onward, a number of seminary graduates pursued their studies in European, British, and American theological schools, coming into contact with a diverse range of intellectual influences, such as Karl Barth and Walter Rauschenbusch.[36] But even before that, Erasmo Braga and José Carlos Rodrigues were incorporating principles of the Social Gospel, the historical criticism, and progressive revelation into Brazilian theology since the 1910s. The first decades of the twentieth century were a period of accelerated social and economic change in Brazil. The Brazilian population nearly doubled between 1890 and 1920. Demographic growth was especially intense in the center-south of the country. Foreign immigration, especially of Italians, Portuguese, and Germans, increased sharply. The coffee-boom and the rapid dissemination of industries in the wake of the Great War changed the economic scenario in cities and the countryside.[37] Social and economic vigor fed into cultural agitation. In São Paulo and Rio de Janeiro, the expansion of publishing houses, the opening of cinemas, the creation of sports associations, and the economic anxieties of the post-WWI era weighed upon elite and popular culture. Working class mobilizations were met with police violence in the early twentieth century, and elite associations in São Paulo launched temperance campaigns to counter the proliferation of bars and growing alcohol consumption.[38] It was in this context of swift social and cultural change and rapid urbanization that

---

[34] Mondragón, *Like Leaven*, 59–60.

[35] Virginia Garrard-Burnett, *Protestantism in Guatemala: Living in the New Jerusalem* (Austin: University of Texas Press, 1998), 80–83.

[36] Silas L. Souza, *Pensamento social e político no protestantismo brasileiro* (São Paulo: Editora Mackenzie, 2005), 115–118.

[37] Boris Fausto, "Brazil: The Social and Political Structure of the First Republic, 1889–1930," in *The Cambridge History of Latin America: volume V, c. 1870 to 1930*, ed. Leslie Bethell (Cambridge: Cambridge University Press, 1986).

[38] Jeffrey Needell, *A Tropical Belle Époque: Elite Culture and Society in Turn-of-the-Century Rio de Janeiro* (Cambridge: Cambridge University Press, 1987); Sidney Chalhoub, *Trabalho, lar e botequim: O cotidiano dos trabalhadores no Rio de Janeiro da Belle Époque* (São Paulo: Editora Brasiliense, 1986).

the protagonists of this chapter appropriated Protestant theology and interwove them to the sociopolitical realities they encountered.

As the previous chapter has shown, Brazilian evangelical ministers began to embrace ideas of the Social Gospel in the 1910s. One of its key proponents, the American Methodist bishop Francis J. McConnell, gave an address titled "Christian Faith in an Age of Doubt" at the Congress on Christian Work in Latin America at the Panama Congress of 1916 that exerted a strong impact on Erasmo Braga and Eduardo Pereira. In McConnell's arguments, the early twentieth-century convergence between the scientific spirit and Christian ethic could overcome the forces of nature, disease, and poverty and alleviate men's anxiety in an age of global conflicts and rapid industrialization.[39] Upon examining the significance of McConnell's address, Pereira stressed that this reciprocity between Christianity and science could, besides solving the problems of health and pauperism, reconcile evangelical Christianity with the Brazilian intelligentsia, struck by waves of incredulity.[40]

It was Braga, however, who became the key advocate of the principles of the Social Gospel in Brazil. After the Panama Congress of 1916 and working as secretary of the Brazilian Committee on Cooperation, Braga traveled widely across the world participating in international missionary meetings in Montevideo, Jerusalem, Oslo, and Havana.[41] Braga's involvement with the early twentieth-century ecumenical movement exerted a decisive influence in his theology throughout the interwar period. Like Pereira, Braga also stressed the importance of McConnell's address at Panama. Propagating the principles of early twentieth-century ecumenism, he argued that only a united evangelical front could alleviate the social problems of Latin America by spreading education, combating infections, and reorganizing labor relations, so that workers received a fair share of profits.[42] Unlike Pereira, though, whose appreciation of McConnell's social Gospel was inserted into a book of anti-Catholic controversy, Braga's criticism of the Catholic Church was milder. Braga was a second-generation evangelical. Whereas first-generation converts frequently portrayed their break with previous religious

---

[39] Francis McConnell, "Christian Faith in an Age of Doubt," in *Christian Work in Latin America*, vol. III (New York: The Missionary Education Movement, 1917), 297–304.

[40] Eduardo C. Pereira, *O problema religioso da America Latina: Estudo dogmatico-historico* (São Paulo: Imprensa Methodista, 1920), 168–171.

[41] Erasmo Braga, *Religião e cultura* (São Paulo: União Cultural Editora, n/d), 14–15.

[42] Erasmo Braga, *Pan-Americanismo: Aspecto religioso* (New York: Missionary Education Movement, 1916), 99–100, 75–76.

backgrounds through a language of strong rupture, their offspring did not and they were able to apply their religious zeal and energy into other areas.[43]

For Braga, what justified the intensification of evangelical missionary work in Brazil was not simply the ubiquitous religious and cultural influence of Catholicism, but a number of social ills: the prevalence of illiteracy among rural and urban workers; outbreaks of syphilis, tuberculosis, leprosy, and malaria; addiction to *cachaça* (distilled sugarcane spirit); lack of public sanitation; and the socially disaggregating effects of rapid industrialization.[44] And the consequences of the expansion of evangelicalism could be seen beyond figures of church growth and membership. In Braga's view, the contributions of missionaries to education was particularly important because in the early years of the Republic the system of primary education of São Paulo had been reorganized according to the model set by Methodist and Presbyterian schools in that state.[45] Also, the evangelical emphasis on marital fidelity and sexual purity challenged what Braga called the "double standards of sexual morality," a widespread custom in the Brazilian countryside that conceived male infidelity as a sign of adult masculinity.[46]

In a conference on comparative religions organized by the Spiritualist Crusade in Rio de Janeiro in 1928, Braga best showed his commitment to the Social Gospel, the ecumenical movement, and their intersections. In his long address, Braga compared the contemporary movement toward evangelical convergence to the sixteenth-century Reformation. Both had been animated by an impulse not of innovation, but of "reversion to primitive Christianity." The best sources of this movement were the life and deeds of Jesus Christ and the Bible. And serious social consequences ensued from that principle, for evangelical Christians sought to "read and vulgarize the historical documents bearing the information of what Jesus did and taught."[47] Absorbed by the preoccupation to make the scriptures accessible to all social classes, Braga affirmed that Protestants had become key promoters of culture and universal literacy in the modern world.[48] Responding to the critics

---

[43] For an analysis of how religious change evolved along generational lines, see Chapter 4 of this text.

[44] Erasmo Braga and Kenneth Grubb, *The Republic of Brazil: A Survey of the Religious Situation* (London: World Dominion Press, 1932), 8–10, 14, 27; Braga, *Pan-Americanismo*, 106.

[45] Braga and Grubb, *The Republic of Brazil*, 31–32. On the education reform of São Paulo, see Fernando Azevedo, *A cultura brasileira: Introdução ao estudo da cultura no Brasil, tomo terceiro*, 3rd ed. (São Paulo: Edições Melhoramentos, 1958), 140.

[46] Braga, *Pan-Americanismo*, 156–157.

[47] Erasmo Braga, "Protestantismo," in *Religiões comparadas*, ed. Gustavo Macedo (Rio de Janeiro: Roland Rohe & Cia, 1929), 79.

[48] Braga, "Protestantismo," 80.

of evangelical Christianity, Braga explained the meaning of Protestant individualism. For him, it was a process of self-discovery and moral liberation by which men and women reconciled their consciousness with God. This process produced "incoercible" individuals, who did not negotiate a single line of their renovated consciousness under the pressures of their degenerate moral surroundings.[49] But such individualism projected itself into social life. For Braga, the revolt against present-day iniquities was an essential feature of the renewed individual Christian consciousness. In his address, Braga enumerated a set of social evils that terrified the contemporary world: the industrialization of human relations, the resurgence of neo-paganism, the distance between capital and work, class and racial conflicts worldwide, secret diplomacy, the emergence of interwar nationalisms, and pornography. A united body of evangelical Christians, intent on overcoming factional and denominational divisions, could coordinate forces on a global scale and Christianize the social order.[50] And here he acknowledged his intellectual debts to Tommy Fallot, Johann Blumhardt, Walter Rauschenbusch, and Francis J. McConnell, precursors and exponents of social Christianity.

Foreign missionaries and Brazilian ministers also responded to processes of social change in different ways in the early twentieth century. In a context of increasing urbanization and human migration, Protestants sometimes thought that the devil inhabited in the cities and idealized life in the countryside. The American Episcopal bishop and missionary Lucien Kinsolving, in an address to a YMCA gathering in Rio de Janeiro in 1903, affirmed that it was in the cities that the three temptations of the day—pornographic literature, gambling, and lasciviousness—made their victims. In the countryside, though, the youth found themselves "sheltered by the domestic home and instructed by the pulpit, where God's prophet proclaims the divine law Sunday after Sunday."[51] For the Presbyterian pastor and philologist Otoniel Mota, born and raised in the countryside of São Paulo, life in the cities had "effeminizing" effects upon the "coward bipeds who swarm in the civilized centers." Even though he worked as a church pastor, seminary professor, and academic in the city of São Paulo, Mota undertook frequent travels to the countryside. These were filled with hunting and horse-riding sessions, aimed at hardening and invigorating his manners softened by urban life.[52] Unlike

---

[49] Braga, "Protestantismo," 91.
[50] Braga, "Protestantismo," 92–96.
[51] Lucien L. Kinsolving, *A razão de ser da Associação Christã de Moços* (Rio de Janeiro: Casa Publicadora Baptista, 1903), 9–15.
[52] Otoniel Mota, *Selvas e choças* (São Paulo: Imprensa Methodista, 1922), 14, 139, 169–170.

an influential group of writers who portrayed the mixed-race *caboclos* of indigenous and white descent and the *caipira* inhabitants of the countryside as degenerate and slothful, Mota idealized the *caipiras*.[53] He represented the *caipira* men and women of the countryside of São Paulo and Minas Gerais as fearless individuals who through their strong and brave characters fought with wild animals, especially the fearsome *onça pintada* (jaguar), settled the wilderness, and transformed indomitable forests into plantations.[54] In this sense, the work of the Rev. Otoniel Mota can be situated within a broader literary and artistic trend in early twentieth-century Brazil that romanticized the virtues of the *caboclo* and *caipira* populations, whose qualities embodied the "authentic" national character.[55]

Such romanticization of pristine rural cultures and traditions was not an exclusive feature of Brazilian Protestants. Evangelical and Catholic missionaries in colonial Congo idealized the African village life in a context of violent colonial occupation, forced labor, cultural change, and demographic crisis, rejecting intellectualism and cosmopolitanism as vices of Western civilization.[56] And nineteenth-century British missionaries in southern Africa, believing that the industrial city disrupted harmonious social relations, projected the image of their own rural, idyllic past as a model for the African future.[57] In contexts of accelerated social and economic change, with their destabilizing effects upon traditional customs and forms of life, missionaries worldwide romanticized mythic pasts and sought to restore old virtues.

The participation of church leaders in the twentieth-century ecumenical movement influenced their ideologies and thinking in the interwar era. Despite this romantic idealization of their society's past, Brazilian Protestants held the aggressive nationalisms of the interwar era in suspicion. Instead, they promoted certain aspects of Wilsonian internationalism. José Carlos Rodrigues translated and published in 1918 some speeches given by American president Woodrow Wilson during the war. In an introduction to

---

[53] Dain Borges, "'Puffy, ugly, slothful and inert': Degeneration in Brazilian Social Thought, 1880–1940," *Journal of Latin American Studies* 25 (1993): 235–256.

[54] Mota, *Selvas e choças*, 67–79.

[55] Barbara Weinstein, *The Color of Modernity: São Paulo and the Making of Race and Nation in Brazil* (Durham, NC: Duke University Press, 2015); Mônica Pimenta Velloso, *A brasilidade verde-amarela: Nacionalismo e regionalismo paulista* (Rio de Janeiro: CPDOC, 1990).

[56] David Maxwell, *Religious Entanglements: Central African Pentecostalism, the Creation of Cultural Knowledge, and the Making of the Luba Katanga* (Madison: University of Wisconsin Press, 2022), ch. 4.

[57] Jean Comaroff and John Comaroff, *Of Revelation and Revolution: Christianity, Colonialism, and Consciousness in South Africa, vol 1* (Chicago: University of Chicago Press, 1991), 74–75.

the volume, Rodrigues compared Wilson to the prophet Isaiah and contemporary America to old Israel: the modern nation and its president-prophet had been endowed with a holy mission to "propagate and defend the rights of men."[58] Rodrigues employed a number of religiously charged metaphors and images in his introduction, stressing the importance of Wilson's Presbyterian upbringing in shaping his character. He portrayed the role of the United States in the Great War as an altruistic, "semi-divine" consecration of a people in favor of lasting and stable peace.[59] And highlighting the importance of the League of Nations in bringing about world peace, he wrote that its creation was:

> a great step towards the attainment of the "Kingdom of God" on earth: the work of Jesus Christ is a slow development, but perpetual, incessant. Nations are divine instruments that ensure the progress of that supreme Kingdom, until the day dreamt by many arrives, in which the regeneration of the world will be so advanced that Christianity itself would become . . . unnecessary, for all aspects of human life would be religious and the Christian Church would be humanity itself. . . . Patriotism, the love to those who are closer to us by blood, noble as it is, must cede to the greater ascendancy of this love to humanity, to its peace, that surpasses race barriers and political markers, and that thus creates a divine Society of peoples, this kingdom that the Council of Nicaea in the fourth century declared would be "without end."[60]

By claiming that the kingdom of God could be achieved through the workings of political institutions, Rodrigues sidelined premillennial dispensationalism. Also, his confidence in universalist markers resonated with the early twentieth-century ecumenical agenda and its attempts to transcend racial, political, and denominational boundaries through the establishment of global organizations that operated in a logic distinct from states, markets, and empires, the political left and right.[61]

---

[58] José C. Rodrigues, ed., *Mensagens, allocuções e discursos do presidente Wilson concernentes á guerra actual* (Rio de Janeiro: Jacintho Ribeiro dos Santos, 1918), 6.

[59] Rodrigues, *Mensagens*, 6-10.

[60] Rodrigues, *Mensagens*, 10-11.

[61] Elisabeth Engel, James Kennedy, and Justin Reynolds, "Editorial—The Theory and Practice of Ecumenism: Christian Global Governance and the Search for World Order, 1900-80," *Journal of Global History* 13 (2018): 157-164.

Erasmo Braga, too, embraced internationalist principles. He believed that in the face of emergent interwar nationalisms, regionalist movements in São Paulo, and the strengthening of race conflicts across the world, schools, publishers, cinema directors, churches, and families should come together and inculcate "an international, cooperativist mind-set in the new generation."[62] To promote this cause, Braga argued, Brazilian educators should adapt geography and history textbooks to fight the "parochial tendency" dominant in Brazilian conceptions of nationality by including studies of international institutions and movements such as the Hague Tribunal and the League of Nations.[63] In an article published in a Portuguese periodical, *Portugal Evangelico*, Braga regarded as diabolical the emergence of a nationalist mentality among peoples of Latin culture that regarded their ethnic heritage, race, and subservience to the Vatican as organically connected. Instead, he advocated the "cosmic" unity of Luso-Brazilian evangelicalism, a religious movement that connected Portuguese-speaking evangelical churches in Brazil, Portugal, the United States, Hawaii, Macau, and Goa.[64]

Otoniel Mota, by his turn, inscribed his critiques of interwar communism and fascism into the conversational style of his tales, replete with images of the natural world. Reproducing one of the hunting stories he heard from an old tax collector in the countryside of São Paulo, Mota dubbed it the "deeds of a Bolshevist tapir." Upon being shot in its back late in the night by one of the members of the hunting crew, the tapir rushed into the tent used by the hunters, threw the cook into a cauldron with hot beans, dragged the tent away, and fell in the midst of the dogs that were tied nearby.[65] Needless to say, he equated Bolshevism to disorder. And in a tale read before the Society of Christian Culture of São Paulo in November 1935, Mota fantasized himself in a dialogue with a *joão de barro* (red ovenbird). Throughout the conversation, the bird set its laborious instincts and oven-like, clay nest as counterexamples to authoritarian regimes. Irreducible in the face of communism, with its violation of private property, and incoercible before fascism, with its rejection of democracy and divinization of political leaders, the *joão de barro* of Mota's story advocated "Christian cooperativism" as a remedy to nationalism.[66]

---

[62] Braga, *Religião e cultura*, 154.
[63] Braga, *Religião e cultura*, 157–158.
[64] Braga, *Religião e cultura*, 109–115. Also published in *Portugal Evangelico*, March 15, 1927.
[65] Mota, *Selvas e choças*, 178–181.
[66] Otoniel Mota, *A filosofia do joão-de-barro: Fantasia educativa lida perante a "Sociedade Cristã de Cultura" na noite de 19 de novembro de 1935* (São Paulo: Estab. Graphico Cruzeiro do Sul, n/d).

Catholic intellectuals and clergymen interacted with interwar nationalism, communism, and broader processes of social and economic turmoil in different ways. In 1922, a group of influential laymen, encouraged by the then archbishop Sebastião Leme, created an association of Catholic intellectuals called *Centro Dom Vital*, named after the bishop of Olinda arrested during the Religious Question of 1874.[67] The center's founder and key thinker, Jackson de Figueiredo, contended against the anarchic and socially destabilizing movements inaugurated by the Reformation, the French Revolution, and international communism, as well as the secularist and anticlerical leanings of Brazil's intellectual elites. Influenced by Blaise Pascal and neo-Thomist philosophy and reacting to the disestablishment of Catholicism by the Republic, Figueiredo sought inspiration in medieval Christendom in his attempts to re-Catholicize the social and political order and to promote a spiritual revolution in the country.[68] Dubbing democratic governments as the "tyranny of incompetence," he and his followers embraced organicist views of society.[69]

Throughout the 1920s and 1930s some of the most influential Catholic clergymen endorsed collectivist political ideologies in Brazil. Their corporatism offered an alternative to Marxist notions of class struggle and resonated with Catholic teachings on social unity and harmony.[70] Influential clerics and lay Catholic intellectuals from the *Centro Dom Vital* associated themselves with the Integralist movement in the 1930s. Founded by the journalist, modernist writer, and Catholic militant Plínio Salgado, the Brazilian Integralist Action took some organizational inspiration from Mussolini's Fascist Party, although it was ideologically and politically closer to the corporatist regimes of Spain and Portugal.[71] Advocating a strong nationalism, emphasizing the importance of social order, fighting communist mobilizations, and upholding Catholic notions of traditionalism, preservation, and social harmony, the Integralist movement echoed some of the

---

[67] On the reorganization of the Catholic Church under the Republic, see Ralph Della Cava, "Catholicism and Society in Twentieth-century Brazil," *Latin American Research Review* 11 (1976): 7–50.

[68] Riolando Azzi, *A neocristandade: Um projeto restaurador* (São Paulo: Paulus, 1994), 105–128. On Figueiredo, see also Francisco Iglésias, *História e ideologia* (São Paulo: Perspectiva, 1971), 109–159.

[69] Azzi, *A neocristandade*, 123–128, at 118.

[70] Kenneth Serbin, "Church and State Reciprocity in Contemporary Brazil: The Convening of the International Eucharistic Congress of 1955 in Rio de Janeiro," *Hispanic American Historical Review* 76 (1996): 721–751.

[71] Paulo Brandi, "Plínio Salgado," in *Dicionário histórico biográfico brasileiro pós 1930* (Rio de Janeiro: Ed. FGV, 2001).

Catholic anxieties of that era.[72] Some influential Catholic activists and clergymen engaged actively with the Integralist Action, including the writer and literary scholar Alceu Amoroso Lima, successor of Figueiredo at the *Centro Dom Vital*, and the Fathers Leonel Franca and Helder Câmara. The latter became one of the key exponents of progressive Catholicism decades later.[73]

Even though Protestant and Catholic responses to religious, social, and political change in the interwar period differed significantly, it would be misleading to situate them as the polar opposites of the political and ideological spectrums. Both valued the principles of social order and harmony over conflict and struggle. Like the Catholics, Protestants bemoaned radical movements such as the French and the Russian revolutions as drivers of anarchy. They praised the fact that, unlike the United States, the Brazilian Empire had been able to abolish slavery without provoking a war, and that unlike France Brazilian republicans were able to overthrow a monarchical government without bloodshed.[74] Catholics and Protestants alike intended to re-spiritualize culture and social life in Brazil, even if from different standpoints, which they viewed as attacked by various flanks including communism, rationalism, and industrialization. It is equally misleading to dismiss the thinking and theologies of Brazilian Protestants as imitative and out of touch with the social challenges of their country. Evangelical concerns with hygiene and sobriety, frequently depicted as markers of social alienation,[75] were set in a context in which temperance and sanitation campaigns loomed large, attracting increasing attention from scientists, writers, and political leaders, and sat at the heart of national projects of modernization.[76] Pastors and missionaries closely followed these public debates. Braga quoted long passages from the reports of Dr. Belisário Pena, a leading exponent of the sanitation agenda, in his attempts to highlight the significance of Protestant missions, while missionaries regarded Pena as a supreme example of healthy patriotism.[77]

---

[72] Helgio Trindade, *Integralismo (o fascismo brasileiro na década de 30)* (São Paulo: Difel, 1974).

[73] Margaret T. Williams, "Integralism and the Brazilian Catholic Church," *Hispanic American Historical Review* 54 (1974): 431–452.

[74] *Brazilian Missions* I, n. 7, pp. 49–50; vol. III, n. 2, pp. 11–13; Eduardo C. Pereira, *Um brado de alarma* (São Paulo: Typ. a vapor de Jorge Seckler & C., 1885).

[75] Pierson, *A Young Church*, 94–104; Rubem Alves, *Protestantism and Repression: A Brazilian Case Study*, trans. John Drury (London: SCM Press, 1985), ch. 6.

[76] Luiz A. de Castro Santos, "O pensamento sanitarista na Primeira República: Uma ideologia de construção de nacionalidade," *Dados* 28 (1985): 193–210; Thomas Skidmore, *Black into White: Race and Nationality in Brazilian Thought* (New York: Oxford University Press, 1974), ch. 6.

[77] Braga and Grubb, *The Republic of Brazil*, 8–10; Philippe Landes, *Dom Aquino: Imperialismo e protestantismo* (Cuyabá: Typ. d'A Penna Evangelica, 1928), 35–36.

Biblical Theology, Higher Criticism, and Biblical Archaeology

Brazilian Protestant ministers upheld an unequivocally evangelical approach to the Bible. Like their counterparts in other corners of the world, they attributed exceptional power to their holy book and viewed it as the ultimate source of authority. For Brazilian evangelicals, the scriptures were particularly relevant not only because they drove them away from the "errors" and "false traditions" of Catholicism. They believed that rigorous criticism and accurate interpretation were key drivers of intellectual reasoning, and powerful tools against ecclesiastical and political despotism.[78] Serious biblical scholarship, attentive to the original languages and properly contextualized in time and space, could be a vigorous instrument in evangelical efforts to Christianize the social order as well as to reconcile Christianity with the Brazilian intelligentsia.[79] Brazilian Protestant intellectuals also viewed biblical scholarship as a dynamic field that constantly refashioned itself in the light of new evidence and methodology.

In 1922, the same year of the foundation of the Catholic *Centro Dom Vital*, the Brazilian Communist Party, and the organization of the Modern Art Week in São Paulo, that important catalyst of the Brazilian modernist movement, Braga published an article titled "The Bible and the Literary Culture." In this text, Braga praised the simultaneous upsurge in the philological, historical-critical, and analytic study of biblical texts, arguing that it could counter the spread of fanaticism and charlatanism produced by obscure and subjective exegeses.[80] Furthermore, Braga argued, such an interest in biblical scholarship in Brazil coincided with the modernist interest in folklore studies and philological research on the literary sources of the Portuguese language. For the Presbyterian pastor, scholars would begin to understand the "residues of humanity's primitive beliefs, the components of our ideas, the elementary forms of our sentiments, and the fundamental processes of our psychology" found in Brazilian philological documentation, only by paying serious attention to the religious elements within them, ultimately formed by the Bible.[81] Braga believed that biblical scholarship would illuminate the modernist interest in cultural archaism and authenticity.

---

[78] Pereira, *O problema religioso*, 31–37, 326, 417–424.
[79] Pereira, *O problema religioso*, 168–172.
[80] Braga, *Religião e cultura*, 51–52. Originally published in *Revista de Cultura Religiosa*, 1922.
[81] Braga, *Religião e cultura*, 53.

Two other elements that further dynamized biblical scholarship and interpretation for Brazilian evangelical intellectuals were archaeology and philology. The field of biblical archaeology emerged in Europe and Britain in the late nineteenth century as a remedy to the skepticism of theologians who embraced the historical-critical method. Archaeological societies mobilized evangelical constituencies and raised funds for expeditions and excavations aimed at confirming Old Testament stories.[82] Braga, however, in his 1928 address to the Conference on Comparative Religions in Rio de Janeiro, showed himself to be an enthusiast of all "scientific innovations" that helped Christians to recover the "original message" of the Bible, and this included biblical archaeology, the historical-critical method, and paleography.[83] Mota published a short tract in 1926, *Archaeology and the Bible: Lights from Gezer*, that illustrated the ways in which Brazilian Protestants appropriated biblical archaeology. In Mota's tract, the discoveries of French archaeologist Charles Clermont-Ganneu, who identified, in 1871, the old city of Gezer mentioned in the book of Joshua, confirmed the "veracity" of some biblical stories but, more significantly, also reshaped the ways Christians read and interpreted the Bible. Archaeological excavations, Mota argued, illuminated the customs and habits of the era of the patriarchs, projecting "intense light over a multitude of texts that are now veritable cruxes for [biblical] commentators."[84]

Philology, on the other hand, was seen as an instrument that could improve Portuguese versions of the Bible and elucidate biblical passages of obscure meanings. In 1932, Mota published a short article in the theological journal *The Expository Times*. Here Mota employed all his erudition to challenge the interpretation of a small puzzle in the first epistle to the Corinthians: that of the veiled women. Contradicting respected New Testament commentators such as Frédéric Godet and Sir William Ramsay, Mota referred to the classical literature of Euripides and Homer, a vast secondary literature in French and English, as well as contemporary biblical scholarship to argue that the veil to which Paul referred in his epistle was not the Jewish veil of his own culture and that it did not cover the face of women.[85] Also, evangelical ministers

---

[82] Keith Whitelam, "The Archaeological Study of the Bible," in *The New Cambridge History of the Bible: Volume 4, from 1750 to the Present*, ed. John Riches (New York: Cambridge University Press, 2015), 139–148; David Gange, "Religion and Science in Late Nineteenth-century British Egyptology," *Historical Journal* 49 (2006): 1083–1103.
[83] Braga, *Religião e cultura*, 74–76.
[84] Otoniel Mota, *A archeologia e a Biblia: Luzes de Gezer* (São Paulo: Irmãos Ferraz, 1926), 12–13.
[85] Otoniel Mota, "The Question of the Unveiled Woman (1 Co. xi, 2–16)," *Expository Times* 44 (1932): 139–141.

showed some dislike of the Portuguese versions of the Bible available for them.[86] To solve this problem, and moving away from the policies of Bible societies, Mota translated a new version of the gospel of Matthew, which included extensive endnotes with historical and linguistic analyses, and wrote a commentary of the book of Acts.[87] In Mota's words, his new translation of Matthew was intended to be, "at the same time, modern and conservative, that is, in a language devoid of certain archaisms, but respecting the thought, the spirit, and the lovely simplicity of the original."[88] In other cases, philological examination of biblical passages led Brazilian theologians into more delicate debates. Mota, for instance, in another short and popular tract published in 1938, argued that the Greek word *aiónios*—translated as "eternal" in Matthew 25:46—did not denote endless, everlasting punishment. Quoting the Oxford theologian Alfred Plummer, Mota argued that the meaning of this Greek expression varied according to context and did not refer to the duration of time. And citing the Cambridge-educated cleric Frederic Farrar, he affirmed that the expression *kólasis aiónios*—translated as *eternal punishment*—actually meant a disciplinary punishment, whose roots were connected to the verb *to prune*: evildoers would be disciplined in order to flourish, not to be thrown into everlasting punishment.[89] Nevertheless, Mota and the majority of Protestant intellectuals of the first half of the twentieth century remained faithful to the evangelical emphasis on the centrality and inspiration of the Bible and rejected accusations of theological modernism.[90]

In the early twentieth century, liberal theologies and the so-called higher criticism began to penetrate the Brazilian evangelical public sphere, challenging the traditional evangelical attachment to the Bible. Responses to these modern sets of Protestant theologies in Brazil varied from outright rejection of their central tenets to their selective incorporation into works of biblical scholarship. Brazilian Methodist ministers reacted bitterly when the American missionary J. L. Bruce preached a sermon at the opening session of the annual Methodist conference in São Paulo in 1905, arguing that

---

[86] See, for instance, Braga, *Religião e cultura*, 53–54, in which Braga argues that the two favorite translations of foreign missionaries (the Almeida and the Brazilian versions) did not match the literary merits of the Figueiredo version, which was a translation from the Vulgate.

[87] *O evangelho de São Matheus, traducção e annotações de Othoniel Motta* (n/p: n/p, 1933); Otoniel Mota, *Breves annotações ao livro dos Actos* (São Paulo: Irmãos Ferraz, n/d).

[88] *O evangelho de São Matheus*, 3.

[89] Otoniel Mota, *Uma passagem interessante: Mateus XXV-46* (São Paulo: Emprêsa Gráfica da "Revista dos Tribunais, 1938).

[90] Mota, *Uma passagem*, 8.

the Bible contained a good number of contradictions and mistakes, and that the gospels did not portray the totality of Christ's actions. Brazilian minister Antonio Ribeiro published a seventy-page tract refuting Bruce's ideas and advocating the idea of verbal inspiration, infallibility, and sufficiency of the Bible.[91] Álvaro Reis, pastor of the Presbyterian Church of Rio de Janeiro, the largest evangelical church of Latin America, went further. In an article published in November 1914 in the Presbyterian periodical *O Puritano*, Reis affirmed that the "Roman apostasy," materialized in the Eucharistic congresses and Catholic modernism, had joined the apostasy of liberal Protestantism, materialized in the higher criticism. "The [Great] war," Reis argued, "is a fruit of this *rationalism*. And it is quite possible that after this enormous carnage, men will remember more and better—that the Word of God is the Truth, and that the 'wisdom of this world is not only foolishness for God', but foolishness and disgrace for the world itself."[92] The argument that the Great War was a fruit of theological liberalism also circulated across Anglophone evangelical networks.[93] Even the young Gilberto Freyre, while still a young Baptist student at Baylor University writing to the Brazilian press in 1919 about his undergraduate studies in Texas, praised the qualities of the American evangelical minister Billy Sunday, who preached "the doctrines of Grace, personal Salvation, Redemption, etc. in their evangelical purity ... without the stains of the 'higher-criticism.'"[94] These men viewed Liberal theologies as drivers of social and political unrest, innovations that obscured the purity and clarity of the gospels.

But another group of Brazilian Protestant intellectuals were able to incorporate central tenets of liberal theologies. Some of them objected to literalist exegeses of the Bible. Mota, for instance, argued that it was an unfortunate and poor literal exegesis of the "Curse of Ham" of Genesis 9 carried out by Catholic priests in colonial Brazil that ultimately "produced the enslavement of a race! How baleful the Bible is when interpreted in the light of such indolent exegesis."[95] The strongest and clearest defense of the higher criticism came not from an ordained minister or theology professor, but a

---

[91] Antonio Ribeiro, *A questão da infallibilidade da Biblia perante a Egreja Methodista do Brasil* (São Paulo: Weiszflog Irmãos, 1908).
[92] *O Puritano*, November 26, 1914, n. 780.
[93] Brian Stanley, *Christianity in the Twentieth Century: A World History* (Princeton, NJ: Princeton University Press, 2018), 28.
[94] Gilberto Freyre, *Tempo de aprendiz*, vol. I (São Paulo: IBRASA, 1979), 51–53.
[95] Otoniel Mota, *Do rancho ao palacio: Evolução da civilização paulista* (São Paulo: Companhia Editora Nacional, 1941), 146–147.

journalist, the influential José Carlos Rodrigues. After his retirement as editor and owner of the *Jornal do Commercio*, the largest and most widely circulated paper in South America, Rodrigues immersed himself in a project he had been preparing for many years: a commentary of the Old Testament. Research for this work took him to the United States and Britain where, as usual, he filled his already vast personal library with books of biblical theology.[96] In 1921, Rodrigues published in Edinburgh, at his own expense, a two-volume commentary on the Old Testament of over thirteen hundred pages. In this work, Rodrigues embraced the higher criticism and the so-called progressive revelation to argue that the Old Testament contained the first set of foundational revelations which God delivered to mankind, before their completion in Jesus Christ.[97]

The first part of Rodrigues's first volume, titled *General Considerations on the Bible*, was published separately in 1918 in Rio de Janeiro. One of the central claims of this book was that the Bible contained a broad set of fundamental religious and moral teachings interwoven with some inaccurate historical data of lesser importance.[98] Rodrigues rejected the validity of a literalist approach to the Bible, which he attributed to the Rabbi of the gospels, enslaved to "the smallest signals of the letters." Christ, in contrast, did not "adhere to this servitude, ... always seeking the *fundamental meaning* of the text, and not its exact words."[99] Also, he criticized both those scientists who refused to attribute any value to the Bible in the light of contemporary biological, astronomical, and geological studies, and the theologians who attempted to establish similarities between the narrative of the Genesis and modern scientific findings. The latter, he contended, believed that "the six days of Creation corresponded to six big *aeons* of geological life, as if these thousands or millions of years had 'mornings and afternoons' as in the [biblical] text."[100] For Rodrigues, no one would find elaborated and accurate scientific and historical explanations in the Bible because the book was not written for that purpose: the Bible was a religious book.[101] He affirmed that Adam and Eve were not the first humans, but symbols; that the stories of

---

[96] Tucker, *Dr. José Carlos Rodrigues*, 18–24.
[97] José C. Rodrigues, *Estudo historico e critico sobre o Velho Testamento*, 2 vols. (Edinburgh: T. & A. Constable, 1921).
[98] José C. Rodrigues, *Considerações geraes sobre a Biblia* (Rio de Janeiro: Imprensa Norwood, 1918), 168–169.
[99] Rodrigues, *Considerações geraes*, 105.
[100] Rodrigues, *Considerações geraes*, 17–18.
[101] Rodrigues, *Considerações geraes*, 13.

Balaam's mule and Samson were legendary but served to inculcate essential religious ideas; and that the Hebrew cosmogony of the Genesis was similar to ancient Babylonian and Mexican myths.[102]

Nevertheless, Rodrigues embraced the idea of biblical inspiration. He defined inspiration as "the influx of God's Spirit into man." The Holy Spirit, however, was not responsible for all the historical and chronological errors of the Bible because the recipients of such inspiration were fallible human beings who were inspired only ethically. The human "receptibility" of these spiritual revelations, Rodrigues argued, did not follow traditional rules, for "a sinner, recently converted, *can* see more transcendent truths than the saint who has been spending his life in the constant practice of good before God."[103] Rodrigues's work of biblical theology embraced certain tenets of Protestant liberal thinking in the early twentieth century but retained its evangelical outlook. The unfolding of biblical prophecies throughout history, he argued, reaffirmed the authority of the Bible. He regarded the teachings of the gospels as sublime expressions of Jesus's simplicity that should be universally available. Rodrigues was also an enthusiast of the work of Bible Societies.[104] Paraphrasing David Martin, Rodrigues and his contemporaries believed in the democratic availability of the *inspiration* of the spirit.[105] In line with a tradition in Brazilian evangelicalism that stretched back to the 1870s, Rodrigues believed in the civilizing power of the Bible, whose influence was best seen in societies that, as he argued, opened and read it vigorously, such as Britain and the United States.[106] In this sense, Brazilian evangelicals were intellectually closer to the modestly liberal Anglophone biblical scholars, who raised the standards of academic theology in Britain and America but remained orthodox in their beliefs, than to German theologians and ecclesiastical historians such as Friedrich Schleiermacher and Adolf von Harnack.[107]

An important question relates to the reach of such ideas. The diffusion of concepts and ideas was usually dependent on a large number of variables, ranging from literacy rates to more mundane affairs, such as the materiality of texts; the demands of authors; and the conditions of publishing houses,

---

[102] Rodrigues, *Considerações geraes*, 20–22.
[103] Rodrigues, *Considerações geraes*, 36–37.
[104] Rodrigues, *Considerações geraes*, 70–82, 116, 147, 165.
[105] Martin, *Forbidden Revolutions*, 10–11.
[106] Rodrigues, *Considerações geraes*, 148–165.
[107] Mark Chapman, "Liberal Readings and Their Conservative Responses," in *The New Cambridge History*, ed. Riches, pp. 208–219. Rodrigues and Pereira frequently quoted from Anglophone bible scholars such as Joseph Lightfoot, William Sanday, Marcus Dods, Crawford H. Toy, and Philip Schaff.

booksellers, and readers.[108] In the early twentieth century, when the evangelical population of Brazil was still small and evangelical ministers were scarce, books of biblical theology did not enjoy much prestige nor arouse great interest. Rodrigues entrusted to his long-time friend and agent of the American Bible Society in Rio de Janeiro, Hugh Tucker, the responsibility of being the custodian of his commentary of the Old Testament.[109] In 1925, two years after Rodrigues's death, Tucker wrote to Jane Rodrigues, the old journalist's English wife, about the fate of his commentary. Of the 286 sets of books shipped from Edinburgh to Rio, 206 had been damaged due to defective packing, with twenty-eight copies of volume one so severely damaged that they were deemed useless. Four years after its publication, the Methodist bookstore of São Paulo, which had kept 130 copies of Rodrigues's work, had been able to sell only ninety-four sets.[110] Nevertheless, parts of Rodrigues's writings on biblical theology circulated more widely. The eighth chapter of his *General Considerations on the Bible* on the methods of Christ's teachings and simplicity of his language was published in the influential *Jornal do Commercio*.[111] Also, a part of Rodrigues's vast personal library containing his books on biblical theology and archaeology were donated to the libraries of the YMCA and the Union Seminary in Rio de Janeiro.[112]

Evangelicalism was a movement of diffusion. Its various agents, both religious specialists and ordinary believers, mobilized their constituencies to subsidize the publication of evangelistic pamphlets, periodicals, and campaigns. Mota, for instance, persuaded members of the Independent Presbyterian Church of São Paulo in 1925 to establish a partnership with an emerging publishing house. The church intended to produce and circulate religious literature of its own, and it arranged the publication of a number of tracts with the Ferraz Brothers publishing house, which printed them at cost and was responsible for sales. The church and the publisher shared equally the profits resulting from an addition of thirty percent on each volume printed.[113] Under these terms, the Independent Church of São Paulo was able to produce with the Ferraz Brothers a number of tracts of biblical

---

[108] Robert Darnton, "What is the History of Books?" *Daedalus* 111 (1982): 65–83; Robert Darnton, "Discourse and Diffusion," *Contributions to the History of Concepts* 1 (2005): 21–28.
[109] Tucker, *Dr. José Carlos Rodrigues*, 19.
[110] H. C. Tucker to Mrs. Rodrigues, Rio de Janeiro, November 19, 1925. BN, Rio de Janeiro. 32,04,01 n 50.
[111] Rodrigues, *Considerações geraes*, 147.
[112] H. C. Tucker to Mrs. Rodrigues, Rio de Janeiro, May 22, 1929. BN, Rio de Janeiro. 32,04,01 n 51.
[113] Otoniel Mota, *Plano de acção* (São Paulo: Irmãos Ferraz, 1925), 10–11.

archaeology and religious controversy that were widely disseminated in the city.[114]

Domesticating Evangelical Christianity

One of the central arguments of this book is that Brazilian evangelicalism emerged out of a constant interaction and negotiation with local cultural idioms and transnational religious ideas and practice. Protestant writers manipulated a vast repertoire of cultural and intellectual traditions, unpacking, disaggregating, and "dismembering" some of their central concepts, and combining them again in different ways.[115] Previous chapters have shown that Brazilian ministers contended with the anticlerical leanings of French Enlightenment philosophers but located notions of natural rights and freedom in the experiences of the early Christian church in their apologetic tracts. In the context of the Great War, Protestant writers such as Eduardo Pereira and Erasmo Braga brought together the internationalist emphasis of the early twentieth-century ecumenical movement with both their anti-Catholic sentiments and notions of Brazilian exceptionalism to convey the message of missionary congresses to the Brazilian public. In doing so, ministers and missionaries translated the fundamental concepts of Protestantism to their Brazilian audiences by locating and domesticating evangelical religion. There are good reasons, therefore, to nuance the interpretations of scholars such as Antonio Gouvêa Mendonça, for whom missionaries and ministers constantly reaffirmed their attachment to American denominationalism and theology, remaining disconnected from the sociocultural realities of Brazil.[116]

What remains to be examined is how Brazilian evangelical intellectuals interwove their religious identity, portrayed as alien by Catholic and nationalist writers, to Brazilian history and culture. Unlike evangelical missionaries in West Africa, China, and the Pacific in the nineteenth and twentieth centuries, for instance, where beliefs and rituals other than Christianity prevailed,

---

[114] Mota, *A archeologia e a Biblia*; Thomas P. Guimarães, *Defesa do protestantismo* (São Paulo: Irmãos Ferraz, 1926); Accacio Coutinho, *Espiritismo ou materialismo?* (São Paulo: Irmãos Ferraz, 1927); E. Magnin, *O espiritismo* (São Paulo: Irmãos Ferraz, 1926).
[115] On intellectual dismemberment, see Christopher Bayly, "Afterword," *Modern Intellectual History* 4 (2007): 163–169.
[116] Antonio G. Mendonça, "O protestantismo no Brasil e suas encruzilhadas," *Revista USP* 67 (2005): 48–67.

their counterparts in Latin America, the Philippines, and parts of Lusophone and Francophone Africa encountered and interacted with Catholicism. Even though these encounters frequently evolved into bitter religious controversies, Protestant leaders as sectarian as Pereira acknowledged that Catholic evangelism had introduced all the fundamental doctrines of Christianity in Brazil: the doctrines of the trinity, the resurrection, the church, sacramental practice, and the final judgment.[117] But apart from these obvious points of contact between two variants of the same religion, evangelical practices and beliefs resonated with a variety of popular traditions in Brazil.

Building on ethnographic studies conducted in São Paulo and Minas Gerais in the 1940s, French historian Émile Léonard argued that a series of popular celebrations, such as the festival of the "three magi" and the *cururu*, an improvised musical dispute involving two singers, had a strong biblical basis because their lyrics were based on the scriptures. For Léonard, these and other festivities facilitated the penetration of Protestant propaganda among the *caipira* population.[118] At least since the 1860s, Catholic priests and lay leaders organized a number of mobilizations of faithful Catholics in Bahia, Pernambuco, Paraíba, and Ceará aimed at restoring old shrines and cemeteries. Also, it was laypeople who staffed the Catholic houses of charity in the Brazilian northeast.[119] Black confraternities in São Paulo and Bahia collected alms for saints among devotees and raised funds for their altars and shrines. Their leaders met with the encroachments of both police chiefs, who viewed such practices as expressions of undesirable African customs, and members of the Catholic hierarchy, who objected to the autonomy of brotherhoods.[120] Therefore, there were a number of antecedents to the so-called Protestant biblicism and activism that informed the reception of evangelical Christianity in Brazil and shaped the religious encounter.

But the deliberate process of weaving evangelical Christianity into Brazilian culture and history was made through a careful observation of

---

[117] Eduardo C. Pereira, *Nossa attitude para com a Egreja Romana* (Rio de Janeiro: Casa Publicadora Baptista, 1916), 2.

[118] Émile G. Léonard, *O protestantismo brasileiro: Estudo de eclesiologia e história social*, 3rd ed. (São Paulo: ASTE, 2002), 95–97.

[119] Dain Borges, "Catholic Vanguard in Brazil," in *Local Church, Global Church: Catholic Activism in Latin America from Rerum Novarum to Vatican II*, ed. Stephen Andes and Julia Young (Washington: Catholic University of America, 2016), 21–49.

[120] Alicia L. Monroe, "To Govern the Church: Autonomy and the Consequences of Self-determination for the Brotherhood of Saint Efigênia and Saint Elesbão of Black Men of São Paulo, Brazil, 1888–1890," *Hispanic American Historical Review* 97 (2017): 63–94; João José Reis, *Divining Slavery and Freedom: The Story of Domingos Sodré, an African Priest in Nineteenth-century Brazil*, trans. H. Sabrina Gledhill (New York: Cambridge University Press, 2015), 9.

the country's customs and traditions. Itinerant work, a standard mode of Protestant evangelism, equipped ministers, missionaries, colporteurs, and converts with an important range of popular customs, practices, and beliefs on the basis of which they built such links. Presbyterian historian Júlio A. Ferreira, describing the long travels of the Rev. Zacarias de Miranda in the countryside of São Paulo between 1881–1884, wrote romantically that "the pioneers were horsemen."[121] The first generations of Portuguese-speaking ministers in Brazil made extensive trips across the Brazilian countryside administering sacraments to scattered congregations, opening new preaching places, and doing evangelistic work.[122] Licensed preachers also undertook lengthy and frequent evangelistic trips in the first years of work, serving a number of churches spread across the Brazilian territory. This was the case of Erasmo Braga, who made preaching tours to Paraná and Minas Gerais after graduation between 1897–1898, spending five months away from home.[123] Nothing quite matches, however, the trip of American Presbyterian missionary Franklin Graham alongside the Brazilian seminarian Antonio dos Santos in 1913. They spent eight months traveling on horseback from the state of Bahia to the border with Bolivia, studying the field and pushing the missionary frontier to the west.[124] In such trips, evangelists and missionaries were usually hosted in the *sítios* of converts or knocked on doors of random houses and asked to stay overnight. That is why foreign missionaries frequently described Brazilians as a hospitable, charitable, and courteous people to their sending bodies in the United States.[125] Also, they gathered information about the customs, language, beliefs, and domestic intimacy of the populations of the countryside. The cover of Mota's book, *Selvas e Choças*, a collection of *caipira* tales and stories published by the Methodist Press of São Paulo in 1922, can be seen a token of evangelical itinerancy (Figure 6.2).[126]

---

[121] Julio A. Ferreira, *Galeria evangélica: Biografias de pastôres presbiterianos que trabalharam no Brasil* (São Paulo: Casa Editora Presbiteriana, 1952), 131–136, at 136.

[122] Relatório Annual de J. F. Dagama apresentado ao Presbyterio do Rio de Janeiro em sessão em São Paulo a 9 de Agosto de 1875; Relatório de M. P. B. de Carvalhosa para o anno de 1875. AHP, São Paulo. Coleção Carvalhosa, Relatórios Pastorais (1866–1875).

[123] Relatório do trabalho do licenciado Erasmo Braga desde junho de 1897 até julho de 1898. AHP, São Paulo. Atas e Relatórios, 1895 a 1903.

[124] Pierson, *A Younger Church*, 56–57.

[125] Robert Speer, *South American Problems* (New York: Student Volunteer Movement for Foreign Missions, 1912), 74; Braga and Grubb, *The Republic of Brazil*, 16.

[126] Catholic missionaries, especially Vincentians and Capuchins, also conducted itinerant work in the interior of Brazil. On the *santas missões*, see Erika Helgen, *Religious Conflict in Brazil: Protestants, Catholics, and the Rise of Religious Pluralism in the Early Twentieth Century* (New Haven, CT: Yale University Press, 2020), 163–198.

THE RISE OF AN EVANGELICAL INTELLIGENTSIA 233

Figure 6.2 The cover of Otoniel Mota's *Selvas e Choças*, published in 1922. Photo taken by the author.

The iconoclast impulse of evangelical Christianity led Protestant ministers to depict some traditional practices and popular beliefs as absurd. A minister, possibly the Brazilian Rev. Antonio Pedro C. Leite, published in the *Imprensa Evangelica* a sequence of articles titled "Popular Superstitions" under the pseudonym *Evangelista* between 1877–1878. The writer collected a series of thirty-seven practices he observed in the countryside of São Paulo and described them in a pejorative, ironic, and amusing form. The eleventh on the list, for instance, informed that "when the morning is foggy and one wants to dissipate the mist, one burns old rags, whose smoke has the virtue of clearing up the day."[127] And another one affirmed that:

> There are two modes by which many Catholics expel cockroaches from their houses.... The first is to invite them three Sundays consecutively to listen to a mass. If they do not go with that, the house owner goes to any place where there are ants called *correcções* [army ants], and invites them in the following terms: —Pals, take a visit to our house for there is a great snack waiting for you. The ants go, and the cockroaches run away.[128]

Brazilian Protestant writers, such as the anonymous *Evangelista* and the Rev. Eduardo Carlos Pereira attributed the prevalence of these superstitions among the Brazilian population to high rates of illiteracy and Catholic creeds. For Pereira, the neo-Catholicism of pope Pius IX revived pre-Christian and medieval paganism, interweaving them with Christianity.[129] And the *Evangelista* argued that the Catholic Church "directly and positively" taught superstitious practices to the Brazilian population via its periodical *O Apostolo* and the colonial Constitutions of the Archbishopric of Bahia.[130]

But whereas Protestant ministers advocated Bible-reading and iconoclasm as effective tools of religious cleansing, they positively sought to inscribe evangelical Christianity into the domestic intimacy of rural families. As Braga wrote in 1916, one of the most remarkable but invisible transformations of the country at that time was the penetration of "the vivifying energy of the Gospel" into the "intimacy of the family, the peasant's rustic shack, the hut of the *sertanejo*," where Christian literature and hymnals "of fairly exotic poetry" were constantly opened and examined.[131] In his tales and memoirs of life in the countryside, Mota highlighted the conversational feature of *caipira*

---

[127] *Imprensa Evangelica*, October 6, 1877, n. 20.
[128] *Imprensa Evangelica*, September 15, 1877, n. 18.
[129] Pereira, *O problema religioso*, 384.
[130] *Imprensa Evangelica*, March 14, 1878, n. 11. For the other articles of the *Popular superstitions* series, see *Imprensa Evangelica*, September 1, 1877, n. 17; November 3, 1877, n. 22; February 14, 1878, n. 7; April 4, 1878, n. 14; April 11, 1878, n. 15; June 6, 1878, n. 23.
[131] Braga, *Pan-Americanismo*, 52–53.

customs and community life, in which neighbors and family members gathered around the fire in the evening to tell anecdotes and stories of fishing and hunting sessions, some quite exaggerated.[132] The writers of conversion narratives and histories of Protestant genealogies portrayed religious change as a process that evolved through intimate conversations with evangelical neighbors, friends, family members, and occasionally a foreign missionary.[133] Pereira's texts, published by the Brazilian Society of Evangelical Tracts since the 1880s, also brought the dialogical trait of *caipira* domesticity to the forefront. Depicting the inhabitants of Minas Gerais and São Paulo as courteous and hospitable, Pereira's stories frequently started with an evangelist traveling through the countryside and asking to stay overnight in houses by the road. The evangelist then engages in a friendly conversation with his hosts over dinner and introduces evangelical doctrines to the family.[134] In his tracts, Pereira frequently took as his starting point certain elements of family Catholic devotions, such as the Lord's Prayer and the veneration of Mary, and argued in conversational style that the dogmas of Mary's immaculate conception and the worship of saints were either medieval or modern creations of Rome, not primitive Christianity. Ultimately, what such evangelical tracts attempted to do was to build upon Christian beliefs that were already there, in rural domestic devotions, and invert the logic of anteriority, claiming that evangelical beliefs and practices were in fact older than Catholic ones.

The familiarity of Brazilian Protestant ministers with the customs, traditions, beliefs, and language of the countryside of São Paulo and Minas also informed their intellectual labor. In fact, a good number of Brazilian Presbyterian ministers working in different parts of the country in the early twentieth century had been born and raised in the states of São Paulo and Minas Gerais. This included, among others, Eduardo C. Pereira, Otoniel Mota, Erasmo Braga, José Zacarias de Miranda, Álvaro Reis, and Mattathias Gomes dos Santos.[135] Some of these ministers combined the strong emphasis on language learning of their seminary training with their

---

[132] Mota, *Selvas e choças*, 53–65.
[133] See Chapter 4 of this text.
[134] Eduardo C. Pereira, *O unico advogado dos peccadores* (São Paulo: Typ. a vapor de Jorge Seckler & C., 1884); Eduardo C. Pereira, *A bemaventurada Virgem Maria* (São Paulo: Typographia King, 1887); Eduardo C. Pereira, *Nosso pae que está nos céos* (São Paulo: Livraria Evangelica, 1902).
[135] Data on their careers can be found in Pierson, *A Younger Church*. On J. Z. Miranda see Ferreira, *Galeria Evangélica*. Places and dates of birth—E. Pereira: Caldas (MG), November 8, 1855; O. Mota: Porto Feliz (SP), April 16, 1878; E. Braga: Rio Claro (SP), April 23, 1877; J. Z. de Miranda: Baependi (SP), November 5, 1851; A. Reis: São Paulo (SP), March 22, 1864; M. G. dos Santos: Campinas (SP), September 11, 1879.

rudimentary ethnographic observations of popular customs and traditions in different ways.

When Pereira and Mota emerged as Brazil's leading linguists in the twentieth century, they incorporated regional variations of the Portuguese language into their works of grammar and philology. As Pereira wrote in a short book of philology, the work of a grammarian was not to determine the rules of standard Portuguese, but that of observing and codifying what was spoken by the majority of the population. It was the method of the natural sciences applied to the science of language. And such work required the observation of how both the learned classes and the common folk used a certain language, modifying it and showing its evolutionary force.[136] In his *Historical Grammar*, Pereira affirmed that grammarians should pay close attention to the historical, phonological, and morphological aspects of the language to account for its changes and adaptations over space and time.[137] He portrayed Portuguese as a living language, enriched by regional variations, incorporation of foreign expressions, and varieties in pronunciations on both sides of the Atlantic, and systematized a few regional variations of the language in São Paulo and Minas Gerais. His best-selling *Expository Grammar*, which reached as many as ninety-six editions and became a standard secondary-school textbook in Brazil, showed how regional variations were consequences of the "evolutionary work of the language" instead of just mistakes.[138] Pereira's grammar offered a host of examples of how regional unorthodox uses of the Portuguese language in the Brazilian countryside resembled earlier modifications of popular Latin, incorporating the sounds of animals and nature into the language or relocating the word stress in accordance to local customs.[139]

The Rev. Otoniel Mota succeeded Pereira in both the pastorate of the Independent Presbyterian Church of São Paulo and as a linguist. Like Pereira, Mota also systematized and explained local uses and regional variations of Portuguese in his books. He explained in his *My Language*, adopted as a textbook in the prestigious Pedro II secondary school of Rio de Janeiro, that *caboclo* adaptations of Portuguese followed long-established

---

[136] Eduardo C. Pereira, *Questões de philologia* (São Paulo: Typographia Falcone, 1907), 20–23.
[137] Eduardo C. Pereira, *Grammatica historica*, 9th ed. (São Paulo: Companhia Editora Nacional, 1935 [1916]).
[138] Eduardo C. Pereira, *Grammatica expositiva: Curso superior*, 26th ed. (São Paulo: Companhia Editora Nacional, n/d [1907]), 13 and 222.
[139] Pereira, *Grammatica expositiva*, 8, 13, 32–37, 113, 128, 148, 164, 264–265.

grammarian principles such as the law of minimal effort and analogy.[140] In suppressing complicated sounds in favor of easier ones, "ordinary people" adapted the Portuguese language and demarcated the evolution from popular Latin, to archaic Portuguese, to its modern form.[141] Mota's work as a linguist fed back into his pastoral and theological endeavors. In a new translation of the gospel of Matthew into Portuguese, Mota applied his philological knowledge to the biblical text and linked scenes, practices, and artifacts of first-century Palestine to twentieth-century Brazil. Throughout the new version Mota affirmed that the clothes of northern Brazil's *vaqueiros* (cowboys) resembled those of John, the Baptist; replaced the word *rede* (fishing net) by *tarrafa* (cast net), more widely used by Brazilian fishermen; and compiled a set of similarities between the customs and material world of Hebrew antiquity and "our people," "our land."[142]

This interest in *caipira* customs and language, an integral part of missionary labor and intellectual production, resonated very closely with the regionalist and modernist movements in São Paulo in the early twentieth century. Brazilian modernism emerged in a context of rapid urban and industrial growth, as well as dizzying cultural diversification. In a context of industrial growth, commercial boom, and intensifying foreign immigration, *paulista* intellectual elites sought to recover old traditions, an "authentic" popular culture, and promote them.[143] Members of the wealthy and influential Prado family, a clan of *paulista* landowners, sponsored tours of Brazilian and foreign artists across the country to observe, study, and promote popular culture, ultimately producing a "re-discovery of Brazil." Those who benefited from the Prados included prestigious playwrights, novelists, and artists such as Afonso Arinos, Mario de Andrade, Tarsila do Amaral, Oswald de Andrade, and the French Blaise Cendrars. These artists were interested in forging a "synthesis composed of historical, modern, ethnic, tropical, national symbols that produced an ultimate effect of 'Brazilianess'" that at times displayed xenophobic sentiments.[144]

The regionalist movement of São Paulo also idealized certain aspects of the Brazilian past, especially the polemical figure of the *bandeirantes*. These were mostly *mamelucos*, men of mixed Portuguese and Amerindian descent

---

[140] Otoniel Mota, *O meu idioma*, 2nd ed. (São Paulo: Weiszflog Irmãos, 1917), 28, 33, 39.
[141] Mota, *O meu idioma*, 11.
[142] Mota, *O evangelho de São Matheus*, 99, 107–108, 120–122.
[143] Sevcenko, *Orfeu extático*, 245–246.
[144] Sevcenko, *Orfeu extático*, 238–244, 277–307, at 299.

who had their home-base in São Paulo and, from the early seventeenth century onward, organized long-distance expeditions to explore the Brazilian territory, enslave indigenous people, and search for precious minerals. Their profitable enslaving of indigenous groups alongside their preference for the Christianized, peaceful ones of the missionary reductions, put them into perennial conflict with the Jesuits.[145] The aggressive, "uncivilized" outlook of the *bandeirantes* made them poor candidates to stand as a national myth of origin. But whereas Catholic missionaries in the colonial period depicted the *bandeirantes* as cruel characters, early twentieth-century *paulista* writers idealized them, recasting the *bandeirantes* as lighter-skinned, proto-capitalist entrepreneurs in contrast to the decadent, parasitical, darker-skinned mulattoes of the Brazilian northeast.[146] São Paulo's colonial past was projected as the cradle of modern Brazil. Scholars of *bandeirante* history appropriated notions of racial difference and insisted that there were few or no traces of African racial and cultural influence in São Paulo, depicting the *bandeirantes* as a "race of giants."[147]

The ambivalent relations of Brazilian evangelicals with racial theories and nationalism also led them into ambivalent relations with modernism and *paulista* regionalism. Braga, one of the founders of the *Paulista Academy of Letters*, showed throughout his career a special suspicion and dislike of interwar nationalism. In his view, churches, schools, the press, and other cultural agents should promote an "internationalist mind-set." For the pastor and educator, and in a clear reference to the regionalism of São Paulo, this was a powerful remedy against the "provincial and parochial tendency" that hindered the progress of the "concept of national solidarity among the units of the federation."[148] It was Otoniel Mota, however, who engaged more closely with *paulista* regionalism, taking part in the movement but maintaining his unique stance. At the same time that scholars of *bandeirante* history rehabilitated the nature of their violent protagonists, the prestigious

---

[145] On the bandeirantes, see Richard Morse, *The Bandeirantes: The Historical Role of the Brazilian Pathfinders* (New York: Alfred A. Knopf, 1965); John Monteiro, *Blacks of the Land: Indian Slavery, Settler Society, and the Portuguese Colonial Enterprise in South America*, trans. James Woodard and Barbara Weinstein (New York: Cambridge University Press, 2018 [1994]).

[146] Barbara Weinstein, "Racializing Regional Difference: São Paulo *versus* Brasil, 1932," in *Race and Nation in Modern Latin America*, ed. Nancy Appelbaum, Anne Macpherson, and Karin A. Rosemblatt (Chapel Hill: University of North Carolina Press, 2003), 237–262, at 243–244, 247–254.

[147] Weinstein, *The Color of Modernity*, 37–39; John Monteiro, "Caçando com gato: Raça, mestiçagem e identidade paulista na obra de Alfredo Ellis Jr.," *Novos Estudos CEBRAP* 38 (1994): 79–88.

[148] Braga, *Religião e cultura*, 154, 157–158.

writer Monteiro Lobato created a literary character that was the opposite of the adventurous slavers: the Jéca Tatú.[149] In his book *Urupês* (1918) Lobato popularized the figure of the Jéca Tatú, whose physical traces and behavior epitomized the *caipira* men: he was a mixed-race *caboclo*, lazy, uneducated, and superstitious, who watched all big political and social transformations in his indifferent squatting position.[150] Lobato's Jéca Tatú was the embodiment of the idea of degeneration, a central concept in Brazilian social thought.[151]

In this context Mota created his own representation of the men and women of the countryside of São Paulo and blurred the boundaries between *caipira* and *bandeirante* identities. His 1922 book, *Selvas e Choças*, included a chapter entitled *Bandeirante*, whose central character was a brave and respectable man known as Jeca Tigre (tiger), a clear contrast to Lobato's *caipira*. In fact, elsewhere in the book Mota referred to a band of "fearless Jecas" in the countryside of São Paulo as "those whom Monteiro Lobato does not know."[152] But Mota's Jeca *bandeirante* was not a slaver or prospector. Instead, he was a man who settled the backlands and tamed wild nature. In the midst of a vigorous and harmful land, Jeca Tigre built his house with his own hands aided by his family and servants, and he said to himself: "we are accommodated. Let there be health and all will be well; praised be God!"[153] The clearing of land with brushfire, which Lobato portrayed as a token of *caipira* backwardness, was to Mota a sign of man's victory over wild nature.[154] And Jeca Tigre's son Tico, upon listening to the stories of his *bandeirante* forefathers during evening talks by the fire, felt them whispering to him a variation of God's commandment to Adam and Eve in the Eden: "Tico... felt that in the bottom of his great and blossoming soul a clear voice said to him: 'You are the heir of this race. Do not let the virile animus of your ancestors perish in you. Be a man, be strong, subdue the jungles and the beasts.'"[155]

Mota's book *From Hut to Palace: Evolution of the Paulista Civilization* dedicated a chapter to the *bandeirante heart*, which was aimed at deconstructing Jesuit depictions of the *bandeirantes* as cruel and violent. Examining the wills and inventories of old *paulista* families, Mota claimed that his forefathers were a benevolent, warm-hearted people who dispensed generous treatment

---

[149] Tatú, in Portuguese, is an animal, the armadillo—a mammal with leathery armor shell.
[150] J. Monteiro Lobato, *Urupês*, 13th ed. (São Paulo: Brasiliense, 1966 [1918]), 277–292.
[151] Borges, "'Puffy, Ugly, Slothful and Inert.'"
[152] Mota, *Selvas e choças*, 165.
[153] Mota, *Selvas e choças*, 68–69.
[154] Mota, *Selvas e choças*, 70.
[155] Mota, *Selvas e choças*, 72.

to indigenous people and African slaves.[156] Once again, he did not depict the *bandeirantes* as the leaders of bands of slavers, prospectors, and pathfinders of the seventeenth and eighteenth centuries, but as the men and women who shaped *paulista* civilization. The hardened and uneducated spirit of the colonial inhabitants of São Paulo was a product of their intellectual isolation and longstanding conflict with a harmful nature.[157] Elsewhere, Mota claimed that the historical presence of African slaves in the plateau of São Paulo was not significant enough to alter the racial composition of the region.[158] All these assertions were in harmony with the regionalist movement. But in Mota's narrative, some of the agents who invigorated São Paulo's trade, agriculture, and intellectual life were immigrants or foreign-born. It was a gypsy woman, Francisca Rodrigues, who first opened a sort of grocery shop in São Paulo, and for him Italian landowners were positively invigorating agricultural production in the state.[159] In this sense, Mota offered a unique interpretation of *paulista* regionalism that brought together various features of evangelical thought of the era. His writings mobilized the missionary repertoire of traditional customs and beliefs of rural populations and, unlike some influential regionalist writers of his era, confirmed the Protestant suspicion of interwar nationalism and racial theories.[160]

Protestant intellectuals attempted to inscribe their religion into Brazilian culture in yet another way. They located evangelical Christianity deep into the Brazilian past. And there were similar efforts in worldwide expressions of the Christian faith. Throughout the nineteenth and twentieth centuries, with the expansion and consolidation of a world-system of nation states, the loyalty of specific Christian minorities to their nations was put in doubt. Ultramontane Catholics in nineteenth-century Britain were accused of being disloyal to the monarchy, and conversion to Christianity in India and China was often deemed as anti-national. In the face of this, Christian converts and religious specialists across the world advocated the ancient roots of their religion.[161] Nineteenth-century Bengali Christian writers discussed historical evidence of St. Thomas's travel to India in order to situate their own

---

[156] Mota, *Do rancho ao palacio*, 127–139.
[157] Mota, *Do rancho*, 111–115, 119–126.
[158] Otoniel Mota, "'Negro Tapanhuno,'" *Revista da Academia Paulista de Letras* 7 (1944): 10–21.
[159] On the "gypsy of 1603," see Mota, *Do rancho*, 108–109; and on Italian ranchers, see Mota, *Selvas e choças*, 172–174.
[160] Also in Mota, *A filosofia do joão-de-barro*.
[161] Peter van der Veer, "Nationalism and Religion," in *The Oxford Handbook of the History of Nationalism*, ed. John Breuilly (Oxford: Oxford University Press, 2013), 655–671, at 660.

society in the apostolic tradition and dismiss the idea of the foreignness of Christianity.[162] In West Africa, Yoruba Christians employed what John Peel has called anticipation and prophesy to inculturate Christianity. Building upon the Yoruba religious culture, these agents claimed that the *orisa* Orunmila prefigured Christ. They also reinterpreted old prophecies of the coming of Europeans and their religion, whose most authoritative sources were the *babalawos*.[163] In Latin America, the issue at stake was the superficial historical anchorage of evangelical Christianity. For Catholic priests and nationalist intellectuals, conversion to Protestantism eroded the traditional order and the alliance between religion and national identity. In the 1930s and 1940s, Mexican Congregationalist Alberto Rembao sought to revert this stigma by asserting the Iberian origins of Protestantism and claiming that late medieval and early modern Spanish mystics influenced the Lutheran Reformation decisively. In Rembao's argument, this history helped to "de-Saxonize" evangelical Christianity and showed that Protestantism was not alien to the *Spanish soul*.[164]

In a similar way, Brazilian Protestants interwove religion, history, and patriotism building upon a solid historical repertoire related to the presence of French Huguenots in sixteenth-century Rio de Janeiro (1555–1567) and Reformed Dutch in seventeenth-century Pernambuco (1630–1654).[165] Despite the historical and geographical limitations of these religious experiences, Protestant writers stressed their importance and attempted to situate Protestantism at the very beginnings of Brazilian history. The book *Brazil and the Brazilians*, written by Presbyterian chaplain James C. Fletcher and Methodist missionary Daniel P. Kidder, recovered the history of the French settlement. Originally published in 1857, it was widely read by American missionaries in Brazil. The book asserted that Rio de Janeiro was the site where the first Protestant service was celebrated in the Americas in 1555: "It was upon this island that ... these French Puritans offered their

---

[162] Shinjini Das, "An Imperial Apostle? St Paul, Protestant Conversion, and South Asian Christianity," *Historical Journal* 61 (2018): 103–130, at 125–126.

[163] J. D. Y. Peel, *Religious Encounter and the Making of the Yoruba* (Bloomington: Indiana University Press, 2000), 299–300.

[164] Mondragón, *Like Leaven*, 107–108.

[165] On the French settlement of Rio, the *France Antarctique*, see H. B. Johnson, "The Portuguese Settlement of Brazil, 1500–1580," in *The Cambridge History of Latin America, vol. I: Colonial Latin America*, ed. Leslie Bethell (Cambridge: Cambridge University Press, 1984), 249–286, at 275–277. On the Dutch colony, see Evan Haefeli, "Breaking the Christian Atlantic: The Legacy of Dutch Tolerance in Brazil," in *The Legacy of Dutch Brazil*, ed. Michiel van Groesen (Cambridge: Cambridge University Press, 2014), 124–145.

prayers and sang their hymns of praise nearly threescore years and ten before a Pilgrim placed his foot on Plymouth Rock, and more than a half century before the Book of Common Prayer was borne to the banks of the James River."[166] In their narrative, Portuguese interest in recovering the territory, Catholic intolerance, and the religious cynicism of Nicolas de Villegaignon, the founder of the French colony, motivated the war between Portuguese colonial authorities and the French. But, to Fletcher and Kidder, Protestantism lived on in Brazil. For them, "the mysterious dealings of Providence" alongside the "faithful prayers... [of] those pious Huguenots" enabled the country, nearly three hundred years later, to benefit from a liberal constitution and an independent government that safeguarded religious freedom.[167]

Decades later, during a series of celebrations of historical events, Protestants carried further this historical anchorage of evangelical Christianity into the depths of Brazilian history. In 1900, during the celebrations of the four hundredth anniversary of the arrival of the Portuguese in the Brazilian coast, José Carlos Rodrigues wrote a history of non-Catholic religions in Brazil. Rodrigues's book was part of a monumental collection that examined various aspects of Brazilian history over the previous four centuries: literature, sciences, the arts, trade, industry, agriculture, mining, and religion. The influential Father Júlio Maria wrote the book on Catholicism. In it, the priest emphasized the centrality of the Catholic Church in the construction of a sense of Brazilian nationality. In his argument, the First Mass and the missionary efforts of the Jesuits embodied the central role played by the Church in cementing the unity of the nation.[168] Countering the Catholic priest, Rodrigues wrote that Portuguese and Catholic rule in the colonial period promoted moral decay. He depicted the Inquisition as a solvent of harmonious social relations, turning citizen against citizen, and children against parents.[169] Despite colonial persecution, intellectual isolation, and the violence of the Inquisition, Rodrigues claimed that the influence of Judaism and Protestantism left an enduring legacy in Brazil, especially in the indigenous communities of Rio de Janeiro and Pernambuco. For Rodrigues, the seeds sown by the French, the Dutch, and the Jews did not fall into a wasteland,

---

[166] James C. Fletcher and Daniel P. Kidder, *Brazil and the Brazilians: Portrayed in Historical and Descriptive Sketches* (Philadelphia: Childs & Peterson, 1857), 54.
[167] Fletcher and Kidder, *Brazil and the Brazilians*, 59–60.
[168] Júlio Maria, "A religião, ordens religiosas, instituições pias e beneficentes no Brasil," in *O livro do centenário (1500–1900)* (Rio de Janeiro: Imprensa Nacional, 1900).
[169] José C. Rodrigues, *Religiões acatholicas no Brazil, 1500–1900*, 2nd ed. (Rio de Janeiro: Escriptorio do Jornal do Commercio, 1904), 44–45, 60.

but grew slowly in different corners of the country. Quoting from colonial texts, Rodrigues claimed that Dutch missionary efforts had transformed the Indians of Pernambuco into Calvinists and Lutherans.[170]

In 1917, Protestants recalled these histories in another context. Commemorating the four hundredth anniversary of the Reformation, an elder of the Presbyterian Church of Rio de Janeiro, Domingos Ribeiro, translated from the French an account of the beliefs and execution of the French Protestants Jean du Bourdel, Matthieu Verneuil, and Pierre Bourdon in Rio under Villegaignon. The last part of this tract featured Braga's translation of the *Guanabara Confession of Faith* written by these men alongside André de la Fon. Braga and Ribeiro portrayed these men as the "proto-martyrs" of Protestant Christianity in Brazil.[171] In the same year, the Independent Presbyterian Church of Rio de Janeiro published a short book commemorating the Reformation. In it, Eduardo Pereira situated the execution of the French Huguenots in Rio de Janeiro into the bloodshed of the era, linking the stories of the martyrs of Guanabara to the martyrs of the English Reformation, including Hugh Latimer and Thomas Cranmer.[172]

Building upon these historical experiences, evangelical intellectuals located Brazilian Protestantism in the very beginning of the history of both the nation and the transnational circuits of the Reformation, representing the evangelical missionary enterprise in modern Brazil as an echo of a distant past. In the late nineteenth and early twentieth centuries, a group of Protestant writers and ministers, including José Carlos Rodrigues and the Rev. Álvaro Reis, depicted the Jesuits as foreign agents of a foreign potentate based in Rome. In the colonial past, Rodrigues wrote, the Jesuits and the Inquisition "mummified" the Portuguese kingdom and its colony.[173] And in the first years of the Brazilian Republic, Reis wrote, they were the anti-patriotic enemies of the new regime, opposed to the principles of religious liberty and the civil marriage.[174] Reis, Braga, Rodrigues, and Pereira all referred to Villegaignon as the "Cain of the Americas" on account of the persecution of his fellow Protestant Frenchmen, and emphasized how the

---

[170] Rodrigues, *Religiões acatholicas*, 27, 71–72, 80–81, 92.

[171] Domingos Ribeiro, *A tragedia de Guanabara, ou Historia dos protomartyres do christianismo no Brasil* (Rio de Janeiro: Typ. Pimenta de Mello, 1917).

[172] *A commemoração do 4º centenário da Reforma—31 de outubro de 1917* (São Paulo: Typographia d'O Estandarte, 1917), 16–17.

[173] Rodrigues, *Religiões acatholicas*, 64.

[174] Álvaro Reis, *José de Anchieta á luz da historia patria* (São Paulo: n/p, 1896); Álvaro Reis, *Anchieta, o carrasco de Bolés á luz da historia patria* (São Paulo: n/p, 1896), 31.

influential Catholic priest José de Anchieta acted as an executioner to the survivors of the French colony.[175] In doing so, they represented religious persecution and the Catholic Inquisition as elements that disaggregated Brazilian society: these practices drove away the economically dynamic Protestants and Jews and shattered the development of the future nation. And establishing a clear contrast to the historical legacy of the Catholic Church, Protestant ministers argued that they were the real patriotic citizens of the Brazilian state, and that their religion was the fittest to promote the development of the nation. In this period, the Catholic Church recruited Vincentian priests from Belgium and France and Maryknoll missionaries from the United States in its efforts to rejuvenate the Church's missionary endeavors in Brazil.[176] Protestant ministers compared this increasing denationalization of the Catholic Church to the nationalization of the evangelical missionary enterprise, claiming that their efforts to educate a local Protestant clergy and revive Christian religion embodied the true patriotic spirit of the Republic.[177]

Conclusion

When the University of São Paulo was founded in 1934, its first professors were recruited from among existing literary academies, scientific institutes, faculties, and secondary schools. Before the specialization of academic disciplines and the professionalization of academic careers, the first generations of university professors straddled multiple areas of expertise and served different academic, political, educational, and religious institutions. In this period, Protestant pastors and seminary professors played an important role in the formative decades of the University of São Paulo, especially in the fields of linguistics and philology.[178] Their interest in these topics stemmed from both the strong and demanding emphasis on language acquisition at Protestant seminaries and the influence of the Revs. Eduardo Carlos Pereira and Erasmo Braga over the earliest generations of Presbyterian pastors in

---

[175] Reis, *Anchieta, o carrasco de Bolés*, 23–25; Rodrigues, *Religiões acatholicas*, 17–20, 26–37; Pereira, *O problema religioso*, 58; Braga, *Pan-Americanismo*, 25.
[176] Della Cava, "Catholicism and Society," 23–24; Serbin, *Needs of the Heart*, 70–72.
[177] Landes, *Dom Aquino*, 38, 57; Rodrigues, *Religiões acatholicas*, 215.
[178] Izidoro Blikstein, "Maurer, Salum e a Romanística: pioneirismo, Sabedoria e humildade," *Estudos Avançados* 8 (1994): 259–262; José de S. Martins, "Penúltimas palavras," *Revista Brasileira de Ciências Sociais* 29 (2014): 195–210.

Brazil. By recovering the trajectories and careers of the early twentieth-century evangelical intelligentsia, this chapter shed light on diachronic processes of intellectual formation in modern Brazil. Its protagonists undertook a different training from that of the country's secular and Catholic intellectual elites and followed different careers. But although the conceptual foundations that informed evangelical notions of national loyalty, regional belonging, and social action differed substantially from those of Brazil's secular and Catholic intelligentsia, they all shared a broader discursive arena and responded to similar processes of social, political, and religious change. Their ideas and discourses circulated in different social arenas but were loosely connected around general debates. Amidst the uncertainties, anxieties, and expectations of the first decades of the twentieth century, religious thinkers elaborated effective responses to processes of social and political change precisely because they were religious: "because they could draw on the ambiguous power of myth and symbol and ritual; because they could mean many things at once and contain many potentialities."[179]

It was the flexibility of such religious languages that provided Brazilian evangelical ministers with the tools to mobilize such a vast array of beliefs, secular ideologies, and popular traditions and forge notions of nationhood as well as forms of social and cultural engagement. Protestant ministers, such as Pereira, Braga, Mota, Reis, and Miranda, fiercely criticized the revival of conservative Catholicism, but they also built upon a set of Catholic practices and beliefs to introduce their own message. They recovered the histories of French and Dutch settlements in colonial Brazil to situate Protestantism deep into Brazilian history. In a context of rapid social change and facing the rise of interwar nationalism, they appropriated strands of social theologies and ecumenical internationalism to craft new conceptions of patriotic behavior. And it is precisely here that one comprehends a remarkable feature of religious movements worldwide: their ability to build upon and re-sacralize not only religious practices and creeds other than theirs, but also secular ideologies. It happened with Yoruba Christians in the nineteenth century, who appropriated the semantic ground created by Islam and *orisa* religious to inculturate Christianity.[180] It happened with Western thinkers in the post-WWII period, such as Jacques Maritain and Gerhard Ritter, for whom

---

[179] Terence Ranger, "Religious Movements and Politics in Sub-Saharan Africa," *African Studies Review* 29 (1986): 1–69, at 51.

[180] Peel, *Religious Encounter*, chs. 7 and 10.

human rights were a Christian legacy to be defended against the violence of revolution, not a fruit of the modern revolutions.[181] And it also featured in the arguments of progressive Catholics in Latin America, to whom liberation theology had been born with the "prophetic cry" of Spanish Dominican friars Antonio de Montesinos and Bartolomé de las Casas in the sixteenth century, not in the 1970s.[182] The Brazilian evangelical writers and ministers of the early twentieth century shared in this impetus, mixing together a wide array of concepts, customs, and images to locate the new religion into Brazilian culture and history. They acted as religious experts who mediated between multiple cultural frameworks and channeled Protestant theologies and identities into local debates and dynamics, projecting the new religion into the public sphere.

---

[181] Samuel Moyn, *The Last Utopia: Human Rights in History* (Cambridge, MA: Belknap Press of Harvard University Press, 2012), 76. On the relationship between conservative Christian movements and human rights, see Samuel Moyn, *Christian Human Rights* (Philadelphia: University of Pennsylvania Press, 2015).

[182] Ivan Petrella, "The Intellectual Roots of Liberation Theology," in *The Cambridge History of Religions in Latin America*, ed. Virginia Garrard-Burnett, Paul Freston, and Stephen Dove (New York: Cambridge University Press, 2016), 359–371, at 359–360.

Conclusion

In 1934, the elder and founder of the Presbyterian Church of Perdizes, Manuel de Melo, the rural *caipira* believer whose conversion was described in Chapter 4, was taken to an evangelical conference in the city of Patrocínio, Minas Gerais. On that occasion, the elderly convert gathered with foreign missionaries, local ministers, leaders, and converts from various cities and villages around western Minas Gerais. In the words of his daughter, Maria de Melo Chaves, that conference represented to Manuel something akin to Moses's journey "from the green plains of Moab unto the top of Mount Nebo, from where he was able to contemplate the 'promised land' that had been the supreme ideal of his life. There he experienced, in its fullness, the value of a life dedicated to the service of the Lord. There he had a new and radiant view of the Gospel of Christ in the social sphere, in the congregation of believers, in the refinement of their spirituality!"[1] For Maria de Melo Chaves, by looking at the expansion of evangelical Christianity in Brazil, Manuel de Melo was contemplating the fruits of his commitment to the missionary enterprise. His congregation thrived, his children were educated, and his religious authority had been tested and confirmed.

Manuel's trajectory and impressions of the Patrocínio conference encapsulate some of the historical transformations described in this book. This is a history that originated in small religious communities scattered across the growing Brazilian cities and the vast countryside and decades later boasted a complex religious bureaucracy comprising educational institutions, seminaries, publishing houses, and large-scale evangelical conferences. In the beginning, the majority of congregations were only occasionally served by missionaries and ordained ministers, affording much space for local leadership. They gathered family members and neighbors in private homes to sing from hymnals, pray, and read together from the Bible, periodicals, tracts, and printed sermons. By the 1930s, the earliest

---

[1] Maria de Melo Chaves, *Bandeirantes da fé* (Belo Horizonte: Associação Evangélica Beneficente de Minas Gerais, 1947), 186–187.

generation of missionaries and pioneer converts, including Manuel de Melo, was passing away. Their social and cultural worlds were also changing and giving space to new religious configurations. Up until the end of his life, Manuel struggled to read the Bible and to write. His children, on the other hand, had been educated in mission schools and acquired some degree of cultural sophistication.

The history of evangelical Christianity in Brazil evolved amidst these complex changing dynamics. This book examined the multiple tensions and interplays between global and local forces, old and new sociocultural configurations, and changing religious alignments that shaped the movement's earliest history. Its chapters looked at the multiple ways in which converts seized the concepts, symbols, practices, and institutions of evangelical missionaries and adapted them to their specific circumstances. Their urge to recover pristine, age-old Christianity echoed the message of evangelicals worldwide, but it also resonated with the agendas of dissenting Catholics and liberal reformers in Brazil, which enabled Protestantism to relate to the religious and political struggles of the country. The evangelical movement in Brazil was connected in various ways to the networks and organizations of the "Protestant International," but it also developed a distinct local flavor and a complex relationship with established customs and cultural idioms.

This analysis of the evangelical publishing enterprise in Brazil illuminates some of the dynamics implicated in processes of religious change. Because Protestants devoted such an inordinate amount of time, money, energy, arguments, and personnel into the publication and circulation of literature, a study of their publishing endeavor reveals crucial aspects of the process of making of evangelical religion. Throughout, I highlighted the centrality of the local agents of religious diffusion and reconstructed the reading practices that emerged at grassroots level in the modern history of the country. I also concentrated on the extensive infrastructures that evangelists and booksellers devised to set Bibles and Christian literature in motion. A close examination of conversion narratives and biographies of early converts sheds light on the changing forms of sociality and cultural transformations involved in religious change, while an analysis of their tracts and books reveals their strategies of conceptual location of evangelical religion. This conclusion returns to some of the discussions of the previous chapters and relates them to the worldwide expansion of evangelical Christianity and to the religious transformations of modern Brazil.

Protestant-Catholic Interactions

In the 1930s, the Catholic Church entered a new era. After decades of bureaucratic expansion and institutional reconstruction since the religious disestablishment of the republican government in 1889, the Church sought to restore its ties to the Brazilian state in the context of Getúlio Vargas's long rule (1930–1945). Since the 1920s, the influential bishop, later cardinal Sebastião Leme encouraged the creation of lay organizations, such as the *Centro Dom Vital* (Dom Vital Center, 1922), which gathered the vanguard of the Catholic intelligentsia, and the *Liga Eleitoral Católica* (Catholic Electoral League, 1932), which encouraged the activism of students and workers. These institutions played an important role in the church–state rapprochement.[2] Vargas's authoritarian corporatism resonated with the Church's teaching on social discipline, order, and unity, and the Constitution of 1934 made a series of concessions to Catholic pressures, including the promulgation of the constitution in the name of God, the indissolubility of marriages, civil recognition of religious marriages, and rights for Catholic unions.[3] These transformations pushed Protestants to flex their organizational muscles. They created stronger interdenominational confederations that fulfilled the dreams of evangelical union described in Chapter 5 and made their first ventures into the realm of formal politics. The Methodist minister Guaracy Silveira, from the Brazilian Socialist Party, was elected to the constitutional assembly of 1934 and in congress he upheld the legacy of Brazil's early republicans to withstand Catholic re-establishment.[4]

By that time evangelicals were still a small religious minority. Erasmo Braga and Kenneth Grubb estimated that in 1930 there were 135,390 communicant members within a larger community of over 700,000 churchgoers and immigrants across the Brazilian territory.[5] It was not much in a county of over 41 million people. But although missionaries, ministers, and evangelists

---

[2] Thomas C. Bruneau, *The Political Transformation of the Brazilian Catholic Church* (London: Cambridge University Press, 1974); Sérgio Miceli, *A elite eclesiástica brasileira: 1890–1930*, 2nd ed. (São Paulo: Companhia das Letras, 2009).

[3] Ralph Della Cava, "Catholicism and Society in Twentieth-century Brazil," *Latin American Research Review* 11 (1976): 7–50; Kenneth Serbin, "Church and State Reciprocity in Contemporary Brazil: The Convening of the International Eucharistic Congress of 1955 in Rio de Janeiro," *The Hispanic American Historical Review* 76 (1996): 721–751.

[4] Paul Freston, "Protestantes e política no Brasil: Da Constituinte ao impeachment." (PhD dissertation, State University of Campinas, 1993), 154–157.

[5] Erasmo Braga and Kenneth Grubb, *The Republic of Brazil: A Survey of the Religious Situation* (London: World Dominion Press, 1932), 140.

were not remarkably successful in terms of conversion and church growth in this period, they served as catalysts of broader transformations that significantly altered the religious scenario of the country. The patterns of reception and resistance to missionary Christianity encountered in Brazil have parallels worldwide. To some extent they are reminiscent of the transformations of the "religious economy" of the Indian Ocean studied by historian Nile Green. In nineteenth-century Bombay, the evangelistic efforts of British and American Protestant missionaries prompted a wide array of responses from Hindu and Muslim religious elites. Christians remained a tiny minority in this period, but their methods and ideologies proved disruptive. On the ideological level, the idea that religious affiliation could be changed by an act of individual choice was revolutionary. On the methodological level, the communication technologies missionaries used, and the scale of their operations, haunted their competitors.[6]

In Brazil, an older heterodox religious tradition conceived the possibility of universal salvation amongst Christians, Jews, and Muslims since the colonial era.[7] The liberal and reformist Jansenist Catholicism that predominated in specific ecclesiastical circles until the mid-nineteenth century resembled Protestantism in its austere piety and attachment to the Bible.[8] Protestant missionaries and evangelists built upon the relative openness of these religious currents, which eased the cultural constraints that limited the individual choice to convert. But Protestants required from converts a steadfast religious commitment that left little room for compromise or relativism. What really unnerved Romanized Catholics were the principles of the free examination of the scriptures and of the universal priesthood. These ideas challenged ecclesiastical hierarchies and empowered ordinary believers to a degree that Catholic leaders considered intolerable. Capuchin friars and village priests burned Bibles and evangelical literature in large bonfires aimed at cleansing their communities from Protestant pollution. Catholic writers depicted Protestantism as the earliest of a series of anarchic transformations, including the French and the Russian revolutions, that unsettled organic social hierarchies and threatened the authority of the Church.

---

[6] Nile Green, *Bombay Islam: The Religious Economy of the West Indian Ocean, 1840–1915* (New York: Cambridge University Press, 2011), ch. 1.

[7] Stuart Schwartz, *All Can Be Saved: Religious Tolerance and Salvation in the Iberian Atlantic World* (New Haven, CT: Yale University Press, 2008).

[8] David Gueiros Vieira, *O protestantismo, a maçonaria e a Questão Religiosa no Brasil* (Brasília: Editora Universidade de Brasília, 1980), 29–32.

But Catholics also responded in a positive way to the large-scale and far-reaching operations of mission and Bible societies. They improved mechanisms of clerical training, mobilized laypeople in the Church's struggle to retain its prestige and power, expanded their bureaucratic apparatus to places where the institutional presence of the Catholic Church was minimal, and organized coordinated attempts to administer sacraments and provide catechetical instruction to far-off communities. Protestant–Catholic competition energized both sides of the Christian divide in modern Brazil, giving rise to new forms of religious mobilization, ecclesiastical organization, and practice. Even though Protestants remained a small religious minority in this period, their endeavors and ideologies generated strong potential for religious change, laying some of the groundwork for Pentecostal expansion decades later.[9] These novel cultural configurations depended largely on the local agents who appropriated the missionary impetus of the era and expanded the new evangelical frontiers.

Hidden Innovators in Brazil's Religious Arena

The local converts and religious elites that feature as protagonists in this book were part of a broader religious minority that disrupted and fragmented the Brazilian religious landscape from below alongside middle-class professionals, foreign immigrants, enslaved Africans, freed persons, and cosmopolitan urban elites. They introduced an array of religious practices, materials, creeds, and faiths in Brazil that consolidated Candomblé, Spiritism, Positivism, Umbanda, and evangelical Christianity. The idea that the "deregulation" of Latin America's religious markets only took off in the post-World War II era lacks historical depth and fails to account for longer history of dissent in the region.[10] These religious innovators built networks of practitioners, clients, and followers amidst sweeping processes of colonial control, social differentiation, and political change since the colonial era.[11]

---

[9] Pedro Feitoza, "Historical Trajectories of Protestantism in Brazil, 1810–1960," in *Brazilian Evangelicalism in the Twenty-first Century: An Inside and Outside Look*, ed. Eric Miller and Ronald Morgan (Cham, Switzerland: Palgrave Macmillan, 2019), 31–63.

[10] Andrew Chesnut, *Competitive Spirits: Latin America's New Religious Economy* (Oxford: Oxford University Press, 2003).

[11] For histories of African religions in Brazil, see João José Reis, *Divining Slavery and Freedom: The Story of Domingos Sodré, an African Priest in Nineteenth-century Brazil*, trans. H. Sabrina Gledhill (New York: Cambridge University Press, 2015); Luis Nicolau Parés, *The Formation of Candomblé:*

In the nineteenth and twentieth centuries, foreign missionaries, Brazilian ministers, evangelists, schoolteachers, Bible-readers, and converts became the distinctive agents of the new religion. Their efforts to spread evangelical Christianity in Brazil spurred a very specific form of secularization. Far from promoting a decline of religious attendance or privatizing religion, evangelicals were interested in creating voluntary communities of faithful believers who deployed modern means of communication to assert their presence in the public sphere. However, in a country that only recently began to accept open religious dissidence after centuries of colonial control, Protestants advocated that Catholicism should retract as the "sole normative source of public political allegiance."[12]

The proselytizing message of Protestants emphasized the need for people to convert: to abandon their devotion to Mary and the saints, to cut ties with the hierarchical model of the Catholic Church, and to change their lives. The communities they engineered gave rise to new social, political, and cultural configurations that reframed the contours of Brazil's religious arena. Like Muslim and Hindu communities in modern India and dissenting churches in England, Brazilian evangelical congregations, schools, seminaries, and organizations of youth and women created free space for lively debate and intellectual exchange.[13] Protestants experimented with democratic practices in such spaces, enabling members to exercise the "universal priesthood of all believers" in various ways, including through representative and electoral ecclesiastical systems. Members of Congregationalist, Baptists, and Christian Brethren churches ensured the independence of local congregations from the institutional control of larger denominational bodies, such as synods, presbyteries, and dioceses, enabling their communities to be rapidly captured from below.

On the other hand, the religious innovations missionaries and evangelists advocated and promoted were reminiscent of the transformations of the

---

Vodun History and Ritual in Brazil, trans. Richard Vernon (Chapel Hill: University of North Carolina Press, 2013); Diana Brown, *Umbanda: Religion and Politics in Urban Brazil* (New York: UMI Research Press, 1994).

[12] Ingrid Creppell, "Secularisation: Religion and the Roots of Innovation in the Political Sphere," in *Religion and the Political Imagination*, ed. Ira Katznelson and Gareth Stedman Jones (Cambridge: Cambridge University Press, 2010), 23–45, at 34.

[13] Christopher Bayly, *Empire and Information: Intelligence Gathering and Social Communication in India, 1780–1870* (Cambridge: Cambridge University Press, 1996), ch. 5; Edward P. Thompson, *The Making of the English Working Class* (London: Penguin Books, 2013 [1963]), 56.

Catholic Church in this era, which was also undergoing a dynamic process of renewal. The interactions that emerged in this period resulted from syntheses of old and new customs in Brazil. Rural *folk* Catholicism shared some features with evangelical Christianity that enabled the new religion to create local roots and expand. Evangelical activism, the dedication of laypeople to the evangelizing enterprise and to religious affairs which has been described as a central component of modern evangelicalism, resonated with the highly participatory culture of Brazilian Catholicism.[14] Catholics gathered in lay associations to raise funds and promote processions and festivals for patron saints, organized *mutirões* to restore rundown chapels and cemeteries, and took part in prayer meetings and religious services in public squares aimed at asserting the public status of their faith. In a different way, the hierarchical model of the Ultramontane reform and the "Restorationist" movement of the twentieth century advanced a strong and zealous anti-Protestant rhetoric, blaming religious fragmentation as a source of disorder and anxiety in Brazilian society.[15] Although Protestantism and Romanized Catholicism became rival varieties of Christian religion, they shared a strong emphasis on the notion of individual conversion, demanding from their adherents an unwavering religious commitment, the abandonment of "ungodly" vices, and a confidence on the tools of modernity, especially the press and independent associations. Brazilian evangelicals built upon such practices and ideas, channeling, reforming, and repackaging their potential. By holding these strands together, these religious innovators were able to balance rupture and continuity, construing Protestantism as a religion that was simultaneously transformative and adaptable.

The innovative force of evangelical religion also manifested itself in other forms. Like the people of the "middling sort" in West and eastern Africa studied by anthropologist Karin Barber, Brazilian evangelicals cultivated a "fervent regard for the capacity of reading and writing to enhance personal and social existence."[16] Protestants depicted their encounter with God as an encounter with the printed word, the holy scriptures. The meditative and reflexive reading of the Bible was seen as a vital tool for the recovery of the

---

[14] On modern evangelicalism, see David Bebbington, *Evangelicalism in Modern Britain: A History from the 1730s to the 1980s* (London: Unwyn Hyman, 1989).

[15] Erika Helgen, *Religious Conflict in Brazil: Protestants, Catholics, and the Rise of Religious Pluralism in the Early Twentieth Century* (New Haven, CT: Yale University Press, 2020).

[16] Karin Barber, "Introduction: Hidden Innovators in Africa," in *Africa's Hidden Histories: Everyday Literacy and the Making of the Self*, ed. Karin Barber (Bloomington: Indiana University Press, 2006), 1–24, at 5.

spiritual energy, egalitarianism, and pristine purity of the early Christian church. In congregations, believers and religious leaders opened the pages of evangelical tracts, periodicals, books, and printed sermons, read them aloud, and discussed them. Their search for spiritual nourishment and consolation generated new reading practices in a country with high rates of illiteracy. This monograph explored some dynamics involved in the consolidation of Protestantism as a book religion in that context. A vast and extensive network of churches, bookstores, and mission stations, connected to one another through the work of itinerant colporteurs, enabled Christian literature to circulate widely and played a central role in linking evangelical religion to literacy. The successes of these propagandists of the book were contingent upon the material circumstances facilitating the circulation of print.

Locating Evangelical Religion

This study has also explored the many ways in which Protestants related the beliefs and practices of evangelical religion to public debates, political transformations, culture, and custom. The evangelical defense of religious disestablishment, the creation of civil registrations of births and marriages, and the secularization of cemeteries resonated with the political agendas of liberal politicians, modernizing reformers, and republican leaders. Scholars such as Jean-Pierre Bastian and José Míguez Bonino reconstructed these connections across Latin America with insightful and meticulous care, showing how evangelical diffusion emerged as an endogenous phenomenon responsive to internal dynamics, rather than an extraneous project driven by foreign agents.[17] But apart from these connections and echoes, this book examined the specific ways in which local ministers and converts appropriated the conceptual, symbolic, and ritual repertoire of evangelical religion in Brazil and adapted them. Its protagonists related religious change to broader processes of sociopolitical modernization. They idealized the primitive Christian church as the supreme model for modern democracies, serving as a contrast to the violence and anticlericalism of the liberal revolutions while simultaneously promoting individual liberties and self-improvement. They claimed that Protestantism met the demands of the emerging Brazilian

---

[17] Jean-Pierre Bastian, *Protestantismos y modernidad latinoamericana: Historia de una minorías religiosas activas en América Latina* (Mexico, DF: Fondo de Cultura Económica, 1994); José Míguez Bonino, *Rostros de protestantismo latinoamericano* (Buenos Aires: Nueva Creacion, 1995).

nation state. It was a religion that encouraged industry and discipline, promoted hierarchical and orderly domestic spaces, cherished the constitutional arrangements of the republic, and whose educational and social institutions embodied civic virtues.

The processes of religious change also developed a complex relationship with established culture. Conversion was experienced and described as a rupture with traditional religion; its climax was reached when converts set fire to or threw away their icons and statues of saints, depicted as polluted objects that contaminated the "true" and spiritual Christian worship. The Protestant emphasis on individual salvation led believers to break away from networks of patronage and godparenthood, which to a certain extent determined chances of personal and professional success in a communitarian society.[18] Missionaries and ministers promoted self-reliance and industry as Christian virtues, encouraging some degree of personal independence. But converts were re-socialized again in religious communities, recreating social relations with fellow believers. The loss of a protective network implicated in the dissolution of social bonds was accompanied by their reconstruction in another environment. And even though Brazilian converts withdrew from processions, festivals of patron saints, and socialization in taverns, they nevertheless took part in village weddings, *mutirões*, street markets, and independent associations. Evangelical conversion itself evolved amidst established forms of socialization, in conversations around the table, the fire, and in the domestic intimacy of rural and urban families. Over time Protestants diversified their repertoire of responses to tradition, idealizing pristine rural communities untouched by the vices of modern cities and seeking to locate Protestantism into the depths of Brazilian past. These ambiguous features enabled evangelical religion to appear as simultaneously modern and traditional, local and global, progressive and conservative.

This focus on the conceptual and cultural location of evangelical religion offers a corrective to the influential thesis that Brazilian evangelicals reproduced the conservative ideologies, politics, and practices of American Protestantism and thus remained out of touch with the social and cultural realities of the country.[19] Quite the opposite occurred. Brazilian evangelicals

---

[18] Richard Graham, *Britain and the Onset of Modernization in Brazil, 1850–1914* (Cambridge: Cambridge University Press, 1968), ch. 11.

[19] Antonio Gouvêa Mendonça, *O celeste porvir: A inserção do protestantismo no Brasil*, 3rd ed. (São Paulo: EdUSP, 2008 [1984]); Antonio Gouvêa Mendonça and Prócoro Velasques Filho, *Introdução ao protestantismo no Brasil* (São Paulo: Edições Loyola, 1990).

drew from various global and local intellectual sources, including British non-conformity, French and Belgian liberal Catholics, and Anglophone academic theology. They brought together a broad and unexpected set of ideas and concepts in public debates with Catholic periodicals, the anticlerical secular elites, nationalist writers, and folklorists. Missionaries and ministers replaced racialized explanations for Brazil's economic "backwardness" with a variety of religious determinism, arguing that Protestantism promoted the values and practices of modernity. In the context of the Great War, they mixed together the call to interdenominational cooperation of the early ecumenical movement with long-held utopias about hemispheric unity that circulated across the Americas. The emerging evangelical intellectual elites educated in mission schools and Protestant seminaries recovered the customs and language of the rural populations of the backlands of São Paulo and Minas Gerais amidst a broader drive to idealize pristine communities spurred by modernist artists and regionalist writers. Brazilian Protestants engaged closely with the public debates and arguments of their era, creating new forms of social and political action.

As historian Frederick Cooper observed, when examining large-scale intellectual exchanges, "we should be asking who talks to whom and what they say" instead of assuming that modern communication technologies and long-distance interactions spread shared ways of thinking.[20] Whenever possible, this monograph reconstructed the specific intricacies involved in the intellectual and cultural entanglements that shaped Brazilian evangelical thought and practice. Evangelicals penetrated the conceptual world of Brazilian society, channeling tenets of Protestant theology and notions of religious change into debates circulating in the country's public sphere.[21] These religious specialists and local converts navigated between multiple cultural and intellectual frameworks and carried out "the conceptual work necessary to domesticate Christianity."[22]

In this way, the sentiment of Manuel de Melo alluded to in the beginning of this conclusion is revealing. It was a sense of propriety and self-confidence

---

[20] Frederick Cooper, "How Global Do We Want Our Intellectual History To Be?" in *Global Intellectual History*, ed. Samuel Moyn and Andrew Sartori (New York: Columbia University Press, 2013), 283–294, at 292.

[21] Pedro Feitoza, "The Middle Line of Truth: Religious and Secular Ideologies in the Making of Brazilian Evangelical Thought, 1870–1930," *Modern Intellectual History* 19 (2022): 1033–1057.

[22] David Maxwell, "Historical Perspectives on Christianity Worldwide: Connections, Comparisons and Consciousness," in *Relocating World Christianity: Interdisciplinary Studies in Universal and Local Expressions of the Christian Faith*, ed. Joel Cabrita, David Maxwell, and Emma Wild-Wood (Boston: Brill, 2017), 47–69, at 50.

that the history he was witnessing and the large religious apparatus he was looking at were, to a certain extent, the fruits of his labor. In the narrative of his daughter, Maria de Melo Chaves, Manuel endured all the hardships characteristic of *caipira* men like him: poverty, lack of formal instruction, and isolation. He also experienced for a time the social estrangement that usually accompanied conversion experiences, and he carried the stigma of being a dissident in a Catholic-majority society. However, over the long run, religious mobility gave way to social mobility. His children were educated in mission colleges and seminaries, found employment in Protestant schools and churches, and were thus able to climb the social ladder. Through the pages of Protestant periodicals and tracts, these individuals attempted to evangelize broad audiences and take part in religious controversies and sociopolitical arguments, participating in the public sphere and entering the stage of civil society as public actors. They resorted to notions of scriptural authority and spiritual inspiration to respond to the sociopolitical challenges of their era and to give meaning and life to their faith amidst wide-ranging processes of historical transformation. They mediated between disparate cultural and intellectual frameworks, and secular and religious domains, to weave the new religion into the social fabric of the country. The history of evangelical Christianity in Brazil unfolded through this lively tension between the transformative dynamic embodied in the language of conversion and its strategies of reconciliation and mediation with local political and religious discourses and traditional culture.

Bibliography and Sources

Manuscript and Archival Sources

1. American Bible Society. Philadelphia, PA, USA

Historical Essay #15, Part V-A&B. Distribution abroad, 1861–1900

2. Arquivo Histórico Presbiteriano. São Paulo, Brazil

Atas e Relatórios, 1895 a 1903
Coleção Carvalhosa, Relatórios Pastorais (1866–1875)
Primeiro Livro de Actas da Igreja de Ubatuba, 1880

3. Bible Society Archives, University Library, University of Cambridge, UK

BSA/D1/2, File C
BSA/D1/2, Foreign correspondence inwards. Robert Reid Kalley, 1839–1877
BSA/D1/7-123 (Agents Book nº 123, South America)
BSA/D1/7-144 (Agents Book nº 144, South America)
BSA/E3/1/4-11
BSA/E3/1/4-7

4. Biblioteca Fernandes Braga, Igreja Evangélica Fluminense. Rio de Janeiro, Brazil

Correspondência Dr. Kalley

5. Biblioteca Nacional. Rio de Janeiro, Brazil

Correspondência de José Carlos Rodrigues, Caixa 001, 32,04,01
Correspondência de José Carlos Rodrigues, Caixa 003, 32,04,03

6. International Baptist Mission Board. Richmond, VA, USA

Solomon Ginsburg papers
Zachary Clay Taylor papers

7. Centro de Documentação e História Rev. Vicente Themudo Lessa. São Paulo, Brazil

Pasta de Fotos

8. New College Library, Special Collections. Edinburgh, UK

CSCW51/7/6/5

9. Presbyterian Historical Society. Philadelphia, PA, USA

Mission Correspondence, South American Letters
RG 360, folder Samuel Rhea Gammon (1865–1928)
RG81-34-21, Latin America Conference, 1912–14

10. School of Oriental and African Studies Library. London, UK

USCL/RTS/03/19-20, Religious Tract Society—Correspondence

Printed Primary Sources

1. Periodicals, Newspapers, and Magazines

A Cigarra
Brazilian Missions
Imprensa Evangelica
Jornal do Commercio
O Apóstolo
O Pulpito Evangelico
O Puritano
Revista da Academia Paulista de Letras
Revista de Cultura Religiosa
Semana Evangélica

2. Reports, Abstracts, and Proceedings

Abstracts of the Annual Reports of the Religious Tract Society. Vols. 78–93. 1877–1892.
Annual Reports of the Board of Foreign Missions of the Presbyterian Church of the United States. Vols. 34–53. 1871–1890.
Annual Reports of the British & Foreign Bible Society, with an Appendix and a List of Subscribers and Benefactors. Vols. 18–53. 1856–1899.
Annual Reports of the Religious Tract Society. Vols. 78–102. 1877–1901.
Brazil: The Quarterly Record of the "Help for Brazil" Mission. N. 54, July 1908.
Proceedings of the Southern Baptist Convention. Vols. 26–35. 1881–1890.
Report of the Centenary Conference on the Protestant Missions to the World, Held in Exeter Hall (June 9th–19th), London, 1888, Vol. II, edited by Rev. James Johnston. London: James Nisbet & Co., 1888.

3. Tracts, Books, and Pamphlets

A Biblia e o povo. Lisbon: Livrarias Evangelicas, 1897.
A commemoração do 4º centenário da Reforma—31 de outubro de 1917. São Paulo: Typographia d'O Estandarte, 1917.
A confissão de fé da Igreja Presbyteriana do Brazil. Rio de Janeiro: Livraria Evangelica, 1876.
A minha conversão: Revelações de uma senhora à sua amiga catholica. Rio de Janeiro: Typographia Universal de Laemmert, 1885.
Atas da Convenção Batista, 1918, apud Duncan A. Reily, *História Documental do Protestantismo no Brasil*. 3rd ed. São Paulo: ASTE, 2003.
Blackford, A. L. "Cultos e casas de culto." In *O Pulpito Evangelico: Volume primeiro, 1874*, 4–17. Rio de Janeiro: Livraria Evangelica, 1874.
Blackford, A. L. *Sketch of the Brazil Mission*. Philadelphia: Presbyterian Board of Education, 1886.
Bomfim, M. *A América Latina: Males de origem*. Rio de Janeiro: Topbooks, 2005 [1905].
Braga, E. "Following Up the Jerusalem Meeting in Brazil." *International Review of Missions* 28 (1929): 261–265.
Braga, E. *Pan-Americanismo: Aspecto religioso*. New York: The Missionary Education Movement, 1916.
Braga, E. "Protestantismo." In *Religiões comparadas*, edited by Gustavo Macedo, 75–96. Rio de Janeiro: Roland Rohe & C., 1929.
Braga, E. *Religião e cultura*. São Paulo: União Cultural Editora, n/d.
Braga, E., and K. Grubb. *The Republic of Brazil: A Survey of the Religious Situation*. London: World Dominion Press, 1932.
Chaves, M. M. *Bandeirantes da fé*. Belo Horizonte: Associação Evangélica Beneficente de Minas Gerais, 1947.

Christian Work in Latin America: Cooperation and the Promotion of Unity, the Training and Efficiency of Missionaries, the Devotional Addresses, the Popular Addresses, Tome III. New York: The Missionary Education Movement, 1917.

Christian Work in Latin America: Survey and Occupation, Message and Method, Education, Tome I. New York: The Missionary Education Movement, 1917.

Collecção das leis do Imperio do Brazil, 1824, parte 1ª. Rio de Janeiro: Imprensa Nacional, 1886.

Collecção das leis do Imperio do Brazil, 1828, parte 1ª. Rio de Janeiro: Typographia Nacional, 1878.

Collecção de hymnos escolhidos. Recife: n/p, 1895.

Conference on Missions in Latin America, March 12 and 13, 1913. Lebanon, PA: Sowers Printing Co., 1913.

Costa, G. A. *A sanctificação do domingo.* São Paulo: n/p, 1891.

Coutinho, A. *Espiritismo ou materialismo?.* São Paulo: Irmãos Ferraz, 1927.

Darlow, T., H. Moule, and A. Jayne. *Historical Catalogue of the Printed Editions of Holy Scripture in the Library of the British and Foreign Bible Society.* London: The Bible House, 1911.

Differença entre catholico e protestante. Rio de Janeiro: Livraria Evangelica, 1889.

do Rio, J. *A alma encantadora das ruas.* São Paulo: Companhia das Letras, 1997 [1906].

Entzminger, W. E. *Fiat Lux ou Resultado do meu exame do "exame" do Snr. Juvêncio Marinho sobre "O Modo do Baptismo."* Rio de Janeiro: Casa Editora Baptista, 1902.

Eschola Americana—32ºanno; Mackenzie College 12º anno. São Paulo: n/p, 1902.

Esher, N. S. C. *Religião do estado: Propaganda pela igualdade de cultos.* Rio de Janeiro: Casa Publicadora Methodista, 1900.

Eu não comprehendo a Bíblia. Lisbon: Typ. De Vicente da Silva & Co., 1897.

Ferreira, M. V. *O Cristo no júri.* São Paulo: Oficinas Gráficas de Saraiva, 1957 [1891].

Fletcher, J. C., and D. P. Kidder. *Brazil and the Brazilians: Portrayed in Historical and Descriptive Sketches.* Philadelphia: Childs & Peterson, 1857.

Franca, L. *A Igreja, a Reforma e a civilização.* 5th ed. Rio de Janeiro: Ed. Agir, 1948 [1922].

Ginsburg, S. *A Wandering Jew in Brazil: An Autobiography of Solomon L. Ginsburg.* Nashville, TN: Sunday School Board, 1922.

Gladstone, W. *Os decretos do Vaticano em suas relações com a lealdade civil: Discussão politica.* Rio de Janeiro: Typographia Universal de Laemmert, 1875.

Glass, F. C. *Adventures with the Bible in Brazil.* London: Pickering & Inglis, 1923.

Glass, F. C. *With the Bible in Brazil: Being the Story of a Few of the Marvellous Incidents Arising from its Circulation There.* London: Morgan & Scott LD., 1914.

Gouvêa, H. *Francisco Lopes Ribeiro.* Rio Claro: Typographia Brasil, 1922.

Gouvêa, H. *Notas biographicas de Henrique Gomes de Oliveira.* 2nd ed. Jaú: Typographia da Casa Mascote, 1911.

Guimarães, T. P. *Defesa do protestantismo.* São Paulo: Irmãos Ferraz, 1926.

Holanda, S. B. *Raízes do Brasil.* São Paulo: Companhia das Letras, 2009 [1936].

Holden, R. *Confissões de fé.* Lisbon and Rio de Janeiro: Calçada dos Mestres and D. F. Ladeira do Barroso, 1906.

Kalley, R. R. *Observações á instrucção pastoral do Exc.mo. Bispo do Porto, D. Americo sobre o protestantismo.* Porto: Imprensa Civilisação de Santos & Lemos, 1879.

Kalley, S. P. *A alegria da casa ou Raios de luz sobre a vida familiar.* Lisbon: Tipografia Eduardo Rosa, 1916 [Rio de Janeiro, 1866].

Kalley, S. P. *O casamento e a vida domestica: seus deveres e suas provas de alegria.* 2nd ed. Lisbon: Typ. e Lith. de Adolpho Modesto & Cª, 1887.

Kidder, D. *Sketches of Residence and Travel in Brazil.* 2 vols. Philadelphia: Sorin & Ball, 1845.

Kinsolving, L. L. *A razão de ser da Associação Christã de Moços.* Rio de Janeiro: Casa Publicadora Baptista, 1903.

Landes, P. *Dom Aquino: Imperialismo e protestantismo.* Cuyabá: Typ. d'A Penna Evangelica, 1928.

Lauresto (Nicolau S. C. Esher). *I—A Maçonaria como Religião, pelo Rev. J. D. Brownlee; II—A Maçonaria perante o Christianismo, pelo Rev. W. Foster; III—"As Sociedades Secretas", uma resolução synodal*. Rio de Janeiro: Casa Publicadora Methodista, 1900.

Laveleye, E. *Do futuro dos povos catholicos: Estudo de economia social*, translated by Miguel Vieira Ferreira. Rio de Janeiro: Typographia Universal de E. & H. Laemmert, 1875.

Macedo, G. "Advertencia." In *Religiões comparadas*, edited by Gustavo Macedo, iii–iv. Rio de Janeiro: Roland Rohe & C., 1929.

Magnin, E. *O espiritismo*. São Paulo: Irmãos Ferraz, 1926.

Manifesto aos nossos irmãos, membros da Igreja Presbyteriana do Brazil. São Paulo: Typ. da Sociedade Brazileira de Tratados Evangelicos, 1892.

Maria, J. "A religião, ordens religiosas, instituições pias e beneficentes no Brasil." In *O livro do centenário (1500–1900)*, 1–134. Rio de Janeiro: Imprensa Nacional, 1900.

McConnell, F. "Christian Faith in an Age of Doubt." In *Christian Work in Latin America*, Vol. III, 297–304. New York: The Missionary Education Movement, 1917.

McNair, S. *O culto*. Lisbon and Rio de Janeiro: Calçada dos Mestres and D. F. Ladeira do Barroso, 1906.

McNair, S. *Os ministros de Deus: seu Senhor, seu serviço e seu sustento*. Lisbon and Rio de Janeiro: Calçada dos Mestres and D. F. Ladeira do Barroso, 1903.

McNair, S. *Que devemos fazer?* .Lisbon and Rio de Janeiro: Calçada dos Mestres and D. F. Ladeira do Barroso, 1906.

McNair, S. *Round South America on the King's Business*. London: Marshall Brothers, 1913.

Miranda, J. Z. *O culto das imagens*. São Paulo: Typ. a vapor de Jorge Seckler & Co., 1885.

Miranda, J. Z. *Procrastinação ou o perigo de adiar a salvação*. São Paulo: Typographia a Vapor de Jorge Seckler & C., 1886.

Monteiro Lobato, J. *Urupês*. 13th ed. São Paulo: Brasiliense, 1966 [1918].

Mota, O. "'Negro Tapanhuno.'" *Revista da Academia Paulista de Letras* 7 (1944): 10–21.

Mota, O. "The Question of the Unveiled Woman (1 Co. xi, 2-16)." *Expository Times* 44 (1932): 139–141.

Mota, O. *A archeologia e a Biblia: Luzes de Gezer*. São Paulo: Irmãos Ferraz, 1926.

Mota, O. *A filosofia do joão-de-barro: Fantasia educativa lida perante a "Sociedade Cristã de Cultura" na noite de 19 de novembro de 1935*. São Paulo: Estab. Graphico Cruzeiro do Sul, n/d.

Mota, O. *Breves annotações ao livro dos Actos*. São Paulo: Irmãos Ferraz, n/d.

Mota, O. *Do rancho ao palacio: Evolução da civilização paulista*. São Paulo: Companhia Editora Nacional, 1941.

Mota, O. *Historietas*. São Paulo: Livraria Técnica, 1946.

Mota, O. *O meu idioma*. 2nd ed. São Paulo and Rio de Janeiro: Weiszflog Irmãos, 1917.

Mota, O. *Plano de acção*. São Paulo: Irmãos Ferraz, 1925.

Mota, O. *Selvas e choças*. São Paulo: Imprensa Methodista, 1922.

Mota, O. *Uma passagem interessante: Mateus XXV-46*. São Paulo: Emprêsa Gráfica da "Revista dos Tribunais, 1938.

O cura e o protestante. Lisbon: Livrarias Evangelicas, 1903.

O Darbysmo, cartas do Dr. Robert R. Kalley. Lisbon: Adolpho, Modesto & C. Impressores, 1891.

O estudo devoto da Biblia. Lisbon: Livrarias Evangelicas, 1899.

O evangelho de São Matheus, traducção e annotações de Othoniel Motta. n/p: n/p, 1933.

O Reverendo pastor evangélico José Manoel da Conceição (supplemento aos mezes de janeiro e fevereiro de 1884). Rio de Janeiro: Typ. a vapor de Leroy King Bookwalter & Comp, 1884.

Oliveira Lima, M. *The Evolution of Brazil Compared with that of Spanish and Anglo-Saxon America*. Stanford, CA: Stanford University Press, 1914.

Oliveira Lima, M. *Pan-Americanismo (Monroe-Bolivar-Roosevelt)*. Rio de Janeiro: H. Garnier, 1907.

Pereira, E. C. *A bemaventurada Virgem Maria*. São Paulo: Typographia King, 1887.

Pereira, E. C. *A divina instituição do baptismo de crianças*. São Paulo: Typographia Commercial de H. Rossi, 1905.

Pereira, E. C. *A lingua*. São Paulo: n/p, 1890.
Pereira, E. C. *A religião christã em suas relações com a escravidão*. São Paulo: Typographia a vapor de Jorge Seckler & C., 1886.
Pereira, E. C. *Balanço historico da Egreja Presbyteriana Independente Brasileira*. São Paulo: Imprensa Methodista, 1921.
Pereira, E. C. *Grammatica expositiva: curso superior*. 26th ed. São Paulo: Companhia Editora Nacional, n/d [1907].
Pereira, E. C. *Grammatica historica*. 9th ed. São Paulo: Companhia Editora Nacional, 1935 [1916].
Pereira, E. C. *Nossa attitude para com a Egreja Romana*. Rio de Janeiro: Casa Publicadora Baptista, 1916.
Pereira, E. C. *Nosso pae que está nos céos*. São Paulo: Edição da Alliança Evangelica de S. Paulo, 1903 [1886].
Pereira, E. C. *Nosso pae que está nos céos*. São Paulo: Livraria Evangelica, 1902.
Pereira, E. C. *O culto dos sanctos e dos anjos*. São Paulo: Typ. de Leroy King Bookwalter & Co., 1884.
Pereira, E. C. *O problema religioso da America Latina: Estudo dogmatico-historico*. São Paulo: Imprensa Methodista, 1920.
Pereira, E. C. *O protestantismo é uma nullidade: Polêmica religiosa*. São Paulo: Typographia Aurora, 1896.
Pereira, E. C. *O unico advogado dos peccadores*. São Paulo: Typographia a Vapor de Jorge Seckler & Comp., 1884.
Pereira, E. C. *Questões de philologia*. São Paulo: Typographia Falcone, 1907.
Pereira, E. C. *Trabalho e economia ou A fidelidade de Deus manifestada na vida de um discipulo*. São Paulo: Typographia a Vapor de Jorge Seckler & Comp., 1885.
Pereira, E. C. *Um brado de alarma*. São Paulo: Typ. a vapor de Jorge Seckler & C., 1885.
Pereira, E. C. *Vem e vê!* São Paulo: n/p, 1891.
Pires, C. *Conversas ao pé-do-fogo*. Itu: Ottoni Editora, 2002 [1921].
Pires, C. *Patacoadas*. Itu: Ottoni Editora, 2002 [1927].
Programma e Regulamento do Instituto de S. Paulo, Escola Americana. São Paulo: Typ. de Leroy King Bookwalter, 1885.
Regional Conferences in Latin America. New York: The Missionary Education Movement, 1917.
Reinkens, J. H. *Profissão de fé dos Velhos-Catholicos na Allemanha*, translated by Miguel Vieira Ferreira. Rio de Janeiro: E. & H. Laemmert, 1874.
Reis, A. *Anchieta, o carrasco de Bolés á luz da historia patria*. São Paulo: n/p, 1896.
Reis, A. *José de Anchieta á luz da historia patria*. São Paulo: n/p, 1896.
Ribeiro, A. *A questão da infallibilidade da Biblia perante a Egreja Methodista do Brasil*. São Paulo: Weiszflog Irmãos, 1908.
Ribeiro, D. *A tragedia de Guanabara, ou Historia dos protomartyres do christianismo no Brasil*. Rio de Janeiro: Typ. Pimenta de Mello, 1917.
Rodrigues, J. C., ed. *Mensagens, allocuções e discursos do presidente Wilson concernentes á guerra actual*. Rio de Janeiro: Jacintho Ribeiro dos Santos, 1918.
Rodrigues, J. C. *Considerações geraes sobre a Biblia*. Rio de Janeiro: Imprensa Norwood, 1918.
Rodrigues, J. C. *Estudo historico e critico sobre o Velho Testamento*, 2 vols. Edinburgh: T. & A. Constable, 1921.
Rodrigues, J. C. *Religiões acatholicas no Brazil, 1500–1900*. 2nd ed. Rio de Janeiro: Escriptorio do Jornal do Commercio, 1904.
Schneider, F. J. "O governo da igreja." In *O Pulpito Evangelico: Volume primeiro, 1874*, 3–29. Rio de Janeiro: Livraria Evangelica, 1874.
Silveira, M. J. *Carta pastoral premunindo os seus diocesanos contra as mutilações, e as adulterações da Bíblia traduzida em português pelo padre João Ferreira D'Almeida; contra os folhetos, e livretos contra a religião, que com a mesma Bíblia se tem espalhado nesta cidade;*

e contra alguns erros, que se tem publicado no país. Bahia: Typ. de Camillo de Lellis Masson & Co., 1862.
Simonton, A. G. *Diário, 1852-1867*. São Paulo: Casa Editora Presbiteriana, 1982.
Speer, R. *South American Problems*. New York: Student Volunteer Movement for Foreign Missions, 1912.
Stiller, E. *Traços historicos e pontos principaes de divergencia das igrejas evangelica protestante e catholica romana*. Rio de Janeiro: E. & H. Laemmert, 1874.
Strossmayer, J. *O papado e a infallibilidade*. São Paulo: Typ. Aurora da Sociedade Brazileira de Tractados Evangélicos, 1897.
Torres, M. G. *Pela graça é que somos salvos mediante a fé*. São Paulo: Typ da Sociedade Brazileira de Tractados Evangélicos, 1894.
Trajano, A. *Quadragesimo anniversario da Egreja Evangelica Presbyteriana do Rio de Janeiro, 1862-1902*. Rio de Janeiro: Casa Editora Presbyteriana, 1902.
Tucker, H. C. *Dr José Carlos Rodrigues [1844-1923]: A Brief Sketch of His Life*. New York: American Bible Society, n/d.
Tucker, H. C. *The Bible in Brazil: Colporter Experiences*. New York: Young People's Missionary Movement of the United States and Canada, 1902.
Whately, E. I. *Objecções à Biblia e a melhor maneira de lhes responder*. Lisbon: Typ. De Vicente da Silva & Co., 1896.

Secondary Sources

1. Bibliography

"Of Bibles and Ballots: Evangelical Churches are Political Players in Brazil." *The Economist*. Special report: Brazil on the Brink (June 5, 2021). https://www.economist.com/special-report/2021/06/05/of-bible-and-ballots.
Abreu, M. "Livros ao mar: Circulação de obras de Belas Artes entre Lisboa e o Rio de Janeiro ao tempo da transferência da corte para o Brasil." *Tempo* 12 (2008): 74-97.
Abreu, M., and Marisa Deaecto, eds. *A circulação transatlântica dos impressos: Conexões*. Campinas: Unicamp, 2014.
Adamovicz, A. L. "Imprensa protestante na Primeira República: Evangelismo, informação e produção cultural. O Jornal Batista (1901-1922)." PhD diss., Universidade de São Paulo, 2008.
Alencastro, L. F., and Maria Luiza Renaux. "Caras e modos dos migrantes e imigrantes." In *História da vida privada no Brasil, Vol. 2: Império*, edited by Luiz Felipe de Alencastro, 291-335. São Paulo: Companhia das Letras, 1997.
Algranti, L. M. *Livros de devoção, atos de censura: Ensaios de história do livro e da leitura na América portuguesa (1750-1821)*. São Paulo: Hucitec, 2004.
Almeida, J. R. P. *História da instrução pública no Brasil (1500-1889)*. São Paulo: EDUC, 1989.
Alonso, A. *Idéias em movimento: A geração de 1870 na crise do Brasil-império*. São Paulo: Paz e Terra, 2002.
Alonso, A. *The Last Abolition: The Brazilian Antislavery Movement, 1868-1888*. New York: Cambridge University Press, 2022.
Alves, R. *Protestantism and Repression: A Brazilian Case Study*, translated by John Drury. London: SCM Press, 1985.
Anderson, B. *Imagined Communities: Reflections on the Origin and Spread of Nationalism*. Rev. ed. London: Verso, 2006 [1991].
Ayala Mora, E. "El origen del nombre América Latina y la tradición católica del siglo XIX." *Anuario Colombiano de Historia Social y de la Cultura* 40 (2013): 213-241.
Azevedo, F. *A cultura brasileira: introdução ao estudo da cultura no Brasil, tomo terceiro*. 3rd ed. São Paulo: Edições Melhoramentos, 1958.

Azevedo, I. B. *A celebração do indivíduo: A formação do pensamento batista brasileiro*. 2nd ed. São Paulo: Edições Vida Nova, 2004.

Azzi, R. *A neocristandade: Um projeto restaurador*. São Paulo: Paulus, 1994.

Baggio, K. G. "A 'outra' América: A América Latina na visão dos intelectuais brasileiros das primeiras décadas republicanas." PhD diss., University of São Paulo, 1998.

Ballantyne, T. *Entanglements of Empire: Missionaries, Maori, and the Question of the Body*. Durham, NC: Duke University Press, 2014.

Barber, K. "Introduction: Hidden Innovators in Africa." In *Africa's Hidden Histories: Everyday Literacy and the Making of the Self*, edited by Karin Barber, 1–24. Bloomington: Indiana University Press, 2006.

Barber, K. *The Anthropology of Texts, Persons and Publics: Oral and Written Culture in Africa and Beyond*. Cambridge: Cambridge University Press, 2007.

Barbosa, J. C. *Slavery and Protestant Missions in Imperial Brazil*, translated by Fraser MacHaffie and Richard Danford. Lanham, MD: University Press of America, 2008.

Barreto, R., Jr. "The Church and Society Movement and the Roots of Public Theology in Brazilian Protestantism." *International Journal of Public Theology* 6 (2012): 70–98.

Basile, M. "O laboratório da nação: A Era Regencial (1831–1840)." In *O Brasil Imperial, Vol. II: 1831–1870*, edited by Keila Grinberg and Ricardo Salles, 53–119. Rio de Janeiro: Civilização Brasileira, 2009.

Bastian, J. P. "Protestantism in Latin America." In *The Church in Latin America, 1492–1992*, edited by Enrique Dussel, 313–350. Tunbridge Wells: Burns & Oates, 1992.

Bastian, J. P. "The Metamorphosis of Latin American Protestant Groups: A Sociohistorical Perspective." *Latin American Research Review* 28 (1993): 33–61.

Bastian, J. P., ed. *Protestantes, liberales y francmasones: Sociedades de ideas y modernidad en América Latina, siglo XIX*. Mexico, DF: Fondo de Cultura Económica, 1990.

Bastian, J. P. *Le protestantisme en Amérique latine: Une approche socio-historique*. Geneva: Labor et Fides, 1994.

Bastian, J. P. *Los dissidentes: Sociedades protestantes y revolución en México, 1872–1911*. Mexico, DF: Fondo de Cultura Económica, 1989.

Bastian, J. P. *Protestantismos y modernidad latinoamericana: Historia de una minorías religiosas activas en América Latina*. Mexico, DF: Fondo de Cultura Económica, 1994.

Bayly, C. "Afterword." *Modern Intellectual History* 4 (2007): 163–169.

Bayly, C. *Empire and Information: Intelligence Gathering and Social Communication in India, 1780–1870*. Cambridge: Cambridge University Press, 1996.

Bayly, C. *Recovering Liberties: Indian Thought in the Age of Liberalism and Empire*. Cambridge: Cambridge University Press, 2012.

Bayly, C. Sven Beckert, Matthew Connelly, Isabel Hofmeyr, Wendy Kozol, and Patricia Seed. "AHR Conversation: On Transnational History." *American Historical Review* 111 (2006): 1441–1464.

Bayly, C. *The Birth of the Modern World, 1780–1914: Global Connections and Comparisons*. Oxford: Blackwell, 2004.

Bebbington, D. *Evangelicalism in Modern Britain: A History from the 1730s to the 1980s*. London: Unwin Hyman, 1989.

Bessone, T. M. "Comércio de livros: Livreiros, livrarias e impressos." *Escritos (Fundação Casa de Rui Barbosa)* 5 (2011): 41–52.

Bethell, L. "Brazil and 'Latin America.'" *Journal of Latin American Studies* 42 (2010): 457–485.

Bethell, L., and José Murilo de Carvalho. "Joaquim Nabuco e os abolicionistas britânicos: Correspondência, 1880–1905." *Estudos Avançados* 23 (2009): 207–229.

Bialecki, J., Naomi Haynes, and Joel Robbins. "The Anthropology of Christianity." *Religion Compass* 2 (2008): 1139–1158.

Blikstein, I. "Maurer, Salum e a Romanística: Pioneirismo, sabedoria e humildade." *Estudos Avançados* 8 (1994): 259–262.

Boehrer, G. "José Carlos Rodrigues and *O Novo Mundo*, 1870-1879." *Journal of Inter-American Studies* 9 (1967): 127-144.
Boehrer, G. "The Church and the Overthrow of the Brazilian Monarchy." *Hispanic American Historical Review* 48 (1968): 380-401.
Boehrer, G. "The Church in the Second Reign, 1840-1889." In *Conflict and Continuity in Brazilian Society*, edited by Henry H. Keith and S. F. Edwards, 113-140. Columbia: University of South Carolina Press, 1969.
Borges, D. "'Puffy, Ugly, Slothful and Inert': Degeneration in Brazilian Social Thought, 1880-1940." *Journal of Latin American Studies* 25 (1993): 235-256.
Borges, D. "Catholic Vanguard in Brazil." In *Local Church, Global Church: Catholic Activism in Latin America from Rerum Novarum to Vatican II*, edited by Stephen Andes and Julia Young, 21-49. Washington: Catholic University of America, 2016.
Borges, D. *The Family in Bahia, Brazil, 1870-1945*. Stanford, CA: Stanford University Press, 1992.
Braga, H. F. *Salmos e hinos: Sua origem e desenvolvimento*. Rio de Janeiro: Igreja Evangélica Fluminense, 1983.
Brandi, P. "Plínio Salgado." In *Dicionário histórico biográfico brasileiro pós 1930*, edited by Alzira Abreu and Israel Beloch. Rio de Janeiro: Ed. FGV, 2001.
Brock, P. "New Christians as Evangelists." In *Missions and Empire*, edited by Norman Etherington, 132-152. Oxford: Oxford University Press, 2005.
Brown, D. *Umbanda: Religion and Politics in Urban Brazil*. New York: UMI Research Press, 1994.
Bruneau, T. C. *The Political Transformation of the Brazilian Catholic Church*. London: Cambridge University Press, 1974.
Brusco, E. "The Reformation of Machismo: Asceticism and Masculinity among Colombian Evangelicals." In *Rethinking Protestantism in Latin America*, edited by Virginia Garrard-Burnett and David Stoll, 143-158. Philadelphia: Temple University Press, 1993.
Brusco, E. *The Reformation of Machismo: Evangelical Conversion and Gender in Colombia*. Austin: University of Texas Press, 1995.
Burke, P. *Popular Culture in Early Modern Europe*. 3rd ed. Farnham: Ashgate, 2009.
Cabrita, J., and David Maxwell. "Introduction: Relocating World Christianity." In *Relocating World Christianity: Interdisciplinary Studies in Universal and Local Expressions of the Christian Faith*, edited by Joel Cabrita, David Maxwell, and Emma Wild-Wood, 1-44. Leiden: Brill, 2017.
Cabrita, J. *Text and Authority in the South African Nazaretha Church*. New York: Cambridge University Press, 2014.
Calvani, C. "Anglicanismo no Brasil." *Revista USP* 67 (2005): 36-47.
Cândido, A. *Os parceiros do Rio Bonito: Estudo sobre o caipira paulista e a transformação dos seus meios de vida*. 11th ed. Rio de Janeiro: Ouro Sobre Azul, 2010.
Cardoso, D. N. "Henry Maxwell Wright (1849-1931): O poeta do amor que salva." *Revista Caminhando* 19 (2014): 61-70.
Carvalho Franco, M. S. *Homens livres na ordem escravocrata*. 4th ed. São Paulo: Editora UNESP, 1997.
Carvalho, J. M. "Radicalismo e republicanism." In *Repensando o Brasil dos oitocentos: Cidadania, política e liberdade*, edited by José Murilo de Carvalho and Lúcia M. Bastos P. das Neves, 19-48. Rio de Janeiro: Civilização Brasileira, 2009.
Carvalho, J. M. *A construção da ordem: A elite política imperial/Teatro de sombras: a política imperial*. 3rd ed. Rio de Janeiro: Civilização Brasileira, 2010.
Carvalho, J. M. *D. Pedro II*. São Paulo: Companhia das Letras, 2007.
Cavalcanti, H. B. "O projeto missionário protestante no Brasil do século 19: Comparando a experiência presbiteriana e batista." *Revista de Estudos da Religião* 4 (2001): 61-93.
Cavalcanti, H. B. "The Right Faith at the Right Time? Determinants of Protestant Mission Success in the 19th-century Brazilian Religious Market." *Journal for the Scientific Study of Religion* 41 (2002): 423-438.

Chalhoub, S. "The Politics of Disease Control: Yellow Fever and Race in Nineteenth-century Rio de Janeiro." *Journal of Latin American Studies* 25 (1993): 441–463.

Chalhoub, S. *Trabalho, lar e botequim: O cotidiano dos trabalhadores no Rio de Janeiro da Belle Époque*. São Paulo: Editora Brasiliense, 1986.

Chapman, M. "Liberal Readings and Their Conservative Responses." In *The New Cambridge History of the Bible: Volume 4, from 1750 to the Present*, edited by John Riches, 208–219. New York: Cambridge University Press, 2015.

Chesnut, A. *Competitive Spirits: Latin America's New Religious Economy*. Oxford: Oxford University Press, 2003.

Clark, C. "From 1848 to Christian Democracy." In *Religion and the Political Imagination*, edited by Ira Katznelson and Gareth Stedman Jones, 190–213. Cambridge: Cambridge University Press, 2010.

Clark, C., and Michael Ledger-Lomas. "The Protestant International." In *Religious Internationals in the Modern World: Globalization and Faith Communities since 1750*, edited by Abigail Green and Vincent Viaene, 23–52. Basingstoke: Palgrave Macmillan, 2012.

Clayton, J. E. "The Legacy of Robert Reid Kalley." *International Bulletin of Missionary Research* 26 (2002): 123–127.

Comaroff, J., and John Comaroff. *Of Revelation and Revolution: Christianity, Colonialism, and Consciousness in South Africa*. Vol. 1. Chicago: University of Chicago Press, 1991.

Cooper, F. "How Global Do We Want Our Intellectual History To Be?" In *Global Intellectual History*, edited by Samuel Moyn and Andrew Sartori, 283–294. New York: Columbia University Press, 2013.

Cooper, F. *Colonialism in Question: Theory, Knowledge, History*. Berkeley: University of California Press, 2005.

Costa, E. V. "Brazil: The Age of Reform, 1870–1889." In *The Cambridge History of Latin America, vol. V: c.1870–1930*, edited by Leslie Bethell, 725–778. Cambridge: Cambridge University Press, 1986.

Costa, E. V. *The Brazilian Empire: Myths and Histories*. Chicago: University of Chicago Press, 1985.

Cowan, B. A. *Moral Majorities across the Americas: Brazil, the United States, and the Creation of the Religious Right*. Chapel Hill: University of North Carolina Press, 2021.

Cox, J. *The British Missionary Enterprise since 1700*. New York: Routledge, 2010.

Crabtree, A. R. *História dos batistas do Brasil até o ano de 1906*. 2nd ed. Rio de Janeiro: Casa Publicadora Batista, 1962 [1937].

Creppell, I. "Secularisation: Religion and the Roots of Innovation in the Political Sphere." In *Religion and the Political Imagination*, edited by Ira Katznelson and Gareth Stedman Jones, 23–45. Cambridge: Cambridge University Press, 2010.

Cruz Costa, J. *A History of Ideas in Brazil: The Development of Philosophy and the Evolution of National History*, translated by Suzette Macedo. Berkeley: University of California Press, 1964.

Darnton, R. "Discourse and Diffusion." *Contributions to the History of Concepts* 1 (2005): 21–28.

Darnton, R. "History of Reading." In *New Perspectives on Historical Writing*, edited by Peter Burke, 157–186. Cambridge: Polity Press, 1991.

Darnton, R. "What is the History of Books? *Daedalus* 111 (1982): 65–83.

Das, S. "An Imperial Apostle? St Paul, Protestant Conversion, and South Asian Christianity." *Historical Journal* 61 (2018): 103–130.

Dawsey, J., and Cyrus Dawsey. "The *Confederados*' Contributions to Brazilian Agriculture, Religion and Education." In *The Confederados: Old South Immigrants in Brazil*, edited by James Dawsey and Cyrus Dawsey, 84–104. Tuscaloosa: University of Alabama Press, 1995.

De Groot, C. F. G. *Brazilian Catholicism and the Ultramontane Reform*. Amsterdam: CEDLA, 1996.

Deiros, P. A. "Protestant Fundamentalism in Latin America." In *Fundamentalisms Observed*, edited by Martin E. Marty and R. Scott Appleby, 142–196. Chicago: University of Chicago Press, 1991.

BIBLIOGRAPHY AND SOURCES

Delap, L., and Maria DiCenzo. "Transatlantic Print Culture: The Anglo-American Feminist Press and Emerging 'Modernities.'" In *Transatlantic Print Culture, 1880–1940: Emerging Media, Emerging Modernisms*, edited by Ann Ardis and Patrick Collier, 48–65. Basingstoke: Palgrave Macmillan, 2008.

Della Cava, R. "Brazilian Messianism and National Institutions: A Reappraisal of Canudos and Joaseiro." *Hispanic American Historical Review* 48 (1968): 402–420.

Della Cava, R. "Catholicism and Society in Twentieth-century Brazil." *Latin American Research Review* 11 (1976): 7–50.

Della Cava, R. *Miracle at Joaseiro*. New York: Columbia University Press, 1970.

Dias, Z. M. "A larva e a borboleta: Notas sobre as [im]possibilidades do protestantismo no interior da cultura brasileira." In *Diálogos cruzados: Religião, história e construção social*, edited by Mauro Passos, 133–147. Belo Horizonte: Argumentum, 2010.

DiVanna, I. "Reading Comte Across the Atlantic: Intellectual Exchanges between France and Brazil and the Question of Slavery." *History of European Ideas* 38 (2012): 452–466.

Dreher, M. N. "Immigrant Protestantism: The Lutheran Church in Latin America." In *The Cambridge History of Religions in Latin America*, edited by Virginia Garrard-Burnett, Paul Freston, and Stephen Dove, 304–318. New York: Cambridge University Press, 2016.

Elbourne, E. "Word Made Flesh: Christianity, Modernity, and Cultural Colonialism in the Work of Jean and John Comaroff." *American Historical Review* 108 (2003): 435–459.

Engel, E., James Kennedy, and Justin Reynolds. "Editorial—The Theory and Practice of Ecumenism: Christian Global Governance and the Search for World Order, 1900–80." *Journal of Global History* 13 (2018): 157–164.

Engelke, M. *A Problem of Presence: Beyond Scripture in an African Church*. Berkeley: University of California Press, 2007.

Englund, H., and James Leach. "Ethnography and the Meta-narratives of Modernity." *Current Anthropology*, 41 (2000): 225–248.

Etherington, N. "Education and Medicine." In *Missions and Empire*, edited by Norman Etherington, 261–284. New York: Oxford University Press, 2005.

Fausto, B. "Brazil: The Social and Political Structure of the First Republic, 1889–1930." In *The Cambridge History of Latin America: Volume V, c. 1870 to 1930*, edited by Leslie Bethell, 779–830. Cambridge: Cambridge University Press, 1986.

Fea, J. *The Bible Cause: A History of the American Bible Society*. New York: Oxford University Press, 2016.

Feitoza, P. "Experiments in Missionary Writing: Protestant Missions and the *Imprensa Evangelica* in Brazil, 1864–1892." *Journal of Ecclesiastical History* 69 (2018): 585–605.

Feitoza, P. "Historical Trajectories of Protestantism in Brazil, 1810–1960." In *Brazilian Evangelicalism in the Twenty-first Century: An Inside and Outside Look*, edited by Eric Miller and Ronald Morgan, 31–63. Cham, Switzerland: Palgrave Macmillan, 2019.

Feitoza, P. "Immigrants, Missionary Networks, and the Rise of a Luso-Brazilian Evangelical Movement, 1850–1900." Paper given at the Christian Missions in Global History Seminar. Institute of Historical Research, University of London, February 2021.

Feitoza, P. "The Middle Line of Truth: Religious and Secular Ideologies in the Making of Brazilian Evangelical Thought, 1870–1930." *Modern Intellectual History* 19 (2022): 1033–1057.

Ferreira, J. A. *Galeria evangélica: Biografias de pastôres presbiterianos que trabalharam no Brasil*. São Paulo: Casa Editora Presbiteriana, 1952.

Ferreira, J. A. *História da Igreja Presbiteriana do Brasil*, vol. I. 2nd ed. São Paulo: Casa Editora Presbiteriana, 1992.

Florez, J. *Lived Religion, Pentecostalism, and Social Activism in Authoritarian Chile: Giving Life to the Faith*. Leiden: Brill, 2021.

Frase, R. "A Sociological Analysis of the Development of Brazilian Protestantism: A Study of Social Change." PhD diss., Princeton Theological Seminary, 1975.

Frase, R. "The Subversion of Missionary Intentions by Cultural Values: The Brazilian Case." *Review of Religious Research* 23 (1981): 180–194.

Freston, P. "Breve história do pentecostalismo brasileiro." In *Nem anjos nem demônios: Interpretações sociológicas do pentecostalismo*, edited by Alberto Antoniazzi et al., 67–159. Petrópolis: Vozes, 1994.
Freston, P. "Pentecostalism in Latin America: Characteristics and Controversies." *Social Compass* 45 (1998): 335–358.
Freston, P. "Protestantes e política no Brasil: Da Constituinte ao impeachment." PhD diss., State University of Campinas, 1993.
Freston, P. "The Many Faces of Evangelical Politics in Latin America." In *Evangelical Christianity and Democracy in Latin America*, edited by Paul Freston, 3–36. Oxford: Oxford University Press, 2008.
Freston, P. "The Protestant Eruption into Modern Brazilian Politics." *Journal of Contemporary Religion* 11 (1996): 147–168.
Freston, P. *Evangelicals and Politics in Asia, Africa and Latin America*. Cambridge: Cambridge University Press, 2001.
Freyre, G. *Order and Progress: Brazil from Monarchy to Republic*, translated by Rod W. Horton. New York: Knopf, 1970.
Freyre, G. *Tempo de aprendiz, vol. I*. São Paulo: IBRASA, 1979.
Fyfe, A. "Commerce and Philanthropy: The Religious Tract Society and the Business of Publishing." *Journal of Victorian Culture* 9 (2004): 164–188.
Gamsa, M. "Translation and the Transnational Circulation of Books." *Journal of World History* 22 (2011): 553–575.
Gange, D. "Religion and Science in Late Nineteenth-century British Egyptology." *Historical Journal* 49 (2006): 1083–1103.
Garrard-Burnett, V. *Protestantism in Guatemala: Living in the New Jerusalem*. Austin: University of Texas Press, 1998.
Gilley, S. "The Papacy." In *The Cambridge History of Christianity: World Christianities, c. 1815–c. 1914*, edited by Sheridan Gilley and Brian Stanley, 13–29. New York: Cambridge University Press, 2006.
Gobat, M. "The Invention of Latin America: A Transnational History of Anti-imperialism, Democracy, and Race." *American Historical Review* 118 (2013): 1345–1375.
Goldman, F. P. *Os pioneiros americanos no Brasil: Educadores, sacerdotes, covos e reis*. São Paulo: Pioneira, 1972.
González, O., and González, J. *Christianity in Latin America: A History*. New York: Cambridge University Press, 2008.
Goodman, D. "Public Sphere and Private Life: Toward a Synthesis of Current Historiographical Approaches to the Old Regime." *History and Theory* 31 (1992): 1–20.
Graham, R. *Britain and the Onset of Modernization in Brazil, 1850–1914*. Cambridge: Cambridge University Press, 1968.
Graham, R. *Patronage and Politics in Nineteenth-century Brazil*. Stanford, CA: Stanford University Press, 1990.
Graham, S. L. "The Vintem Riot and Political Culture: Rio de Janeiro, 1880." *Hispanic American Historical Review* 60 (1980): 431–449.
Grass, T. *Gathering to His Name: The Story of Open Brethren in Britain and Ireland*. Milton Keynes: Paternoster, 2006.
Green, A., and Viaene, V. "Introduction: Rethinking Religion and Globalization." In *Religious Internationals in the Modern World: Globalization and Faith Communities since 1750*, edited by Abigail Green and Vincent Viaene, 1–19. Basingstoke: Palgrave Macmillan, 2012.
Green, N. *Bombay Islam: The Religious Economy of the West Indian Ocean, 1840–1915*. New York: Cambridge University Press, 2011.
Griffiths, G. "'Trained to Tell the Truth': Missionaries, Converts, and Narration." In *Missions and Empire*, edited by Norman Etherington, 153–172. New York: Oxford University Press, 2005.
Guerra, F. X. *Modernidad y independencias: Ensayos sobre las revoluciones hispánicas*. Madrid: Encuentro, 2009.

Guimarães, H. *Os leitores de Machado de Assis: O romance machadiano e o público de literatura no século 19*. São Paulo: Nankin/EDUSP, 2004.

Guimarães, M. L. S. "Nação e civilização nos trópicos: O Instituto Histórico e Geográfico Brasileiro e o projeto de uma história nacional." *Estudos Históricos* 1 (1988): 5–27.

Habermas, J. *The Structural Transformation of the Public Sphere: An Inquiry into a Category of Bourgeois Society*, translated by Thomas Burger. Cambridge: Polity Press, 1989 [1962].

Haefeli, E. "Breaking the Christian Atlantic: The Legacy of Dutch Tolerance in Brazil." In *The Legacy of Dutch Brazil*, edited by Michiel van Groesen, 124–145. Cambridge: Cambridge University Press, 2014.

Hale, C. "Political and Social Ideas in Latin America, 1870–1930." In *The Cambridge History of Latin America. Vol. IV: c. 1870–1930*, edited by Leslie Bethell, 367–441. Cambridge: Cambridge University Press, 1986.

Hallewell, L. *Books in Brazil: A History of the Publishing Trade*. Metuchen, NJ: The Scarecrow Press, 1982.

Harries, P. "Missionaries, Marxists and Magic: Power and the Politics of Literacy in South-east Africa." *Journal of Soutern African Studies* 27 (2001): 405–427.

Harries, P., and David Maxwell. "Introduction: The Spiritual in the Secular." In *The Spiritual in the Secular: Missionaries and Knowledge about Africa*, edited by Patrick Harries and David Maxwell, 1–29. Grand Rapids, MI: W. B. Eerdmans Publishing Co., 2012.

Harris, P. "Denominationalism and Democracy: Ecclesiastical Issues Underlying Rufus Anderson's Three Self Program." In *North American Foreign Missions, 1810–1914: Theology, Theory, and Policy*, edited by Wilbert R. Shenk, 61–85. Grand Rapids, MI: William B. Eerdmans Publishing Co., 2004.

Harris, R. *Lourdes: Body and Spirit in the Secular Age*. London: Penguin, 1999.

Hartch, T. *The Rebirth of Latin American Christianity*. New York: Oxford University Press, 2014.

Hefner, R. "Introduction: World Building and the Rationality of Conversion." In *Conversion to Christianity: Historical and Anthropological Perspectives on a Great Transformation*, edited by Robert Hefner, 3–44. Berkeley: University of California Press, 1993.

Heimann, M. "Catholic Revivalism in Worship and Devotion." In *The Cambridge History of Christianity: World Christianities, c. 1815–c. 1914*, edited by Sheridan Gilley and Brian Stanley, 70–83. New York: Cambridge University Press, 2006.

Helgen, E. *Religious Conflict in Brazil: Protestants, Catholics, and the Rise of Religious Pluralism in the Early Twentieth Century*. New Haven, CT: Yale University Press, 2020.

Hempton, D. *Methodism: Empire of the Spirit*. New Haven, CT: Yale University Press, 2005.

Hermann, J. "Religião e política no alvorecer da República: Os movimentos de Juazeiro, Canudos e Contestado." In *O tempo do liberalismo oligárquico: Da Proclamação da República à Revolução de 1930*, edited by Jorge Ferreira and Lucilia de A. Neves Delgado, 10th ed., 111–52. Rio de Janeiro: Civilização Brasileira, 2018.

Hill, C. L. "Conceptual Universalization in the Transnational Nineteenth Century." In *Global Intellectual History*, edited by Samuel Moyn and Andrew Sartori, 134–158. New York: Columbia University Press, 2013.

Hill, C. *The World Turned Upside Down: Radical Ideas during the English Revolution*. Harmondsworth: Penguin, 1978.

Hilsdorf, M. L. *História da educação brasileira: Leituras*. São Paulo: Pioneira, 2003.

Hofmeyr, I. "Bunyan in Africa: Text and Transition." *Interventions* 3 (2001): 322–335.

Hofmeyr, I. "Inventing the World: Transnationalism, Transmission and Christian Textualities." In *Mixed Messages: Materiality, Textuality, Missions*, edited by Jamie Scott and Gareth Griffiths, 19–35. New York: Palgrave Macmillan, 2005.

Hofmeyr, I. *Gandhi's Printing Press: Experiments in Slow Reading*. Cambridge, MA: Harvard University Press, 2013.

Hofmeyr, I. *The Portable Bunyan: A Transnational History of The Pilgrim's Progress*. Princeton, NJ: Princeton University Press, 2004.

Hogg, W. R. *Ecumenical Foundations: A History of the International Missionary Council and its Nineteenth-century Background*. Eugene, OR: Wipf and Stock, 2002 [1952].
Horton, R. "African conversion." *Africa* 41 (1971): 85–108.
Howsam, L. "The Bible Society and the Book Trade." In *Sowing the Word: The Cultural Impact of the British and Foreign Bible Society, 1804–2004*, Stephen Batalden, Kathleen Cann, and John Dean, 24–37. Sheffield: Sheffield Phoenix, 2004.
Howsam, L. *Cheap Bibles: Nineteenth-century Publishing and the British and Foreign Bible Society*. Cambridge: Cambridge University Press, 1991.
Hunter, E. "Recovering Liberties in Twentieth-century Africa." CRASSH Work in Progress Seminar, Cambridge UK, October 2018.
Hunter, E. *Political Thought and the Public Sphere in Tanzania: Freedom, Democracy and Citizenship in the Era of Decolonization*. New York: Cambridge University Press, 2015.
Hutchison, W. R. *Errands to the World: American Protestant Thought and Foreign Missions*. Chicago: University of Chicago Press, 1987.
Iglésias, F. *História e ideologia*. São Paulo: Perspectiva, 1971.
Ivereigh, A. "Introduction." In *The Politics of Religion in an Age of Revival: Studies in Nineteenth-century Europe and Latin America*, edited by Austen Ivereigh, 1–21. London: Institute of Latin American Studies, 2000.
Johnson, H. B. "The Portuguese Settlement of Brazil, 1500–80." In *The Cambridge History of Latin America, Vol. I: Colonial Latin America*, edited by Leslie Bethell, 249–286. Cambridge: Cambridge University Press, 1984.
Johnston, A. *Missionary Writing and Empire, 1800–1860*. Cambridge: Cambridge University Press, 2003.
Kapila, S. "Preface." *Modern Intellectual History* 4 (2007): 3–6.
Karasch, M. C. *Slave Life in Rio de Janeiro, 1808–1850*. Princeton, NJ: Princeton University Press, 1987.
Kennedy, J. L. *Cincoenta annos de methodismo no Brasil*. São Paulo: Imprensa Methodista, 1928.
Kidd, C. *The Forging of Races: Race and Scripture in the Protestant Atlantic World, 1600–2000*. New York: Cambridge University Press, 2006.
Killingray, D. "Passing On the Gospel: Indigenous Mission in Africa." *Transformation* 28 (2011): 93–102.
Kirkendall, A. *Class Mates: Male Student Culture and the Making of a Political Class in Nineteenth-century Brazil*. Lincoln: University of Nebraska Press, 2002.
Kirkpatrick, D. C. "C. René Padilla and the Origins of Integral Mission in Post-war Latin America." *Journal of Ecclesiastical History* 67 (2016): 351–371.
Kirkpatrick, D. C. *A Gospel for the Poor: Global Social Christianity and the Latin American Evangelical Left*. Philadelphia: University of Pennsylvania Press, 2019.
Kirsch, T. *Spirits and Letters: Reading, Writing and Charisma in African Christianity*. New York: Berghahn Books, 2008.
Klug, J. "Imigração no sul do Brasil." In *O Brasil Imperial, vol. III: 1870–1889*, edited by Keila Grinberg and Ricardo Salles, 201–231. Rio de Janeiro: Civilização Brasileira, 2009.
Kothe, M. G. "O Brasil no século XIX: Restrições aos grupos não católicos." In *História em movimento: Temas e perguntas*, edited by Albene M. Menezes, 92–103. Brasília: Thesaurus, 1999.
Larsen, T. "Defining and Locating Evangelicalism." In *The Cambridge Companion to Evangelical Theology*, edited by Timothy Larsen and Daniel J. Treier, 1–14. Cambridge: Cambridge University Press, 2007.
Latourette, K. S. "Ecumenical Bearings of the Missionary Movement and the International Missionary Council." In *A History of the Ecumenical Movement, 1517–1948*, edited by Ruth Rouse and Stephen Neill, 351–402. London: SPCK, 1954.
Lehmann, D. *Struggle for the Spirit: Religious Transformation and Popular Culture in Brazil and Latin America*. Cambridge: Polity Press, 1996.

Léonard, E. G. "L'illuminisme dans un protestantisme de constitution récente." *Revue de l'Histoire de Religions* 1 (1952): 26–83.
Léonard, E. G. *Iluminismo num protestantismo de constituição recente*. São Bernardo do Campo, SP: UMESP, 1988.
Léonard, E. G. *O protestantismo brasileiro: Estudo de eclesiologia e história social*, 3rd ed. São Paulo: ASTE, 2002 [1963].
Leonel, J. *História da leitura e protestantismo brasileiro*. São Paulo: Editora Mackenzie, 2010.
Leonel, J., Ivanilson Bezerra da Silva, and Silas Luiz de Souza, eds. *O jornal 'Imprensa Evangelica' e o protestantismo brasileiro*. Votorantim, SP: Linha Fina, 2020.
Lessa, V. T. *Annaes da 1ª Egreja Presbyteriana de São Paulo (1863–1903): Subsidios para a historia do presbiterianismo brasileiro*. São Paulo: Edição da 1ª Igreja Presbiteriana Independente de São Paulo, 1938.
Levine, R. "'Mud-Hut Jerusalem': Canudos Revisited." In *The Abolition of Slavery and the Aftermath of Emancipation in Brazil*, edited by Rebecca Scott, 119–166. Durham, NC: Duke University Press, 1988.
Levine, R. *Vale of Tears: Revisiting the Canudos Massacre in Northeastern Brazil, 1893–1897*. Berkeley: University of California Press, 1992.
Lewis, D., ed. *The Blackwell Dictionary of Evangelical Biography: 1730–1860*. 2 vols. Oxford: Blackwell, 1995.
Lindenfeld, D. "Indigenous Encounters with Christian Missionaries in China and West Africa, 1800–1920: A Comparative Study." *Journal of World History* 16 (2005): 327–369.
Lindenfeld, D., and Miles Richardson. "Introduction." In Beyond conversion and Syncretism: Indigenous Encounters with Missionary Christianity, 1800–2000, edited by David Lindenfeld and Miles Richardson, 1–24. New York: Berghahn Books, 2012.
Martin, D. *Forbidden Revolutions: Pentecostalism in Latin America and Catholicism in Eastern Europe*. London: SPCK, 1996.
Martin, D. *Tongues of Fire: The Explosion of Protestantism in Latin America*. Oxford: Basil Blackwell, 1990.
Martin, R. *Evangelicals United: Ecumenical Stirrings in pre-Victorian Britain, 1795–1830*. Metuchen, NJ: The Scarecrow Press, 1983.
Martins, J. S. "Penúltimas palavras." *Revista Brasileira de Ciências Sociais* 29 (2014): 195–210.
Maspoli, A. *Religião, educação e progresso*. São Paulo: Editora Mackenzie, 2001.
Matos, Alderi Souza. *Erasmo Braga, o protestantismo e a sociedade brasileira: Perspectivas sobre a missão da igreja*. São Paulo: Cultura Cristã, 2008.
Maurer Jr., T. H. "Professor Otoniel Mota (1878–1951)." *Revista de História* 3 (1951): 478–479.
Maxwell, D. "'Sacred History, Social History': Traditions and Texts in the Making of a Southern African Transnational Religious Movement." *Comparative Studies in Society and History* 43 (2001): 502–524.
Maxwell, D. "Continuity and Change in the Luba Christian Movement, Katanga, Belgian Congo, c. 1915–50." *Journal of Ecclesiastical History* 69 (2018): 326–344.
Maxwell, D. "Historical Perspectives on Christianity Worldwide: Connections, Comparisons and Consciousness." In *Relocating World Christianity: Interdisciplinary Studies in Universal and Local Expressions of the Christian Faith*, edited by Joel Cabrita, David Maxwell, and Emma Wild-Wood, 47–69. Leiden: Brill, 2017.
Maxwell, D. "Historicizing Christian Independency: The Southern African Pentecostal Movement, c. 1908–60." *Journal of African History* 40 (1999): 243–264.
Maxwell, D. "The Creation of Lubaland: Missionary Science and Christian Literacy in the Making of the Luba Katanga in Belgian Congo." *Journal of Eastern African Studies* 10 (2016): 367–392.
Maxwell, D. "The Missionary Movement in African and World History: Mission Sources and Religious Encounter." *Historical Journal* 58 (2015): 901–930.
Maxwell, D. *African Gifts of the Spirit: Pentecostalism and the Rise of Zimbabwean Transnational Religious Movement*. Oxford: James Currey, 2006.

Maxwell, D. *Religious Entanglements: Central African Pentecostalism, the Creation of Cultural Knowledge, and the Making of the Luba Katanga*. Madison: University of Wisconsin Press, 2022.

McGuinness, A. "Searching for 'Latin America': Race and Sovereignty in the Americas in the 1850s." In *Race and Nation in Modern Latin America*, edited by Nancy Appelbaum, Anne Macpherson, and Karin A. Rosemblatt, 87–107. Chapel Hill: University of North Carolina Press, 2003.

Mendes, L. "The Bachelor's Library: Pornographic Books on the Brazil-Europe Circuit in the Late Nineteenth Century." In *The Transatlantic Circulation of Novels between Europe and Brazil, 1789–1914*, edited by Márcia Abreu, 79–100. Cham, Switzerland: Palgrave Macmillan, 2017.

Mendonça, A. G. "O protestantismo no Brasil e suas encruzilhadas." *Revista USP* 67 (2005): 48–67.

Mendonça, A. G., and P. Velasques Filho. *Introdução ao protestantismo no Brasil*. São Paulo: Edições Loyola, 1990.

Mendonça, A. G. *O celeste porvir: A inserção do protestantismo no Brasil*. 3rd ed. São Paulo: Editora da Universidade de São Paulo, 2008 [1984].

Meyer, B. "'Make a Complete Break with the Past': Memory and Post-colonial Modernity in Ghanaian Pentecostalist Discourse." *Journal of Religion in Africa* 28 (1998): 316–349.

Miceli, S. *A elite eclesiástica brasileira: 1890–1930*. 2nd ed. São Paulo: Companhia das Letras, 2009.

Miceli, S. *Intelectuais e classe dirigente no Brasil (1920–1945)*. São Paulo e Rio de Janeiro: DIFEL, 1979.

Míguez Bonino, J. *Rostros del protestantismo latinoamericano*. Buenos Aires: Nueva Creación, 1995.

Mondragón, C. *Like Leaven in the Dough: Protestant Social Thought in Latin America, 1920–1950*, translated by Daniel Miller and Ben Post. Madison, NJ: Fairleigh Dickinson University Press, 2011.

Monroe, A. L. "To Govern the Church: Autonomy and the Consequences of Self-determination for the Brotherhood of Saint Efigênia and Saint Elesbão of Black Men of São Paulo, Brazil, 1888–1890." *Hispanic American Historical Review* 97 (2017): 63–94.

Monteiro, D. T. *Errantes do novo século: Um estudo sobre o surto milenarista do Contestado*. São Paulo: Duas Cidades, 1974.

Monteiro, J. "Caçando com gato: Raça, mestiçagem e identidade paulista na obra de Alfredo Ellis Jr." *Novos Estudos CEBRAP* 38 (1994): 79–88.

Monteiro, J. *Blacks of the Land: Indian Slavery, Settler Society, and the Portuguese Colonial Enterprise in South America*, translated by James Woodard and Barbara Weinstein. New York: Cambridge University Press, 2018 [1994].

Morel, M. *As transformações dos espaços públicos: Imprensa, atores políticos e sociabilidades na cidade imperial (1820–1840)*. São Paulo: Hucitec, 2005.

Morse, R. *The Bandeirantes: The Historical Role of the Brazilian Pathfinders*. New York: Alfred A. Knopf, 1965.

Moura, S., and José M. G. Almeida. "A Igreja na Primeira República." In *História Geral da Civilização Brasileira, vol. 2, tomo III*, edited by Boris Fausto, 312–342. Rio de Janeiro and São Paulo: DIFEL, 1977.

Moyn, S., and Andrew Sartori. "Approaches to Global Intellectual History." In *Global Intellectual History*, edited by Samuel Moyn and Andrew Sartori, 3–30. New York: Columbia University Press, 2013.

Moyn, S. *Christian Human Rights*. Philadelphia: University of Pennsylvania Press, 2015.

Moyn, S. *The Last Utopia: Human Rights in History*. Cambridge, MA: The Belknap Press of Harvard University Press, 2012.

Nachman, R. "Positivism, Modernization, and the Middle Class in Brazil." *Hispanic American Historical Review* 57 (1977): 1–23.

Needell, J. *A Tropical Belle Époque: Elite Culture and Society in Turn-of-the-century Rio de Janeiro.* Cambridge: Cambridge University Press, 1987.
Neves, G. P. "A religião do Império e a Igreja." In *O Brasil Imperial, vol. I: 1808–1831*, edited by Keila Grinberg and Ricardo Salles, 377–428. Rio de Janeiro: Civilização Brasileira, 2009.
Neves, G. P. "Igreja." In *Dicionário do Brasil colonial (1500–1808)*, edited by Ronaldo Vainfas, 292–296. Rio de Janeiro: Objetiva, 2001.
Neves, L. M. B. P. *Corcundas e constitucionais: A cultura política da independência (1820–1822).* Rio de Janeiro: Revan/FAPERJ, 2003.
Pang, E. S., and Ron Seckinger. "The Mandarins of Imperial Brazil." *Comparative Studies in Society and History* 14 (1972): 215–244.
Parés, L. N. *The Formation of Candomblé: Vodun History and Ritual in Brazil*, translated by Richard Vernon. Chapel Hill: University of North Carolina Press, 2013.
Peel, J. D. Y. "Conversion and Tradition in Two African Societies: Ijebu and Buganda." *Past & Present* 77 (1977): 108–141.
Peel, J. D. Y. "For Who Hath Despised The Day Of Small Things? Missionary Narratives and Historical Anthropology." *Comparative Studies in Society and History* 37 (1995): 581–607.
Peel, J. D. Y. "The Pastor and the *Babalawo*: The Interaction of Religions in Nineteenth-century Yorubaland." *Africa* 60 (1990): 338–369.
Peel, J. D. Y. *Religious Encounter and the Making of the Yoruba.* Bloomington: Indiana University Press, 2000.
Petrella, I. "The Intellectual Roots of Liberation Theology." In *The Cambridge History of Religions in Latin America*, edited by Virginia Garrard-Burnett, Paul Freston, and Stephen Dove, 359–371. New York: Cambridge University Press, 2016.
Phelan, J. L. "Pan-Latinism, French Intervention in Mexico (1861–7) and the Genesis of the Idea of Latin America." In *Conciencia y autenticidad históricas: escritas en homenaje a Edmundo O'Gorman*, edited by Juan A. Ortega y Medina, 279–298. Mexico City: UNAM, 1968.
Piccato, P. "Public Sphere in Latin America: A Review of the Historiography." *Social History* 35 (2010): 165–192.
Piedra Solano, A. *Evangelização protestante na américa latina: Análise das razões que justificaram e promoveram a expansão protestante*, vol. 2. São Leopoldo: Sinodal, 2008.
Pierson, P. E. *A Younger Church in Search of Maturity: Presbyterianism in Brazil from 1910 to 1959.* San Antonio: Trinity University Press, 1974.
Plou, D. S. "Ecumenical History of Latin America." In *A History of the Ecumenical Movement: Volume 3, 1968–2000*, edited by John Briggs, Mercy A. Oduyoye, and Georges Tsetsis. Geneva: World Council of Churches, 2004.
Porter, A. *Religion versus Empire? British Protestant Missionaries and Overseas Expansion, 1700–1914.* Manchester: Manchester University Press, 2004.
Prado, M. L. *Utopias latino-americanas: Política, sociedade, cultura.* São Paulo: Contexto, 2021.
Premack, L. "'The Holy Rollers are Invading our Territory': Southern Baptist Missionaries and the Early Years of Pentecostalism in Brazil." *Journal of Religious History* 35 (2011): 1–23.
Racine, K. "Commercial Christianity: The British and Foreign Bible Society's Interest in Spanish America, 1805–1830." *Bulletin of Latin American Research* 27, supplement 1 (2008): 78–98.
Ramón Solans, F. J. "The Creation of a Latin American Catholic Church: Vatican Authority and Political Imagination, 1854–1899." *Journal of Ecclesiastical History* 71 (2020): 316–336.
Ramos, G. "Conversion of Indigenous People in the Peruvian Andes: Politics and Historical Understanding." *History Compass* 14 (2016): 359–369.
Ranger, T. "Religious Movements and Politics in sub-Saharan Africa." *African Studies Review* 29 (1986): 1–69.
Ranger, T. *Are We Not Also Men? The Samkange Family & African Politics in Zimbabwe, 1920–64.* Harare: James Currey, 1995.
Reily, D. A. *História documental do protestantismo no Brasil* 3rd ed. São Paulo: ASTE, 2003.

Reis, J. J. "'Nos achamos em campo a tratar da liberdade': A resistência escrava no Brasil oitocentista." In *Viagem incompleta: a experiência brasileira, 1500-2000,* edited by Carlos G. Mota, 241-263. São Paulo: Editora SENAC, 2000.

Reis, J. J. *Divining Slavery and Freedom: The Story of Domingos Sodré, an African Priest in Nineteenth-century Brazil,* translated by H. Sabrina Gledhill. New York: Cambridge University Press, 2015.

Reis, J. J. *Slave Rebellion in Brazil: The Muslim Uprising of 1835 in Bahia,* translated by Arthur Brakel. Baltimore: Johns Hopkins University Press, 1993.

Ribeiro, B. *José Manoel da Conceição e a reforma evangélica.* São Paulo: Livraria O Semeador, 1995.

Ribeiro, B. *Protestantismo e cultura brasileira: Aspectos culturais da implantação do protestantismo no Brasil.* São Paulo: Casa Editora Presbiteriana, 1981.

Ribeiro, B. *Protestantismo no Brasil monárquico (1822-1888): Aspectos culturais da aceitação do protestantismo no Brasil.* São Paulo: Pioneira, 1973.

Robbins, J. "Continuity Thinking and the Problem of Christian Culture: Belief, Time, and the Anthropology of Christianity." *Current Anthropology* 48 (2007): 5-17.

Robert, D. "Rufus Anderson." In *The Blackwell Dictionary of Evangelical Biography: 1730-1860,* 2 vols., edited by Donald Lewis, vol. I, 19-21. Oxford: Blackwell, 1995.

Robert, D. "The 'Christian Home' as a Cornerstone of Anglo-American Missionary Thought and Practice." In *Converting Colonialism: Visions and Realities in Mission History, 1706-1914,* edited by Dana Robert, 134-165. Grand Rapids, MI: William B. Eerdmans Publishing Co., 2008.

Rocha, J. G. *Lembranças do passado.* 4 vols. Rio de Janeiro: Centro Brasileiro de Publicidade, 1941.

Rodrigues, C. "Sepulturas e sepultamentos do protestantes como uma questão de cidadania na crise do Império (1869-1889)." *Revista de História Regional* 13 (2008): 23-38.

Rospocher, M. "Beyond the Public Sphere: A Historiographical Transition." In *Beyond the Public Sphere: Opinions, Publics, Spaces in Early Modern Europe,* edited by Massimo Rospocher, 9-30. Bologna: Duncker & Humboldt, 2012.

Rouse, R., and Stephen Neill, eds. *A History of the Ecumenical Movement, 1517-1948.* London: SPCK, 1954.

Sabato, H. "Citizenship, Political Participation and the Formation of the Public Sphere in Buenos Aires 1850s-1880s." *Past & Present* 136 (1992): 139-163.

Sabato, H. *The Many and the Few: Political Participation in Republican Buenos Aires.* Stanford, CA: Stanford University Press, 2001.

Salinas, D. *Latin American Evangelical Theology in the 1970s: The Golden Decade.* Leiden: Brill, 2009.

Salinas, D. *Taking Up the Mantle: Latin American Evangelical Theology in the 20th Century.* Carlisle: Langham Global Library, 2017.

Samson, J. *Race and Redemption: British Missionaries Encounter Pacific Peoples, 1797-1920.* Grand Rapids, MI: William B. Eerdmans Publishing Company, 2017.

Sanders, J. *The Vanguard of the Atlantic World: Creating Modernity, Nation, and Democracy in Nineteenth-century Latin America.* Durham, NC: Duke University Press, 2014.

Santos, L. A. C. "O pensamento sanitarista na Primeira República: Uma ideologia de construção de nacionalidade." *Dados* 28 (1985): 193-210.

Santos, L. A. *Os mascates da fé: História dos evangélicos no Brasil (1855 a 1900).* Curitiba: CRV, 2017.

Santos, L. C. V. G. *O Brasil entre a América e a Europa: O império e o interamericanismo (do Congresso do Panamá à Conferência de Washington).* São Paulo: Editora UNESP, 2004.

Schwarcz, L. M. *The Spectacle of the Races: Scientists, Institutions, and the Race Question in Brazil, 1870-1930,* translated by Leland Guyer. New York: Hill and Wang, 1999.

Schwartz, S. *All Can Be Saved: Religious Tolerance and Salvation in the Iberian Atlantic World.* New Haven, CT: Yale University Press, 2008.

Serbin, K. "Church and State Reciprocity in Contemporary Brazil: The Convening of the International Eucharistic Congress of 1955 in Rio de Janeiro." *Hispanic American Historical Review* 76 (1996): 721–751.

Serbin, K. *Needs of the Heart: A Social and Cultural History of Brazil's Clergy and Seminaries.* Notre Dame: University of Notre Dame Press, 2006.

Sevcenko, N. *Orfeu extático na metrópole: São Paulo, sociedade e cultura nos frementes anos 20.* São Paulo: Companhia das Letras, 1992.

Sharkey, H. J. "The British and Foreign Society in Port Said and the Suez Canal." *Journal of Imperial and Commonwealth History* 39 (2011): 439–456.

Shenk, W. R. "Rufus Anderson and Henry Venn: A Special Relationship?" *International Bulletin of Missionary Research* 5 (1981): 168–172.

Sigmund, P. *Liberation Theology at the Crossroads: Democracy or Revolution?* New York: Oxford University Press, 1990.

Silva, E., Lyndon Santos, and Vasni Almeida, eds. *Fiel é a palavra: Leituras históricas dos evangélicos protestantes no Brasil.* Feira de Santana: UEFS Editora, 2011.

Sinclair, J., and Arturo Piedra Solano. "The Dawn of Ecumenism in Latin America: Robert Speer, Presbyterians, and the Panama Conference of 1916." *Journal of Presbyterian History* 77 (1999): 1–11.

Sivasundaram, S. *Nature and the Godly Empire: Science and Evangelical Mission in the Pacific, 1795–1850.* Cambridge: Cambridge University Press, 2005.

Skidmore, T. "Racial Ideas and Social Policy in Brazil, 1870–1940." In *The Idea of Race in Latin America, 1870–1940*, edited by Richard Graham, 7–36. Austin: University of Texas Press, 1990.

Skidmore, T. *Black into White: Race and Nationality in Brazilian Thought.* New York: Oxford University Press, 1974.

Smilde, D. *Reason to Believe: Cultural Agency in Latin American Evangelicalism.* Berkeley: University of California Press, 2007.

Smith, R. C. *Improvised Continent: Pan-Americanism and Cultural Exchange.* Philadelphia: University of Pennsylvania Press, 2017.

Souza, S. L. *Pensamento social e político no protestantismo brasileiro.* São Paulo: Editora Mackenzie, 2005.

Spyer, J. *Povo de Deus: Quem são os evangélicos e por que eles importam.* São Paulo: Geração Editorial, 2020.

Stanley, B. "Christian Missions and the Enlightenment: A Reevaluation." In *Christian Missions and the Enlightenment*, edited by Brian Stanley, 1–21. Grand Rapids, MI: W. B. Eerdmans Publishing Co., 2001.

Stanley, B. *Christianity in the Twentieth Century: A World History.* Princeton, NJ: Princeton University Press, 2018.

Stanley, B. *The World Missionary Conference, Edinburgh 1910.* Grand Rapids, MI: Eerdmans, 2009.

Sullivan-González, D. "Religious Devotion, Rebellion, and Messianic Movements: Popular Catholicism in the Nineteenth Century." In *The Cambridge History of Religions in Latin America*, edited by Virginia Garrard-Burnett, Paul Freston, and Stephen Dove, 269–285. New York: Cambridge University Press, 2016.

Suttles, D. "Schism on the Prairie: The Case of the Free Portuguese Church of Jacksonville, Illinois." *Journal of Presbyterian History* 75 (1997): 211–222.

Taylor, C. "Religious Mobilizations." *Public Culture* 18 (2006): 281–300.

Tenorio-Trillo, M. *Latin America: The Allure and Power of an Idea.* Chicago: University of Chicago Press, 2017.

Thompson, E. P. *The Making of the English Working Class.* London: Penguin Books, 2013 [1963].

Thornton, M. C. *The Church and Freemasonry in Brazil, 1872–1875: A Study in Regalism.* Washington: Catholic University of America Press, 1948.

Trindade, H. *Integralismo (o fascismo brasileiro na década de 30)*. São Paulo: Difel, 1974.
Uribe-Uran, V. "The Birth of a Public Sphere in Latin America during the Age of Revolution." *Comparative Studies in Society and History* 42 (2000): 425–457.
van der Veer, P. "Introduction." In *Conversion to Modernities: The Globalization of Christianity*, edited by Peter van der Veer, 1–21. New York: Routledge, 1996.
van der Veer, P. "Nationalism and Religion." In *The Oxford Handbook of the History of Nationalism*, edited by John Breuilly, 655–671. Oxford: Oxford University Press, 2013.
Velasques Filho, P. "'Sim' a Deus e 'não' à vida: Conversão e disciplina no protestantismo brasileiro." In *Introdução ao protestantismo no Brasil*, edited by Antonio Gouvêa Mendonça and Prócoro Velasques Filho, 205–232. São Paulo: Edições Loyola, 1990.
Velloso, M. P. *A brasilidade verde-amarela: Nacionalismo e regionalismo paulista*. Rio de Janeiro: CPDOC, 1990.
Viaene, V. "Nineteenth-century Catholic Internationalism and its Predecessors." In *Religious Internationals in the Modern World: Globalization and Faith Communities since 1750*, edited by Abigail Green and Vincent Viaene, 82–110. Basingstoke: Palgrave Macmillan, 2012.
Vieira, D. G. "Liberalismo, masonería y protestantismo en Brasil, siglo XIX." In *Protestantes, liberales y francmasones: Sociedades de ideas y modernidad en América Latina, siglo XIX*, edited by Jean-Pierre Bastian, 39–66. Mexico, DF: Fondo de Cultura Económica, 1990.
Vieira, D. G. *O protestantismo, a maçonaria e a Questão Religiosa no Brasil*. Brasília: Editora UnB, 1980.
Wacker, G. *Heaven Below: Early Pentecostals and American Culture*. Cambridge, MA: Harvard University Press, 2001.
Warner, M. *Publics and Counterpublics*. New York: Zone Books, 2005.
Weber, M. *The Protestant Ethic and the Spirit of Capitalism*, translated by Talcott Parsons. New York: Routledge, 2001 [1905].
Wedemann, W. "A History of Protestant Missions to Brazil, 1850–1914." PhD diss., Southern Baptist Theological Seminary, 1977.
Weinstein, B. "Racializing Regional Difference: São Paulo *versus* Brasil, 1932." In *Race and Nation in Modern Latin America*, edited by Nancy Appelbaum, Anne Macpherson, and Karin A. Rosemblatt, 237–262. Chapel Hill: University of North Carolina Press, 2003.
Weinstein, B. *The Color of Modernity: São Paulo and the Making of Race and Nation in Brazil*. Durham, NC: Duke University Press, 2015.
Whitelam, K. "The Archaeological Study of the Bible." In *The New Cambridge History of the Bible: Volume 4, from 1750 to the Present*, edited by John Riches, 139–148. New York: Cambridge University Press, 2015.
Willems, E. "Protestantism as a Factor of Culture Change in Brazil." *Economic Development and Cultural Change* 3 (1955): 321–333.
Willems, E. *Followers of the New Faith: Culture Change and the Rise of Protestantism in Brazil and Chile*. Nashville, TN: Vanderbilt University Press, 1967.
Williams, C. P. "Henry Venn." In *The Blackwell Dictionary of Evangelical Biography: 1730–1860*. 2 vols., edited by Donald Lewis, vol. II, 1138–1140. Oxford: Blackwell, 1995.
Williams, M. T. "Integralism and the Brazilian Catholic Church." *Hispanic American Historical Review* 54 (1974): 431–452.
Woodard, J. "Pages from a Yellow Press: Print Culture, Public Life and Political Genealogies in Modern Brazil." *Journal of Latin American Studies* 46 (2014): 353–379.
Woodard, J. *A Place in Politics: São Paulo, Brazil, from Seigneurial Republicanism to Regionalist Revolt*. Durham, NC: Duke University Press, 2009.
Zaret, D. "Religion, Science, and Printing in the Public Sphere in Seventeenth-century England." In *Habermas and the Public Sphere*, edited by Craig Calhoun, 212–235. Cambridge, MA: MIT Press, 1992.

2. Reference works

Dicionário Cronológico de Autores Portugueses, vol. I. Mem Martins, PT: Publicações Europa-América, 1985.
Dicionário de história religiosa de Portugal, vol. 4. Lisbon: Círculo de Leitores, 2000.
Silva, I. F. *Diccionario bibliographico portuguez: Estudos de Innocêncio Francisco da Silva*, tome VIII. Lisbon: Imprensa Nacional, 1867.

Index

Tables and figures are indicated by an italic *t* and *f* following the page number.

abolitionists and abolitionism, 4–5, 15, 53–55, 96–97, 108–9, 121–22
abolition of slavery, 50–51, 53–54, 68, 109–10, 113, 222
Abreu e Lima, José Inácio, 49–50
ABS. *See* American Bible Society
African Friend, The, 53–54
African religions, 16–17, 23, 251–52
Albuquerque, Antônio Teixeira de, 48–49
Almeida, Egydio Pereira de, 44–45
Almeida, João Ferreira de, 82–83
Almeida translation of the Bible, 63, 82–83, 85–86, 170–71, 225n.88
Amaral, Tarsila do, 237
American Bible Society (ABS), 20–21, 26, 48–49, 61, 75, 165, 211–12, 228–29
  Almeida translation of the Bible, 82–83
  Catholic opposition to Bibles from, 84–85
  colporteurs, 58–59, 68–69, 78–80, 79n.77, 82
  distribution figures, 63–65
  Panama Congress, 179
American Board of Commissioners for Foreign Missions, 40–41
American Civil War, 25, 27, 53–54
American Legation, 61
American School (later, Mackenzie Institute/College), 44–46, 209–10
American Seamen's Friend Society, 61
Anchieta, José de, 243–44
Anderson, Benedict, 93–94
Anderson, Rufus, 40–41
Andrade, Mario de, 237
Andrade, Oswald de, 237
Anglicans and Anglicanism
  British immigrants, 23, 24
  ecumenical movement, 203
  establishment of, 24
  interactions with BFBS, 61–62
  missionary outreach to chaplains, 26
Anglo-Catholics, 25, 178
Anjos, Manoel dos, 71–74, 76–77, 78–79
Apocryphal books, 62, 82–83, 89–90

Apóstolo, O, 84–85, 104, 107, 234
Archaeology and the Bible (Mota), 224
Arinos, Afonso, 237
Arrested Reformation, The (Muir), 180
Assemblies of God, 129, 174
Assis, Machado de, 108–9
Azevedo, Aluísio de, 108–9

"bachelor's library," 87–88
Bagby, Anne, 28, 168, 171–72
Bagby, William, 28, 52–53, 168, 171–72
Baillot, Augusto, 209–10
Ballantyne, Tony, 6–7
bandeirantes, 162–63, 237–40
Baptists and Baptist churches
  abolitionist movement, 53–54
  American Confederate immigrants, 25, 53–54
  appeal of, 31–32
  Assemblies of God, 174
  civilizing effects of Christian literature, 2–3
  collaboration and competition, 168–69, 170–72
  conversion of various social classes, 135
  correspondence with Bible Societies, 71
  denominational differentiation, 28–29, 48–49, 124–25, 139–40, 170–74, 172n.26, 203
  early missionaries and congregations, 28–29, 31*f*, 168
  factional divisions, 170–71, 174
  growth of, 173–74
  hydrolatry controversy, 173–74
  independence and autonomy of local churches, 173–74, 252
  local fundraising, 38–39
  membership figures, 29
  Panama Congress, 179
  political issues and transformations, 52–54
  Proclamation of the Republic, 113
  publishing enterprise, 47–49, 172, 187–88
  schools and education, 44–45, 47, 173–74
  worldwide evangelical network, 55–56
yellow fever, 77–78

280 INDEX

Barber, Karin, 15–16, 252–53
Barbosa, José Carlos, 53–54
Barbosa, José Maria, 126
Barbosa, Ruy, 190–91
Barreto, João Paulo (João do Rio), 58, 68
Bastian, Jean-Pierre, 9–10, 51, 96–98, 203, 254–55
Bastos, Aureliano Tavares, 103
Batista, Cícero Romão, 176–77
beatas and *beatos*, 175–77
Bebbington, David, 11–13
Berg, Daniel, 174
BFBS. *See* British and Foreign Bible Society
BFM-PCUSA (Board of Foreign Missions of the Presbyterian Church of the United States of America), 35–36, 47, 205
"Bible and the Literary Culture, The" (Braga), 223
Bible and Tract Societies. *See* Bible Societies; names of specific societies
Bible production and distribution, 2–3, 4, 5–6, 18, 47–48, 55. *See also* colporteurs; translation
  American Bible Society, 63–65, 84–85
  Baptist churches, 48–49
  British and Foreign Bible Society, 62–65, 64t
  colporteurs, 58–60
  early missionaries, 26
  illiteracy, 75–76
  journey from printer to reader, 68–69
  Presbyterian churches, 39–40
  prices, 78–79
Bible-readers, 3–4, 40, 43–44, 75–76, 208, 251–52
Bible Societies, 58–60, 228. *See also names of specific societies*
  Catholic reaction to, 81–87
  denominational alliances, 71
  imagined communities, 93–94
  Lusophone networks, 90–91, 94
  negative association of with Bibles, 84–85
Bilbao, Francisco, 183–84
Blackford, Alexander, 27, 32–33, 34, 40, 43–44, 85–86, 107–8, 152
Blackford, Elizabeth (Nannie), 27, 43–44
Blessed Virgin Mary, The (Pereira), 117–18
Board of Foreign Missions of the Presbyterian Church of the United States of America (BFM-PCUSA), 35–36, 47, 205
Bolívar, Simón, 193–95
Bolsonaro, Jair, 7
Bomfim, Manoel, 190–91
Bonino, José Míguez, 165–66, 254–55

Bossuet, Jacques-Bénigne, 106–7
Bourdel, Jean du, 243
Bourdon, Pierre, 243
Bowen, Thomas Jefferson, 56
Braga, Erasmo, 1–2, 19, 46–47, 90–91, 155–56, 159, 160, 167, 188–90, 191–99, 201–4, 205, 209–11, 214–17, 220, 222, 230, 231–32, 234–36, 236n.137, 238–39, 243–46, 249
Braga, João Ribeiro de Carvalho, 34–35, 46, 66–67, 159
Braga, Remigio, 209–10
Brazil and the Brazilians (Fletcher and Kidder), 51–52, 195–96, 241–42
Brazilian Baptist Convention, 203
Brazilian Evangelical Church, 96, 211–12
Brazilian Evangelical Confederation, 204
Brazilian Historical and Geographical Institute (IHGB), 51–52
Brazilian Missions, 109–10
Brazilian Society of Evangelical Tracts (BSET), 2–3, 18–19, 35–36, 115–25, 234–35
  critique of Catholicism, 116–19, 120
  critique of elite liberal intellectualism, 120–22
  founding of, 115–16
  moral teachings and reformation of conduct, 122–24
  publishing house, 115–16
British and Foreign Bible Society (BFBS), 18, 58–60, 61–68, 126, 129–30, 169–70, 211–12
  advertising strategies, 86–87
  Almeida translation of the Bible, 63, 82–83, 85–86
  avoidance of denominational conflict, 62
  Bible as instrument of social improvement, 67–68
  Bible distribution, 62–65, 64t
  Bible translation, 62
  'Bíblia' versus 'As Escrituras Sagradas,' 86–87
  Catholic opposition to Bibles from, 82–85
  colporteurs, 68–74, 75–80, 81, 82–84, 85–87, 88, 90, 152–53
  early agents, 61
  "false Bibles," 82–85, 86
  Figueiredo translation of the Latin Vulgate, 82–83, 170–71
  foundation of, 62–63
  objectives of, 62–63
  organizational structure of, 62–63
  price of Bibles, 78–79
  social and economic improvement for staff, 76–77

time lag between dissemination and
    conversions, 67
  transatlantic exchange of literature, 90–91
Brown, Marcia, 211n.24
Bruce, J. L., 225–26
Brusco, Elizabeth, 8–9
BSET. *See* Brazilian Society of
  Evangelical Tracts

caboclos, 161, 217–18, 236–37, 238–39
caipiras, 145–46, 150, 151–52, 153–54, 155–57,
    159–60, 161–63, 217–18, 231–32, 234–35,
    237, 238–39, 247, 256–57
Calvinists and Calvinism, 22–23, 241–42
Câmara, Helder, 221–22
Camillo (colporteur), 68–69, 70*f*
Campos, Benedito Ferraz, 34–35
Campos, Caetano, 211n.24
Carroll, Henry, 180–81
Carvalho, José Martin de, 63, 68, 69–74, 76–79,
    85–87, 152–53
Carvalho, José Murilo de, 74–75
Carvalhosa, Modesto P., 34, 37–38, 44, 157–58
Casas, Bartolomé de las, 245–46
Casas de Caridade, 175
Castilho, José, 146
Castro, Emilio, 152
catechisms, 3–6, 17–18, 43–44, 208–9
cateretês, 141, 141n.38
Catholics and Catholicism. *See also* conversion;
    *names of specific Catholics and
    institutions*
  Christian cooperation, 165, 167, 179–82,
    185–89, 199
  church–state rapprochement, 249
  collectivist political ideologies, 221–22
  conversion to Protestantism, 134
  disestablishment, 79–80, 96–99, 113–15,
    177
  ecclesiastical materialism, 116–19
  educational institutions, 39, 113–14
  education of clergy, 100–1, 113–14, 184, 251
  elite reactions to political, social, and
    economic turmoil, 221–22
  First Vatican Council, 18–19, 98–99, 101–2,
    117–18, 120, 129–30, 157–58, 177
  historical anchorage, 241–42
  Immaculate Conception, 187–88
  Latin America concept, 184
  lay engagement and involvement, 39, 99–100,
    175–76, 249, 251, 252–53
  Marian pietism, 98–99, 110–11, 117–18,
    163–64, 187–88

  official religion, 22–23, 136
  opposition to Protestantism, 2–3, 52–53,
    77, 79–87, 135, 167–68, 190–91, 204,
    250, 252–53
  outreach of immigrant priests, 123–24,
    156, 243–44
  Papal Infallibility, 98–99, 101–2, 106–7, 110–
    11, 117–18, 120, 187–88, 199
  Pentecostal derivation of practices
    from, 8–9
  political issues and transformations, 9–10,
    21, 22–24, 37, 39, 50–51, 52, 79–80, 96–99,
    101, 103–5, 107, 110–11, 113–15, 129–
    30, 249
  popular messianic movements, 174–77
  Protestant critique of, 4–5, 20–21, 25, 48–50,
    101–13, 116–19, 120, 129–30, 167, 177,
    185–88, 204, 234
  reaction to colporteurs and Bible Societies,
    63, 77, 79–88, 169–70
  reading and writing in worship, 74–75
  religious freedom/liberty, 22–24
  religious mobilization, 98–99, 175–76
  Religious Question, 101, 103–5, 107, 110–11,
    113–14, 129–30, 177, 221
  renewal and reform, 4–5, 15, 18–19, 21, 26,
    97–103, 116–18, 124–25, 135, 156, 174–75,
    188–89, 204, 252–53
  Romanization, 81, 96–97, 100–1, 112–13,
    120, 207, 250, 252–53
  rural folk Catholicism, 56–57, 252–53
  state patronage, 24, 37, 103, 113–14
  Ultramontanism, 80–81, 84–85, 99, 100,
    101–2, 103, 129–30, 175–77, 188–89, 240–
    41, 252–53
CCLA (Committee on Cooperation in Latin
  America), 182–83, 184–85, 201–2, 203–
  4, 205
cemeteries, secularization of, 23, 49–50, 53–54,
  56–57, 103, 113, 136–37, 254–55
Cendrars, Blaise, 237
Centro de Documentação e História Vicente
  Themudo Lessa (CDH-VTL), 4–5
Centro Dom Vital, 221–22, 223, 249
Cerqueira Leite, Antônio Pedro de
  (*Evangelista*), 34–35, 47–48, 233–34
Cerqueira Leite, Remigio de, 115–16
Chamberlain, George, 32–33, 34–35, 37–38, 56,
  196, 208–9, 211–12
Chaves, Maria de Melo, 139–41, 142–43, 146–
  47, 159, 160–63, 247–48, 256–57
Chaves, Marta de Melo, 142–43
Christian Brethren. *See* Plymouth Brethren

Christian cooperation, 19, 165–204
  anti-Protestant rhetoric and mobilization, 174–78
  Braga's book, 189–90, 191–202
  Brazilian exceptionalism, 195–96, 230
  Catholic messianic movements, 174–77
  collaboration and competition, 167–74
  Committee on Cooperation in Latin America, 182–83, 184–85
  critique versus collaboration with Catholicism, 167, 179–82, 185–89, 199
  doctrinal and ritual differences, 170–73
  Latin America concept, 182–84, 185–86
  nationalism versus, 220
  New York Conference, 179–86
  pacts of missionary cooperation, 169, 172
  Panama Congress, 165–67, 168, 184–88
  Pan-Americanism, 165–67, 184–85, 189–92, 193–95, 196–97, 202
  Pereira's book, 189–90, 191, 192–93, 194–98, 199–201
  print and literacy, 169–70
  science and Christianity, 197–201
  shared evangelical characteristics, 174–75
  World Missionary Conference, 177–80, 182–83, 184–86, 187–89
"Christian Faith in an Age of Doubt" (McConnell), 215–16
Christian Religion in its Relations with Slavery, The (Pereira), 54
Church, the Reformation, and Civilization, The (Franca), 204
Church Missionary Society, 40–41
civil registration of marriages and births, 23, 50, 53–54, 57, 103, 113, 136–37, 254–55
Clermont-Ganneu, Charles, 224
coffee industry, 21, 31–32, 56–57, 135, 214–15
Colégio Piracicabano, 211n.24
Collegio Pío Latino Americano, 100, 184
colporteurs, 2–4, 18, 26–27, 33, 39–40, 48–49, 58–60, 61–63, 66–67, 68–87
  advertising strategies, 86–87
  American Bible Society, 58–59, 68–69, 78–80, 79n.77, 82
  'Bíblia' versus 'As Escrituras Sagradas,' 86–87
  British and Foreign Bible Society, 68–74, 75–80, 81, 82–84, 85–87, 88, 90
  Catholic reaction to, 77, 79–87
  class and education of, 71–74
  dealings with public authorities, 79–81, 82–83
  discouragement, 77
  dismissal of, 152
  economic crises, 78–79
  exchanging Bibles for goods, 78–79
  "false Bibles," 82–85, 86
  images of, 70f, 70f, 72f, 73f
  imagined communities, 93–94
  journey of Bibles from printer to reader, 68–69
  literacy, 71–74
  missionaries following at heels of, 93
  negative association of with Bibles, 84–85
  ordeals and obstacles experienced by, 77–81
  race of, 71–74
  responsibilities of, 68–69
  salaries, 76–77, 152–53
  social and economic improvement for, 76–77
  travel and transport, 68–69, 70f, 77
  yellow fever, 77–78
Comaroff, Jean, 143–44
Comaroff, John, 143–44
Committee on Cooperation in Latin America (CCLA), 182–83, 184–85, 201–2, 203–4, 205
Comte, Auguste, 114–15
Conceição, José Manoel da, 34, 148–49
Conference on Comparative Religions (1928), 1–2, 216–17, 224
Congregationalists and Congregationalism. *See also names of specific Congregationalists*
  abolitionist movement, 53–54
  civilizing effects of Christian literature, 2–3
  collaboration and competition, 167–68, 171–72
  colporteurs, 69–71
  conduct of converts, 152
  conversion of various social classes, 32–33, 135
  ecumenical movement, 203
  education of pastorate, 124–25
  independence and autonomy of local churches, 252
  missionaries, 26–27
  political issues and transformations, 51–53, 113
  publishing enterprise, 47–48
Conselheiro, Antônio (Antônio Mendes Maciel), 175–76
Constitutions of Brazil, 22–24, 79–81, 103, 113–14, 136, 180–81, 249
conversion, 18–19, 131–64, 252–53, 255. *See also names of specific converts*
  academic study of, 133–34
  break with family heritage, 134
  caipiras, 145–46, 150, 151–52, 153–54, 155–56, 159–60, 161–62

cleanliness and organization, 150–53
contempt for former beliefs and practices, 146, 149–50, 153–54, 157–58
conversation and persuasion, 143–50
cultural discontinuity and continuity thinking, 133–34
dissolution and reconstitution of social bonds, 138–43
family and community life, 155–56
festive culture, 140–41
first- versus second-generation converts, 133–34, 139–40, 153–54, 156–63, 215–16
imagery from natural world and everyday life, 146–47
kin and co-parenthood networks, 146
manifestations of divine providence and aid, 143
nostalgia about early rural converts, 161–62
primitivism, 134, 156–58
printed conversion narratives, 147–50
recovering the image of the *bandeirantes*, 162–63
reformation of manners and morals, 150–56
religious bureaucracies as compensation for lost social networks, 141–43
renewal versus rupture, 134
selective response to customs, 140–41
social and political contexts of, 135–38
time lag between dissemination and conversions, 67
conversion narratives, 3–5, 6, 18–19, 67, 131–33, 147–50, 248
Cooper, Frederick, 256
co-parenthood, 138–39, 141–42, 146, 163–64
Corfield, Richard, 61–62
Corrêa, João da Costa, 27–28, 168–69
Correio Mercantil, 92–93
Costa, Antônio de Macedo, 82, 101, 104
Costa, Guilherme da, 122–23
Couto, Nicolau Soares do, 211–12
Craik, Henry, 125–26

Daffin, Robert, 146–47
Dagama, João, 29, 32–34, 37–38, 43–44, 75–76
Darby, John Nelson, 125–27
Darwin, Charles, 199–200
Deiros, Pablo A., 212–13
Díaz, Porfirio, 9–10
Differences Between Catholics and Protestants, 111–12
Dornelas, José, 145–46
Duffield, A., 61–62

Echo da Verdade, 48–49
ecumenical movement, 165–67, 178, 203, 215–17, 218–19, 230, 245–46, 255–56. *See also* names of specific conferences
Edinburgh Conference. *See* World Missionary Conference
educational institutions. *See* schools and educational institutions
electoral reform (1881), 23
Elliot, Samuel, 75–76
Enlightenment, 121–22, 130, 230
Entzminger, William Edwin, 172
Episcopalians and Episcopalianism
 collaboration and competition, 167–68
 early missionaries and congregations, 24, 28, 167–69
 Panama Congress, 179
Estandarte, O, 35–36
Evangelical Bookshop, 111–12
evangelical intelligentsia, 205–46
 biblical archaeology, 224
 biblical scholarship, 223–24
 Catholic and secular intelligentsia versus, 205–8
 conservatism and fundamentalism, 212–13
 domesticating evangelical Christianity, 230–44
 ecumenical movement, 215–17, 218–19, 230
 higher criticism, 225–28
 historical anchorage, 240–44
 internationalism, 218–20, 238–39
 interwar nationalism, 218–21, 222, 238–40
 liberal theologies, 225–28
 non-seminary trained intellectuals, 211–12
 philology, 224–25, 236–37
 regionalism, 238–40
 regional variations of Portuguese, 236–37
 romanticization of rural cultures and traditions, 217–19
 science and Christianity, 215
 seminary-educated elite, 205, 207–11
 social and political theologies, 212–22
 Social Gospel, 214–16
 University of São Paulo, 244–45
 women, 211
Evangelista (Antonio Pedro de Cerqueira Leite), 34–35, 47–48, 233–34
Expository Grammar (Pereira), 46, 236
Expository Times, The, 224–25

Faria, Daniel, 127
Ferraz Brothers, 229–30
Ferreira, Júlio A., 231–32

Ferreira, Miguel Vieira, 91–92, 96, 103, 106–7, 134, 211–12
Figueiredo, Antonio Pereira de, 82–83, 170–71
Figueiredo, Jackson de, 221
Figueiredo translation of the Latin Vulgate Bible, 82–83, 149–50, 170–71, 225n.88
First Vatican Council (Vatican I), 18–19, 98–99, 101–2, 117–18, 120, 129–30, 157–58, 177
Fletcher, James C., 20–21, 26, 27, 51–52, 61, 195–96, 241–42
Fluminense Evangelical Church (Igreja Evangélica Fluminense), 1–2
  collaboration with BFBS, 69–71
  colporteurs, 69–71
  education for black people and freed-slaves, 53–54
  founding of, 26–27
  Plymouth Brethren, 126
  social class of members, 71–74
Fon, André de la, 243
Franca, Leonel, 204, 221–22
Frase, Ronald, 8, 31–32, 135
Freemasonry, 9–10, 51, 80–81, 96–97, 101, 104, 171n.19, 175–77
French Revolution, 121–22, 221, 250
Freston, Paul, 11–13
Freyre, Gilberto, 225–26
From Hut to Palace (Mota), 239–40
functionalism, 8–9, 137–38
Fundamentalism Project, The, 212–13
Future of the Catholic Peoples, The (Laveleye), 91–92, 106–8, 111–13, 189–90

Gammon, Samuel, 44–45, 142–43
Gammon Institute, 159
Gamsa, Mark, 15–16
Garnier, Baptiste Louis, 111
General Considerations on the Bible (Rodrigues), 227–29
Geographical Society of New York, 196
Ginsburg, Solomon, 38–39, 128–29, 171–72, 172n.26
Gladstone, William, 110–13, 199
Glass, Frederick, 68–69, 71–74, 75, 131–33, 152–53
Gobineau, Arthur de, 108–9
godparenthood, 139–40, 255
Góes e Vasconcellos, Zacarias de, 103–4
Gomes, Henrique, 156–57, 159, 161
Gouvêa, Antonio Francisco de, 146
Gouvêa, Herculano de, 159, 160–61
Gouvêa, Severino de, 159
Graham, Franklin, 231–32

Graham, Richard, 138–39
Great War (World War I), 165, 167, 177–78, 197, 214–15, 225–26, 230
Green, Nile, 249–50
Griffiths, Gareth, 6
Groves, Anthony, 125–26
Grubb, Kenneth, 249
Guanabara Confession of Faith, 243
Gymnasium of São Paulo, 46, 209–10

Habermas, Jürgen, 13–14
Hendrix, Eugene, 180–81
Hermann, Jacqueline, 113–14
higher criticism, 199–200, 225–28
Historical Grammar (Pereira), 236
Historical Traces and Main Points of Divergence of the Evangelical Protestant and Roman Catholic Churches (Stiller), 104–7, 111–12
History of the Popes, 149–50
Hofmeyr, Isabel, 15–16, 59–60
Holanda, Sérgio Buarque de, 190–91
Holden, Caterina, 127
Holden, Richard, 61–62, 63, 67–68, 69–71, 76–77, 82, 85–86, 89–90, 91–92, 126–27, 129
Howard, Jorge P., 213–14
Howell, John Beatty, 47–48, 208–9
Huguenots, 22–23, 241–42, 243
Hunter, Emma, 13
hymns and hymnals, 3–4, 5–6, 47–48, 128–29, 138, 150–51, 171–72, 197–98, 234–35, 241–42, 247–48

Ibiapina, José Maria, 175–76
iconoclasm, 1–2, 89–90, 116–17, 120, 134, 146, 149–50, 163–64, 233–35, 255
I Do Not Understand the Bible, 65t
Igreja Evangélica Fluminense. *See* Fluminense Evangelical Church
IHGB (Brazilian Historical and Geographical Institute), 51–52
immigration, 3–4, 9–10, 21, 23, 24–26, 50–51, 55, 56–57, 214–15
  from America, 25, 27–28, 53–54, 56–57
  from Germany, 3–4, 24–25, 27, 135, 167–68
  from Japan, 46n.106
  missionary view of melting pot, 55
  outreach of immigrant priests, 123–24, 156, 243–44
  from Portugal, 26–27, 33
  from Switzerland, 24–25, 167–68
  "whitening" of Brazilian society, 24–25, 50–51, 108–9

imperialism, 80–81, 167, 183–84, 190–91, 196–97
Imprensa Evangelica, 18–19, 130
  BSET, 115–16
  circulation of, 39–40
  contributors to, 35–36, 47–48, 115–16, 169–70, 233–34
  conversion narrative supplements, 148–50
  critique of Catholicism, 101–3, 104, 111–12
  critique of traditional practices and popular beliefs, 233–34
  moving headquarters of, 47–48
  RTS, 88–89
  secularization of cemeteries, 49–50
  used as packing paper, 66–67
Independent Presbyterian Church, 4–5, 211–12, 229–30, 236–37, 243
indigenous peoples and cultures
  autonomy of local churches, 40–41
  conversion, 143–45
  indigenous languages, 58–59, 213–14
  missionary reports, 6–7
  reading and development of indigenous mind, 16–17
  subjugation and notions of inferiority, 6, 40–41, 108–10, 162, 191–92, 237–38
  transnational dimension of public sphere, 14–15
individualism, 114–15, 129, 150–51, 154–55, 165–66, 191–93, 203, 212–14, 216–17
  individual and private reading practices, 16–18, 21, 62–63, 65t, 67, 81, 84–85, 90–91, 150
  individual faith, conversion, and salvation, 11–13, 65–67, 99, 118–19, 138–40, 141–42, 146–47, 249–50, 252–53, 255
infant baptism, 28–29, 48–49, 124–25, 139–40, 170–71, 172
Inman, Samuel, 184–85
Inquisition, 185–86, 191–92, 242–44
Integralist movement, 202–3, 221–22
International School, 27, 44–45, 71
Isabel (princess), 52
itinerant booksellers. *See* colporteurs

Jansenism, 148–49, 250
Jéca Tatú, 238–39, 239n.151
Jefferson, Thomas, 194–95
Jews and Judaism, 120–21, 180–81, 242–44
joão de barro (red ovenbird), 146–47, 220
Joaquim, Antonio, 157–58
Johnston, Anna, 6
Jones, Sylvester, 180–81

Jornal Baptista, O, 172
Jornal do Commercio, 165, 226–27, 228–29
Joy of the House, The (Kalley), 150–51

Kalley, Robert, 26–27, 53–54, 63, 69–74, 80–81, 85–86, 90, 91–93, 92n.139, 126–27, 152
Kalley, Sarah, 69–71, 150–51
Kidder, Daniel P., 20–21, 26, 51–52, 195–96, 241–42
Killingray, David, 144–45
Kinsolving, Lucien, 28, 123–24, 187, 217–18
Kirsch, Thomas, 66–67
Koselleck, Reinhart, 13–14
Kyle, John, 181–82

Laemmert, Eduard, 111
Laemmert, Heinrich, 111
Laemmert Brothers' publishing house, 111
Lane, Edward, 27, 71, 85–86, 89
La Plata Mission, 27–28, 168–69
Latin America concept, 182–84, 185–86, 186n.84
Laveleye, Émile de, 91–92, 106–8, 111–13, 121–22, 189–90
League of Nations, 218–19, 220
Lehmann, David, 8–9, 37–39
Leme, Sebastião, 220–21, 249
Lemos, Miguel, 114–15
Lenington, Robert, 115–16, 208–9
Léonard, Émile, 231
Lessa, Vicente Themudo, 209–10
liberation theology, 202–3, 221–22, 245–46
Liga Eleitoral Católica, 249
Lima, Alceu Amoroso, 221–22
Lima, Joaquim Fernandes de, 66–67
Lima, Manoel de Oliveira, 190–91
literacy and reading. *See also* publishing enterprise; *names of specific Bible Societies, denominations, and written works*
  awareness of, 74–75
  Bible-readers, 3–4, 40, 43–44, 75–76, 208, 251–52
  Brazilian consumption of Christian literature versus other Lusophone countries, 90–91
  campaigns for universal literacy, 213–14, 216–17
  civilizing and uplifting power of, 2–3, 16–18, 68, 228, 253–54
  collective reading and listening, 5–6, 16–18, 74–76, 159, 205–48, 253–54
  colporteurs, 71–74, 94–95
  conversion and, 3–4, 65–67, 94–95, 131, 147–50

literacy and reading (cont.)
  evangelicals as agents of literacy, 2, 3–4
  illiteracy, 5–6, 32–33, 40, 41–42, 63–65, 71–76, 234, 253–54
  individual and private reading practices, 16–18, 21, 62–63, 65t, 67, 81, 84–85, 90–91, 150
  lay involvement, 39–40
  objectives of, 2–3
  possession and hysteria through reading, 83–84
  power and prestige associated with, 74–75, 143
  reading and writing in worship, 74–77
  schools and education, 42–44, 47, 142–43
  study of Christian literacy, 6–7, 16–17
Lobato, Monteiro, 108–9, 238–39
Lopes Ribeiro, Francisco, 141, 159, 161
Louis XIV, 106–7
Loyson, Père Hyacinthe, 199
Lusophone world, 18, 55–56, 65t, 90–95, 126
  Catholic opposition to Protestant "false Bibles," 83–84
  Protestant networks, 90–91, 94, 126
  religious discourse and debate, 107–8
Lutherans and Lutheranism, 240–41, 242–43
  collaboration with Bible Societies, 71
  immigration, 24–25, 135, 167–68
  mission work, 25

Maciel, Antônio Mendes (Antônio Conselheiro), 175–76
Mackenzie, John Theron, 44–45
Mackenzie Institute/College (formerly, American School), 44–46, 209–10
Magalhães, Benjamin Constant de, 114–15
Magalhães, Luiza, 209–10
mamelucos, 237–38
maps
  Brazil at the start of the Republic, 30f
  early nuclei and congregations, 30f, 31f
Maria, Júlio, 241–42
Marian pietism, 98–99, 110–11, 117–18, 163–64, 187–88
Maritain, Jacques, 245–46
Marquis of Paraná, 32–33
Martin, David, 8–10, 45–46, 205–6, 228
Martin, Roger, 89
Mathew, George Buckley, 80–81
McConnell, Francis J., 199–200, 215–16
McNair, Stuart, 127–30
Melo, David, 139–40, 146
Melo, Manuel de, 139–41, 150–51, 157–58, 159, 247–48, 256–57
Mendonça, Antônio Gouvêa, 5–6, 8, 31–32, 40–41, 135, 140–41, 212–13, 230
Menezes, Manoel Antônio de, 168–69
Mesquita, Cândido J. de, 34
Methodists and Methodism. *See also names of specific Methodists*
  abolitionist movement, 53–54
  collaboration and competition, 167–69, 171–72, 171n.19
  conversion of various social classes, 135
  correspondence with Bible Societies, 71
  early missionaries and congregations, 20–21, 25–26, 27–28, 168–69
  ecumenical movement, 203
  higher criticism, 225–26
  institution building, 128–29
  Panama Congress, 179, 180–81, 184–85
  political issues and transformations, 53–54, 204, 249
  publishing enterprise, 51–52, 189–90, 211n.24, 228–29, 231–32
  schools and education, 44–45, 216
Military School of Rio de Janeiro, 114–15
Miranda, Antonio, 79–80
Miranda, José Zacarias de, 34–35, 47, 115–18, 122–24, 129–30, 208–9, 235–36, 236n.137, 245–46
Miranda, Zacarias de, 231–32
missionaries. *See also* Christian cooperation; conversion; literacy and reading; political issues and transformations; publishing enterprise; schools and educational institutions; social issues and transformations; *names of specific missionaries, denominations, and conferences*
  abolitionist movement, 53–54
  analysis of missionary reporting and sources, 5–7
  early, 4, 20–21, 24, 25–29, 30f, 31f, 167–69, 247–48
  evangelical and missionary imagination, 2, 21–22, 55, 68, 75, 79–80, 93–94, 132–33, 156–57, 165, 195–96
  following at heels of colporteurs, 93
  impressions of Brazil, 20–21
  pacts of cooperation, 169, 172
  role of female missionaries, 201–2
missionary conferences. *See* New York Conference; Panama Congress on Christian Work in Latin America; World Missionary Conference

Missionary Education Movement, 189–90
modernism, 221–22, 223, 224–26, 237, 238–39, 255–56
modernization, 42–43, 50–51, 56–57, 112–13, 114–15, 123–24, 129–30, 138–39, 222, 254–55
Mondragón, Carlos, 203
Monroe Doctrine, 190–91, 193–94, 196–97
Montesinos, Antonio de, 245–46
Monteverde, Anita de, 201–2
Monteverde, Eduardo, 184–85
Moody, Dwight, 128–29
Morris, James, 28
Morton, George, 27
Mota, Otoniel, 209–11, 217–18, 220, 224–25, 226–27, 229–30, 231–32, 234–37, 236n.137, 239–40, 245–46
Mota translation of Matthew, 224–25, 236–37
Mott, John, 178, 184–85
Muir, William, 180
Müller, George, 125–26
Muslims and Islam, 74–75, 245–46
Mussolini, Benito, 221–22
mutirões, 140–41, 146–47, 175, 252–53, 255
My Conversion: Revelations of a Lady to her Catholic Friend, 149–50
My Language (Mota), 236–37

Nabuco, Joaquim, 190–91
Neves, Antônio dos Santos, 47–48
Newman, Junius, 27–28
New York Conference (1913), 167, 179–86
Nina Rodrigues, Raimundo, 108–9
Nobiling, Oskar, 209–10
non-denominational bodies, 4, 62, 127–28, 186. *See also* British and Foreign Bible Society
Novo Mundo, O, 54, 103
Nueva Democracia, La, 203

Oliveira, Henrique Gomes, 141, 146
Oliveira, Vital, 101, 103–4, 221
Origin of Species, The (Darwin), 199–200
Our Attitude Towards the Roman Church (Pereira), 187–88, 194–95
Our Father in Heaven (Pereira), 145–46

pacts of missionary cooperation, 169, 172
pamphlets. *See* literacy and reading; publishing enterprise; tracts and pamphlets; *names of specific tracts and pamphlets*
Panama Congress of 1826, 193–94
Panama Congress on Christian Work in Latin America (1916), 165–67, 168, 184–88, 193–97, 203, 205, 211–12

Braga's book on, 189–90, 191–92, 193–94, 195–96, 197–99, 201–2
Brazilian exceptionalism, 195–96
capitalist economic rationality, 165–67
commissions, 184–86
Committee on Cooperation in Latin America, 182–83, 184–85, 201–2
critique of Catholicism, 167, 185–88
delegates, 184–85
development of, 179–83, 184–85
disseminating findings and strategies of, 187–88
division following, 187–88
effects of, 165–66
Latin America concept, 185–86
objectives of, 165–66
Pan-Americanism, 165–67, 184–85, 197, 202
Pereira's book on, 189–90, 193, 194–200, 204
political issues and transformations, 186
role of female missionaries, 201–2
science and Christianity, 197–99
Social Gospel, 165–66, 215–17
social issues and transformations, 186, 201–2
Pan-Americanism, 165–67, 184–85, 189–92, 193–95, 196–97, 202
Pan-Americanism: Religious Aspect (Braga), 189–90
Papal Infallibility, 98–99, 101–2, 106–7, 110–11, 117–18, 120, 187–88, 199
Pascal, Blaise, 221
Paulista Academy of Letters, 211, 238–39
paulista regionalism, 162, 237–40
Pedro Feliz, 131, 132–33, 132*f*
Pedro II, 24–25, 26, 29, 37, 44–45, 51–52, 61, 79–80, 100, 113, 236–37
Peel, John, 6–7, 144–45, 240–41
Pena, Belisário, 222
Pentecostals and Pentecostalism
Assemblies of God, 129, 174
cultural policies and national pride, 162–63
derivation of practices from Catholicism, 8–9
direct evangelism, 173–74
dispensational premillennialism, 129
education, 45–46, 205–6
groundwork for growth of, 251
mainline Protestant views of, 129, 203
materiality of texts, 66–67
primitivism, 11–13
reactionary fundamentalism, 212–13
study of, 8–9, 38–39, 45–46
surfacing of "buried intelligentsia," 205–6

Pereira, Eduardo Carlos, 2–3, 19, 34–36, 36f,
    46, 47–48, 54–55, 109–10, 112–13, 115–18,
    119–22, 129–30, 145–46, 167, 187–90, 191,
    192–93, 194–98, 199–201, 202–3, 204,
    208–10, 215–16, 229n.109, 230–31, 234–
    36, 236n.137, 243–46
Pereira Barreto, Luis, 114–15
periodicals, 2–6, 15–16, 17–18, 48–49, 55–56.
    See also names of specific periodicals
  Catholic, 80–81, 83–85
  colporteurs, 59–60
  Religious Tract Society and, 89–90
Phelan, John, 183–84
Piccato, Pablo, 13, 14–15
Pierson, Paul, 212–13
Pilgrim's Progress, The, 92–93
Pires, Cornélio, 145–46, 150, 159
Pius IX, 50–51, 98–99, 100, 102, 110–11,
    112–13, 124–25, 129–30, 177, 184, 187–88,
    199, 234
Plymouth Brethren, 18–19, 91–92, 96–97,
    125–29, 252
political issues and transformations, 5–6, 8–10,
    18, 19, 21, 22–24, 39, 51–54, 113, 204, 249.
    See also names of specific denominations
  Catholic church–state rapprochement, 249
  Catholic disestablishment, 79–80, 96–99,
    113–15, 177
  Catholic elite reactions to political, social,
    and economic turmoil, 221–22
  contexts of conversion, 135–38
  debate and dissent in the public sphere, 49–
    55, 130, 189–90, 251–52, 256–57
  evangelical intelligentsia, 212–22
  formal Protestant political involvement, 249
  official religion, 22–23, 136
  Panama Congress, 186
  Proclamation of the Republic (1889), 24, 29,
    34–35, 52, 68, 79–80, 97–98, 113, 114–
    15, 136
  Religious Question, 101, 103–5, 107, 110–11,
    113–14, 129–30, 177, 221
  state patronage, 24, 37, 103, 113–14
polygenism, 109–10, 200–1
"Popular Superstitions" (Cerqueira Leite), 233–34
Portales, José Eyzaguirre, 100, 184
Portugal Evangelico, 220
Positivists and Positivism, 42–43, 81, 101, 114–15,
    121–22, 175, 176–77, 199–200, 207, 251–52
Prado family, 237
Pregador Cristão, O, 88, 89
premillennial dispensationalism, 129, 212–13, 219
Presbyterians and Presbyterianism

abolition of slavery and abolitionism, 53–54,
    113
Apocryphal books, 62
appeal of, 31–32
Bible-readers, 40, 75–76
Bibles printed in Lisbon versus in London, 86
collaboration and competition, 167–69, 171–72
conduct of converts, 152
conversion of various social classes, 32–33,
    135
conversion via texts used as packing paper,
    66–67
correspondence with BFBS, 71
critique of Baptist doctrine, 173
denominational differentiation, 28–29, 124–25
early missionaries and congregations, 4, 20–
    21, 25–27, 28–29, 30f, 168–69
ecumenical movement, 203
Foreign Board of Missions, 178–79
independence and autonomy of local
    churches, 2–3, 35–36, 40, 205
infant baptism, 139–40
institution building, 33, 37–38, 40, 173–
    74, 205
lay engagement and involvement, 34, 39–40
literacy, 44
local fundraising, 38–39
local leadership, 34–36, 39–40
membership figures, 29, 39–40
modern liberalism and the Enlightenment,
    121–22
national synod, 29
Panama Congress, 179, 180–81, 189–90
political issues and transformations, 51–52
Proclamation of the Republic, 113
publishing enterprise, 47–48, 115–
    16, 124–25
Religious Tract Society and, 89
schools and education, 40, 43–47,
    211n.24, 216
seminary education, 208–9
social transformations, 55
training of pastorate, 173–74
women's education, 211
World Missionary Conference, 178–79
worldwide evangelical network, 56
yellow fever, 77–78
Priest and the Protestant, The, 111–12
primitivism, 1–2, 11–13, 106–7, 118–19, 134,
    156–58, 216–17, 248, 253–55
Proclamation of the Republic (1889), 24, 29,
    34–35, 52, 68, 79–80, 97–98, 113, 114–
    15, 136

Protestant evangelical Christianity, 2–3, 146, 247–57. *See also* political issues and transformations; schools and educational institutions; social issues and transformations; *names of specific Protestants, denominations, societies, and conferences*
  association with and centrality of the Bible, 84–85, 119–20, 158, 187–88, 199–200, 212–14, 223, 224–26
  atonement and crucicentrism, 11–13, 118–19, 145–46, 169–70
  attachment to and power of the written word (book religion), 1–2, 4, 65–66, 65t, 253–54
  categorizing in ideological and theological spectrums, 96–98
  Catholic opposition to, 2–3, 77, 79–87, 135
  Christian cooperation, 19, 165–204
  civilizing effects of Christian literature, 68, 228
  concept of race, 107–10
  conceptual exchanges, 11
  conversion, 18–19, 32–33, 131–64
  countering corruptive intellectual trends, 114–16
  critique of Catholicism, 4–5, 20–21, 25, 48–50, 101–13, 116–19, 120, 129–30, 177, 204, 234
  critique of elite liberal intellectualism, 120–22, 130
  denominational differentiation, 28–29, 118–19
  differing research perspectives on, 8–10
  dissolution and reconstitution of social bonds, 255
  domesticating, 230–44
  early missionaries and congregations, 20–21, 26–29, 30f, 31f, 231–32, 247–48
  explanations for early acceptance of, 31–33
  "false Bibles" controversy, 2–3, 82–85, 86, 91–92
  first wave of expansion in Brazil, 18, 20–57
  formal political involvement, 249
  foursquare definition of, 11–13
  grassroots dynamics of, 11
  growth of, 2, 3–4, 7
  iconoclasm, 1–2, 89–90, 116–17, 120, 134, 146, 149–50, 163–64, 233–35
  imagined communities, 93–94
  immigration, 23, 24–25
  importance of reading, 16–18
  independence and autonomy of local churches, 35–36, 40–41
  individualism and self-reliance, 11–13, 84–85, 118–19, 138–40, 212–14, 216–17, 255
  institution building, 18, 37–42, 129
  intelligentsia, 205–46
  justification by faith, 109–10, 119, 125–26, 187–88
  lay engagement and involvement, 33–34, 37–40, 41–42
  literature to counteract immoral influences, 87–88, 96
  local leadership, 33, 34–36, 39–41
  local tithing and fundraising, 37–39
  locating evangelical religion, 254–57
  membership figures, 29, 39–40, 249–50
  millenarian expectations, 94
  mixed-race populations, 19, 145–46, 154, 162, 217–18, 237–39
  modernization, 42–43, 50–51, 56–57, 112–13, 114–15, 123–24, 129–30, 138–39, 222, 254–55
  morality and reformation of conduct, 2–3, 67–68, 87–88, 96, 109–10, 120–24, 129–30, 138, 146–47, 150–56, 158–59, 201–2, 212–13, 216–17
  os bíblias, 2–3, 84–85
  Positivism and, 114–15
  premillennial dispensationalism, 129, 212–13, 219
  primitivism, 1–2, 11–13, 106–7, 118–19, 156–58, 216–17, 248, 253–55
  Proclamation of the Republic, 113
  public sphere, 9–10, 13–18
  publishing enterprise, 18, 47–56
  Reformation figures versus Church Fathers, 102, 120
  religious diversification, 18–19, 103–13
  religious freedom/liberty, 22–24
  religious innovation, 251–54
  religious specialists, 33, 34–35, 256
  Spiritism and, 114–15
  terminology, 11–13, 105
  time lag between dissemination and conversions, 67
  universal priesthood, 129, 250, 252
  Westminster Confession of Faith, 124–25
  worldwide networks and community, 22–23, 38–39, 55–56, 57, 58–59, 90–91, 94, 104, 107–8, 126–27, 197, 205, 212, 248
Psalms and Hymns, 128–29
publishing enterprise, 3–4, 18, 33, 34, 47–56, 248. *See also* literacy and reading; *names of specific institutions, writers, and publications*

publishing enterprise (cont.)
    abolitionist movement, 53–54
    analysis of missionary reporting and sources, 5–7
    artisanal printing presses, 3–4
    attachment to and power of the written word (book religion), 1–2, 4, 65–67, 65t
    booksellers and popular books, 58
    circulation of texts, 15–18
    civilizing and uplifting power of print materials, 2–3, 16–18, 67–68, 228, 253–54
    conversion via texts used as packing paper, 66–67
    denominational differences and competition, 48–49
    evangelical print culture, 2
    high cost of books, 63–65
    immoral publications, 87–88, 96
    introduction of printed matter in Brazil, 74–75
    local writers and workers, 47–48
    Lusophone world, 55–56
    materiality of texts, 15–18, 66–67, 83–84
    Plymouth Brethren, 127
    political issues and transformations, 49–55, 96–97
    purposes of, 2–3
    religious diversification, 96–97
    religious freedom/liberty, 49–53
    social transformations, 54
    theological discourse and debate, 4
    women's participation in, 211
    worldwide evangelical network, 55–56
Publishing House of the Assembly of God, 129
Puritano, O, 173, 177, 178–79, 225–26
Puritans and Puritanism, 62, 106–7, 241–42

Quakers, 106–7
Quirino, José, 146

race. *See also* indigenous peoples and cultures; slavery
    amicable negotiation and accord, 193–95
    degeneration, 108–9, 110–11
    differentiation of Latin and the Anglo-Saxon races, 191–93, 202
    Latin America concept, 183–84
    mixed-race populations, 19, 145–46, 154, 162, 217–18, 237–39
    polygenism, 200–1
    scientific racism, 108–10, 154
Ransom, John James, 27–28, 168–69
reading. *See* literacy and reading

red ovenbird (*joão de barro*), 146–47, 220
Reformation, 102, 120, 180–81, 188–89, 216–17, 221, 242–44
Regency Period, 26–27
regionalist movement, 162–63, 220, 237–41
Reinkens, Joseph, 110–12, 117–18
Reis, Álvaro, 38–39, 178–79, 189–90, 225–26, 235–36, 236n.137, 243–44, 245–46
Reis, João José, 23
religious freedom/liberty, 9–10, 22–24, 49–53, 103–4, 113, 136–37, 177, 191–92, 241–42, 243–44
religious persecution, 21, 22–23, 26–27, 33–34, 51–53, 79–80, 137, 191–92, 242–44
Religious Problem of Latin America, The (Pereira), 189–90
Religious Question, 101, 103–5, 107, 110–11, 113–14, 129–30, 177, 221
Religious Tract Society (RTS), 18, 59–60, 87–93
    adaptability, 89–90
    BFBS colporteurs, 88, 90
    Catholic opposition to tracts from, 87–88
    collaboration with established organizations, 88
    founding of, 87–88
    images in tracts and books, 89–90
    literature to counteract immoral influences, 87–88
    objectives of, 89
    religious discourse and debate, 91–92, 107–8
    sponsorship of periodicals, 89–90
    transatlantic exchange, 90–91
    withholding support to evangelistic work, 89
Rembao, Alberto, 240–41
Reverend and Evangelical Pastor José Manoel da Conceição, The, 148–49
Revista de Missões Nacionais (Review of National Missions), 35–36, 109–10
Ribeiro, Antonio, 225–26
Ribeiro, Domingos, 243
Rio, João do (João Paulo Barreto), 58, 68
Ritter, Gerhard, 245–46
Robbins, Joel, 133
Rodrigues, Jane, 228–29
Rodrigues, José Carlos, 54, 103, 126, 165, 184–85, 199–200, 211–12, 214–15, 218–19, 226–29, 229n.109, 241–42, 243–44
Romanized Catholicism, 81, 96–97, 100–1, 112–13, 120, 207, 250, 252–53
Romero, Sílvio, 190–91
RTS. *See* Religious Tract Society
rural folk Catholicism, 56–57, 252–53

INDEX 291

Salgado, Plínio, 221–22
Samson, David, 49–50
Samson, Jane, 200
San Martín, José de, 194–95
Santos, Antonio dos, 231–32
Santos, João Manoel Gonçalves dos, 47–48, 63, 67, 68, 69–71, 75–76, 77–78, 79–80, 85–87, 88, 90, 94, 169–70, 236n.137
Santos, Mattathias Gomes dos, 173, 235–36
SBC. *See* Southern Baptist Convention
Schaff, Phillip, 172
Schneider, Francis, 112–13
schools and educational institutions, 5–6, 32–33, 34, 42–47
   Bibles and tracts as primers, 58–59
   conversion and retention, 45–46
   education of Catholic clergy, 100–1, 113–14, 184, 251
   education of ministers and intellectuals, 46
   education of slaves and freed-slaves, 53–54, 56
   establishment and maintenance of, 43–45
   ideal of Christian civilization, 42–43
   literacy, 44
   local fundraising, 43–45
   modernization, 42–43
   objectives of, 43–44
   opportunities provided by, 46–47
   Positivism, 114–15
   religious bureaucracies as compensation for lost social networks, 141–43, 158–59
   second-generation converts, 159–60
   seminary-educated Protestant elite, 205, 207–11
   social and economic improvement for colporteurs and superintendents, 76–77
   state of schools in nineteenth-century Brazil, 37
   women's education, 211
Schwartz, Stuart, 157–58
scientific racism, 108–10, 154
SCPK (Society for Propagating Christian Knowledge), 178
Second Vatican Council (Vatican II), 202–3
secret societies, 9–10, 13–14
Selvas e Choças (Mota), 231–32, 233f, 239
Série Braga (Braga), 46
sertanejos, 146–47, 154, 161, 162–63, 234–35
Shankey, Ira, 128–29
Sharkey, Heather, 60
Shenk, Wilbert, 40–41
Shorter Catechism, 43–44, 208–9
Silva, Antonio da, 82–83
Silveira, Guaracy, 204, 249

Silveira, Manuel Joaquim da, 82
Simonton, Ashbel, 20–21, 27, 89
sitiantes, 135, 140–41, 145–46
slavery
   abolitionists and abolitionism, 4–5, 15, 53–55, 96–97, 108–9, 121–22
   abolition of, 50–51, 68, 109–10, 113, 222
   bandeirantes, 162, 237–40
   "Curse of Ham," 226–27
   educating and evangelizing slaves and freed-slaves, 53–54, 56, 109–10, 113
   immigration and, 24–25, 50–51
   racial theories, 108–10
   reading and writing in worship, 74–75, 94–95
   slave revolts, 26–27
Smilde, David, 8–9
Smith, George, 180–81
Smith, John Rockwell, 209–10
Soares, Manoel, 85–86
social issues and transformations, 3–4, 8–11, 15, 18, 19, 21–22, 31–33, 44, 47, 51–54, 56–57, 113, 204, 249. *See also* race; schools and educational institutions; *names of specific denominations*
   Bible and Christianity as source of social progress and improvement, 67–68, 109–10, 112–13, 121–22, 123–24, 129–30, 161–62
   Catholic messianic movements, 175
   Christian cooperation and ecumenical conferences, 165–67, 186, 191–93, 198–99, 201–2
   conversion, 71–74, 135–43, 153–54, 158–59, 163–64
   ecumenical movement, 215–17
   everyday use of reading and writing, 74–75, 94–95
   Habermasian model of the public sphere, 13–15
   individualism and, 212–14
   missionary imagination, 55
   Panama Congress, 186, 201–2
   Positivism, 114–15
   publishing enterprise, 54, 55, 74–76
   religious bureaucracies as compensation for lost social networks, 141–43, 158–59
   religious change and, 8, 9–10
   rise of social theologies, 202–3
   schools and educational institutions, 76–77, 141–43, 158–59
   social contexts of conversion, 32–33
   Social Gospel, 165–66, 214–17
   social mobility, 44, 47, 76–77, 101, 118–19, 150–51, 160, 175, 256–57

292 INDEX

societies of thought, 9–10, 51, 96–97
Society for Propagating Christian Knowledge (SCPK), 178
Society of Christian Culture, 220
Solano, Arturo Piedra, 165–66
Soper, Edwin, 52–54
South American Missionary Society, 88
Southern Baptist Convention (SBC)
  Foreign Mission Board, 38–39, 48–49, 56
  missionaries, 28, 52–53, 56, 167–68
  sectarianism, 171–72
Souza, Paulino Soares de, 50
Souza e Silva, Manoel de, 83–84
Spaulding, Justin, 26
Speer, Robert, 178–80, 182–83, 184–85
Spiritists and Spiritism, 114–15, 175, 251–52
spiritual autobiographies. *See* conversion narratives
Spiritualist Crusade of Rio de Janeiro, 1–2
Spurgeon's College, 63
Stanley, Brian, 178, 197–98
Stewart, Robert, 90–91
Stiller, Erich, 104–7, 111–13
Strong, Josiah, 184–85
Strossmayer, Josip, 120, 199
Structural Transformation of the Public Sphere, The (Habermas), 13
Sunday, Billy, 225–26
Syllabus, 110–11, 187–88

Tambaram Conference (1938), 193
Taylor, Hudson, 125–26
Taylor, Kate, 28, 55, 168, 171–72
Taylor, Laura, 44–45
Taylor, Zachary, 28, 29, 48–49, 52–54, 168, 170–72
Teixeira Mendes, 114–15
Theological Institute of São Paulo, 208–10, 210f
Thorman, Canuto, 209–10
three-self program, 40–41
Torres, Miguel, 34–35, 47–48, 115–16
Torres Caicedo, José María, 183–84
tracts and pamphlets, 2–6, 18–19, 96–97. *See also* literacy and reading; publishing enterprise; *names of specific tracts and pamphlets*
  Baptist, 48–49
  biblical archaeology and religious controversy, 229–30
  colporteurs, 58–60
  conversation and conversion, 145–46
  critique of Catholicism, 104–8, 110–12, 116–19, 120

  critique of elite liberal intellectualism, 120–22
  interdenominational publishing, 169–70
  local production and translation of, 55
  Lusophone world, 55–56, 65t
  moral teachings and reformation of conduct, 122–24
  objectives of, 17–18
  Religious Tract Society, 87–93
  slavery and abolitionism, 53–54
Trajano, Antônio, 34–35
translation, 55, 92–93, 96–97, 106–7, 110–11, 124–25, 211–12, 218–19, 243
  Almeida translation, 63, 82–83, 85–86, 170–71, 225n.88
  Brazilian Society of Evangelical Tracts, 120
  British and Foreign Bible Society, 62–63, 82–83, 85–86
  early Baptist materials, 48–49
  Figueiredo translation, 82–83, 149–50, 170–71, 225n.88
  hymns, 128–29
  indigenous languages, 58–59
  Japanese immigration, 46n.106
  Mota translation of Matthew, 224–25, 236–37
  Panama Congress, 187–88, 189–90
  philology, 224–25
  regional variations of Portuguese, 236–37
  Religious Tract Society, 91–92
Treaty of Commerce and Navigation, 22–23
Trinitarian Bible Society, 170–71
Tucker, Hugh, 20–58, 67, 68–69, 75, 79–81, 93, 228–29
Typographia Aurora, 115–16

Ultramontanism, 80–81, 84–85, 99, 100, 101–2, 103, 129–30, 175–77, 188–89, 240–41, 252–53
universal priesthood, 129, 250, 252
University of São Paulo, 211, 244–45
Uribe-Uran, Victor, 14–15
Urupês (Lobato), 238–39

Vanorden, Emmanuel, 87–88, 96, 111, 168–69
Vargas, Getúlio, 204, 249
Vatican I. *See* First Vatican Council
Vatican II (Second Vatican Council), 202–3
Vaughan, Julio Ribeiro, 47–48
Veer, Peter van der, 138–39
Venn, Henry, 40–41
Verneuil, Matthieu, 243
Vianna, Manoel, 69–71, 72f, 83–84
Viçoso, Antônio Ferreira, 100

Vieira, David Gueiros, 96–97
Villegaignon, Nicolas de, 241–42, 243–44
Vingren, Gunnar, 174

Wacker, Grant, 129
Warner, Michael, 15–16
Watts, Martha, 211n.24
Weber, Max, 106–7
Wesley, John, 121–22
Westminster Confession of Faith, 43–44, 124–25
Willems, Emilio, 8, 155
Wilson, Woodrow, 218–19
With the Bible in Brazil (Glass), 71–74
World Missionary Conference (Edinburgh Conference) (1910), 19, 38–39, 165–66, 168, 177–80, 189–90, 194–95
    ecumenical movement and, 178
    negotiated terms of, 178–79, 182–83
    objections to, 178–80
    science and Christianity, 197–98
    similarities and differences between other conferences and, 182–83, 184–86, 187–89
World War I. *See* Great War
Worship of Images, The (Miranda), 116–17
Worship of Saints and Angels, The (Pereira), 116–17
Wright, Henry Maxwell, 128–29

Xavier, Innocencio, 40, 43–44

yellow fever, 44–45, 77–78
Young, Reginald, 131–32
Young Men's Christian Association (YMCA), 165, 211–12, 217–18, 228–29